Nostradamus

A LIFE AND MYTH

Nostradamus

A LIFE AND MYTH

THE FIRST COMPLETE BIOGRAPHY
OF THE WORLD'S MOST FAMOUS
AND CONTROVERSIAL PROPHET

John Hogue

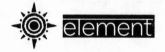

Element
An Imprint of HarperCollins*Publishers*
77–85 Fulham Palace Road,
Hammersmith, London W6 8JB

The website address is: www.thorsonselement.com

and *Element* are trademarks of
HarperCollins*Publishers* Ltd

First published by Element 2003

1 3 5 7 9 10 8 6 4 2

A catalogue record of this book is
available from the British Library

ISBN 0 00 714051 7

Printed and bound in USA by
R R Donnelley, Harrisonburg, USA

Contents

To that which no memory can destroy.

ACKNOWLEDGMENTS

First, I would like to thank all those intrepid editors, designers, and proofreaders at Thorsons/Element for, as Nostradamus would say, "drinking most of the smoke of the lamp [of scholarship]" of long hours inherently endured while accomplishing the goal of tight deadlines. Chief among the people working at Thorsons/Element, I would like to thank the coven of dear wiccans (the wise women, that is) who made this book possible: Belinda Budge (Publishing Director), Louise McNamara (Senior Editor, and new mother), Katy Carrington (Senior Commissioning Editor) for her patience, vision, and deadline extensions; and last but not least, Kate Latham (Project Editor) who, with humor and great aplomb, saw to it that the creative journey of this book came to its successful conclusion.

Also I would like to thank my Thorsons editor, Matthew Cory; and dear thanks also go to my freelance conceptual editor, Larry Boggs, who managed once again to un-dot my Ts and uncross my eyes.

Great thanks and gratitude must also be delivered to all those scholars of Nostradamus yet living, who fall into three categories: the first and second being sympathetic supporters or avowed enemies of my interpretations, and the third being all those scholars caught in the cross-fire. I render sincere thanks to you all, including Bernard Chevignard, Michel Chomarat, Peter Lemesurier, James (the Amazing) Randi, J.R. Jochmans, and J.H. Brennan. You are all my teachers, whether you see yourselves as my supporters or (especially) as my enemies.

Thanks must also be rendered to the late 20th-century Nostradamian scholars upon whose shoulders no sympathetic or debunking scholars can perch themselves high and crow: Edgar Leoni, Steward Robb, and Dr. Edgar Leroy of St.-Rémy.

Many thanks also to Jacqueline Allemand, the curator of Maison de Nostradamus in Salon-en-Provence, for all her help in tracking down crucial French publications of Nostradamus' literary and prophetic works along with important commentaries and critical publications.

Many thanks to my best mate and agent, Ronald S. Tanner.

A personal thanks to my special friends for all their love and encouragement: Nadine (Satgyan) Joyau, Robert (Diwamani) Mutter, Talia Toni Marcus, Madir (Thackeray), Nancy White, and Mother Vipassana. Finally, silent gratitude must go to the peaceful anima of my little island in the archipelago of Puget Sound, for mothering me through this most challenging writing marathon.

An Eccentric Man for All Seasons

~

The 16th-century French doctor Michel de Nostradamus, and his obscure yet hypnotic prophecies, have cast their spell on the world over the last four-and-a-half centuries. He has become a wellspring for wisdom and waggishness for a broad range of diverse historical figures and colorful characters. He is a brunt of jokes by Jay Leno of NBC's *Tonight Show* and was the theatrical device of a cigar-waving Orson Welles, giving one of his better melodramatic performances as the host in a documentary, uttering facts, fables, and smoke rings as captivating and cloudy as Nostradamus' own writings. Nostradamus has been the inspiration for something as benign and silly as the Nostra Doormouse of holiday cards, while others exploited his prophecies for deadlier purposes. Josef Goebbels used the prophecies of Nostradamus as a Nazi propaganda weapon during World War II, while Britain's legendary prime minister Winston Churchill retaliated with his own platoon of interpreters, until even Louis B. Meher, the movie mogul of

MGM Studios, put Nostradamus on the silver screen in his film shorts to boost American morale.

Today, many dismiss Nostradamus as a freak of urban legends and reject his interpreters and avid students as victims of another reconstituted alluvium of New Age sewage. Nonetheless, he has had (and still has) millions of admirers and defenders. Some of them were kings and queens of France, including such rulers as Henry IV, Louis XIII, Louis XIV, and Emperor Napoleon's wife – the Empress Josephine. Respected literary giants such as Victor Hugo have tried to decipher him. World leaders have invoked his name to change destiny.

Nostradamus and his prophecies just won't go away. At the moment when it seems as if the tangle of biographical fact and myth about the man and the chaos of his cryptic prophecies should drive one away, lightning bolts of what appear to be prescient genius cut through his nebulous narrative of tomorrow.

Was Nostradamus a fraud or a true prophetic savant?

One thing is certain: it is safe to say that the man who launched the Nostradamian phenomenon has made good on at least one of his 1,500 or more predictions – that greater and lingering fame would come after his death. Indeed, after his passing in 1566, his "afterlife" has made his name far more famous and enduring than when he was alive. It cannot be denied, even by his greatest debunkers, that Nostradamus is one of the best-known historical figures of the past millennium.

When we, and the controversy of Nostradamus, entered a new millennium, many interpreters and dilettantes of Nostradamus mistakenly believed his prophecies foretold the end of the world – a strangely popular but patently unqualified myth, since Nostradamus had dated the end of the world 1,797 years ahead in the year 3797. Nevertheless, a peaceful turning of New Year's Day 2000 exposed Nostradamus in the minds of many believers and skeptics as a prophetic failure and charlatan. Then on 11 September 2001, the debate about this man and myth came back before global scrutiny. No sooner had the twin towers of the World Trade Center collapsed into billowing, apocalyptic clouds of debris, than Reuters News Agency broadcast across the planet a prophecy attributed to Nostradamus about "hollow mountains" falling in the "City of York." The lines of the purported prophecy – much like what we know about the man Nostradamus – were a blend of myth and fact. Fake lines like "the city of York" drew people in, yet these were sewn together with stolen lines of two actual Nostradamus prophecies – the same prophecies that for decades many interpreters, including this author, believed forecast a future nuclear or terrorist attack on New York's lower Manhattan financial district.

A prophetic hoax about an attack on the "City of York" rode on the back of these real quatrain (four-line) prophecies about what many believe is an attack on New York:

> *At forty-five degrees latitude, the sky will burn,*
> *Fire approaches the great new city.*
> *Immediately a huge, scattered flame leaps up,*
> *When they want verification from the Normans* [the French].

> *Garden of the world near the new city,*
> *In the path of the hollow mountains:*
> *It will be seized and plunged into a boiling cauldron,*
> *Drinking by force the waters poisoned by sulfur.*
>
> (QUATRAIN 97, CENTURY 6 AND QUATRAIN 49, CENTURY 10,
> *THE PROPHECIES OF M. MICHEL DE NOSTRADAMUS.*)[1]

When you have two prescient-sounding yet general provocations that include images like "fire approaching" a "new city" at "forty-five degrees latitude" in the "path" of "hollow mountains" near a "garden of the word," the hackles can rise – especially if you apply present-day facts to conveniently join together the dots of a 450-year-old prophetic rant to see what you want to see. Does one brush it all off as a coincidence that the city of "new" York is near latitude 45 degrees, or that the first Boeing 757 hijacked by terrorists cut into the North Tower of the World Trade Center in "a huge, scattered flame" at a 45-degree angle? Is it just the law of chance fooling a prophetically sympathetic mind when the second hijacked airliner passed over New Jersey (also known as the "Garden" state) and swerved at high speed toward the South Tower of the "World" Trade Center building exactly over the "Path" subway tunnel before slamming into the second man-made peak of "hollow mountains"? And when Nostradamus describes his vision of "hollow mountains" being "seized and plunged" into a "boiling cauldron," are we conned yet again by a new generation of sycophants tagging events of their time on to cryptic ravings; or is it more than a coincidence that each tower as it fell looked as if it were seized by the hand of an invisible force and plunged into the boiling cauldron of its own debris cloud? Are the "Normans" some retroactive allusion to the people of Normandy, or is this, as Nostradamian scholars believe, a code name for the French, whose intelligence agents on 10 September were indeed frantically warning their opposites in Washington D.C. that a terrorist attack on America was imminent?

Do we have a 16th-century charlatan catching us in our projections when the multiple meanings of Renaissance French can satisfy what we want to see? The word Nostradamus uses for "cauldron" is *cuue* (spelled *cuve* in Modern French). It can mean a number of things beyond "cauldron" such as "tank" or "tub." Is the skeptic right when he brushes off any application of this word to the fall of the twin towers? Is the skeptic right to suggest waggishly that we might as well say Nostradamus is predicting some future disaster in a jacuzzi; or, is it not a little disturbing to one's flippant reason to discover that the World Trade Center was built on a huge, rectangular cement box of watertight floor and walls known as "the tub"?

Welcome to the debate.

It could be said that Nostradamus the man planted the seed of Nostradamus the Myth in April 1554 (on Friday the Thirteenth, no less) when it is believed his secretary began transcribing his bizarre history of the future. The Myth was born 12 years later, in 1566, when family and friends laid his lifeless body behind the wall of his favorite chapel outside of town.

Ever since that day, Nostradamus has enjoyed an afterlife.

In life, he painstakingly manufactured a literary chaos that would turn the cloudy quatrains and half-page-long sentences of his prophetic prose narratives into a *tabular* upon which each generation of interpreters could project their hopes, fears, and expectations. Moreover, for centuries now, biographers, blind believers, debunkers, and "prophegandists" have helped it along, with accurate and inaccurate dissemination of his prophetic legacy.

In the process the man and his life have all but disappeared in the giant shadow cast by his own controversial prophecies.

So just who was Nostradamus?

The new millennium and the "9/11" attacks have sparked the greatest debate yet about the efficacy of this man and his prophecies. There could be no better time to release a book that reassesses what we know about Nostradamus, the man.

The present book is the first complete and full-bodied biography and historical reassessment in over 60 years. This publication celebrates the 500-year anniversary of the birth of history's most famous and controversial prophet.

How the Memory Replaced the Man

✌

Biographies are not about real people. They are about the memories we collect in their name. Some recollections are negative, others reverent; some attempt to be objective, but even an unbiased biographer depends on material coming from those supporters and detractors who are not. Once recorded, a memory of someone changes with time. One era praises, another condemns – and so the slant on the dissemination of the facts goes, depending on the way history is filtered by the attitudes of each new era. The shadow of a man's life is ever made of the darkness of print on the paper of biographies. If we think we get a true taste of the real article, perhaps we are doing what the Zen master said – "eating pictures of rice cakes." Can memories at any time adequately compare themselves to the mystery and reality we hold at this very moment, as living, breathing human beings?

If a fair and balanced telling of any life story must pass the gauntlet of memory and prejudice, the problem is exacerbated in the case of writing biographies of controversial figures such as Nostradamus. The surviving corroborative sources are few, while the strong emotions and dogmatic beliefs his name conjures are (and always were) many. The majority of the details of Nostradamus' ancestry and biographical information are posted to us in three identifiable tiers of hunting and gathering down a long 500-year road through history. We first begin with the auto-biographical record of Nostradamus and the surviving accounts of three eyewitnesses from the 16th century: his brother, Jehan de Nostredame (1522–c. 1577),[2] his eldest son, César de Nostredame (1556–1629)[3] and his secretary and self-professed first disciple, Jean-Aymes (Aimé) de Chavigny (d. 1604).[4] The second posting, if you will, comes from 17th-century biographers Etienne Jaubert[5] and Theophile de Garencières.[6] However, much of what they convey to us as documented biographical information unfortunately comes with little or none of their sources intact, thanks to time's inexorable destruction and the misplacement of historical archives.

The first complete biography of Nostradamus comes from the early 18th century. Pierre-Joseph de Haitze published *La Vie de Nostradamus* in 1712. It is the source for over half of the stock biographical information extant today, and it appears to be based on recollections passed down in two unpublished manuscripts written by Palamèdes Tronc de Coudoulet, the great-grandson of Pierre Tronc de Coudoulet – one of Nostradamus' closest friends and cronies later in his life. The 19th-century researcher F. Buget,[7] who claims to have seen the Coudoulet manuscripts before they disappeared, attests to their authenticity and general veracity when judged against his own research. Unfortunately, much of Buget's material is unverifiable thanks no doubt again to the appetite of termite time and the march of archival housecleaners.

The third tier of hunter-gatherers relaying biographical facts consists of a number of intrepid scholars stirring the dust-motes of archival halls throughout the 20th century. Chief among these are the critical and balanced examinations of modern scholars, such as Edgar Leoni,[8] who defined himself as an "advanced amateur" Nostradamian scholar. Then there are Michel Chomarat,[9] Pierre Brind'Amour,[10] Peter Lemesurier,[11] and the authors of more cynical examinations, such as Dr. Edgar Leroy[12] and the professional magician-turned-crusader against all things paranormal, James Randi.[13]

Before we begin to piece together a facsimile of a man out of these various postings of memories, it would be good to heed the insight of Norman Mailer:

I think it's very good to get rid of the notion that because you've accumulated some facts, therefore you're factual.[14]

If a purely objective and factual biography of anyone is beyond any biographer's honest grasp, then what can we learn from the story of someone's life? Perhaps we can experience a history of the essential, if not the undiluted factual history of a human being. We might gain an understanding of that higher history that is myth. To me, biographer Daniel Grotta, in his biography of J.R.R. Tolkien, defined the difference between factual and mythological history in the simplest terms when he said, "To tell the past is history; but to explain the past, and to make it meaningful to the present, is mythology."[15]

Thus I present to you the surviving shards of base metal memories of the real Nostradamus, in the hope that once reconstructed these fragments will yield their share of mythology's gold and make the life and myth of Nostradamus meaningful to you in this ever-present moment.

John Hogue
(4 April 2003)

CHAPTER ONE

Born in the Land
of Troubadour Kings

❦

Of Havens and Heritage

Retrace the tearful trail of Nostradamus' Jewish ancestors and you
will eventually find yourself back in late 14th-century Spain, cow-
ering before a zealot priest named Fernando Martinez. In 1391,
Father Martinez cast the first stone that shattered the fragile
glasshouse of Spanish Gentile tolerance of their Jewish neighbors.
Martinez' persuasive fire-and-brimstone speeches marked the end
of a 672-year interlude between persecutions that began with the
Moorish conquest of most of the Spanish peninsula in the year
719, from when a succession of Moorish caliphs had decreed that
Jews and Christians be given the second-citizen status of protected peoples provided under Islamic law. Although burdened with
special taxes, a distinctive costume identifying their minority
status, and other restrictions – including a stringent ban on proselytizing – the Caliphs had granted Christians and Jews freedom
of worship, and their cultural identity and traditions were for the
most part protected.

I

By the final decade of the 14th century, Christian armies had effectively pushed the Moors out of most of Spain. It was not long before the rich legacy of cultural diversity of language, culture, and intermarriage of Moors, Christians, and Jews in Spain fell victim to old prejudices and fears crossing over the Pyrenees mountains from Christian Europe. The anti-Semitic call for expulsion was now heard again in Spain. Christian priests, such as Father Martinez, and the laity demanded *limpieza di sangre* – a cleansing of contaminated blood.

Every pure-blooded Christian knew that the Jews were what St. Gregory called "slayers of the Lord" and St. Jerome called "vipers." Even meek and mild St. Bernard of Clairvaux defined the Jews as a "degraded and perfidious people." The proto-fascists of late medieval Spain upheld St. John Chrysotom's words that: "The Jews sacrifice their children to Satan … They are worse than wild beasts … the synagogue is a brothel, a den of scoundrels, the temple of demons devoted to idolatrous cults, a criminal assembly of Jews, a place of meeting for the assassins of Christ!"[1]

The call to a new pogrom by Father Martinez saw thousands of Jews killed in a wave of massacres across Spain. The survivors were given the choice either to stay and be forcibly baptized as Christians or to leave their homes and livelihoods for places unknown. Most of them converted and grudgingly went to church, while others continued to practice their religion and their kosher dietary restrictions in secret until the 1470s. But then the Church, led by Tomás de Torquemada, the first Inquisitor General of Spain, launched a new Jew-hunt, bringing on the mass murder and complete expulsion of Jews from Spain during the Spanish Inquisition.

It is suggested that Nostradamus' ancestors in the 1390s had seen the signs of things to come and joined the first Diaspora from Spain a century before Torquemada's rack and flaming stakes decimated the descendants of those foolish enough to remain. The outcasts made their way east over the muddy tracks of the high mountain passes down into south-western France, where many settled into the Jewish community at Carcassonne. An accounting of Nostradamus' paternal lineage begins there, with an early ancestor named Astruge de Carcassonne, whose son Vital married Astrugie Massip. Their son Davin possibly converted to Christianity and changed his name to Arnauton de Velorgues. According to the skeptical inquirer Dr. Edgar Leroy, he may have married a woman named Venguessonne. Nostradamian encyclopedist Peter Lemesurier, however, believes the vague archival fragment is an appellation for "Ben Guesson" or "son of Guesson." That would make Guesson and Guessonnett linguistic echoes reverberating back to a Spanish Jewish ancestor named Guasón ("Joker"). Further, he speculates with some measure of a scholar's tongue-in-"cheekiness" that if there is a genetic disposition to humor in the bloodline of Nostradamus, it will surface again in the birth of the "irrepressible young Michel."[2]

Just when Nostradamus' ancestors wandered eastwards into Provence from Carcassonne is not known. The move was certainly motivated by word of mouth that there was a renewed openness for the settlement of Jews in the lands of the last troubadour king, René "the Good" (1409–80). A tolerant ruler who liked to wear a turban and Arabic robes, his family (the House of Anjou) had once adopted many native cultural influences when they held Crusader citadels in the Holy Land. René counted many Moors and Saracens among his courtiers. His Edict of 1454 granted Jews in Provence the freedom to practice commerce, the arts, and medicine. They could be notaries or financial agents, and openly practice their religion. It is likely that the family of Guesson (or Gassonet) had moved into Provence sometime before (probably well before) the mid-1450s.[3]

Afterwards they put down roots in Provence's autonomous Papal enclave of Avignon, where Guy Gassonet married Stella Crescas. When she died, he married a devout Jewess named Benastrugue. Archival evidence at Orange marks the year 1463 as the time Guy Gassonet recanted his Jewish origin to become a baptized Christian, taking the name Peyrot (Pierre) de Nostredame. Benastrugue rejected Christianity and received from her "saved" husband her 15 minutes (or better, her 15 words) of historic fame in the archives of Orange when Pierre officially repudiated her as his wife. He then married the submissive Blanche de Sainte-Marie, and they had at least six surviving children, including Nostradamus' future father, Jaume; his uncles, François and Pierre; and three aunts, Catherine, Bartholomée, and Marguerite.

Lemesurier makes an educated guess that Guy Gassonet picked the name Peyrot (Pierre) after his bishop, and the surname *de Nostredame* ("of Our Lady") on the day of his conversion, which he believes could have been on 2 July 1463, the date on which the Feast of the Visitation of the Virgin Mary was celebrated. Lemesurier further believes Pierre and his new Christian wife, Blanche, argued over what name to pick for the family, Blanche believing Pierre should adopt his wife's family name, de Sainte-Marie ("of St. Mary").[4] Although such speculation has merit, without solid proof there is a danger of unintentionally adding to the dense tissue of myths already surrounding Nostradamus' life and lineage. At the risk of further fueling the debate, I would only add one more possibility: Peyrot, being a man, could not bring himself to adopt his wife's name; thus *de Nostredame* (or the Latin *de nostra domina*) was a compromise.

Advanced amateur scholar Edgar Leoni points to Depping's speculation in his history of the Jews[5] that Nostradamus' paternal grandfather, Pierre de Nostredame, came from Italian Jews known as *Nostradone*, or *Nostradonna*. Occult scholar Manly P. Hall proposes that the family of Nostra Donna entered Italy as refugees from Andalusia, Spain, and that Piedro Nostra-Donna moved to Arles, Provence, where he practiced medicine and Gallicized his name to Peyrot de Nostredame.

While Hall does not supply his source for this theory, Depping clearly takes his lead from Pierre's future grandson and Provençal historian, Jehan de Nostredame, who recorded in his *Chronique de Provence* that by the year 1469 his grandfather addressed himself as "Pierre de Nostredame or Nostradone."

Pierre de Nostredame, so the speculation goes, was a "famous doctor and astrologer" of Arles, well versed "in the Hebrew and Greek languages." According to Jehan, his paternal grandfather quarreled with the city's pharmacists. They gathered before the city magistrates to protest against doctor Nostredame because he had the gall to concoct his own drugs and not call upon their services. Pharmacists in the 16th century were notorious for skimping on the ingredients of doctors' recipes to save money and inflate their profits. So, rather than "falsifying his drugs" as charged by his competitors, Pierre may have made his own to ensure that his patients would be protected from quacks. In any case, Gentile physicians and pharmacists applied pressure on the city magistrates to have him driven out of Arles. It is equally possible that these efforts were motivated by Pierre's Jewish origin, along with his success and independent outlook as a doctor. Such anti-Semitic motivations are not far-fetched, considering that a council of magistrates and priests held at Arles in the 13th century invented the first yellow identification patches for Jews.

In 1940, in an attempt to buttress these speculations, Charles Reynaud-Plense pored over Provençal archives searching for objective evidence of "Nostradonna" hailing from Italy. He found nothing to back up Jehan de Nostredame's "Nostredone"-from-Arles story. He did, however, find references to another Jewish doctor named Abraham Solomon, who is mentioned both in departmental archives (*L'Encyclopédie du Département des Bouches-du-Rhône*)[6] and in the writings of Nostradamus' son, César de Nostredame (in his *L'Histoire et Chronique de Provence*). Solomon, it seems, was King René's personal physician. Reynaud-Plense's comprehensive research[7] identifies him as the descendant of Sephardic refugees landing in Marseilles sometime after the Spanish massacres of 1391. Although the archival report states that

Solomon was "ennobled and baptized," no surviving document exists identifying him as Pierre de Nostredame. Reynaud-Plense did not leave it at that. He was clearly influenced by the 19th-century Nostradamian scholar F. Buget, who made the Solomon/ Nostredame link in articles published in 1862, from documentation that, unfortunately, had disappeared by the following century.

Thus, upon these fragile factual threads hangs a popular legend that places Nostradamus' paternal grandfather among the notable caravanserai of poet-knights, troubadours, artists, physicians, and Judeo-Christian and Saracen philosophers and healers that followed King René's renaissance court about the western Mediterranean on royal visits to his far-flung dominions.[8] And fragile though these threads may be, the legend does not skimp on detail, or even plausibility. Continuing with this scenario, it is while in service to this vagabond court that speculation helps us stretch out Pierre's hand in friendship to Nostradamus' maternal great-grandfather: the recently baptized Jew taking the Christian name Jean de Saint-Rémy. The tale goes that Dr. Saint-Rémy earned his role as King René's personal physician by curing his ailing laundress, Charlotte the Turk.[9] King René's son Jean, Duke of Calabria and Lorraine, had taken an interest in retaining Pierre de Nostredame, recently run out of Arles, as his personal physician. The two physicians met, became fast friends, and followed their royal charges in René's traveling court, enriching their purses and obtaining a knowledge of medicine, astrology, and cultures that spanned southern Europe. In 1470, Jean was poisoned in Barcelona just as he was closing negotiations to add this Spanish principality of Catalonia to his other realms. We are told that one of his last wishes was to bequeath his loyal physician, Pierre de Nostredame, to his father. The days of travel ended as the king, old and broken-hearted, moved his doctors and the court permanently to Tarascon, in Provence.

Around the same time that Reynaud-Plense was propounding the court physicians' story, another scholar, Dr. Edgar Leroy of

Saint-Rémy, rifled through other records and, finding nothing supporting the Solomon/Nostradonna connection, concluded the story is sheer bunk. Instead, he suggested that Nostradamus is indeed the grandson of Peyrot (Pierre) de Nostredame – the product of a long line of recently baptized Jewish grain dealers from Avignon; and that Nostradamus' father, named Jaume (or Jacques) de Nostredame, was also a grain dealer who left the business in 1495 and moved to St.-Rémy to marry Reynière de Saint-Rémy, the daughter of Jean de Saint-Rémy, Nostradamus' maternal grandfather.

This record implies to Leroy that Saint-Rémy's association with the court of King René had a less romantic context, and that pleasant family legends of great-grandfather Jean tending to the health of Provence's last troubadour king are no more than wishful thinking. According to Leroy, Jean, the Christianized Jew, was a failed physician of the town and the king's appointed treasurer of the town of St.-Rémy. He was nominally the king's tax collector, not his doctor. It must be added that less flattering studies of the "good" King René depict him as a skinflint when it came to his subjects. He drained their finances, dispensing money generously in patronage of artists, scholars, and to retired Jewish doctors of the taxing kind, such as Saint-Rémy – the latter being charged with reaching ever deeper into the pockets of their neighbors in St.-Rémy to fund the king's many expensive cultural and artistic projects.

Leroy may have rushed to judgment himself. An avowed anti-Nostradamian before he began his research, he made his conclusions on what documentation survives or can be found; but its incompleteness can mislead an investigator, particularly a biased one. A retired physician and tax collector today could have been a court-physician to the king yesterday. There is nothing in the surviving records proving that Jean de Saint-Rémy was anything but a respected, if financially strapped, physician of the town from which he adopted his new Christian name.[10] It is also not impudent speculation to assume that some of the elements of the "physicians-at-court" story have a basis in fact. Yes, there is no comprehensive proof that Nostradamus' maternal great-grandfather was Abraham Solomon, or that he was "at" court, but there is more than a good chance (if not a surviving record) that he could have attended to the aging king's health on the frequent royal progressions of his court through the town of St. Rémy. Clearly, Nostradamus' maternal great-grandfather was well enough educated and sufficiently knowledgeable from long experience and travels to pass on to his great-grandson an intellectual brilliance and sense of geography far beyond his tender age.

The smattering of objective facts used as a basis for speculation and counter-speculation concerning Nostradamus' ancestors does at least converge on the little town of St.-Rémy. All sides agree that the doctors – or the grain dealer and town treasurer's families – settled there by the 1480s. Jean de Saint-Rémy appears in the records as the town treasurer in 1481. Perhaps coincidentally, his appearance there does support the stock biographies that claim he and Peyrot de Nostredame left the king's court at Tarascon upon his death the year before. The records also show Jean's son, René (who, by the way, is named in honor of the king), married Beatrice Tourrel, before he died sometime around the year 1479.

Reynière de Saint-Rémy, the daughter of the late René de Saint-Rémy, would marry Jaume de Nostredame, the son of Peyrot.[II] Nostradamus' father was a successful merchant at the time of his marriage and his wealth and properties no doubt increased from this match with the daughter of the town treasurer and money-lender. By 1503, Jaume would become a notary public, signing himself as *Jacobus de nostra domina*. He would also take on the responsibilities of scribe, bailiff, and clerk of the town court.

Nostradamus' parents, it could be said, would be blackmailed to become Christians. King René died in 1480, and was succeeded by his nephew Charles of Maine. Charles' death in 1486 brought an end to both male lines of the first and second House of Anjou, which automatically saw the kingdoms of Provence and Maine become possessions of the French Crown. Tolerance for the Jews died with them.

By 1488, Charles VIII of France ordered the Jews of Provence to become baptized. When his son Louis XII took the throne, he made this more than a threat by signing the Edict of 26 September 1501, demanding that all Jews become baptized within three months, or else leave Provence, or, worse, suffer "severe penalties."

The entire de Nostredame clan chose baptism rather than exile from their adopted land.[12] In public, they masqueraded as model Christians while secretly persevering with their private beliefs and Jewish heritage at home. Into this atmosphere of living a double life, Nostradamus was born.

The Devil is in the Astrological Details

St.-Rémy's most famous son, Michel de Nostredame, was born a few minutes after noon, the day before the eve of *Calendo* – the name in the Provençal tongue for Christmas. The Julian calendar calculations used at that time would mark his appearance on Thursday, 14 December (23 December by modern Gregorian reckoning) in the year 1503.

Today, Nostradamus' birthplace is marked by a municipal plaque on the pockmarked limestone face of a block of a house nestled against the city wall on the narrow Rue Hoche. Its appearance certainly rubs one's expectations raw when you consider biographical accounts that little Michel's father was then a prosperous grain merchant, no doubt well-heeled with the dowry of his mother. Then again, this may be only the first modest house of newlyweds freed from better family accommodation elsewhere in town that have since been lost to memory; or the plaque may be advertising the wrong address.

If this is the house of Michel de Nostredame's birth, then the pockmarked stone slabs we can see now were likely hidden under a fresh blush of ocher plaster, which would have soaked in the soft, greenish winter sunlight and shadow for which St.-Rémy is famous. Nostradamus' maternal great-grandfather and paternal grandfather came to see the child on the day of his birth. Into the trembling hands of Jean de Saint-Rémy, his daughter deposited a tiny rosy-cheeked baby of peaches and cream complexion, wrapped in swaddling clothes. On that first day, it was too early for Jean de Saint-Rémy and Peyrot de Nostredame to encounter in the squinting face of the newborn his most distinctive feature – his penetrating and hypnotic gray eyes.

Certainly, his father, the notary, would have made note of the time of birth to plot the child's horoscope. Astrology was widely used by the upper classes to plot a map of potential destiny using calculations based on the position of the stars. The newborn's maternal great-grandfather had been a doctor before becoming town treasurer, and all doctors of the day were trained astrologers. It was popularly believed that the movements of planets and stars in the cosmos had a direct influence on the human body, and could not only reveal its strengths and weaknesses, but could also influence the type of herbs and medicines for appropriate healing, and mark the time a physician should use them to greatest effect. If not Peyrot, then at least Jean de Saint-Rémy would have drawn little Michel's horoscope or had it commissioned.

The general paradigm of God's universe held by people of the Western world at the time of Michel de Nostredame's birth defined the universe in a finite cast that satisfied their limited understanding. This picture is in some ways quite foreign to us. There was a great and ordered vault of heaven, which serenely revolved above the trials and tribulations of life. The cosmic orbs of sun, moon, and the planets plotted their steady courses between Heaven and Earth to mark its seasons and cycles in God's great and immutable timepiece that had run 5,500 years or so since He created the world and the universe. That universe consisted of the Earth at its center, around which the sun, moon, and planets passed in orbit along the unchangeable boundaries of concentric spheres. The sphere nearest to Earth, its edge defined by the orbit of the moon, was the realm of fire and air wherein God permitted change and chaos to play in the fire-brush of comets – the bearded stars – and the sharp blaze of meteors. The sphere farthest from Earth is where God painted his stars. Beyond the stellar veil of this outermost sphere, the Lord dwelt in Paradise.

The limitations at the beginning of the 21st century are on a grander scale. For us the perceptible universe has existed 13.5 billion years back in time, stretching chaotic clouds of galaxies 27 billion or more light years from end to end. By comparison, Jean de Saint-Rémy's cosmos was a breathtaking little bubble in God's Paradise, with a radius of 50 million miles from Earth to the stars, which the Lord had created some 4,000 years or so before the birth of Christ. Beyond a few minor disputes as to the details, that model of the universe had become the established astronomical dogma since the Greek astronomer and astrologer Claudius Ptolemaeus (Ptolemy) of Alexandria, Egypt, advanced his astronomical theory of the order and functioning of the heavenly bodies in the 2nd century C.E.

Horoscopes were calculated with the use of an ephemeris, consisting of tables of astrological data to plot the movements of planets and constellations at the time of birth. In the baby's case, the natal horoscope could be plotted either at or a few minutes after noontime.[13] To calculate the position of Michel's birth as it related to the planets and stars, latitude tables were required, but no longitude was calculated at that time. The world had yet to agree to a common meridian, such as Greenwich Mean Time. Unlike today's circular charts, the birth chart was set down in pen and parchment on a square divided into 12 triangles. These represented the houses – or 12 departments or dimensions – of life and destiny. The manner in which the time and location of the planets and constellations at birth fall within the 12 houses helps the astrologer interpret their influence on the subject's destiny and potentials. You could say that objective astronomical information of the placement of planets and stars at birth passes through the intuitive and subjective artistry of the interpreter in a form of mathematical poetry. It is not science as defined today, but the feelings of a human heart cannot always be measured and weighed.

We do not know what poetry of potential Jean de Saint-Rémy discovered, as he plotted the chart of the newborn Michel in the quieter days following the Christmas festivals of 1503, as no written record of his findings (let alone the natal horoscope itself) survives. Even so, the natal information survives, even if the reflections of Saint-Rémy do not, so some of the following astrological insights we can draw 500 years later may well agree with many of those of baby Michel's great-grandfather.

First, he might have noticed an auspicious conjunction of the Sun (ruler of the character) with Mercury (messenger of intellect) at high noon, the time of Michel's birth. This can be a portent of a great astrologer and seer. This conjunction sits in the ninth house, representing higher intellect and spiritual understanding, and is in the sign of Capricorn. Capricorn gives the child a seriousness of demeanor, a love of scholarship and learning and, if well directed, will give the boy a taciturn and dignified nature. If Jean had plotted the boy's ascendant, as I believe he must, he would immediately have noticed a powerful T-square aspect of the Aries ascendant and Virgo descendant at 90 degrees from the Midheaven conjunction. The square can be an aspect of malevolence or affliction, but if it is borne by a great and diligent soul, a square can act as a friction point of revelation. It defines the life-challenges Michel would have to transcend to obtain divine grace. The child would require effective guidance in order to direct and tame his gift of prophecy in the harness and halter of cogent letters and words. This could be a difficult undertaking, for the fates would conspire in such a square to vex his original mind with ill-conceived language skills unless he found the appropriate patient mentor who could nurse him past the initial impediments to learning and letters. A good teacher of the liberal arts would be required.

Jean de Saint-Rémy's concerns might next have settled on the dramatic positioning of his great-grandson's natal Moon in Scorpio, which unfortunately sits in the house of its detriment, the eighth. The Moon is the ruler of temperament, and if there are no mitigating aspects with other houses and planets, then emotions could become the boy's undoing in life. He could be willful, possessive, and jealous to the extreme, hold grudges and dominate others by dark arts. The Moon's position in the eighth house, ruled by Mars, could doubly magnify his emotional desires and the temptation to lust. Much energy and emotional attention could settle, for better or worse, on partnerships, and Michel could be fortune's foil of inheritance, dowry, and marriage. However, if properly taught, the subject might transform these base metals of his Moon position into the alchemical gold of hard and tempered understanding and careful discernment of friends, lovers, and enemies. It would not be an easy path, but, as a wise man once said, the sword may first complain of having to go into the furnace fire, but later on celebrates the cool and sharpened strength forged by tribulation's flame. The boy's Moon could awaken in him powers of otherworldly perception. It is the sign of the medium, the spirit oracle, or, if ill-directed, the sign of the necromancer and Satan's spawn.

Though emotion's ruler wallows in the eighth house of detrimental Scorpio, the angels of its higher potential are clasped by the harmonious trine configuration of the Moon with the conjoined Jupiter, Saturn, and Mars in the sign of Cancer. Through this trine, with the combined power of his Midheaven conjunction, the higher aspects of Scorpio's ruling planet of Mars might mitigate the trials and temptations of a scary and sensuous Scorpio Moon. Rather than an entity ruled by animal passions and secret grudges of the impetuous god of war and intemperance, the boy might awaken within himself, through this great trine, the enlightened *Mage*. The more base the "mettle," the greater the alchemical potential of a magician's higher nature.

It all depends on who might give the boy the right motivation and direction in life. His nature would be deep, naturally introspective, and hard to fathom, thanks to his many planets in the water element (the Moon, Mars, Jupiter, and Saturn – the latter three all in retrograde motion). He could be prone to violent outbursts of emotion and temper if he were to lack self-control (the ascendant in Aries), but Venus in Aquarius in the eleventh house counterbalances the tendency toward tantrums with attunement toward charm and diplomacy. He could also be progressive in his views, if not eccentric, and he would perhaps endure a young man's fair share of lustfulness – a string of shallow dalliances with women – before marriage. While charming Venus might grant him many friends, coming to bask in his outwardly effervescent personality, inside there might live another man hiding a secret world. A Moon in Scorpio could give him an instinctive knowledge and desire to penetrate the mysteries behind unseen phenomena. If harmoniously combined with the retrograde conjunction of Jupiter, Saturn, and Mars in Cancer these would provide him the courage, persistence, and love of ritual needed for practicing magic and prophecy, as well as providing the intellectual muscle for scholarship. Jovial Jupiter would also bless the boy with a good sense of humor – an attribute lacking in most prognosticators.

The conjunction is in the sign and fourth house of home and hearth, and so a proper and nourishing upbringing in this his childhood home – and, later, a harmonious and well-arranged marriage – would be necessary for there to be real success in life. He would have to watch the mischief-making of Mars in his fourth house which may result in his home life being marred by arguments and discord – but Saturn's justice and Jupiter's wisdom could heal any lingering wounds.

Finally, Jean de Saint-Rémy would likely have taken note of the north and south lunar nodes of his great-grandson's chart for some indication of what practical direction the boy's future career should take. He would see his north node (also called the Head of the Dragon in Divine Astrology,[14] or the wheel of fortune) sitting in Pisces, and the south node (or Tail of the Dragon, or wheel of atonement and penance) sitting in Virgo. Pisces gives the child great intuition, whereas Virgo could encourage him to apply his intuition towards medicine and the healing arts.

Jean de Saint-Rémy might well have concluded that his great-grandson was destined for an extraordinary life – perhaps that of a respected astrologer and physician. However, the gifts of original insight could deliver a destiny fraught with danger and tragedy if the powerful contrasts of his inner and outer nature were not harmonized. Thus it is safe to say that his great-grandfather waited patiently yet eagerly for the latent tendencies of the child's intellect to flesh themselves out.

The Conditioning of a Mage

The mind and heart of all newborn children depend on their mother, father, and extended family for the means to imprint a necessary identity to survive in this world. We begin a long life-time habit of gathering other people's experiences, mistaking them as our own. We instinctively bond ourselves to kin and later have a childlike trust exploited by those well-meaning – and not so well-meaning – family and authority figures. The light of child-hood's adult-confounding intelligence soon dims. We obey and learn to insulate ourselves from the world in ways marked by the sentiments of the times, yet we call it perception. We come to our reactions and reasons for being without remembering how other people began weaving a costume called "personality," wrapping and buttoning the constricting garment tight around our innocent nakedness of spirit.

No loving parent intends to smother their child's soul, but we forget that underneath the costume and the mask of personality we wear is an ever-present, naked *isness*. Sometimes it slips out momentarily, and the original face and form of that never-birthed and never-dying beingness emerges. Unfortunately, history leaves behind only the discarded garments of personality for scholars to rummage through, tug, and tear at.

Michel de Nostredame's principal biographers, Jehan and César de Nostredame, and Jean-Aymes de Chavigny, report that he enjoyed an idyllic childhood. It appears that his parents and grandparents gave him financial security and a good home. In other words, his initial indoctrination into the ways of fashioning a persona – or, as that Latin word means, "mask" – went smoothly.

No doubt he had his share of character-building moments and childhood traumas, but these rags of memory have been lost to us. The earliest biographers tell us that the mind of little Michel displayed signs of intuitive and intellectual awareness at quite an early age. It is safe to assume that he possessed, with childhood's energetic magnification, the physical and psychological attributes later noted by eyewitnesses of his middle and old age.[15] Little Michel must have betrayed his acute senses in the quick blink and turn of his gray-eyed gaze to the direction of sights, smells, and sounds of his home. He would soon flare his nose in delight of rich smells of Provençal cooking. He would prick his ears to the slow and opened vowel gavotte of his mother's tongue, augmented by the music of the family's gossip and the captivating, yet bewildering boiling marmalade babble that was the Provençal language. He would also hear for the first time the unctuous lilt of Latin, and, on occasion, the sweet swinging song of the king's French spoken by his father's friends and business associates.

The house that welcomed Michel into the world was ever a matrix of town activity. Jaume de Nostradamus, being a public notary and the town's court scribe, held an important position in the discourse and communications of St.-Rémy. He was one of the few adults in the town and its environs who could read and write, even among the nobility. The members of St.-Rémy's bourgeoisie and noble classes would pass over his threshold, perhaps sample his wine and his wife's cooking, and require the services of his quill pen for communications as varied as a love letter or a last will and testament. In this way, little Michel watched, listened and apparently soon understood the recorded and notarized passage of births and marriages, the milestones of happiness, the subpoenas of dispute, the declarations of heritage and death. His awakening senses, bathed in this atmosphere of Provençal cooking and mental gymnastics, would become sharpened and applied in two lifelong passions: cooking and writing.

Michel became acquainted with the cozy and closed-in street life of St.-Rémy. In the Renaissance period, living quarters were usually crowded. The upper floors were a place for sleeping, the first floor for business and eating – but the streets were where one stretched out one's body, sharpened one's wits, and seized and experienced life. There one found the merchants in their ground-floor shops along the narrowest of lanes (sometimes only the width of a small wagon). The town's famous gentle light soaked down from the multi-storied, biscuit-colored walls and sun-burnt terra-cotta roof tiles to wash itself in milky pink and yellow hues around the hustle of produce sellers, butchers, and fishmongers. It is in the streets, meeting and playing with life as a child, that Michel's mind received the imprint of its Provençal national characteristics. Medieval accounts from French princes passing through the region on their way to the crusades could apply equally to the Provençal native at the dawn of the 16th century. Provençals were generous and welcoming to strangers in times of peace and plenty, prudent and industrious when surviving times of war and famine. They were better lovers than warriors, and willing to eat roots of stalks and vegetables in times of famine. Hence came the proverb: "The Frenchman for fighting, but the Provençal for victuals." They were talkative and lively – as different from the French in customs, character, costume, and food "as a duck is to a chicken."[16]

As he observed the passionate bartering for goods at the market, Michel undoubtedly learned that the Provençal not only absorbed the olive skin and raven hair of the ancient Greeks, and the love for freedom of speech born of their ancient experiments with democracy, but also their cunning ways and (dare we say) chicanery. These characteristics certainly formed the general impression of many outside observers. As an adult, Michel would have such stereotypical judgments whispered behind his back by the more staid and stiff northerners of France.

His first language was the poetic native tongue of Provençal, a dialect of Gallo-Latinized French, richly spiced and blended as it was with the consonant tang and vowel coos of Greek words. His hearth and home was *oustaou*; the daily loaves of bread were called *artoun*. One of the household's servants carried them from market in a wicker *canasto* (basket), and if Michel had one too many helpings of *artoun,* his mother might call him *boufaire* (gluttonous). If his childhood antics displeased his great-grandfather, he would caution him not to be *matou* (foolish).

Michel could see the dilapidated 14th-century gothic spire of St. Rémy's Saint-Martin Cathedral from his street. (The spire was later renovated in the 17th century.) He was baptized there. There he frequently attended mass alongside his newly Christianized family and relatives, and he fell in love with the solemnity, grandeur, and love of God. There too, the Greek language held its spell on Provençal life. Michel may have showed his noted aptitude for picking up languages by asking his father and grand-fathers to explain French religious words of Greek origin, such as *psaume, liturgie, homélie,* and *catholique.* Under the gothic-arched canopy of St. Martin's stone roof, the divine cosmos would be personified, and reduced to traditional dimensions by imposing men in robes bending down at him, crosses swinging in his face.

Michel's first encounters with his luscious homeland beyond the town walls, the wide and fertile farmlands and verdant mead-ows of the Rhône river valley, must have been something of an epiphany. From what was recorded of his later life, we can assume that Michel loved playing in and contemplating the cornucopia of wild flowers and the purple fire of wild *lavendo* (lavender) fields. Evenings would see the boy coming home from each foray, with a relative in tow, a walking and prattling scent bag of *Herbes de Provence.*

At the time of Michel's childhood, unlike the rest of Europe, the land of Provence was free from roving soldiers, but teaming with roving troubadours and poets. The sensuously bucolic yet fictional account of life in Provence in the 1480s written by 19th-century English novelist, Sir Walter Scott, in *Anne of Geierstein,* could approximate some of the ambience of the Provence of Michel's childhood:

The greatest singularity was the absence of armed men and soldiers in the peaceful country. In England, no one stirred without his longbow, sword, and buckler. In France, the hind wore armor even betwixt the stilts of the plough. In Germany you could not look along a mile of road without seeing clouds of dust from which emerged waving feathers and flashing armor. But in Provence all was quiet and peaceful, as if the music of the land had lulled to sleep all wrathful passions. Now and then a mounted cavalier would pass, harp at saddle-bow or carried by an attendant, attesting his character as Troubadour. The short sword, worn on the left thigh, was for show rather than use.[17]

Chavigny said Michel possessed a photographic memory and could comprehend "the meaning of all manner of small, curious facts which interested him."[18] Sympathetic biographers claim that Jean encouraged Michel's mysterious talent for prophecy, adding that the ancestral gift came from his maternal great-grandfather's side of the family.[19] Jean convinced Michel's parents to let the boy live at his house, where the boy could take instruction in rudimentary mathematics and learn to read and write Greek, Latin and Hebrew. We are told that the eager pupil showed a superior aptitude for mathematics and a great love and mastery of the "celestial sciences" of astronomy and astrology.

One might picture the boy and his great-grandfather on one of their walks among the herbs and purple heath, picking their way along the uneven road out of the town of Saint-Rémy to walk in the nearby hills or visit the ancient Roman ruins of nearby Glanum. On hot afternoons, they might seek the cool shade of what were popularly called *Les Antiques* – the graceful remains of a Roman arch of atypically esthetic Greek architectural subtlety, placed beside a more ostentatious columned tower of a Latin mausoleum. The old man reclining on the steps of the latter in the shade might discourse on herbs, Provence's rich classical history and its mythology.

In the evening back at home, after guests and other family members had retired, one can imagine the two sitting together in private. The old man shakes off his public pose as a devout Christian and dips into the deep meanings of the family's Hebrew legacy. He speaks of the Tree of Life and its forbidden knowledge, and tells the young boy that anyone can use this tree of the Jewish Cabala to become self-aware with the light of God. Michel would be indoctrinated into a family secret – that his ancestors were priests of the tribe of Issachar. They were ancient astronomers and adepts in prediction by means the celestial science of Astrology.

In the Old Testament, I Chronicles 12:32 defines these priests as skilled in the reading of "the signs of times to discover what course Israel should follow."[20] Smith and Fuller's *Dictionary of the Bible* says they accomplished this by using geometry and astronomy to set the time, record the past and forecast the future by means of "ascertaining the periods of the sun and moon, the intercalation of months, and dates of solemn feasts, and the interpretation of the signs of the heavens." Jean de Saint-Rémy might have had to explain to the puzzled boy why the God of his Jewish ancestors openly accepted their practice of astrology when the priests of their new faith were more ambivalent. Jean might have quoted

Maimonides, an ancient Jewish philosopher, who said: "For as much as God hath created these stars and spheres to govern the world and hath set them on high and hath imparted honor unto them, and they are ministers that minister before Him, it is [reasonable] that men should laud and glorify and give them honor."

A line of thinking initiated by biographers such as Renuncio Boscolo[21] has Jean presenting the boy with a chest of family heirlooms. Inside are actual papyri and vellum secret books, salvaged and copied from, perhaps, the dog-eared scrolls of past diasporas leading all the way back to the sack of Jerusalem in 70 B.C.E. The cause for such imaginative speculation arises from the few cryptic comments made by Nostradamus himself decades later, in 1555, when dedicating the *Preface* to his prophecies to his son, César. In this dedication he confessed that he had in his possession "several volumes [of occult philosophy] which had been hidden for a great many centuries."[22] Whether these were Jewish scriptures on occult magic, or works of Cabalists, or whether they included the works of Gentile magicians, is kept secret for reasons obvious to anyone under the scrutiny of the justices of the Church for heresy. Nor do we know the definitive moment when young Michel first saw these manuscripts. It could have just as easily been before or after his great-grandfather died, or while visiting some secret library of the occult underground in his future travels. He could even have purchased them openly (if cautiously) from under the counter of a Christianized Jewish book dealer in Avignon, Florence, or Marseilles.

Jean de Saint-Rémy's last lesson was his own death. He imparted to Michel the pain of loss and it struck home with the hammer blow of undertakers nailing shut the coffin, an awareness of mortality's shadow following all who lived. Upon Jean's death, Michel, now entering adolescence, was returned to his parents' home. Whether this was the same crowded hovel on the Rue Hoche or, as others surmise, a new and larger home on the Rue du Berri is disputed, but the household was more pressed for space than before, and perhaps Michel had to get used to a less pampered life, jostling for space and attention alongside a growing number of siblings. By the time Michel was 10 years old they included his elder sister, Delphine, brothers Jehan, Pierre, and Hector – with Louis (b. 1522), Betrand, Jean, and finally Antoine (b. 1523) still on the way. Biographers who theorize that Michel's paternal grand-father, Peyrot de Nostredame, was a retired physician rather than a grain dealer say that he continued Michel's daily instruction on all subjects: classical literature, history, geography, medicine, astrology, and herbal folk medicine. Noted occult researcher and historian, Joseph Robert Jochmans, believes evidence of a paternal connection to the tribe of Issachar is hidden in the adopted name of grandfather Peyrot. The Christian name "Nostredame" adopt-ed by the family of Jews upon their forced conversion is a code for "we give ours" (*Nostra-dame*) or "we are given" (*nous donné*), implying the gift of prophecy shared by those of the priestly tribe.[23] *Soli Deo* is the Latin motto of the House de Nostredame. Thus the members of the family give their secrets and "are given" their gift of second sight by "God alone."[24]

A gift from God, be it authentic or presumed, must be shared. A messianic urge, be it either a neurosis adopted from a frustrated apostle of Jewish mysticism, or an authentic sense of destiny awakened by a great-grandfather and mentor, must have stirred the inner heart of the adolescent to believe that God had some great use for him – a mission too great to be tucked away in the bucolic little town of St.-Rémy. A preliminary and comprehensive education had expanded the mind and deepened the intellectual thirst of Michel de Nostredame. To quench this thirst, he must search a larger world beyond the familiar fields and limestone promontories of *La Ville Verte*, his sleepy hometown. At present, he endured his siblings and the perpetual state of postponement and impatience that was adolescence, biding his time, and dream-ing of the day he would ride through the crumbling Roman arch outside of town to seek out his destiny.

CHAPTER TWO

The Itinerant Apothecary

∽

Le Petit Astrologue

When Michel was 16, his grandfather Peyrot deemed him ready
to leave home and begin his formal education. In the year 1519,
perhaps in the early spring, Jaume de Nostredame and his son,
Michel, saddled pack mules with the youth's few books and
belongings. After receiving pensive and tearful embraces from
family members, father and son mounted their horses and headed
off through the narrow streets of St.-Rémy on their westward
journey to Tarascon – a day's ride away.

The average travel radius from one's birthplace during the
Renaissance was rarely beyond 15 miles. It is not known how many
times – if ever – Michel had traveled beyond his hometown up to
this point. He may have ridden with his father on one-day rides
to cities such as Tarascon. Perhaps he was already familiar with
Avignon and its university – his final destination and his father's
choice for a study of liberal arts. Be that as it may, father and son
likely took the most frequently traveled route to Avignon along
the right bank of the meandering Rhône river until they saw
the crenellated walls and machicolated towers of the capital of the

Papal Enclave in Provence, situated on the confluence of the Rhône and Durance rivers. Avignon's ancient name *Avenius* means "the city of the river and the wind." The northern blast of the region's mistral winds hurried through the streets, and the Rhône frequently flooded during the early 16th century. In those days, the promontory, with its vast heap of a papal palace fortress, appeared as an island when seen against the river's shallow floodplains and waterlogged thickets and marches.

One can imagine that the youth and his father paused to admire the ancient walled city. Avignon was known to be one of the busiest centers of learning since the Middle Ages, and was still basking in the afterglow of having been the capital of Christendom where a succession of seven popes ruled for 70 years in the previous century. Manly P. Hall, in his biographical examination of the world's prophets, *Sages and Seers*, believes Jaume de Nostredame chose Avignon's "second-rate university" (Hall's term) for his son's formal education, mainly out of convenience and for its cosmopolitan atmosphere. It is safe to assume that Michel de Nostredame lodged with relatives, and if we examine the medical and religious literature of the day we might glean some idea of what instruction his father gave his relatives for handling Michel. He would expect that they submit the youth to regular physical exercise, and the heat of awakening sexuality at age 14 onwards made him the subject of debate of parents and theologians alike as to when he should start going to confessional and receive the sacrament of penance. The copious notes taken down in confessors' manuals of that day, recording the desire to touch and be touched by the opposite sex, may have included the unnamed and hushed confessions of Michel.[1] His father would see to it that his relatives allowed Michel time to socialize with others of his age and social station with proper adult supervision.

Hall provides interesting speculation on what university life in Avignon was like during the early 16th century. With his help, we can surmise that Michel found his first years of formal schooling tedious. The professors were the despots of their classroom empires, set upon thrones high above the class to pontificate at the students. Hall tells us that some professors, "bundled in their voluminous robes," sat in imperious silence. Their assistants would act as major-domos of learning, announcing the lessons, reading the lectures and quizzing the pupils, while the remote professors looked (or dozed) on. Books as well as stationery were rare, as most parchment was "brought by camel caravans from Arabia."[2] You could not pull a book off the shelves of Avignon's library – they were chained and nailed to the walls for safekeeping. University learning in France and Provence was also chained to the dogmas of the Catholic Church, especially at Avignon, which derived most of its faculty from the priests and its financial backing directly from the popes in Rome.

Michel studied the classical *trivium* of philosophy, grammar, and rhetoric under the watchful eyes of the priests. Garencières cites from sources long lost to our scrutiny that Michel was a good student: "Such was his memory that he could recite his lessons, word for word, having heard them once."[3]

"This sovereign body imposed no serious limitations to nominal education," states Hall. "It often permitted wandering professors to hold classes, and the faculty at Avignon was frequently augmented by teachers who had graduated from Moorish universities in Spain. The latter brought with them a specialized knowledge of natural history, algebra and optics."[4]

In his free time, he could be found in Avignon's renowned papal library rattling the chains of a wide selection of classical writers and neo-Platonists, along with translations and paraphrases of occult and astronomical works.[5] It is said by Chavigny that the student's love for the celestial sciences earned him the nickname "little astrologer" from his schoolmates.

The expansive and silent mystery of starry nights and their ordered movements, even viewed in the heart of Avignon from the parapets of the papal palace, must have appeared in a bejeweled splendor that in these modern times, in an age of polluted and floodlit skies, we can only imagine. Perhaps the biographer of a contemporary physician-turned-astronomer, Jean Fernel (d. 1558), describes the celestial fire in the belly the youth might have felt:

Contemplation of the stars and heavenly bodies excites such a wonder and charm in the human mind that once fascinated by it, we are caught in the toils of an enduring and delighted slavery, which holds us in bondage and serfdom.[6]

A passion for the stars would naturally lead young Michel to seek a politically and religiously correct avenue for its study. It must be remembered that the Renaissance period held a keen interest in resurrecting the knowledge of the classical and pagan world, as well as encouraging a renewed and heady inquiry into the phenomenal and political sciences and the arts.

But there was a catch (you might call it a "Catechism-22"). The Justices of the Church preyed on those free thinkers who dared press their giddy humor for humanism beyond Catholicism's dogmatic envelope. In other words, freethinking was fine, skeptical inquiry encouraged, as long as thinking and inquiry did not shine its revelatory perception too brightly on any flaws in the dogmas and fundamental beliefs of the Holy Church. The barrier between a study of astronomy and a practice of heretical astrology was vague, and depended on the level of intolerance and reaction of the moment, but it could lead to a destruction of one's career, and, at worst, if summoned before an inquisition, could threaten one's very existence. A study of astrology-cum-astronomy was not deemed heretical as long as you knew the theologically correct balancing act between calculating and predicting phenomena, and events from the "three Ms" – the marvelous, the miraculous, and the magical world. For instance, a Christianized claimant to the heritage of the Jewish Issachar tribe could conjure revelations from the planets and stars to heal the human body in a diagnostic effort.

That, says canon law, was a "marvelous" (ordinary-world) use, and therefore had the Church's imprimatur. However, if you did not leave the summoning of spirits solely to God and his angels, you were committing a "magical" act. You would then be a demono-logue, a conjuror, an occultist worthy of being burned at the stake. If you dared predict what was next in God's plans through the cyclic engine of His cosmos, you would be in spiritual error, and would be thumb-screwed until you recanted. Medicine, therefore, was a relatively safe haven for the study of celestial sciences.

The University of Avignon had had a medical faculty since 1510. It is not known to what extent, if any, Michel studied medicine while at Avignon. We do have it from Chavigny's report on his early life that he publicly made known his desire to become an astronomer. He even went as far as defending the ideas of Nicholas Copernicus (1473–1543). He was heard telling students that God's theologians and priests may have the position of Earth at the cen-ter of the universe all wrong: that in fact the Earth rotates daily on its axis and moves, with other planets, around the Sun.

Skeptics like to note that Chavigny shows Michel defending Copernicus a full 15 years before the latter published his theory in *De Revolutionibus Orbium Coelestrium* in 1543. Chavigny, in their view, is either suffering from a false memory of the dates, or is cooking up a story to enhance his own stature as the disciple of a great man.

In 1512, Copernicus published *Commentariolus*, a paper that openly considered the possibility that the Earth and the planets could orbit the Sun. It is known of the Renaissance that theories and concepts sprung from both word of mouth and correspon-dence between scholars at different centers of learning, long before the first publication made these ideas "official" history. Therefore, it is possible that Chavigny is right, and Michel de Nostredame in his impetuous youth evoked the name of Copernicus and his rumored thoughts, if not his published theory. (Astronomical heresies were not the only thing whispered or brawled over by students at Avignon in 1520. Three years before Michel's enrollment, Martin Luther nailed his 95 theses on the doors of the Wittenberg Cathedral, launching the Protestant Reformation. Pope Leo X issued a papal bull condemning Lutheran doctrines and gave Luther 60 days to recant under pain of excommunication. Luther publicly burned the bull, along with a volume of canon law.)

The controversy stirred by the adolescent Nostredame's intellectual rebellion was serious enough to have him sent home. Perhaps an "act of God" postponed a more serious encounter with church authorities. The archives at Avignon report the outbreak of plague in 1520, warranting the temporary closure of the university. Once back home, in the safety of his parents' house in St.-Rémy, he faced something of a family crisis. His parents feared for their son, born from a family of ex-Jews who at any moment could become the scapegoats of the growing religious tensions between Christian sects. Grandfather Peyrot and his father gave the youth a pointed lecture on the virtues of holding his tongue. It was an attribute of Michel de Nostredame that he rarely made the same mistake twice. But what of his future career? An astronomer lived at best a financially insecure life. Some biographers believe that Nostredame wanted to apply his astronomical skill as an author of almanacs. At the time the genre was a highly competitive field, as the reading fare during the early days of the printing revolution was dominated by a multitude of such authors – most of them quacks. But star augury predicting the coming year's weather, harvests, political woes, and plagues was definitely out. You might damage your reputation as a scholar if you were wrong too often, or bring trouble at your door if your documented political and religious forebodings were right too often.

Nostredame honored his parents, and apparently at last understood the dangers of being a Christianized Jew. It was popularly reasoned by a number of biographers that he decided that he should become a healer or a physician – and in that profession he could cloak his exploration of politically and religiously incorrect mysteries under the protection of a doctor's cap and robes. But if we follow this premise, our story flies free of the facts, and gives rise to one of the greatest myths promulgated by Nostradamus biographers.

The myth goes like this: Michel de Nostredame attended the Medical University at Montpellier in 1522. He obtained his baccalaureate degree in 1525 in the same year that an outbreak of the bubonic plague across southern France forced the faculty to close the university. The professors and licensed students (including Nostredame) spread across the countryside and offered their services during the emergency. Finally, he returned to Montpellier in 1529 to finish his doctorate studies once the danger had passed.

A long overdue re-examination of archival records and Nostradamus' own written reflections about his early years strongly imply that after leaving Avignon he did not arrive to study medicine at Montpellier for nearly another decade. So what was he doing prior to 3 October 1529 when the ledger of new students records his entry into the University?

The University of Direct Experience

No one so far has unearthed a record in the archives of Montpellier proving that Nostradamus enrolled as a student before 1529. Does this mean he was never there before this time? Early biographers say he was, but until a dated record surfaces to prove this, the story must remain in doubt. This "two sojourns at Montpellier University" story is probably based on later biographers, relying on the confessions of Chavigny and potentially embellished accounts from old age passed on by Pierre Tronc de Coudoulet (a crony of Nostredame) to his great grandson Palamèdes. The latter appear in that hard-to-test biographical source, Pierre-Joseph de Haitze's 18th-century life story of Nostradamus – a document lost to scholars of the 21st century, but upheld by biographers of the 19th century who claimed to have read it.

During the final decades of the 20th century, Michel Chomarat, the founder and director of *Association des Amis de Michel Nostradamus,* has been the primary champion for saving the memory of Nostradamus from centuries of loose biographical and brazenly mythical accounts. Chomarat's collection of over 2,000 surviving documentary and archival fragments of the prophet's life puts the whole story of the first Montpellier visit into question. His work inspired Peter Lemesurier to bring to our attention what he believes is a key quote from Michel de Nostredame, recorded later in life, that finally buries the first sojourn story.

Sometime around 1552, Nostredame confessed in the *Proeme* of his book *Traité des fardemens et confitures* (A treatise on cosmetics and preservatives)[7] that he wandered "through a number of lands and countries, from 1521 to 1529, constantly on the move in search of the understanding and knowledge of the sources and origins of plants [planets][8] and other medicinal herbs."

His comment implies that there were intellectual seeds of wanderlust planted at an early age. Exactly by whom or when is open to conjecture. Whether his great-grandfather or grandfather were doctors at court or simply grain dealers, at the very least they traveled extensively throughout Provence. And if Jean de Saint-Rémy and Peyrot de Nostredame were indeed physicians wandering the western Mediterranean with the court of King René, then they might have fostered in young Michel the romantic allure of trekking through distant lands. Perhaps the old men spoke of adventures in places geographically as far removed as Calabria and Catalan. The boy might have memorized the names of friends (perhaps even distant family relations) and secret contacts in the Christianized Jewish underground for later use.

Time spent in Avignon's library might have opened a Pandora's box of wayfaring desires. A professed early interest in herbs and their healing properties might have set his bookish mind on a collision course with the tomes of the most famous itinerant doctor of his day, a man whose life was as large and vivid as his name: the

Honorable Philippus Theophrastus Aureolus Bombastus ab Hohenheim, Eremita (1493?–1541) – "Paracelsus" (beyond Celsus)[9] for short. This contentious and fiery Swiss physician was a professor of theology, master of the Jewish Cabala and alchemy, and miraculous healer (if he said so himself). He was probably history's first modern medical scientist. Paracelsus had passed through southern France a decade before and made his mark on the memory of faculty and students at the Medical University of Montpellier where he once taught medicine. Some of Paracelsus' students could have taught Nostredame at nearby Avignon. A young man, such as Nostredame, with a natural scent for contrariness, might have sought out and absorbed stories of Paracelsus' travels and occult experiments and considered his rebellious medical theories. Paracelsus frequently put into question contemporary medical dogma based on the theories of Galen, a 2nd-century Greek physician. Although in future writings Nostredame never mentioned Paracelsus directly, many of his medical and occult opinions so closely parallel those of the corpulent Bombastus that it is safe to say he was exposed early to Paracelsus' idea – indeed his belief in the emphatic necessity – that real seekers of truth must wander the roads of the world.

"A doctor must be a traveler. Knowledge is experience," declared Paracelsus. University study alone is incomplete. That was the Paracelsian rule. A doctor or herbalist must leave the main roads and mainstream centers of dogma. Seek out wise women, gypsies, sorcerers, wandering tribes, old robbers, and take their lessons from these riffraff.

"For many years I studied at the universities of Germany, Italy and France, seeking to discover the foundations of medicine," wrote Paracelsus. "However, I did not content myself with their teachings and writings and books, but continued my travels to Granada and Lisbon, through Spain and England, through Brandenburg, Prussia, Lithuania, Poland, Hungary, Wallachia, Transylvania, Croatia, the Wendian Mark [Livonia], and yet other countries which there is no need mention here ... I went not only to the doctors, but also to the barbers, bath keepers, learned physicians, magicians and women."[10]

Nostredame did not rely exclusively on this independent thinker, hard drinker and notorious carouser through the nether regions of Renaissance life. His uncompromising passion for free speech and the questioning of authority, together with his libertine ways, often saw Paracelsus cast out of many of the lands he visited before he had plumbed their secrets. More mainstream and classically correct medical giants may have also provoked Nostredame's wandering *medicus* bug. Among these may have been the father of medicine, Hippocrates (c. 460–357 B.C.E.), who advised young doctors to travel from town to town in search of the experience that grounds a doctor's reputation in actual deeds.

One disquieting element lurks in the Chomarat/Lemesurier theory. Did Michel de Nostredame spend these next nine years in constant wanderings, collecting medical and herbal knowledge, inventing cures, creating medical tools, and (as some sympathetic biographers say) gaining a reputation as a healer of the sick (which often preceded his arrival in a new town) – all without a license to practice medicine? The stock biographies portray him as a legally licensed medical practitioner *by 1525*, after plague closed Montpellier University – *not* when it shut the oak doors of academia in Avignon in 1520. Yet, by his own admission, he had already been beating a path to his own brand of medical research and practice for four years, and was probably trying his healing experiments on plague victims by the second general outbreak in 1525. Certainly, the early 16th century had (literally) far fewer degrees of licensing than today, but let it not be assumed by those who rely on Hollywood accounts of the time that unlicensed doctors (or better, quacks) were widely tolerated. A dilettante could not easily tap into the brain trust of degreed physicians without suspicion or complaint. To people in the generally illiterate and unlettered world of the Renaissance, knowledge was status, and it was often withheld from those who had not passed through the rigorous initiation of University learning cliques.

Consider the possible outcome if Michel de Nostredame had had the temerity to seek admittance into Montpellier as a student in 1529 after nine years of practicing medicine without a license. The faculty of that day were considered reasonably tolerant of anti-Galenist theories, but as arch-conservatives when it came to guarding their degrees of licensed medical knowledge. Thomas Platter, a student of Montpellier during the 1590s, once noted: "If an unlicensed doctor is found, or a hawker of ointments, the doctors and the students have the right without further ado to set him backwards on an ass with the tail in his hands for a bridle, and to drive him round the town; which delights the populace, who pelt the fellow with mud and rubbish until he is filthy from head to foot."[11]

Platter then relates that in one case they caught an unlicensed person and locked him in the anatomy theatre while they went to search for an ass. His wife ran crying around the town that the students were preparing to dissect her husband alive. The city magistrates were so convinced by her wretched pleas that the quack was taken from Platter and his fellow students by force.

Controversy was aroused by the documented appearance of Michel de Nostredame at Montpellier in 1529, as we will see, but he certainly did not ride out of town backwards on a donkey. He must have been a licensed apothecary at least, or sometime early in his nine-year journey studied and passed his *per intentionem* exams and the final oral interrogation of *les points rigoreux* and received his license to practice medicine. Lemesurier fancies that he could have received his apothecary license as early as 1520, while studying at Avignon.

Life on the Renaissance Road

Accounts of Michel de Nostredame's travels during this period usually tell of the bare bones – or better, the epitaphs of bare stone-walled cities through which he passed on his crusade to learn and test his ideas on healing and herbal properties. To grasp, but briefly, the warm hand of Nostredame's life at this time depends on evoking the atmosphere of road life out of memoirs and accounts of contemporary merchants and physicians who stirred the same dust and splashed along the same muddy tracks from 1521 to 1529.

Travelers in the era that enjoyed the enlightenment of Leonardo da Vinci and Michelangelo sometimes rode on horse, but mostly trudged along on foot, just like wayfarers of the Middle Ages. The first unsprung and primitive carriages appeared in the middle to latter days of the 16th century. Saddle sores were the bane of young and old wayfarers alike. If Michel de Nostredame sought freedom from the ache and pain of the saddle, he could rock along on the hardwood seats in the goods or farm wagon that was the wheeled transport of the day. Those who could not ride, such as the rare lady of wealth on the road, or infirm and aged nobility, or the well-to-do merchant, would choose to be trundled along on a litter. Young Nostredame would have ridden a horse or mule, which he either owned or replaced at each destination with a fresh animal. One or two pack mules might have followed a few paces behind him, encumbered with his books, astrolabe, medicines, chests of dried herbs, and equipment for making recipes for food, healing balms and even perfumes. A change of clothes might have included the red robes of a student doctor if his license to heal had been granted in some university along the road, or the garb used by one either posing as or being a licensed apothecary. He would wear loose-fitting shirts and coat and leather breeches on journeys. A broad hat hid his face in the shade from the southern sun.

Nostredame would have been armed. The roads of the early 16th century had their share of brigands. They were often unemployed soldiers – former mercenaries of King Francis I's interminable wars with Charles V, the Hapsburg Emperor of the Holy Roman Empire, over Italy. A lone merchant, or a young and placid healer, might have looked indistinguishable from a soldier, armed with his intimidating sword in a buckler. He would have been a fool to travel alone. Few wayfarers ventured beyond the walls of a town until a good number of them had assembled, and in some cases they even hired and shared the cost of heavily armed escorts. Nostredame would have learned tricks to save his valuables, such as sewing coins in the lining of his clothes. A thief ransacking his mule train might overlook coins hidden inside string ball pin cushions filled with needles in his sewing chest. Nostredame's money must have literally stank, since other valuables and coins would be hidden under the false bottom of chests painted over and stuffed with stinking ointments for scabs and ulcers, or stuffed with animal specimens and rotting plants sufficiently repugnant to all the senses that a brigand would toss them to one side. Would robbery have happened often to him? Not likely, it seems. Merchants and chroniclers of the day share the view that bad food and diseases were a vagabond's greatest danger.

The Renaissance road, if you could call it one, was a gash cut by footfalls of primitive trains of packhorses and the barefoot pad of peasants, and grooved and rutted by the rare wheel of a wagon. Few if any had the shade of tall plane trees that southwest France enjoyed in later centuries. On sunny days traffic on the roads generated clouds of dust when they were disturbed; on rainy days, these somber scars became impassable bogs. No one would want to linger on such roads for too long. If your horse and pack animals were fit, and your riding skills keen, an average day's journey on the road could cover 40 kilometers (25 miles).

Few travelers in the 1520s consulted maps, and those regional maps that existed seldom displayed accurate geography. Latitude lines could be calculated from an ephemeris or almanac pamphlet, but were rarely seen on a map – longitude lines not at all; neither would you find the roads marked on them. The Renaissance cartographer would not even attempt to sketch them in. The whims of storms, the tread of armies with their heavy artillery carriages and huge baggage trains, tended to plow under and swamp roads for half the year. A merchant traveler relied on the locals for directions and advice on the condition of roads. Travelogues of the day were long lists of itineraries, consisting of town names, watering holes, hamlets, and inns. You would recite these to the local innkeeper, parish priest, notary, or tax collector, hoping they could verify their existence and point out where they were.

Long-term traveling made one a jack of all dialects in the Tower of Babel that was France and the many regional twists of tongue of other Mediterranean lands. Nostredame's knowledge of Latin and the King's French (still a minority language in French dominions) would make him easily conversant with the higher urban classes and city magistrates. Latin remained the official language of French state government up until 1539, when French replaced it. He would have to master a number of regional dialects to make himself understood in the countryside. Language changed from one village to the next. One can imagine his frustration was similar to the northern Frenchman, Charles de Rouelles, who during his travels across France in the mid-16th century complained that he had to learn eight different ways to say "yes" or "no."

You could be sure a town was near if you came across the T-shaped signpost of the law looming ahead: a gibbet, often dangling the fly-spotted remains of a criminal. The display of these rank robbers was intended to advertise the efficiency of the nearby civic constabulary, sweeping the surrounding countryside free of cut-throats and thieves. However, a grove of gibbets had the opposite effect on travelers. The number indicated just how many brigands must still be at large, lurking along the lonelier stretches of the next day's trail beyond the town.

If your language skills were good, the road you were to follow had not disappeared in the last fortnight's thundershower, and the mule you owned or rented did not go lame, then your long day's journey from the last city gate might end with a sight of the long shadow of the gibbet stretched across the town gate of your destination. There you would meet "friendly" guards and customs officers. A kingdom's cities drew customs duty, as borders and territorial security were still abstract concepts. Merchants did not usually require passports, so everyone was a merchant if they could get away with it. Nostredame's permits (whatever they might have been) were studied and his baggage inspected, as were his letters of introduction from citizen sponsors. When he eventually became a licensed apothecary it probably helped him overcome the quarantine hurdle that few surmounted if they admitted to having passed through regions infected with pestilence in the last 40 days. All members of classes lower than the nobility had their travel weapons impounded.

You would be wise to plan arrival at your destination well before sundown, because the gates of every city were closed from dusk till dawn – even to the city's citizens who were unfortunate enough to miscalculate their journey time. Much could be ascertained by the aware traveler as to the civic health of a settlement by what one found at its gate. If the town was heavily stricken with the bubonic scourge, the magistrates had the guards nail shut all portals except the main gate. There the guards checked travelers one at a time for any signs of contagion.

Because not making it through a city gate by sundown was a common occurrence, Michel made his acquaintance with – and later gave his heart and confessions to – those generous gray-robed monks associated with various charitable hostels in the Franciscan monasteries scattered outside town walls. He would bed down on straw in a stable or stretch out on a simple wooden pallet until sunrise, when guards and customs officials again opened their city gates.

Once permitted entry there were some generic attributes you would expect to see in a typical, self-sufficient French Renaissance town. The streets would generally be narrow. The warrens of layman's hovels and upper-class houses alike would pile and press together in multiple stories conveying a sense of being crowded almost to bursting point. The streets were mostly of dirt and gravel; cobblestones were a luxury. All of the streets were victim to the contents of water closets flung from windows above, especially in the morning when the call *Gare l'eau!* ("Look out for the water!") echoed down the tenements.

Most towns of 4,000 or more souls were self-reliant in the basics of life: food markets, mercantile shops, and artisans of hoof, human maintenance, beam, arch, and brick. You bought your needs with the novel idea of a national and interchangeable golden crown currency called the *ecu*. One *ecu* had the value of three *livres* (roughly equivalent to 4.5 euros or U.S. dollars, or £3 sterling). You could divide *livres* into *sous* and *deniers*. If you had gold coins of other lands you could barter, but beware the merchant's balancing scales. Measuring standards were as free-style as the languages and dialects, and the weight of gold, produce, or a shank of meat varied from town to town.

The average town marketplace was the source of life's sustenance as much as it was the doorway to death from pestilence and sickness. Below the tables of merchant stalls stacked with fly-ridden produce, salted fish and meats, ran the offal of slaughtered animals and the waste and refuse of rotten and discarded vegetables. These garbage heaps beside the available fare often came to life with the stealthy transit of rats, scratching loose their plague-infested fleas to mix with other pests in the rubbish (such as typhous lice). There they waited to hitch a ride on another rat, or spring on a human ankle. The human hosts were oblivious to the danger, generally thinking that disease lived in foul odors that they could neutralize with pungent oils, amulets and perfume – not cleanliness.

The streets were crowded and lively by day. Lower-class mothers encouraged their children to soil their faces, feet and hands while they played, believing that bathing took away a child's vitality, whereas grime protected them from disease. Fetid and perfumed smells and smoke issued from butchers, artisan workshops, perfumeries, and fish and meat quarters, all abuzz with flies and conversation. Life paraded on the streets in lace and threadbare costumes, or huddled in commerce. The press of humanity defied the vast, and generally unpopulated, void beyond the perimeter of parapet and towered walls. There were fewer than 700 million souls on Earth in the 1520s. Many a lonely sojourner welcomed the riot of town life in a thinly peopled, pre-industrial world.

The Renaissance saw a boom in the hostel and inn business and could hardly keep up with expanding commerce. Given the frequency of late arrivals to locked city gates, new inns were mostly built outside the city walls. But the state of hospitality, food and bedding was a mixed one. Except for the infrequent invitation to stay and dine with the upper classes, the meals on the roadside inns provided Nostredame with a diet that consisted predominantly of cereals and grains, such as barley, rye, oats, and wheat, made into bread slices that floated in a watery vegetable soup. Meat would be scarce and expensive, and when it did appear it would soon rot if not consumed. The average family ate meat six times a year. The higher classes undoubtedly ate more because they could afford to salt their meat. Livestock populations in the Renaissance were surprisingly small, because animals often did not survive the winters. A well-stocked butcher's shop was a luxury of the larger towns. Cheese and butter were to be had by the well-coined wayfarer – but few others. The wine was usually sour, and the tables and kitchens were smoky, smelly, and dirty. A perusal of Nostredame's future observations on medicine, hygiene, and food preparation indicate that he was perhaps more aware and sensitive than most to the dangers of bad food and the dirty reality of the roadside tavern.

There is no surviving account of the young apothecary suffering illnesses while on his travels. His noted robust health carried him through the gauntlet of the gastronomic "demons" of the Renaissance dinner table – what Nicholas de la Chesnaye, a French doctor of civil and canon law, satirized in his play *A Condemnation of Feasting* as Apoplexy, Paralysis, Epilepsy, Pleurisy, Colic, and Gout. Michel de Nostredame used his growing understanding of traditional and folk remedies to keep fit by calling upon Chesnaye's "angels," the healing balms named "Pill, Enema and Bleeding."[12]

Far cleaner and more hospitable inns certainly existed. Nostredame would find them when riding westward along the Mediterranean coast of Languedoc and Aquitaine on the well-traveled, ancient trade routes, sometimes marked out by the ground-down cobblestones of a ruined Roman road. After supper and a nightcap of wine, the innkeeper would direct him to a bed where he seldom slept alone. The "someone" with whom he slept would be another dusty, sweat-wrung, lice-bitten male traveler, sharing the cost of a straw stuffed mattress.

Life on the open road was a man's world. Rarely did one see women endure its iniquities and dangers; they were at home looking after their households and tending to children and the family business while their husbands and male kin were on the road selling their wares. However, sightings of women increased on the approaches to important holy shrines, or on Sundays when country dwellers and townsfolk traveled to the local place of worship. At other times one might cross their path on the way from farmstead to the town market. A dedicated traveler like Nostredame might have shared the road with women of gypsy bands, or seen them dangling their legs off the back of wagons of touring *commedia dell'arte* companies. At times of war he might have seen them in great numbers as army camp followers – wives, mistresses, prostitutes, food gatherers, laundresses, and nurses picking their way through the muddy ruts of a ravaged pathway trod by the mercenary armies.

Michel de Nostredame's sexual life was kept hidden from inquisitive contemporaries as well as future biographers. In later years, Chavigny reported that his aging employer "abhorred vice and chastised it severely." The young Nostredame had more temptations on the road. Across Europe a traveler could settle into the waters of crowded mixed public baths in a splashing and carousing atmosphere. There were many municipal brothels in French cities, as well as those on church-owned properties, indirectly financed and encouraged by them. The secular and priestly authorities tried to find a practical – and profitable – solution between the era's tug-of-war between repressive piety and licentious release, the cleric and the municipal authority, or their "Madame," pocketing a fee for the coffers of either holy pope or the public fund. They reasoned that their pimping was a service "for common utility," "in the interest of the public good," "for enhancing the good, piety and honor of the whole commune,"[13] and so on. The tavern-cum-brothels of licensed prostitutes did keep the fees low for food, drink and "fun." They hired midwives approved by either the priest or municipal authorities to give their wenches frequent medical inspections and, as Hale says, keep troublemakers "immobilized for whole evenings at a time."

Maybe Nostredame's public abhorrence of lust in later life was motivated by guilt-ridden memories of sexual pleasures enjoyed in his youth as a vagabond bachelor. Perhaps the repentant older man's outward righteousness was a reaction to repressed memories of the life of a young man on the road, caught in a taxable circle of sin and repentance by municipal and Church authorities who provided the brothels for a fee and the confessional the morning after for a tithe, keeping a young man ever-spinning in a cycle of God, guilt, to God again.

Wanderlust for Knowledge

The intimate reflections of Michel de Nostredame on countless mornings after saddling his mule and modest baggage train remain guarded secrets on the dark side of his Scorpio natal moon. His itinerary spanning nine years on the road is only slightly better documented.

It can be assumed that sometime in the early spring of 1521, Nostredame navigated his mount and pack animals westwards

beyond St.-Rémy; but just where and when he visited his next destinations is open to conjecture. There are numerous geographical
references in his medical prose and prophetic works – most of
them appearing in the latter. They reveal hardly any autobio-
graphical details to us, except that his predictions of a town's
future are written with the matter-of-fact informality of one who
has slept there. It cannot be ruled out that a sizable number of the
625 references in his prophecies to geographical locales, including
major countries, cities, and even the smallest of hamlets, were
known to him. If we make a list of the number of locales of his
day he mentions – starting with France and then radiating out
to the regions beyond Provence – we get the following potential
destinations:[14]

France	270
Italy and its surrounding islands	113
Spain and Portugal	34
Germany and Central Europe	43
Britain, Belgium, Holland and Scandinavia	26
Greece and Eastern Europe	63
North Africa and the Middle East	55
North and South America	11

It is certain that Nostredame never set foot in the New World. The
last entry, and others suggesting locales "in" the stars, suggest that
many of the place names in his prophecies may not come from
firsthand encounters.

A desire to understand herbal and medical arts, if not the need
to gain a doctorate's license, certainly drew him to tap the body of
medical learning that was the University of Montpellier, located 50
miles west of St.-Rémy. Long before the city established its prestigious medical school, it was one of southern France's chief centers
for the warehousing and trade of oriental herbs and spices. When
the bubonic plague finally settled over southwest France between

1520 and 1525, observing and understanding its pathology and experimenting with cures became a dominant obsession of the bold explorer as he entered his early 20s. From Montpellier, he might have followed the plague's trail northeast to the neighboring city of Nîmes. He would have seen a city with its famous Roman amphitheater fused into the masonry of the medieval city walls, and marveled at a line of broken abutments delineating the far more expansive city limits of its glory days as a Greek trading post and later jewel of the Roman Empire. Crowded against the foundations of its Romanesque towers, Nîmes would have presented before the young healer an extreme vision of the squalor and overcrowding endured by most large Renaissance cities. Between 1500 and 1600, Europe underwent a population explosion, jumping from an estimated 60 million to 80 million. The agrarian society of the 16th century had come to the limits of its technological ability to expand agriculture into marginal lands. Most of its widely scattered medium-sized towns of 6–12,000 souls were already too overpopulated to sustain sufficient agricultural employment. The lack of farming jobs especially burdened larger and well-established commercial and industrial centers like Nîmes with the press of unemployed agrarian laborers and their families.

When plague broke out in Southern France in the 1520s, the overcrowding of Nîmes made life within its walls one of the era's most pestilence-ridden arenas. Nostredame the apothecary may have been there more than once during his nine-year travels, learning from experienced apothecaries how to properly identify, mix and compose remedies (some accepted, others likely considered radical or bogus) to heal the sick. References in his prophecies to Nîmes describe, perhaps firsthand, his opinion of the town when he called it "an asylum of the unhealthy."[15]

Nîmes was once the Greco-Roman colony town of *Nemausus,* a pagan spa resort that drew to its delicate temples and curative spring the elite of ancient occult adepts, magicians, necromancers and astrologers. Nostredame in his prophetic writings shows he was well aware of – and perhaps actively involved in – the search for treasure buried under the town's Roman substructure. Nîmes' Convent of St. Sauveur-de-la-Fontaine stood upon the foundations of a temple to the Goddess Diana and a basilica built by Emperor Hadrian, dedicated to his stepmother, the Empress Plotina. Nostredame believed the temple held the gold-and-silver lamp of Emperor Trajan.[16]

He also dug deep into the layers of more subtle treasures. Occult Nîmes still endured. What Christianity had rebuilt and buried in the façade of ancient *Nemausus* still lived in the whispered rituals and secret studies of any number of Jewish physicians or apothecaries who by day brandished their crosses and Christian names, and by night donned the sacred robes and emblems to teach Nostredame their forbidden curriculum.

Nostredame proceeded again through Montpellier, riding west along the coast of Languedoc, moving through towns frequently named in his prophecies, such as Agde and Béziers, and tarrying for a longer time in the city of Narbonne, where the fatalities from the plague were particularly numerous and the Jewish occult underground was active. Later, he would write two prophecies about the low silhouette of a disease-ridden French galley bringing a pestilence to the three towns via the harbor of Agde.[17] Perhaps the prophecy, warning of one million deaths from that future plague, was inspired in part by Nostredame's post-traumatic memory of the sick and dying of Agde, Béziers, and Narbonne from plagues past.

He must have made frequent sorties into the villages dotting the surrounding countryside on a hunt for cures and folk medicine secrets. He would have encountered the truism much distained by the all-male medical elite of his day: "How many savants in Medicine have been outdone by a simple old peasant woman, who with a single plant or herb has found a remedy for illnesses despaired of by physicians?"[18] We can take *Traité des fardemens et confitures* and its catalogue of remedies as a litmus test of what

Michel de Nostredame considered the good cures opposed to the quack "vulgar cures" of illiterate peasants. Those he published seem to focus on the less harmful recipes used for cleaning teeth, or making skin moisturizers, fragrant soaps, beauty creams, cosmetics, and hair dyes. The many ways to preserve fruits, create jellies, or make purgatives also dominate his medical literature. Nostredame tramped through the fields and farms gaining the trust and loosening the tongues of sunbaked, craggy peasant women, no doubt encountering similar outrages in the name of healing to those seen in *Erreurs populaires*, published in 1578 by Laurent Joubert, Chancellor of the Faculty of Medicine at the University of Montpellier. If on some rare occasion a midwife had allowed this wandering apothecary inside to witness a woman in labor, he might have seen the expectant mother sitting over a hot cauldron. If that did not work, the midwife might have placed her husband's hat on her belly, as midwives outside Montpellier did, to initiate the baby's exodus from the womb. He heard the same false medical proverbs in a dozen French dialects and regions, such as, "the comet presages plague"; "who goes to bed thirsty arises healthy"; "a sick person's bedclothes should never be changed"; or "what pleases the mouth is soft on the stomach."

A medical doctor in those days usually left pediatrics to the women, surgery to the layman dentist and cobbler, and lowly drug making to the apothecary. University-trained physicians like Joubert lumped together nosy and inquisitive apothecaries, such as Nostredame, as self-educated yet "presumptuous" dilettantes, no better than midwives and surgeons competing and encroaching upon the territory of the degreed physicians.

After Narbonne, Nostredame's next recorded destination was Carcassonne, with its picturesque medieval fortified sandstone walls and conical orange towers at its eastern gates. These gates would be closed to him and heavily guarded, as the city was heavily visited by pestilence. Even the stock biographical evidence sets his appearance there around 1525 or a little later, as a licensed *medicin* from the disbanded student body of Montpellier. Whether at that time he actually was a medical student licensed to practice medicine, or was just licensed to mix the medicines, the city gates did not remain closed for long, and the overwhelmed town apothecaries welcomed him inside. These may have included descendants of Astruge de Carcassonne, or Davin Arnauton de Velorgues – ancestors of his father's family. They could be what Manly P. Hall calls the "Rabbins and Talmudists" from which Nostredame took further study and continued collecting useful medical experiences by fighting the plague firsthand at Carcassonne.

Nostredame and his remedies came to the attention, he says, of "the gracious Lord Bishop of Carcassonne, Ammanien de Foys," who, it seems, enjoyed numerous applications of a "very potent and effective" composition "for maintaining the health of the human body."[19] Nostredame most likely attended his first audiences with the wan Bishop at the ecclesiastical palace (since destroyed) near Carcassonne's four-cornered Bishop's Tower. The two may have discussed medical and religious matters while walking up and down the wide lists on the outer ramparts, in the shadow of Carcassonne's Tour de l'Inquisition, while taking in the marvelous western views of the Aude river winding up into the foothills of the far-off Pyrenees. Already in his prime, the Bishop's spiritual duties and political fights had depressed him and ground him down. De Foys' gaze was melancholic and tired, his face empty of blood and transparent. Nostredame prescribed a kind of pomade he called "the Elixir of Life."

The cure-all promises written by Nostradamus nearly a quarter-century later hint at the placebo effect the young man's self-confidence might have had on the bishop when "Master Michel" (as people started to call the young apothecary after his stay at Narbonne and Carcassonne) squeezed his patient's hand, aimed a gray-eyed gaze upon him and prepared to speak about his remedy. If we take this passage from *Traité des fardemens et confitures* out of third person to second person, it might sound more like

Nostredame's relentless summary of hypnotic suggestions that comforted the bishop after he took his first sip from the cup of Nostredame's Elixir of Life:

No matter how sad or melancholy [you] may be [you] will become happy and of good cheer, or, if fearful and easily afraid, [you] will be resolute and courageous, or, if [you] are quiet, [you] will become talkative. [Your] natural characteristics will also be changed, for if [you are] somewhat roguish, [you] will become kind and gentle, as [you] were just thirty years old; if [your] beard is starting to turn gray, it slows down the aging process considerably, preserves the complexion but not the years, gladdens the heart and the whole person so completely, as if it were the first day that [you] had come into the world. It makes the breath smell very sweet ... and does not cause any unnatural fever or make [you] feel unwell. It arrests headaches, drives away pains in the side and greatly increases the production of semen. It maintains the four humors in such harmony and uniformity that if [you] did not possess them from [your] birth [you] might live forever. But the One who taught us how we are born into the world, He has also taught us to die. The pleasure, however, which this composition brings to a man refreshes [you] to such an extent that it so lengthens [your] life and adds so greatly to it that no chance event, however intense it may be, can stop someone who uses it from living as long as the old heathens. For if [you are] susceptible to consumption, whatever form it may take, [you] will escape from its danger and be free of it. It also protects [you] from noisome pestilence and if [you have] been infected, for no longer than ten hours, [you] will survive. For greater safety, though, [you] should go at least three miles from the unclean and polluted place, then [you] will be certain that it will pose no danger or cause after-effects. Thus, its properties deserve great praise.[20]

Half balm and half blarney, the homily had its effect on de Foys. A half-teaspoon of this pomade compound consisting of lapis lazuli, coral and gold, stirred into a glass of wine – drunk one-and-a-half hours before lunch – apparently put the pink flush of youth back in the Bishop's waxy cheeks. If the pale Bishop had died of poisoning, our story would end right here with the burning of the freelance healer for witchcraft.

If indeed Michel de Nostredame's memory was photographic, then, as is often the case with savants, it was a highly selective memory. For instance, our protagonist shows a dyslexic's difficulty in remembering people's names. The "Bishop" of Carcassonne from 1521 to 1545 was one Martin de Saint-André. A Bishop Amédée (Ammanien?) de Foix was in Mâcon from 1557 to 1579. He was initially ordered by the Papal Legate at Avignon to run the See at Carcassonne in 1552, the same year Nostradamus' recipes for the Elixir of Life were written down. However, de Foix (or "de Foys") was a victim of last-minute Ecclesiastical shuffling and became Bishop of Mâcon instead – several years after the "elixir" account was published. Nostradamus could have incorrectly remembered their meeting on a later date in Avignon or Mâcon, rather than Carcassonne. Then again, perhaps the mind of the middle-aged Nostradamus, known for his unsubtle and turgid flattery when armed with a pen, did accurately remember their meeting, even if he did not remember the proper ecclesiastical rank of the young and sickly "Monsignor" le Foys at Carcassonne, who may have served the true Bishop Marin de Saint-André in the 1520s. A closer examination of the original French texts shows Nostredame loaded up his introduction of de Foys' with all the titles he would eventually hold: *monseigneur le reuerendisme Euesque de Carcassone, monseigneur Ammanien de Foys.*

After leaving Carcassonne, Nostredame rode northwest through Castelnaudry. He settled down for several months in picturesque Toulouse, the capital of Languedoc, constructed of mellow pink stone, straddling the Garonne. Toulouse was another center of Jewish learning where he showed marked success in curing the plague. Beyond the sun-parched wine country and dry pine-forested hills of Toulouse he followed the Garonne river past

Montauban and Agen to the Atlantic province of Aquitaine (the "land of waters"). One might imagine he would leave the Garonne to pick and categorize the herbs growing along the well-watered fields and pasturelands dotted by tawny-colored promontories topped by medieval castles. Eventually he would travel westward into the Gironde, perhaps taking a rented boat to the river dock-yards of Aquitaine's capital, Bordeaux, where he would encounter the fearful atmosphere of a particularly severe attack of the plague.

Apparently, his reputation as a healer had already preceded him. A delegation of the city's magistrates begged him to stay and save their city. They may have already been aware, either by letters of introduction or from rumors passed down from Toulouse, that the young man had invented a new contraption for fumigating the evil humors of the plague with a brass pump that powdered the air with strong and bracing perfumes consisting of combinations of many new and unique healing herbs.

The medically minded of that day intermingled with the real culprits of pestilence – filth and rats – as they ran around the towns on errands of mercy in their macabre attire. They would wear leather cuirasses (back and breast plates, to ward off a demon's invisible plague arrows), goggles, wide-brimmed hats and long, beaked leather masks stuffed with pungent herbs and garlic. Doctors and apothecaries believed, like the ancient Romans before them, that the pestilence came from foul air and that it required thorough fumigation. Usually they burned the herbs in acrid fogs to the point of suffocating the afflicted. If the plague visitation was particularly terrible and the sick were too numerous, they were shut into a large building, such as the town Hôtel de Ville or a *hospital* run by religious or monastic orders outside the city walls. Inside they lay in soiled bedding in an overcrowded tangle, the window shutters closed to keep the pestilential airs within. Into this medical black comedy of well-meaning ignorance stepped the young Nostredame with his brass pump. It resembled a palm-pumped perfume bottle that spread clouds of pure-smelling herbs to purge (although it only masked) the foul airs of the plague around the patients.

A quarter-century later Nostradamus assessed the state of the apothecary trade in *Traité des fardemens et confitures*:

So if anyone has a desire to live a long life in happiness and good health … let him be on his guard and not trust every apothecary, for although it is true that there are good ones among them, for every good one there are 100 to 1,000 bad ones. For several among them are not worth what they charge and others, although they have enough money and are of exceedingly good standing, are avaricious, selfish and cunning. For because they are concerned they might not make as much as they would wish, they do not use half or even a third of the ingredients. Many of them are ignorant, incompetent and have no desire to learn anything, which is a dreadful crime for such people. Others, however, are very dour and slovenly and act in a very negligent manner with everything they touch. On the other hand, I will not say that there are not some among them who have none of these faults, who in the first place have ability and a good conscience and who are not lacking in skill, but they are careless in their profession and commission anyone with the task, who may carry it out badly. For I must acknowledge that there are some who will do something properly, but they are rare birds and it does not happen very often. For instance, I have traveled extensively throughout the whole kingdom of France and have met many apothecaries and become acquainted with them, but I have seen them do so many unspeakable things that I believe one could not find [outside] the pharmaceutical art any other trade in which there is more malpractice and conscience so sorely tried … Nevertheless, I have been in many places where the noble art of medicine was very much in vogue and excellent work was carried out, but it does not happen everywhere, as is indeed the case today.[21]

He observed firsthand the scandalous treatment of good physicians by their pharmacists while a journeyman apothecary, and later on suffered the brunt of foul treatment directly when he was himself a physician:

Now and then it happens that a doctor goes to an apothecary's premises and, in order to look after his patient's interests, would like to see the medicine himself and weigh out what is necessary, particularly if the apothecary is inexperienced. What happens? If the apothecary happens to be an ignorant idiot, rash, conceited and reckless, seemingly friendly, arrogant, useless, an eccentric ass (for good and bad are to be found everywhere), he will reply to this young doctor as follows: "Why do you want to cause me all this confusion? Do you perhaps think that I am not an honorable man? You should know that I will make it much better than you can prescribe, therefore stick to your own profession and calling and do not interfere with our medicines! Because we make it better!" – from that and 1,000 other stupid remarks which they make you will understand that I cannot write the twelfth part of the things done by such idiots. It is true, however, that among them I have met very honest and stalwart men, well versed in their art and exceptionally well instructed in it, who have remained true to it.[22]

After Bordeaux, Nostredame headed north as far as the windswept Atlantic port of La Rochelle; beyond that, his prose accounts state that he traveled "extensively throughout the whole kingdom of France," but mention few specific locales. The density of French geographical place names decorating his many prophecies is the only circumstantial hint of destinations after La Rochelle. Mark these entries on a map, connect the dots, and we may have Nostredame's Tour de France: a huge and meandering course arching through the west-central Atlantic regions of the Loire Valley, with a detour through Angoulême and Limoges, then through Poitiers and Tours, making another detour down the Loire River to Nantes via Angers. Then the trail continues north up the Loire valley to Orléans, then northeast to Chartres, Evreux, and as far into Normandy as Rouen. At any time during this leg of the journey, he may have detoured to see nearby Paris. From Rouen, via Breteuil, Guise, and a dogleg turn to the left via Arras, he must have encountered his first experiences of the English, who at the time held the port of Calais. Did he journey across the English Channel? If he did he never confessed to it, but one wonders, because there are a large number of geographic entries to English places in his prophecies.

If we turn back from the English Channel, we might journey eastward along the place names and fortress towns hugging the northern frontiers of France. We take another dogleg to the right at Metz, heading south through Champagne country to Nancy, then Langres, to move about through a cluster of towns at the head of the Rhône Valley around Dôle, Chalon-sur-Saone, and perhaps Mâcon (where he may have cured Ammanien de Foys, at a later time than at Carcassonne). Finally, the last leg of the journey takes us down the eastern edge of French dominions with ever more numerous geographic references to a passage south along the Rhone River Valley, finally to settle into the dense swarm of towns and place names around the eastern half of Provence around Avignon.

It is in Avignon that our speculative navigation hits an objective landfall of recorded facts. Seven or more years into his wanderings across France, around 1528, he surfaces at the place of his first formal education and brush with Church authorities. His biographers tell us that he spent many hours at the University library poring over its wide selection of occult books, including Marsilio Ficino's translation of *De mysteriis Aegyptiorum*, which is often cited as the latter-day Nostradamus' bible for instruction in ritual magic used to conjure visions of the future. The Church authorities summon him on an errand of mercy to the bedside of none other than the Papal Legate (the Pope's Viceroy in Avignon), Cardinal de Claremont.

While at Avignon we have the first documented account concerning Nostredame's life-long passion for culinary delights. He invents a quince jelly recipe, we are told, of "such sovereign beauty" to mark the occasion of a visit of Philip de Villiers de l'Isle-Adam, Grand Master of the Knights of St. John. It is so much admired by the Legate and Grand Master that his dessert eventually finds itself at the dinner table of the French king, Francis I.

The recipe required Michel to pour 1.5 kilos of sugar into a boiling pot of 12–14 sliced quinces; he continued to boil this mixture until this mixture of near-diabetic sweetness and fruit mingle into an aromatic mush ready for straining. Next, the young master would take an overturned stool and tie a fine cloth to the legs to strain the pulp without pressing. The gathered juice would slowly be cooked under a small flame. Once well cooked, he would put a drop onto a plate to observe whether the jelly was going to be as stiff as a pearl. A little more boiling and the jelly would be poured into a glass to cool. If the cooking process was done carefully, the jelly would not require red sandalwood or rosewater. By the time it was presented to the Cardinal Clairmont's or Master Philip de Villiers' dinner table, it would have turned a vibrant red, like that of red wine or a fiery ruby. Nostradamian interpreter Erika Cheetam relates that she prepared some for her dinner table and found it far too sweet for her 20th-century taste buds. It must be remembered that sugar was a rare and expensive delicacy, used more for medicine than for culinary purposes. Nostredame's excess denotes the degree of sweet honor and expense that was dispensed to the taste buds of the high-born and wealthy. Modern food historian Anne Daguin of St.-Rémy relates an interesting, albeit non-sourced, story that Nostredame's interest in new techniques for cooking sugars led to spending winters in Toulon, among the galleys of the Islamic Corsairs and Ottoman Turks.[23] She does not give us a specific date, and for the present perhaps the story should be relegated to fascinating hearsay.

By the end of 1528, the plague across southern France had subsided, and Michel de Nostredame rode home to the warm embrace of parents and kin back in St-Rémy. A new appraisal of archived records indicates that he had more on his mind than celebrating his twenty-fifth birthday along with the solemn festivals and harvest feasts of *Calendo*. He was on a mission to convince his father to advance his inheritance so he could finance his next ambition – to become a Physician.

CHAPTER THREE

The Turning of the Dream

∽

A License to Heal

Nostredame's father died in early 1547. An examination of a document in the archives of St.-Rémy, dated 6 February of that year, lists the heirs of the late notary public. The name of his eldest son, Michel, is inexplicably missing. Were father and son no longer on speaking terms? Lemesurier believes Michel de Nostredame sought an advance of his inheritance from a willing and proud father.[1] Sometime in the year 1529, and a full five years before his father drew up his Last Will and Testament, there was no need to list Michel in his will because he chose to follow the custom where a son, at age 25, could request a fixed estimate of his inheritance in advance of his father's demise. True, a father usually granted this form of patrimonial advance to married sons and daughters, not to bachelor sons, but men of the family Nostredame were not indisposed to bending the rules when a vision for the future was at stake. Perhaps Jaume preferred that his bachelor son advance his skills for healing and herbal cures and win for himself and his family the prestige of a Doctorate in medicine. Let wedding bells and children come later. Jaume de Nostredame solemnly acquiesced to a once-only draw of around 500 gold crowns – a sum that would more than cover his son's entry into a prestigious medical university such as at Montpellier.

By the autumn of 1529, the plague emergency had passed, allowing the surviving faculty to reopen the University of Montpellier. Notwithstanding certain accounts of Nostredame's appearance at Montpellier a full seven years earlier, the only surviving university documents declare him present and accountable to study for his doctorate degree in October 1529. There is nothing in the existent paperwork that indicates he came before the faculty without the minimum requirements for enrollment. So it is safe to assume that he handed over to the procurator of students, Dr. Guillaume Rondelet, the proper licenses and letters of invitation, if not as a legally practicing student physician, at least as a licensed apothecary ready to advance his career as a fully-fledged physician.[2]

It would not be this issue that set the young man on a collision course with the medical faculty, as seen scratched on parchment for posterity. The young Nostredame's arrogance had preceded him into the procurator's office in words uttered to students he met, perhaps on Montpellier's splendid promenade of the Place de Peyron – words which were likely whispered along a trail of gossips all the way to the ears of Rondelet.

Rumor became a black mark of objective impropriety, drying on Michel de Nostredame's first entry of registration in the *scolasticorum* (the ledger for professors and students) on 3 October 1529. History forever records the slashing cuts of ink from the hand of the procurator, Guillaume Rondelet, as he violently crossed out the inscription *Master "Mickey" de nostra domina* and later wrote along the margins in a cooler hand his opinion of the 25-year-old upstart:

Of the one that you see inscribed here, and who has been crossed out, listen well reader. We have been informed by chance by an apothecary of the city and by some students who have heard him say bad things about doctors, that is why by decree of the corporation, it was given to me to cross him out of the book of the students.

GUILLAUME RONDELET, PROCURATOR

Introducing himself as a "master" is even more offensive and audacious if it comes from an itinerant apothecary, self-taught, and without a license from the University of Montpellier or perhaps from anyone else, to practice medicine. It seems that the cocky young man backed arrogance with the success of his pharmaceutical concoctions, adding the sting of jealousy to the justification of the corporation's decision to cross him off.

Enemies come hand in hand with supporters and patrons, one being Antoine Romier. A few weeks later we find tempers at the faculty had cooled, perhaps apologies tendered, and we find Nostredame registered in the book of professors and students:

I ... [The Latin verb for "petitioning" is crossed out and he starts again on another track] little Michel [or Mickey] de Nostredame, of the country of Provence, of the city of St.-Rémy, of the diocese of Avignon, have come to study at the University of Montpellier, of which I agree to observe the rules, the rights and the privileges, both present and future. I have paid the registration fees and have chosen Antoine Romier as my patron, the 23rd day of October 1529.

MICHALETUS DE NOSTRA DOMINA

The young man was allowed to enroll but he was not admitted to the traditional *becjaune* (yellow-beak, or baby chick) ritual for new students, perhaps as a punishment for his statements against doctors, nor was he invited to the Inn of Castelnau to participate in the rather rowdy and randy burlesque show followed by a raucous fraternal feast. Facetious wit aside, a party animal Michel de Nostredame was not; moreover, approaching a well-worn and experienced age of 26 years, he was already "old" in the eyes of the average carousing and mischief-making student. We have no record that Nostredame had any association with the other famous Montpellier medical student of that day: the salt-and-pepper bristled, wily, imp-eyed novelist (10 years Nostredamus' senior), and legendary womanizer, François Rabelais. The author of the satires *Gargantua* and *Pantagruel* signed himself into the ledger of students in September the following year. Perhaps neither man wrote anything (even disparaging) about the other because one, a former monk and blossoming novelist and satirist, caroused with the always-on-spring-break, Dionysian student body by night, and attended classes a year behind the class of the other more retreating and reflective student.

∞

As the body of a hanged man lay open on the large wooden table, displaying its bloody meat and organs to the indoor coliseum of red-robed, pale-faced medical students, the good butcher, Dr. Rondelet, head of the anatomy classes at the University of Montpellier, kneaded, poked, cut and probed the convict's corpse with gory, confident hands. He laid out pages of muscle in tendon bindings, pronouncing in a calm voice as he folded over reams of ruined flesh and organs, the generally false yet established dogma of how the human body functioned. The students braced their stomachs and leaned forward on their hard benches, listening to a litany of terms scarce changed since Aristotle fathered the concept of anatomical study hundreds of years before the birth of Christ; then Galen, a physician from the Imperial Roman era a few centuries later, itemized and organized those false assumptions by category.

A surprising number of young ladies crowded the gallery above the students, their eyes filled with morbid and, in some cases, lascivious curiosity as they peered over perfumed fans and handkerchiefs at the naked corpse of the hanged man. They listened to Rondelet pontificate in Latin like a priest at mass, noting the solemn music of his speech with much awe and little comprehension. The students, Michel de Nostredame among them, listened to his lecture and committed notes to memory.

Thus, Rondelet confidently led a new class of medical students astray. He harnessed and rode their minds away from the existence of the human cardiovascular system and any concept of blood flow, to stable them tightly in Galen's fairy tale of the four humors. In brief, Hippocrates and Galen reasoned that if the outer cosmos consisted of the four elements of fire, air, earth, and water, so too should the inner body of the human being consist of four elements or "humors" of blood, phlegm, choler (yellow bile), and melancholy (black bile). If you survived the slings and arrows of war – or, worse, the one-in-three chance of surviving the fragility of childhood – your natural span of life was believed to depend not on the blood coursing through your veins (few at the time believed blood could do this), but on balancing the four humors: the hot, the dry, the cold, and the moist, digested into the juices and vapors absorbed into the body from what you ate. When out of balance or over-dominant, these humors became the source of character and mood traits, such as being "phlegmatic," "sanguine," or having a "dry" wit. A woman in deep depression had the "vapors," or "melancholia."

Clearly, Nostredame already took this gospel of the four humors to heart, diagnosing the wan state of the Bishop of Carcassonne in the context of restoring the balance of humors through his Elixir of Life. He explains:

Since the soul of medicine is none other than natural heat and when that fails, life lingers no longer, so, by means of this composition [the Elixir], a melancholy complexion is changed into a sanguine one, although the two humors are radically opposed to each other. For just as smoke undergoes a transformation from when it is a hot and damp substance to when it becomes soot and cold and dry, with the attributes of earthly things, so this composition rejuvenates the people who use it.[3]

A closer examination of his words in future writings might help us separate objective fact from the myth of Nostredame the doctrinal rebel. The staple 20th-century biographies praise young Nostredame's seemingly advanced ideas of cleanliness, including his regimen of fresh bedding for the sick, sufficient exposure to fresh air, frequent bathing and the drinking of ample and unpolluted water. How original in the 1520s was such an awareness of human hygiene? His teachers made Nostredame clasp his copy of the Hippocratic Corpus close to his breast as the physician's bible. He would find inside its pages many gospels of healing and cleanliness written back in the 5th century B.C.E. that some biographers believe to be 20th-century medical wisdom. Such ideas are in the *Treatise on Epidemics* and the *Treatise on Air, Water, and Places* penned by Hippocrates, and sanctioned by the medical orthodoxy of Montpellier's faculty, where one already finds Nostredame's "progressive" views concerning climate's influence on health. It is from "Hippocrates 101" that we get Nostredame's "advanced" medical philosophy.

We might wax romantic about a man practicing something akin to modern holistic medicine over four centuries ago, commending this physician who, like progressive holistic practitioners today, relied on keeping the body-mind in balance and health by using purgatives and naturopathic remedies to stimulate its own healing powers. However, the "progressive" understanding that we associate with homeopathy was already ancient in Nostredame's times. It came from Galen, that Greco-Roman compiler and indexer of classical medicine. Rational Aristotle, with his irrational belief that women had fewer teeth than men, taught Nostredame about the human body. Prudent Hippocrates gave our savant his legendary caution about not bleeding patients suffering the plague. Perhaps his great-grandfather Jean passed other progressive views of hygiene down to him from family memory, discovered by Sephardic and Islamic doctors from the golden age of Muslim-dominated Spain. Thus Nostredame's advanced angle on Jewish medical ethics was no more "new" than when Moses Maimonides wrote them down in his *Code of Maimonides*, three centuries earlier.

Although Nostredame's medical philosophies were far less original than his myth-makers claim, there are signs in his surviving medical writings that suggest his approaches to some aspects of the accepted medical dogma may have been grounds for passionate debate and even, perhaps, the threat of censure. Evidence shows that he had a young man's distaste for salaried and sedentary career teachers. If the faculty had tried to tame this promising student's way of seeing medicine with the eyes of an apothecary, they did not succeed. The showdown would come early in the new decade, when, it is thought, Michel de Nostredame was ready to face *Les Tiduane* – his doctorate exams.

∽

A large crowd gathered in the great hall to observe the already famous young man's oral examinations before the entire faculty, student body and the citizens of Montpellier. The candidate was required to present a list of twelve subjects for interrogation. Of these half a dozen would be chosen – three by lot, and three more by the Chancellor of the University. His sympathetic biographers tell us that Nostredame expertly countered arguments against his unorthodox practices, stressing his successes as defense. Manly P. Hall believes the interrogator was, by custom, the patron chosen by the student, making him Antoine Romier, one of the most learned doctors of the time. A patron might salvo tough questions set to befuddle the neophyte, yet in his heart wish his protégé would succeed.

We can only guess what subjects these questions covered, as there is no surviving record. Some of the innovations Romier challenged may have included the same criticisms pouring out of Nostredame's quill a quarter-century later: that too often Galen's newfound zealots during the Renaissance's resurgent interest in all things classical took his theoretical views far too literally. Some of the faculty might have murmured their displeasure at this pharmacist-friendly physician-in-training's point of view, and the label "Paracelsist," either openly whispered or collectively thought, might have thickened the air. A growing number of University faculty members were sympathetic. Before the century was out some of the subsequent flocks of "yellow-beaks" would attain their doctorates in medicine and effectively undermine Galen's mistaken views on the cardiovascular system and render his other errors "humorless," so to speak. Nostredame's direct experience of healing on the road for nine years had made him naturally sympathetic to the ancient Alexandrian Empiricists, such a Menodotus of Nicomedia, whose paraphrase on the works of Galen he would later retranslate. Rather than utter the name of a living contemporary, such as Paracelsus, it is more likely the young man cited in his defense less controversial theorists, such as Menodotus. He expressed the accepted minority view that a doctor, while honoring Galen's contributions, should take stock in the empirical proofs of success in healing through herbal mixtures that show positive results. In other words, one should not function as an automaton of belief in *a priori* theories in the name of Galen, for to do so (as Nostredame would later write) would go against Galen's own caveats against dogmatism.

Because the Christian Church favored Galen's medical theories as theologically correct, the young Nostredame would need to exercise great care when answering questions from his patron before Montpellier University's board of medical judges and the attending Bishop of Montpellier. He would need to praise Galen to the satisfaction of physicians and priests, while diplomatically putting into question those who would uphold Galen's theories as incontrovertible. He must have read how Galen, over 1,000 years before, had despaired of the rising righteousness of members of a new monotheistic cult called Christianity, who tended to believe medical theories without testing them and who were "unwilling to surrender their beliefs to philosophical inquiry."

Whatever were the specific pearls or stones tossed at his oral examination at the accepted dogmas of the day, Michel de Nostredame's examination proved successful. He received full medical privileges in a ritual called the *actus triumphalis*. The bells of the St. Firmin rang the night before the induction, to celebrate the advent of a new physician into Christendom. Early the next morning the faculty in the splendor of their red robes and raiment followed a vanguard of musicians on a procession to the lodgings of Michel de Nostredame, escorting him through the crowds of gathering citizens of Montpellier to the Cathedral of St. Firmin. Once inside, and with great pomp and circumstance, the Chancellor awarded him the distinctive cap with a red pom-pom and the golden ring of a doctor of medicine. The golden girdle of the physician was fastened around his waist and he was handed a personalized copy of the book of Hippocrates. Henceforth, little "Mickey" de Nostredame would be remembered by his Latinized surname: *Nostradamus*.

A Mentor and a Marriage

The word "disaster" comes from *desastre*, old French for "from the stars." The whispered phrase fell fearfully from the mouths of the superstitious French farmers trudging home across rain-soaked fields and the soggy ruins of crops in the year 1531. On early evenings when towering thunderheads cast their hailstones upon the land with unseasonable harshness, the night would bring out a comet's ghostly torch to survey the wreck that had become the year's harvests. Gazing at the evening sky at that bearded beacon of apocalyptic fire, the peasants and townspeople, illiterate or educated, shuttered themselves away from its light, and from the queer cold of yet another shortened growing season. Many would wonder what this evil omen would bring to a kingdom already sorely vexed by a decade of God's wrath.

Nostradamus, a new member of the faculty at the University of Montpellier, probably spent many evenings with head aloft, gazing at the spectral fire of what was later called the Great Comet of 1531. He might have been seen as a fixture upon Montpellier's ramparts or peering out from a high window of the spire of the church of St. Firmin. An understanding of what he might have felt about such celestial portents would be echoed in his future written confessions. The medical discourses are coy, but the prophetic narratives and poetry reveal that he did indeed believe comets were signs from God of great changes in the fortunes of individuals and kingdoms.

Historical records of 1531 reveal the general belief in France that the Great Comet was a harbinger of greater woe. Certainly, there was enough lingering woe from the 1520s to make the passage of this comet an object of mass-hysterical superstition. (In fact, this was the same comet which, on its regular 75.5-year orbit around the sun, would appear two-and-a-quarter centuries later to the English astronomer, Sir Edmond Halley, who named it Halley's Comet after himself.) Farmers and prognosticators in their almanacs of the 1520s complained of ever-shortening growing seasons and colder winters. Plagues upon the crops and humanity also increased steadily, as did famine. Most of the almanac writers would say that God was angry with France and was punishing her for her sins. Today we know that divine wrath did not destabilize weather patterns from the 1520s through the rest of the century (especially after 1560); a climatic phenomenon known as the Little Ice Age was to blame.

If asked when life in France began to lurch towards trouble, Dr. Nostradamus might have tendered the popular view that bad weather and worsening times came in 1525 as a direct result of a French military disaster. The army of King Francis I and his teenage sons met the Imperial forces of the "Holy" Roman

Emperor, Charles V, on the fields of sunny Pavia. Both monarchs, and their fathers and grandfathers before them, had emptied the blood and coin of their kingdoms in decades of wars fought over who would dominate the Italian peninsula. At Pavia, the courageous phalanx of French pike men and armored knights met for the first time the withering fire of the Holy Roman Empire's musketeers. The decimation complete, the survivors of the French army recoiled from the fields of Pavia in a complete rout, and France soon learned that it was a land without a king or heirs – Francis I and his sons were now prisoners of Charles V! The ransom for their eventual return gouged deep into the royal coffers, and hefty taxes were levied as compensation. For a time the French economy was hamstrung.

After Pavia, the weather suddenly worsened. Crops failed across the kingdom, and the plagues of 1525 fluttered with invisible demon wings down upon southern France, there to feed on their victims for four terrible years. With the new decade's advent, God seemed to be satiated in his wrath. The weather improved, the plague abated, and even the economy improved, but, by the onset of 1531, the weather took another turn for the worse. In addition, another "plague" was seen by many to be making its way down northern trade routes – this one a pestilence of the spirit. A plague of Lutheranism, like the comet, was passing across France.

Change was coming to France, and to Nostradamus in particular. It is not known to what extent the passing of this comet catalyzed his lifelong interest in understanding how history's wars, plagues, and milestones seem to recur eternally on Earth under the configurations of predictable astronomical cycles of the stars. Indeed, it is not known if Nostradamus had considered what Halley later proved – that the great comet of 1531 was the same stellar emissary seen in the skies at the time of a number of significant historical events. It appeared on the eve of Julius Caesar's assassination in 48 B.C.E. On its next pass in 66 C.E., Josephus saw it over the skies of Jerusalem and called it "a star that resembleth a sword." Four years later, Jerusalem was put to the sword in a rebellion against Imperial Rome. Josephus and Nostradamus' ancestors alike marked the advent of the Jewish Diaspora from Palestine on the appearance of that comet. You can see its tail stitched in fiery cloth on the Bayonne tapestry auguring the Norman invasion of England in 1066, and it is said that the comet inspired Genghis Khan to conquer the world in the 1300s. It was this same ball of ice, pulled to ever more waxing and bedazzled brilliance by the sun's gravity, that was now – in 1531 – seen by Nostradamus in Europe and by Incan astrologers of Peru. In the latter's case, they believed it was a sign of Godly displeasure with their Empire's most recent and ruinous civil war. In the following year, either by coincidence or by divine intent, Pizarro and a handful of mounted Conquistadors would conquer and enslave the Incas.

In the future, it would be the bane of Millerite evangelists, who falsely predicted the end of the world during its advent in 1835 – while others praised it as a sign marking the birth of the Bahá'í religion a few years later. The passage of Halley's Comet through the skies of 1910 presaged World War I in 1914, the subsequent rise of Communism, and the fall of 1,500 years of European monarchy. Can Halley's Comet be blamed for all of these events? Maybe comets merely cast a weird light punctuating history's concurrent paroxysms with more significance than they deserve. Nostradamus may have looked into his own natal chart to find that the planet Saturn, the grim reaper and reality-giver of astrology, had made its first complete 29-year revolution to the position it held at the moment of his birth around the time the comet appeared. Thus, comet, Saturn, and stars conjoined an interpretation demanding that he reflect, review, and prepare for a dramatic change in his life.

∞

It is reported by various biographical sources that upon receiving his doctor's ring, the young Nostradamus was invited to join the faculty of Montpellier. He would remain there until restrictions imposed on his liberal wanderings from the accepted text resolved him, in 1532 (a year following the advent of the Great Comet), at the age of 29, to saddle up his mule and once again take to the road.

Manly P. Hall presents us with one of the better speculative descriptions of the wandering doctor venturing forth in the spring from sunny Montpellier, heading west on the dusty graveled road with his mule and pack animals:

As Doctor Nostradamus jogged along the road on his docile mule, he presented a picture typical of innumerable physicians of his day. His square scholar's hat had been exchanged for a broad-brimmed, all-weather headgear. His doctor's long gown was tucked up around the stirrups. He rode in the midst of a traveling apothecary shop, the various parts of which dangled about him in a well-ordered confusion. There were books and bundles, a small portable furnace, bottles, jars, and boxes. A few choice specimens from the dissecting room also shared space with the customary mortar and pestle. An elaborate case contained the five surgical instruments, and, should the occasion require, the latter also served as cutlery. They also had other uses. Physicians were known to have defended their lives against brigandage with their favorite scalpels.

The most difficult piece of equipment to transport was the birth chair. In Nostradamus' time the presence of this cumbersome device was the true index of the progressive general practitioner.[4]

To the last observation, Hall feeds us some durable myths about young Dr. Nostradamus the pediatrician. Perhaps such educated guesses were the background for Boeser's scripted scenes for the Orion Classic movie *Nostradamus* of the good doctor bringing his own children into the world. Women and their care dominate the medical writings and beauty recipes of Nostradamus in later decades, but none indicate that he progressed beyond the boundaries of his station as a physician and blundered into the realm ruled by the midwife.

Biological clocks of the 16th century ticked with a far more rapid rhythm than today, thanks to a poor diet, hard life on the road, and the rubbish-strewn city streets. At 29, Nostradamus, having obtained a mainstream education and a laudable degree from Montpellier, had the credibility that anyone in need of a physician would honor. At last, any respectable father of marriageable daughters would invite him as a fine prospect for courtship and marriage.

Some might find it strange that he would point his mule in the opposite direction to his homeland of Provence. We can only guess that better memories waited for him in the wake of his last journey west. It was time to collect on them, see them afresh, and settle down in the town that provided profitable contacts, and an agreeability of climate and construction.

Young Dr. Nostradamus made another circuit through the cities of his past successes: Narbonne, Carcassonne, Toulouse, Bordeaux, and La Rochelle. Eugene Bareste writes in homilies, not without credence, that peasants and townspeople hailed the reappearance of their heroic apothecary-turned-doctor like a king returning in triumph to the scene of his earlier successes. After La Rochelle, Nostradamus backtracked through Bordeaux via Agen to Toulouse, where he began establishing a permanent practice. He chose a particularly old Romanesque house on the Rue Triperie, in the center of town, noted for its strange glyphs and ornamentations, but now lost to us in the mayhem and destruction of the French Revolution two-and-a-half centuries later.

One day in 1533, a postman rolled up to this queer relic of a medieval house in Toulouse. He was a wagoner of good will, because no postal system existed. Alternatively, it could be that a hired courier, moonlighting from the royal duties or passing along the usual letters of credit for wealthy merchants and bankers, was hired to hand Dr. Nostradamus a special missive. It was written in a flourishing hand by none other than one of the greatest thinkers and botanists of the Renaissance.

The letter came from Julius-César Scaliger, inviting the doctor to visit him in Agen. He was intrigued to discourse with the physician so highly praised for the cures he achieved by means of his "plague gun."[5] Chavigny tells us that Nostradamus' reply was "at once ingenious, learned and spirited."[6] It most likely displayed the young man's knowledge of Latin and Greek, and particularly a substantial knowledge of flowers, herbs, and cures. Nostradamus' extensive hands-on research into French flora is very likely what attracted Scaliger. The young doctor saddled his mule and came riding to meet this legend and would shortly be drawn into Scaliger's voracious and charismatic presence. Soon the young man's herbal secrets would be surrendered to the old scholar's life-long passion to redefine the science of Botany by reclassifying plants by their particular characteristics rather than by their medicinal and culinary properties.

Scaliger was sometimes called Giulio Cesare della Scala! Or Jules-César de l'Escalle! Or his favorite Latinized pseudonym, *Julius Caesar Scaliger* – but remember to speak his name as an exclamation! It stands for the slap of a book closing on others when he lectures his audience (of one or more). He is "alpha," everyone else is "omega"; disagree and suffer the consequences. He possessed an able and brilliant intellect that could back up his braggadocio. The bright color of his mind outshined that of others of his day. Not that the lucid color of intellectual stars, such as his victims Erasmus or Rabelais, did not contribute equally enlightening and profound textures to the rich tapestry of the Renaissance. Still, none of them blazed with the overbearing brilliance of the man impatiently, eagerly waiting for the arrival of Nostradamus from Toulouse. When Scaliger shone, no one else's color could be seen – or mattered – and for the most part, when blazing specifically at the targets of his intellectual interest, no other color shone clearer.

Nostradamus would later confess in writing that Scaliger was second only to Erasmus in learning. Being "second" was not what this strongly opinionated, self-promoting genius would want us to believe. The first half of his life, as we have received it, is more myth than fact. He claimed to be the scion of the La Scala family of Milan with an illustrious scholastic résumé. His detractors tell us he was the son of a Veronese schoolteacher who received his medical doctorate at the substandard University of Padua.

Scaliger, ever the autocratic autobiographer, wove interesting tales, suffering neither fools nor cynics. He had been a soldier and captain in the service of the Holy Roman Emperor Maximilian for 17 years. Between wars and military exploits, he had learned the art of woodcut drawing and printing from none other than Albrecht Dürer. He had lost both his father and brother while fighting side-by-side with them at the Battle of Ravenna, but received the highest orders of chivalry from the hand of the emperor himself. His wounds in battle and the onset of gout forced him back into civilian life.

Then begins the more credible second half of his life as a bona fide scholar, widely versed in philology and the natural sciences. His doubtful stories of his ancestry aside, he is recognized today as one of the foremost and innovative modern thinkers on the physics and metaphysics of Aristotle. After studying for many years in Italy, in 1525 Scaliger was invited to come and live in Agen as the physician of Bishop Leonardo della Rovere, the nephew of the nepotistic Pope Julius II, the same pontiff who cajoled and badgered Michelangelo for over a decade to complete his painting on the roof of the Sistine Chapel at the Vatican. Scaliger used the merit of his intellect rather than the notable patronage of successive Agenois Bishops of the House Rovere to attract many of the greatest minds from the Renaissance centers of learning to visit his remote corner of southwest France. Chief among the plentiful creations of literate larvae his queen-bee intellect composed in his study at Agen was *Commentarii in Hippocratis Librum de*

Insomniis; also, *De Causis Linguae Latinae Liberi XVIII.* The latter is hailed as the first significant work on the syntax of the Latin language. Later came a translation of Aristotle's history of animals, *Exercitationum Exortericarum Liber Quintus Decimus de Subtilitate ad Hieronymum Cardanum.* Then would come the loquacious drones that together comprised his seven-volume epic on Poetics; then a succession of commentaries on Aristotle and Theophrastus. Scaliger's queen-bee sting was never sharper and more wounding of others than in his counterattack of Erasmus' *Ciceronianus.* The title impishly implies Erasmus' gluteus-maximum pun-ishment of a critique, published in 1528, protesting against the slavish imitation of the style and vocabulary of the Roman orator Marcus Tullius Cicero. Scaliger replied with *Oratio pro Cicerone* – two transcripts of notoriously vituperative speeches made in 1531.

The whole Renaissance thinking world was still abuzz over Scaliger's brilliant deflation of Erasmus' ballooning prestige when Nostradamus followed the lazy curve of the Garonne down its fertile shallow river valley and caught sight of Agen with its gothic spires and pleasant blend of English wood-beamed and French earthen-brick buildings with their black slate and red tile roofs. His new impressions of the city and the flowery, radiant countryside of Gascony were more pleasing than before. Agen was the doorway to Aquitaine; it prospered as a matrix of the Atlantic and Mediterranean parts of southwest France. Nostradamus must have seen it on numerous occasions while on his way west to Bordeaux and La Rochelle, or back again east to Toulouse. Agen also enjoyed the best balance of dry and sunny Mediterranean and wet and luscious Atlantic maritime climates. Perhaps the agreeable climate and Agen's charms were magnified in Nostradamus' mind by an eager expectation to tap into the intellectual cornucopia of knowledge that was Julius Caesar Scaliger.

His first impressions of Scaliger were of a pair of large, razor-sharp eyes peering out over an aquiline nose. A waterfall of curls cascading down a long thick beard was no less captivating. Was he

Moses come alive from Michelangelo's statue? Admiration was immediate and mutual. If we employ Nostradamus' reflections in later years to reconstruct their first and subsequent meetings, he treasured Scaliger as a Renaissance Cicero in eloquence, a poet to match ancient Maro, and a fellow physician twice as august and masterful as Galen times two. The young doctor equally enchanted the old scholar with the wits to back up rumors of his advanced knowledge of plants, philosophy, poetry, and medicine.

They became fast friends. The doctor delighted in sharpening his wits with the mercurial mind of Scaliger, and in 1533 he summoned for his belongings to be moved from Toulouse for a permanent stay in lodgings in Agen – either at the home of his mentor, nestled against the northwestern walls of the charming city, or a short walk away. Agen not only had a new physician, but its citizens prided themselves with the prestige of not one but two famous men of learning decorating their city. It must be remembered that men of learning were the superstars in the Renaissance. Where the modern Agenois prides himself on his soccer stars, their ancestors, 24 generations earlier, cheered on their men of letters and philosophy.

Nostradamus' medical practice flourished in the giant shadow of his new mentor. Soon the wealthiest families in town were parading their daughters of marriageable age before his eye. Just who would catch his fancy and stir his heart? Was he seeking a love-match or the usual arranged and mercenary mainstream marriage, and a dowry that filled wooden chests with gold rather than filling his heart with joy? Whether trophy-wife or a true love, Nostradamus' attraction to available women might well have been conditioned by the popular Renaissance laundry list for beauty:

Three things white: the skin, the teeth, the hands. Three black: the eyes, the eyebrows, the eyelashes. Three red: the lips, the cheeks, the nails. Three long: the body, the hair, the hands. Three short: the teeth, the ears, the feet. Three narrow: the mouth, the waist, the ankle. Three big: the arms, the thighs, the calf. Three small: the breast, the nose, the head.[7]

High foreheads were objects of desire in those days. Nostradamus was born with one. The woman of his dreams, if she did not possess by nature's grace a high hairline, either shaved or plucked one into existence. The lengths and the pains taken (quite literally) by women to fashion and squeeze into the model of the era's whims of what was attractive, far outstripped the suffering of modern slaves of fashionable beauty. Petrarch (1304–74), an early classical Renaissance poet avidly read and quoted by Nostradamus himself, said of women that they suffered as much from vanity as martyrs endure for faith. Young women might endure at every step the sharp pinch from a metal corset – really a key-tightened vice. It strangled her waist, and made a pancake out of too blossoming a breast. If the young man stole a satisfied glance at the fair complexion of her face, neck and arms, she might thank the slices of raw veal, regularly recharged in a bowl of milk, that her nurse had applied to her arms and face the evening before, while she lay prone. Other chemical and biological attacks on blemishes might include alum, lemon juice washes, the pulpy juices of peach stones, a sanding with breadcrumbs cleansed with vinegar distilled with animal droppings. Facial, leg and arm hair suffered the apocalyptic application of lime, orpiment, gum arabic, and ant eggs. After these treatments, the following morning our young lady's skin might receive a whitening cosmetic promising to preserve her smiling looks in a powder mask made with a dab of toxic metals, such as lead and mercury.

Beyond the physical allurements, the mind of Nostradamus and his future mate would most likely acquiesce to – or, perhaps, chafe against – the religious dogma instilled from childhood that men were the masters and women the weak, and that women were the cause of man's fall from grace with God. Nostradamus might have reasoned that women were more emotionally hysterical. They suffered in childbearing and endured life more miserably than men. As a doctor classically trained in Galen's humoric system, Nostradamus would view women as composed of cold and wet humors, men of hot and dry. To some degree he supported the belief that emotional frigidity followed by an attack of weeping wet vapors proved that women fell victim to changeable moods and a weakness for deceiving others, and that in general they were creatures of unpredictable and tricky temperament.[8] When women were deserving of God's punishment, sometimes men needed to be God's agents for retribution. Men followed the Renaissance proverb: "A woman, a dog, and a walnut tree, the more you beat them, the better they be."

More enlightenment existed in the upper classes who paraded their fetching daughters before this new disciple of Scaliger. Women of higher birth were encouraged to read and write. A well-to-do Agenois merchant's daughter was sometimes trained at home in her father's profession so that she could run her husband's business. Still, many a great male-chauvinist mind of the Renaissance disparaged the education of young women as "topsy-turvydom." A man might tolerate a woman learning, but never as a teacher.

Finally a marriage was arranged, says Chavigny, to a young Gascon lady "of high estate, very beautiful and very amiable." Strangely enough, neither Nostradamus nor his sympathetic future secretary and biographer make any mention of her name in their writings. Some biographers believe her name was Adriète de Loubéjac.[9] Skeptics of this assertion suggested that the old Scaliger's fetching but orphaned 16-year-old wife is mistaken for that of Nostradamus. Scaliger married Andriète de Roques-Lobéjac when he was, for the times, an elderly man of 46. (In that day of far shorter life spans, men believed old age came around the age of 42, on the heels of lost virility.) There is a third possibility: Nostradamus' "Adriète" could be a relation of Scaliger's wife – perhaps a cousin or even a half-sister. It is safe to say that

Nostradamus' bride was not as young as Scaliger's wife. According to custom, marriage was delayed for as long as possible if one was well-off and higher born. Nostradamus, at age 30, was at the prime age for professionals in the liberal arts to marry. He had finished his apprenticeship, received his doctorate, and established a practice with enough financial success to provide for a marriage. We can safely assume that his betrothed would not be some child bride, but rather between the ages of 23 and 25.

It is reported to us that the newlyweds and her family were quite happy with their match. Because young girls of the day devoured books about Italian lovers and the troubadour romance novels of Provence, maybe Mademoiselle Adriète had found in the captivating gray eyes of her dark-haired and fair-skinned Provençal, the prospect of a man of means as well as mystery. Vows passed beneath the arched gothic, chandelier-candled halls of one of Agen's many beautiful churches. Later, the satisfied new relations blessed the bride and groom and made for their homes. The newlyweds knelt together before their new bed, saying their prayers, before their sheets and bedclothes became tangled in cool and humid feminine humors bubbling in the grip of hot and dry Mediterranean passions. Within two years, God's good fortune had blessed the couple with the birth of a beautiful boy and girl.

"This too shall pass ..."

For the next three years, Nostradamus spent idyllic days at Scaliger's house, surrounded by some of the greatest minds in Europe, and pleasant nights nourished in the love and security of a happy home. It is while participating in Scaliger's frequent meeting of Renaissance minds, called his "school of philosophers," that Nostradamus may have first met a lifelong and admiring acquaintance, Jean Dorat, from nearby Limoges. At the time he was an up-and-coming scholar of Greek. Scaliger, the undisputed master of classical grammar of his generation, smoothed the rough edges of Dorat's unquestioned talent as a poet.

Boulenger, in his 1933 biography of Nostradamus, describes his physical appearance at this time as "more small than large, more corpulent than lean, and he had a face which could be observed with pleasure. His forehead was wide and high, his cheeks always ruddy, his nose aquiline, his hair a dark chestnut, his beard long and forked, producing the best effect. His face was smiling and open, very pleasing to younger women, while the older ones were not frightened by it."[10]

Boulenger took as his model an illustration, composed in the 18th century from research and speculation, giving us a facsimile of Nostradamus in his early 30s.[11] It depicts him having a wide and robust, almost satyric face with a short, curly beard fringing the broad chin. It is the portrait of a fulfilled, confident, virile young man entering his prime. The jaw is set; the measuring gaze aims from beneath the pulled bowstring of a skeptical brow, ready to release a sharpened arrow of intelligence to pierce the statement or deflate the attitude of a suffered fool. Nostradamus' portrait is reminiscent of earlier paintings rendered of his mentor as a younger man. The similarity conjures up visions of a disciple emulating the master – a son, in hero worship of a father. He is high and mighty in a great man's glow and displays the feline conceit of a disciple who confidently presumes he will be the heir to some future legacy of enlightenment.

There were a few minor blemishes to his happy picture-perfect life. An outbreak of plague in 1534, a year after Nostradamus settled in Agen, found the two physicians working feverishly to heal the sick. After the danger had past, neither Nostradamus' newfound influence with the city magistrates, nor that of Scaliger (he was soon appointed a Consul and Juror of Agen), could compel them to drain the swamps outside of town. Both doctors complained about the fermenting and fetid stench of the swamps occasionally corrupting the air within the walls of the town with the evil fever of plague. In modern terms, the dire humors in the marshland mists of late spring and early summer were clouds of winged vectors. The infestation of mosquitoes gradually worsened along with the weather patterns of the 1530s. It brought longer rainy seasons to Agen, stretching into summer, increasing the frequency of the city's periodic bouts of malaria. Faced with a wall of bureaucratic foot-dragging, Scaliger and Nostradamus threatened to take their fame and honor to another town if something was not done. The good people of Agen were apparently not ready to pay for such a civic improvement, but were more disposed to appoint a delegation bearing gifts and empty promises – in other words, bribes and praise were heaped upon Nostradamus and Scaliger. Anger vented and egos appeased, the two physicians graciously declined the gifts and advised the delegates to distribute them to the aged and infirm of the city. We have a story from Manly P. Hall of Scaliger and his disciple returning on horseback from their boycott of Agen to long lines of grateful and enthusiastic Gascons, cheering the passage of the pair as they returned home. At some point in their enthusiasm, the crowd lifted the pair off their horses and carried them through the streets, parading them around the city like conquering Caesars.[12]

Another "fever" of sorts entered Agen around this time. Its spiritually charged vectors rode down the dusty or muddy tracks from Geneva, Switzerland, carrying a holy book contaminated with vernacular French rather than the inscrutable Latin only a priest could read and dispense. The "pestilence" spread fast, stealing hearts away from the Catholic fold at secret evangelical gatherings, often held at night. People disappeared for a time, their hearts shot through by "plague arrows" aimed by wandering Protestant ministers – who convinced the most zealous to travel back to Geneva and take instruction from the "beast" himself, the young John Calvin (1509–64). Once the victim's infection with this new and damned foreign strain of Lutheran doctrine was beyond all hope of recanting, they would steal back in greater numbers to their homes, villages and towns to infect others with their Calvinism.

By 1536, the fever of the Reformed Church spread to Agen via Foix and Toulouse. The devoutly Catholic Agenois citizens could now recognize and despair its symptoms appearing in neighbors and kin, who spoke in tongues of blasphemous intent, calling the Holy Father a "king of sinful Babylon" and the church "a den of idolaters." On Sundays, they marched in throngs down the streets of Agen singing loud and defiantly from their vernacular hymnals. Catholics believed they dressed in somber attire to match their black-and-white opposition to the only true and universal religion of Christ and his Vicar in Rome. "You mean your Antichrist Papist wallowing in the whore that is Rome?!" was often the Calvinist adherent's retort.

Life in once-pleasant Agen was showing the strain. A sizable and influential minority could be counted as lost. The Catholic majority noted the ominous trend of Calvinism's greater infection rate through the ranks of the city's higher and more educated classes, its magistrates, its consuls and authority figures. They saw the insidious symptoms spreading to the justices, nobility and skilled artisans and merchants upon whom daily life, law, commerce, and order in the town depended.

There is an unsettling and ominous atmosphere that settles down upon a house divided by religion. An invisible barrier falls behind the gaze of the parent, beloved brother, sister, wife, husband, or child. And, after arguments and tears subside, those in the stunned and emotionally contracted household go about their daily business with the shadow of their religious differences haunting the air. It is an invisible distance no one openly acknowledges, but everyone feels and despairs of. All anticipate with gathering dread the inevitable separation, the end of family ties, and the end of financial and emotional security that must come in the wake of fundamental religious differences. But most of all, those who truly believe their alienated loved ones are lost – truly and eternally lost

– know a pain and helplessness that prayers cannot assuage, and pleading attempts at rescue cannot convert.

People in today's modern, secular societies may not conceive how profoundly disturbing the advent of religious divisions was to society and daily life in early 16th-century Europe. Religion had been a unifying force for all classes and peoples for over 1,000 years. No matter how many wars and plagues Europeans endured, for the most part they all had the same God and the same belief in the same path to salvation. It glued civilized society together. Except for the isolated explosion and suppression of the Waldesian or Cathar heresies, everyone shared Christ and the same creed. They shared the same crucifix upon their breast, the holy relics of saints, statues on countless private and public altars, and their lives revolved around the churches in every town. Everyone, high-born or low, waited for Judgment Day, all desired the same paradise, obeyed the same priesthood, endured the same penances, fasts, and festivals.

Then came the Protestant Reformation.

Nostradamus, it seems, remained a champion of the Roman Catholic faith. Later in life, he publicly protested that despite his unorthodox studies of the paranormal, he was ever devout to the Roman Church and its sanctified doctrines. Certainly, his definition of what was Catholic ("universal") at times strayed quite far from the mainstream, but nonetheless he remained a Catholic in his own mind. At the time of the religious debates he might have agreed with his contemporary, Dr. Jean de Vauzelles of Lyon, who in 1533 suggested that Martin Luther was a scourge sent by God to rid the Church of hypocrisy and corruption. Nostradamus could have defended the Roman Catholic faith's need to respond to the heresy of Calvinism by renewing itself in the virtue and sanctity of its age-old doctrines. Yet he must have felt a sickening heartache at times – even a sharp stab of suppressed anger – when it seemed his mentor, Scaliger, was playing more John Calvin's rather than the devil's advocate. Perhaps the younger man, presuming he had tapped into the full capacity of Scaliger's intellect, grew ever more impatient with his mentor's long-winded and opinionated discourses – especially when he seemed more interested in syntax than in making sense.

In 1538, a virulent, and most likely bubonic, plague visited Agen, carrying off new believers and old to their just or unjust deserts in the afterlife. Whatever holy passions had thickened the atmosphere at Scaliger's house, a greater evil poisoned the air, requiring Nostradamus to put aside disputes over Calvin and the Pope and lift up Hippocrates as everyone's savior, as now all sinners and saved alike needed his wisdom to recover or to remain healthy. Nostradamus sprang to action with all the confidence and energy of old. Each day he bade farewell to his young family, thanking the Lord for their continued good health, while death stalked the households of Agen. One day he might have returned from his tour of wealthy patients to find his wife and children burning with the fever. Their slide was as sudden as it was rapid. Every healing technique failed to cure them. Perhaps he mistook a case of mosquito-born malaria from the swamps for the plague – a common oversight of doctors. He would not have known that the deadliest forms of malaria dry up and flame out the life-force of their victims in less than 12 hours.

This darkest moment of grief on the most terrible day in the life of Nostradamus remains opaque to biographers. They only report that he could not save the lives of his wife and children. News of the doctor's personal tragedy spread throughout the town. It was a great scandal. The magical hands and potions of the famous healer had failed! Most of his patients deserted him. The superstitious Catholics might have reasoned that he was secretly a Calvinist heretic in league with the devil; the superstitious Calvinists might have whispered that God had punished yet another necromancing papist for practicing his satanic arts. Who else but a man making a pact with the devil could miraculously heal thousands yet could not save his own children and wife?

At this vulnerable juncture, when Nostradamus reeled with grief and self-doubt, Julius Caesar Scaliger chose to attack and conquer. We are told they had a most violent quarrel – over what is not recorded by either man. Scaliger was notorious for breaking his friendships. He seems to have had that cruel streak which some quick-minded and intellectually dominant people possess. Scaliger could have chosen this moment to use his acidly critical mind to undermine his disciple's sense of self, either because Nostradamus was deemed nothing more than an initially promising intellectual turning into a "mouse," or because he was an intellectual threat. But maybe the cause for the ruthless attack was visceral: if Nostradamus' Adriète and her children were indeed blood relations of Scaliger's wife then he took his personal stake in the tragedy as an excuse to strike out at the grieving and vulnerable scapegoat with singular cruelty.

Scaliger's more famous and intellectually formidable son, Joseph-Justus Scaliger (1540–1609), gives us a clue to lingering thoughts his father held about Nostradamus. The son, one of 16 children Scaliger would sire, was born two years after the altercation. Still, there might be a taint, subconsciously at least, of the father's sin of anti-Semitism in the son's written condemnation of Nostradamus in the 1560s, when he defined him as "a dirty rascal, charlatan, a humbug of Jewish sorcery and malevolence."

Not long after Adriète and her children were buried, her family demanded Nostradamus return her dowry. Perhaps Scaliger encouraged this demand, if the dead Adriète had indeed been blood relation to his own wife. Nostradamus refused, and the family took him to the city court where Scaliger was a jurist. They won what was most likely a very public and sensational case.

Nostradamus never retaliated. His praise of Scaliger in print was all flowers and deferential honor. There is most likely a typographical error in the 1557 edition of his homily to him in *Traité des fardemens et confitures*. Nostradamus possibly did not intend to call his mentor *Squaliger* for posterity – but he did not advise his publishers to correct the mistake either.

Casting Demons and the First Stone

The chapter of life in Agen that began with an invitation to share the fruits of learning ended with a summons to explain a sin. Four years before tragedy struck, Nostradamus was involved in an incident with a workman of Agen casting a bronze statue of the Blessed Virgin Mary. Apparently, Nostradamus had made a careless remark about his workmanship, bruising the artisan's ego. The workman would not forget; after endlessly simmering over the slight, he sought the proper emissary for revenge.

At a later date the workman made his peace in confession to a priest and to God before taking his grievance to Agen's lay justices of the offices of the Inquisition. He told them that Dr. Nostradamus had called his bronze casting of the Mother of God demonic! The dossier – transcribed, signed and sealed – was filed away for the time being. One has to be careful. In happier days the new doctor of Agen had a powerful friend in the Town Consul and Jurist, Dr. Scaliger, and others. Later on, the agents of the Church in Agen felt either that the time was right or that the doctor's protection and prestige were sufficiently weakened by scandal and tragedy to send their report on Dr. Nostradamus' heretical words for consideration by the Dominican fathers and their lay justices at the Inquisition district's main offices at Toulouse. This chance remark took a full three years to make its way from Agen to Toulouse and back again. It might have announced its arrival with a knock on the grieving doctor's door and thrust itself before his disbelieving face in the form of an inquest, signed by the Inquisition's agents at the town's judicial offices. He was requested to appear and explain his intent in calling a bronze statue of the Holy Mother a "demon."

Nostradamus may have found himself in the same courtroom where he had recently suffered the public embarrassment of losing a case to retain his late wife's dowry. He faced a preliminary hearing on a charge of heresy before the workman, the interrogators, and a notary's sharpened quill so that his explanation would be recorded for later examination by the Church justices in Toulouse. His pro-Catholic early biographers and apologists tell us Nostradamus had explained that in saying this fellow was "casting devils" he only meant to chide the workman for the grotesque quality of his work. No theological opinion was being expressed. Nostradamus' later recorded flourishes of charm and diplomacy must have been on verbal overdrive on that day. No doubt he publicly apologized to the workman for his remark before the inscrutable judges waxed and sealed their report and sent it to Toulouse.

The Church authorities in Toulouse read the report, but remained suspicious of him, because such religiously seditious comparisons of holy relics of the Church to graven images of Satan were freely declared by a growing number of Protestants in the region. In fact, at the very time Nostradamus made his comments back in 1534, it was known that John Calvin himself was in the neighboring kingdom of Navarre, training evangelists to spread his doctrines while he completed the final touches to his theological manifesto *Christianae Religionis Institutio* under the protection of the converted royal House of Navarre.

Another ominous knock on Nostradamus' door punctuated the scourges that had toppled his ambitions, soiled his reputation and strangled his happiness in 1538. A lay officer of the Inquisition was at his door delivering an official summons for Dr. Nostradamus to prepare himself to make his way to Toulouse where he would explain himself before the Church Inquisitors.

He would certainly have considered, even obsessed on, what was waiting for him in Toulouse. An inquest could quickly become a trial, requiring he stay either under house arrest or in prison after each hearing, awaiting the outcome in days, weeks or months. There would be a good chance that he would face fair jurists, such as the distinguished judge Simon Reynier, who would later preside over the century's most notorious case of stolen identity.[13] Nostradamus had lived in Toulouse long enough to be aware of the Church Justices there, and of the Conciergie, where all plaintiffs, other than debtors or those owing fines, must submit to sitting and sleeping with leg irons chained to the wall.

He made haste to pack his mules and carry his necessary belongings for the journey – but he was not heading for Toulouse. He stole away in secret, leaving Agen under the cover of night. Nursing his grief and stunned by the sudden passing of his life's dreams into sullen nightmares, Nostradamus vanished into the Jewish Diaspora.

CHAPTER FOUR

The Plague Doctor

∞

An Exodus to Prophetic Mythos

Little is heard from Nostradamus for the next six years. It seems he was astride his mule, moving quickly enough from town to town to stay ahead of history's record and gather as little moss of emotional attachment and ecclesiastical suspicion as possible. In 1539, the apothecary Leonard Bandon of Bordeaux logs Nostradamus' name and opinions concerning the qualities of black and gray amber used at the time for tinctures.[1] Upon such rare documentation – all there is outside of Nostradamus' own scant accounts of geographical locales in his medical journals – biographers build their story of the lost six years.

He continued to make his living as an itinerant doctor, staying at the houses of colleagues and apothecaries – especially those Jewish converts to Christianity who (in some cases) belonged to a flourishing occult underground predisposed to give temporary shelter to a newly widowed and occult kindred spirit in trouble with the Inquisition. There is some speculation that Nostradamus tried rebuilding his life and his medical practice in Bordeaux in 1539, but it appears that he suddenly rode off shortly thereafter.

No reasons are given – or survive. The direction he takes is unknown.

We might follow a trail of bitter cherries left in passages of *Traité des fardemens et confitures* to mark some places passed. Nostradamus was obsessed with the sweet desires of the stomach – in particular, finding ever better ways to cook up fruit preserves of bitter black cherries of "the most delectable taste, which will keep for a long while."[2] In a rare moment of owning to where he had been, Nostradamus, on the trail of the perfect black cherry jelly, says he had "seen it made in Toulouse, Bordeaux and [La] Rochelle." Toulouse, the district seat of the Inquisition, seems an unlikely place to have been seen in 1539. After Bordeaux he might have ridden north to La Rochelle, but another written extract could point his mule south, abandoning France altogether to hide out for an extended period among the black cherry confectioners and sweetmeat makers of Valencia, Spain:

I have often seen preserved things from Valencia, which were extraordinarily good ... Their sugar is inferior [to] ours, but they are more skilled in the art of preservation. The same is true of their sweet meats in the manner in which they finish them, for when the sugar has been thoroughly absorbed and all bad and harmful moisture has been removed, they completely get rid of this sugar (which has become blackened through repeated boiling) and use a very beautiful one, which then makes the confectionery exceptionally attractive and excellent.[3]

In other references to his black-cherry pilgrimage, Nostradamus rides a mule east, indicating he passed through Turin, Genoa, Venice, Savona, and the French province of Languedoc, yet he qualifies that these accounts had come "more recently" to the composing of *Traité des fardemens* (1552). He is speaking of his tour through Italy in 1548–9. This does not rule out earlier trips to Italy as an itinerant apothecary (1521–9), or again as a doctor and widower (1538–44). A handful of surviving correspondence from the late 1550s and early 1560s between Nostradamus and various German merchants seeking astrology readings could imply he made these contacts face-to-face, decades earlier when riding into the patchwork kingdoms of Germany and the principalities of the Hapsburgs.

J.R. Jochmans is the staunchest champion of the theory that Nostradamus traveled as far south as Egypt and as far east as Jerusalem. Jochmans surmises that while in the Holy Land, he stayed in the city of Safed, a center of Cabalistic learning and medieval Jewish mysticism.[4] It is true that, though less frequent, pilgrimages to the Holy Land were still common during the Renaissance. The Ottoman Empire tolerated the comings and goings of small bands of wealthy pilgrims who could afford the expensive journey via the ports of Marseilles or Venice; the chief destination was the Holy Sepulcher in Jerusalem.[5]

Sometime in the mid-1550s, Nostradamus would compose, but was unable to publish, *Orus Apollo*, an eccentric and cryptic discourse on Egyptian hieroglyphs. Jochmans believes passages displaying Nostradamus' understanding of hidden aspects of prophetic and architectural Egyptian mathematics make it circumstantially "likely" that he visited the ancient Egyptian ruins of the Temple of Isis at Philae, and contemplated the sacred remains of Saqqara near the desolation that was once great Memphis.[6]

Bardo Kidogo indirectly puts into question Jochmans' travel theories and, by extension, any theory of wide-ranging travels based on the detailed listing and description of geographic localities by Nostradamus.[7] Kidogo says that great 16th-century commentators on distant lands such as Nostradamus and Shakespeare "might have been up a gum tree" had it not been for the vast collection of travelogues left by the classical writer Plutarch (C.E. 50–120). Nostradamus refers to him a number of times, and clearly Plutarch's voluminous listings and descriptions of his explorations of Greece, the Holy Land, North Africa, Italy, and Gaul aided Nostradamus' gazetteer. Nor did Nostradamus need to go to

Greece and be initiated as a priest in the tradition of the Delphic oracle to learn its secrets. Plutarch, again an initiate in the Delphic mysteries, handed it down. Nostradamus' surprisingly detailed accounts of England come not from a direct experience of the damp northern climate, advancing the arthritic complaints from his Southern French bones; Plutarch had suffered it for him and written it all down. By the same token, in order to source his *Orus Apollo* it did not take Nostradamus in a burnoose to acquire the detailed measurements of ancient Egypt's pyramidal prophecies of stone. He need only have gone to a library in Florence and study a copy of the 4th-century B.C.E. *Hieroglyphia* by Horapollon of Phaenebytis. He could have accessed Cabalists and adepts of Jewish astronomical prophecy aplenty in Marseilles, Nîmes, Toulouse, Bordeaux, and Carcassonne without going to Safed. Islamic thinkers taught in nearby Avignon, and Nostradamus' extensive knowledge of Arabic medicine and herbs could have come from as close to home as his great-grandfather's house down the lane in St.-Rémy – not North Africa.

Beyond his passion for preserves, some circumstantial geographic evidence of his travels during his lost years might be pieced together from potentially apocryphal accounts of an awakening of his ancestral gift of prophetic sight. The first record of an astrological prediction comes from Nostradamus passing through the mountain village of Saint-Bonnet de Champsaur, nestled against the French Alps just north of Provence. It is said he drew the horoscope of the baby son of Madame de Lesdiguières, predicting the boy would become "first in the kingdom." François de Lesdiguières (1543–1626) did indeed become Constable of France in 1622, at age 79.

Nostradamus, on his exodus north through Champagne, is said to have had a run-in with Calvinists at Bar-le-Duc, where it is believed he publicly condemned their foreign and Lutheran doctrines.[8] Afterwards he rode as far north as Florinville (just across the French border in Luxemburg) and was lodged at the Château de Fains, the estate of Lord Florinville. It is said that he healed Florinville's ailing grandmother from an unrecorded ailment that other doctors deemed hopeless to cure. After the crisis had passed, Florinville and the doctor took a stroll through the Château grounds – and, many would add, took a detour into the realm of myth and legend.

From Etienne Jaubert's *Eclaircissement* (1656; pp. 40–41) comes the following account:

In the same place, visiting Monsieur and Madame de Florinville, I learned from them that Michel Nostradamus had lodged there and had treated there Madame de Florinville, grandmother of the said Lord of Florinville, who is still alive, to whom happened this story which, to be entertaining, he tells in diverse places:

Monsieur de Florinville, taking a walk in the courtyard of his château, in the company of Nostradamus, saw two little suckling pigs, one white, and the other black. At the sight of them, he asked Nostradamus for sport what would happen to these two animals. To which the latter replied at once: "We will eat the black one and the wolf will eat the white one."

Monsieur de Florinville, wishing to make a liar of the prophet, secretly commanded his cook to kill the white one and present it at supper. He killed the white one, dressed it and put it on the spit ready for roasting at the appropriate hour. However, while he was on an errand outside the kitchen, a little wolf's cub that was being nourished to tame it entered and ate the rumps of the little white pig ready to be roasted. When the cook returned, fearing to be scolded by his master, he took the black one, killed it, prepared it and served it for supper. Thereupon Monsieur de Florinville, believing he had won the day, knowing nothing of the accident which had occurred, said to Nostradamus: "Well, sir, we are now eating the white pig, and the wolf will not touch it here." "I do not believe it," said Nostradamus; "it is the black one which is on the table." As soon as the cook was made to come in he confessed the accident which provided the company with another more agreeable dish.

Edgar Leoni observes that if Florinville was 20 at the time, and if Jaubert heard the story from Florinville before he recorded it in his *Eclaircissement*, that would still make Florinville a veritable Methuselah for those short-lived days. He would be well over 100 years old! Jaubert, being a typically sincere but occasionally sloppy Nostradamian scholar, relies on the current generation of Lord and Madame Florinville for this story. Jaubert chases his story with the following aperitif: "All France recounts diverse events predicted by [Nostradamus], but not wishing to write anything without being assured about it, I omit them."

Common (and kosher) sense must chime in. Lemesurier and other skeptics of this tale question how Nostradamus, a first-generation Christianized Jew steeped in Hebrew mysticism, would dare pitch into pork at Florinville's table. I would reply that few orthodox Jewish mystics dabbled in classical "gentile" magic rituals. There is no indication in Nostradamus' copious surviving recipes that he was orthodox and kosher-bound in his culinary passions either. He seemed to act with food as he did in magical practices: he sampled everything that interested him, be it pig or prophecy.

A satisfying dinner and divination session was followed by another potentially apocryphal story. Before parting with Florinville, we are told that Nostradamus gazed up at a thickly forested hill in the distance and declared that under its forested back people of the future would find a hidden treasure. However, no one would unearth this treasure by seeking it. Manly P. Hall tells us that many years later, archaeologists in search of the ruins of an ancient pagan temple atop the hill "found pieces of money in the very place indicated by [Nostradamus]."[9]

The location of one of the less plausible legends comes from another ruin – the often ravaged Cistercian Abbey of Orval monastery, on the grounds of the present-day commune of Villiers-devant-Orval in Belgian Luxembourg, just a few miles southeast of Florinville. God-fearing Chantillon burned part of it down in 1637 during the Thirty Years War. In 1793, God-jeering French Revolutionaries leveled the place, after which prophetic frauds plundered its reputation. Two manuscripts purportedly "discovered" in the 19th century claimed that *The Prophecy of Philip Oliverius, printed in 1542* and *The Prophecy of Orval, printed in 1544* were left by our bereft doctor under an assumed name while passing time healing his grief through prayer and meditation at the monastery. Nostradamus may have spent some time there, but the manuscripts predicting the rise of Napoleon Bonaparte appear to be written in another hand and in an alien style. Lemesurier places the journey north to the Abbey of Orval, via Bar-le-Duc, around 1542, but finds both monastery and prophecy stories "highly dubious."[10] He cannot imagine how in that day, peace and solitude could be found alongside one of Europe's most disputed borders.

Actually, Nostradamus could. It must be remembered that hostilities in the Italian wars had ceased by 1538 and would not resume until 1543, when Francis I broke the Truce of Nice and invaded Piedmont. Charles V reacted with an invasion of Picardy via Flanders – over 100 miles to the west of sleepy and peaceful Orval. It would seem that beyond the fuzzy math of the Florinville story, a peaceful sojourn in the fields and abbeys of that area – far more peaceful indeed than Nostradamus' homeland – *could* be had in 1542. With the armies of Charles V encamped around Avignon in the late 1530s,[11] Nostradamus would be wise to have headed to the northeastern frontiers after the Agen period rather than home to Provence.

The Cistercian monks of the Abbey of Orval had a custom. They regarded anyone knocking at their door asking for sanctuary as a messenger from God. The monks would lie prostrate on the stone floor before the new guest. (They take the position of Moses; the guest the burning bush.) The guest, surrendering to the house rules, would react to this welcome with a subtle blend of humility and a burden of divine expectation. Prayer and contemplation replaced sleep. Morning Mass required rising at 2 a.m.; the days were spent in silence, punctuated by the bell tower chiming the next session of solitude, prayer, simple meals and fasting.

A monastery can be the destination of the hopeless, or a safe harbor for disillusioned victims of life's tragedies. For a rare few a monastic retreat becomes a peaceful waystation wherein they settle into and grow acquainted with being the vessel of a vast and shattering new perception of reality. Perhaps, after he left Florinville's hospitality, Nostradamus made less than a half-day's ride southeast to leave the world's distractions for a while and sink under the covers of meditation and isolation. At Orval he could plumb the black cistern of his secret mind and drink from the "melancholy passion" of his awakening "lymphatic" spirit.[12] There, in seclusion and prayer, the psychic encounter commenced. He fought the demons of grief and regret. He peeled life's thwarted expectations off his soul as if he was peeling his own skin and surrendering unto God until all was given – an inner equilibrium of dark and fiery, dank and divine humors restored.

Perhaps this is what happened to him under the protection and care of Cistercian monks at Orval. The order had a weakness for divine emissaries and among its ranks there were many Catholic mystics and noted prophetic seers, such as St. Malachy.[13] The Cistercian monks possibly encouraged him to believe that his awakening powers of prediction were a gift from God.

No one knows exactly how and when melancholia's storm of pain settled to mirror the moon of Nostradamus' cool and collected temperament. It is frequently recorded in the biographies of great psychics that a profound life-crisis can provide the existential shock that awakens a second sight and a new mystical understanding. Those looking from the outside say the person suffered a nervous breakdown; the mystic will refer to it as a "breakthrough." The break with the old usually comes when life glares back its unforgiving reflection of all the illusory things we expect from it, such as security, justice, abiding love, or abiding "anything" in a mortal guise. If the revelation is clear and the attachment to lost illusions becomes too painful to bear, then we seek that which abides beyond the flipping of the two-sided coin of life, the random joys and sadnesses.

A vagabond may have more opportunities to discover the key to unlock that which abides within. He is "there" wherever he goes. Constant movement and change can make an intuitive traveler aware of the presence inside of an utter peace and calmness that is never restless and does not change.

Flip over the coin face from tragedy to transcendence to tragedy again. Who is turning the coin? What threads the beads of past, present and future together? Nostradamus might have grasped the answer and rode home.

Pestilential Sojourn

By 1544, Nostradamus reappears in more trustworthy reports and archives. He had moved to the teeming and congested port of Marseilles in this ancient crossroads of the French Riviera, and must have lived somewhere near the crowded quays – perhaps even finding lodging in its wall of multistoried apartments rising from the narrow streets. The old port which had harbored ancient Phoenician galleys, greeted Massalian Greek colonists, released the faith of Mary Magdalene's gaggle of seafaring missionaries, and suffered the fire-and-brimstone of Moorish and Saracen fleets, brought to Nostradamus a rich supply to fill his two important needs: knowledge and work. The first, in the form of tools and tomes of classical magic, probably came into Nostradamus' hands via Marseilles' bookshops.

But the same ships that brought Nostradamus his tools also transported the plague, which rode on the backs of rats that scuttled amongst the rubbish piles and stacked boxes of goods and library treasures along the docks. In the 1540s Marseilles had a burgeoning trade in healing the sick. Her population was regularly decimated by the plague. Long before the medieval scourge of the Black Death used the port as a doorway into Europe in 1345, the city had been France's chief and most ancient doorway for disease.

Nostradamus set up his medical practice once again. He would never be short of clients, yet it seems the doctors of Marseilles were highly competitive and combative. His account of life there in *Traités des fardemens* directs great vehemence towards the majority of his colleagues.

Among all the places I have visited, however, I know of none where medicine is held in worse esteem and carried out in a more dreadful manner than Marseilles, apart from two or three apothecaries, and the position would be much worse if the doctors of medicine were not so honest and learned. There is a M. Louis Serre, a renowned and learned man and, like Hippocrates, able to predict the outcome of an illness, who is doing as much as he can there and spares no effort to ensure that [the manufacture of medicines is] done correctly and without deception.[14]

Some biographers expand on this quote, speculating that Dr. Serre became a new mentor, honing Nostradamus' understanding of Hippocratic theory and his plague-healing skills just as a new outbreak in late 1544 showed ominous signs of spreading with a virulence not seen since he had followed its devastating trail as a young apothecary 20 years before.

Breath Fresheners versus the Plague

The public records of towns and abbeys across the Midi record the early onset of incessant and heavy winter rains in November 1544.

The unusually rancorous winter of 1544–5 visited upon Provence some of the worst floods in its recorded history. The ancient levees, first laid out by the Greeks and Romans along the Bouche de Rhône district, hemorrhaged and bled kilometer-long muddy cascades across the plains. The swollen rivers beneath Provence's gray winter skies were soon dotted with bloated corpses of animals and people. By spring, the rains and floodwaters had receded, leaving behind the region's worst pestilence of the 16th century.

It can be assumed that Nostradamus and Louis Serre tirelessly marked their days in 1545 with a steadily mounting caseload, punctuated by an escalation of nasty scenes with colleagues. Cries of the dying mingled with those of protest from apothecaries bickering over the stringent recipe instructions from Serre and Nostradamus. One might imagine that a fervent knock on Nostradamus' door in early June of 1546 might have tapped out in his mind a warning of impending danger. Would life in this disagreeable city reach its climax with a summons to face the Justices of the Church? Instead, the summons came in the form of a letter from the city consuls and magistrates of Aix-en-Provence, pleading for him to journey post-haste to help stop the plague from carrying off their stricken town.

The pestilence spreading across Provence had arrived in Aix in the spring of 1546 after a second and unusually grim winter of chill rains and flooding. Neither prayers in the comforting shadows of the great Cathedral of Saint Sauver, nor cures at the ancient hot springs of the city[15] could stop the black boils left by the invisible touch of the plague as it tagged more and more citizens, great and small, Calvinist and Catholic, for feverish death.

The summons may have come with another letter written by someone who lobbied hardest to bring Dr. Nostradamus to Aix – his brother Jehan de Nostredame. At the time Jehan was a politically ambitious solicitor of nearby St.-Rémy, and a frequent visitor to Aix to prosecute court cases. He might have influenced powerful friends in the Provençal Parliament to summon his older brother, the famous healer.[16]

Nostradamus handed over his patients to Serre, and rode north-west to Aix. He passed through peaceful and surprisingly plague-free farms and villages to make his presence known to the tense quarantine guards at the city gates. They may have bid him pass through the gates with a look and gesture that made him feel that he was passing through the gates of hell.

Tales handed down to César, his yet unborn son, might be inserted here to best describe the initial impact of the disaster on his father's first day inside Aix:

Persons stricken by the furor of this malady completely abandoned all hope of recovery, wrap themselves in two white winding sheets, and give forth – even while they live – their sad and lamentable eulogies. (An unheard of thing!) The houses are abandoned and empty, men disfig-ured, women in tears, children bewildered, old folk astonished, the bravest vanquished and animals pursued. The palace is shut and locked, justice silent and deserted. Themis[17] absent and mute, the stretcher-bearers and street porters work on credit. The shops shut, arts halted, temples solitary and the priests all confused. In brief, all the streets were villous, wild and full of weeds because of the bleak absence of man and beast for the 270 days that the evil lasted.[18]

Nostradamus soon found out from the magistrates that he was vir-tually the only medical person left in town. He instructed them to collect the surviving medical men and apothecaries, possibly mak-ing the city's Hôtel de Ville (city hall) his base of operations and medicine manufacture. Shortly, Nostradamus would demand and receive emergency dictatorial powers from the city magistrates. He would use them to hasten the transport and burial of corpses in the cemeteries, and press any man into service in the stretcher-bearing teams carrying the living to collection stations outside the town walls. He would also make frequent tours throughout the town to diagnose the sick in their homes. After diagnosis he had the power to expel and quarantine the afflicted of any class, either to their own quarantined houses, identified by a painted white cross or mark of some kind, or to makeshift hospitals outside the city walls. Nostradamus and the magistrates would invoke the usual restrictions (wasting much time and energy policing them) – putting a halt on trade and public assembly in the open air, and prohibiting livestock within the city walls. All travelers to Aix were turned away if they could not provide verifiable proof that they had not been through infected towns. Such documents would be smeared with an acrid herbal oil before the quarantine officers could read the dripping, stinking mess. The hardest task was collecting and controlling those men who carried out the dead. They were usually brigands, cutthroats, and murderers pressed into service out of the town jail. The townspeople feared and loathed the body-bearers. They reeked like vultures of the plague's foul humors and often carried out more than just the dearly departed. One might have added to the famous call "Bring out your dead!" the codicil "… and your jewels, silver, coins and expensive clothing."

Many resisted the summons to the crowded and pestilential atmosphere of the hospitals outside the walls, for it was known that few survived their convalescence. They were stuffed like sardines into rooms, with windows sealed to keep the pestilence from getting out to the nostrils of the healthy. Nostradamus' Hippocratic philosophy, recently reinforced and emboldened to a zealous degree by practicing with Dr. Serre, would see him on frequent visits to the hospitals fighting for the acquisition of wholesome food, uncontaminated spring water, clean quarters, and fresh bedding for his patients. He would command they open the shutters wide and take down the canvas nailed across windows to allow in fresh and purifying air. To those modern scholars who believe his instructions on moderate diets for the afflicted, sparing in fatty meats, are a myth of imaginative Nostradamian writers, they need only look more carefully at passages in Nostradamus' own writings.[19]

Nostradamus recorded a detailed account of his battle with the pestilence in Aix, six years later in 1552. It appears in various editions of *Traité des fardemens et confitures*,[20] and it is primarily upon the efficacy of this vivid narrative that historians acknowledge Nostradamus as one of the most significant healers of the 16th century, despite the controversy of his of soothsaying in later life.

In the year 1546, I was summoned by the city, Aix-en-Provence, to rescue the citizens from the plague – and this was in a contract from the city magistrates and the government. A great and horrendous outbreak of the plague had begun there at the end of May and would eventually last a full nine months.

The people died in a way one has never experienced before, while they were eating and drinking. The cemeteries were so flooded with corpses that you could not find any consecrated ground to bury the dead. On the second day of the infection, a majority of the plague stricken people became crazy and started running amok. However, these mad ones did not get pustules, but one did see pustules develop on the other infected people who did not go crazy. The latter group died very quickly, sometimes while they were in mid-sentence with the word frozen on their lips. Immediately after their death, their bodies were covered with black pustules. The other ones who died in madness had urine that took on the subtle color of white wine. After the death of these, the violet-colored, stagnant blood was gathering under their skin until half of their body was as blue as the sky.

Any contact with the sick was so dangerous that everybody who only approached them at five paces was stricken with the plague. More of them had the blisters of *the carbons*[21] on their breasts and on their back and on their legs. The skin around the pustules was black as coal. Those that had it on their back were tortured by a horrible itching. The majority of them had no chance to survive. Everybody who had the blisters on their chest died. The few patients who developed the first lesions of the disease behind their ears could more often expect to live for six more days rather than seven.

Scholars of Nostradamus incessantly counter and parry in battles of pure speculation as to whether he wore the outlandish anti-plague costumes of the day. Did he roam the city streets of Aix wearing a leather gown and leather armor? Did he creep up on his patients with a broad-rimmed hat, below which lurked a fearful stare through bug-eyed goggles out of a terrifying bird-beaked leather mask, and the Ibex proboscis that was filled with aromatic herbs to ward off the smell of the evil plague floating in the air? When making his diagnosis, did he probe his patient with a stick held in leather-gloved and garlic-smeared hand, and spit garbled instructions with a mouth worrying a garlic clove, while straining to hear the patient's questions through ears stuffed with pungent herb-saturated cotton balls?

There is no mention of wearing such outfits by Nostradamus himself, but he certainly indicates a fear of getting too close to his patients, implying that at least some protective gear was warranted. Nostradamus may have approached his patients dressed more like an ordinary human being, exuding an aura of confidence and health, but he may have also stunk of garlic and soaked himself in powerful herbal perfumes of his own making, perhaps wearing gloves and tying a cloth or rubber scarf over his mouth and nose. His account gives circumstantial evidence that some of Aix's citizens developed the bubonic plague's highly contagious and deadly pneumonic stage. Death did indeed float on the air, not as some foul humor, but in an aerosol of germs launched in a radius of "five paces" by sneezes and coughs.

Less than a decade after administering to the plague victims of Aix, Nostradamus would write the following prophecy: "The lost thing is found, hidden for so many centuries. Pasteur will be honored as a demigod. This happens when the moon completes her great cycle. He will be dishonored by other rumors as foul as farting."[22]

While harried physicians since the days of Hippocrates and Galen had fought an invisible enemy in the air with their primitive tools, perfumes, frightening costumes – and their false assumptions – the healers from the 2nd century B.C.E. to the 16th century were partly correct: the plethora of viral and bacteriological diseases they lumped together under the all-inclusive label of "pestilence" often *are* in the air, even if they are not "of" the air. Perhaps this is the "lost thing," or secret, Nostradamus became aware of after his battle with the plague in the streets of Aix in 1546. He wrote the above prophecy in 1554, at a time when he had all but retired from medical practice to pursue other interests. Later editions of *Traité des fardemens* in 1557 show no change in his prescription for the plague, which indicates either that he did not care to update it or that his prediction was a real glimpse into the future that did not reveal to him exactly what the "lost thing" was, just that a fellow named "Pasteur" would know and people of his day would nickname him "demigod." Pasteur would discover the secret when the current grand lunar cycle, which began in 1535, completed itself in far-off 1889. Call it a fantastically good guess, or a glimpse into the future, but it is a fact that Dr. Louis Pasteur discovered and confirmed that germs pollute the atmosphere and spread diseases, not evil humors or invisible plague demons with darts and arrows. Perhaps Nostradamus, who himself was a passionate investigator into preserving foods and fruits from corruptions he could not define, was on track to discover or at least imagine that something more than "humors" tainted flesh and food alike.

Any effort to promote such a prophecy as evidence favoring an advanced intuitive or theoretical sense of medicine on Dr. Nostradamus' part might not sit well with some scholars. Still, one has to wonder. The prophecy seems to name Pasteur, then dates 1889 as an important year (indeed, it is the year marking the creation of the Institut Pasteur), and then calls the father of pasteurization a "demigod" just as the *Encyclopedia Britannica* of 1889 did. There is also Nostradamus' crude coda to consider. The dead demigod of medicine faces a fresh and most devastating foul wind of rumor in our own times. Princeton historian Gerald Geison, in his book *The Private Science of Louis Pasteur*, re-examined Pasteur's notes and discovered a disturbing revelation. Pasteur not only tested his rabies vaccine on a nine-year-old boy bitten by a rabid dog, as is popularly believed, but apparently he did not make thorough tests beforehand as he publicly claimed. In other words, the demigod Pasteur played demi-demon Dr. Mengele, testing his experimental rabies treatment on a child with little or no preliminary tests on animals. Fortunately his experiments worked and changed the medical world.

We resume Nostradamus' account about fighting the plague outbreak in Aix:

In the beginning, barely anybody would survive the plague. If somebody would have the malady, neither bleedings, stimulants, hymns nor anything else had any more effect than doing nothing at all. There was a harvest of human beings, in every sense of the word. The fury of the disease was spreading like a wild fire and there was no way to escape it. When we [himself and the city magistrates] had first searched the whole town and gave the order to have the plague victims thrown out beyond the city walls, the next day we would discover even more sick people than before. There was no remedy that would have prevented it. However, everybody who had my medicament carried in their mouths would stay healthy. Towards the end of the plague's visitation, we find by manifest experience that this remedy arrested the contagion for one month.

I do not know to what extent the next strange fact belongs to the subject of this story, but several affirmed their belief during the time that this malignant and horrible plague was a divine punishment. They believed this because beyond the proximity of one kilometer in circumference of Aix-en-Provence only good health was enjoyed in the neighboring villages and farms while the whole town was so plagued that even to look at an infected person would be enough to be infected oneself.

Foods were there in over-abundance and could be purchased at very low prices. But death came galloping so suddenly, that a father scarcely had time to recognize his children before passing away. Several fathers abandoned their wives and children when they knew they were wounded by the pestilence. Many of those plague-stricken people who became deranged threw themselves into the well; others hurled themselves onto the street cobblestones out of an upstairs window. Others who got coal blisters on the shoulders and the chest suffered day and night from violent bleeding out of the nose until they finally died. Pregnant women had miscarriages and died after the fourth day. We found that the child died suddenly and its body was covered with lesions or blotches of a violet color as if the blood was spread over all the surface of the body.

In brief, the desolation was so great that often people died with the gold and silver clutched in their hands, for want [and] lack of a glass of water. When I began giving the medicaments to the first patients brought to me, they where in such a horrible condition that many of them expired with the medication in their mouths.

If, in a state of prophetic ecstasy, Nostradamus did predict the advent of Pasteur, this passage shows little sign that outside of his reveries he was anything more than a medical creature of his day. He describes the plague "wounding" its victims. Is it a literal wounding with invisible plague arrows or a metaphorical one? Had he any inkling of germ contagion if he sincerely subscribed to the popular 16th-century superstition that a plague victim could pass a contagion with merely a look? Moreover, Nostradamus cautiously cites the superstition popularly held by townspeople and doctors alike that the plague was a divine punishment. His prophecies, written a decade hence, implicate him as a firm believer in the holistic impact of evil deeds, begetting famines and plagues in their wake. The growing minority of Calvinists of Aix and across Provence did believe the plague was divine retribution against their Catholic neighbors. The Catholic majority in the Parliament of Aix regularly sanctioned, forgave and forgot the perpetrators of the first small-scale massacres of Calvinists, along with Waldesian heretics, across Provence in the mid-1540s. Of course, the Calvinists succumbing to the plague while under the pro-Catholic Dr. Nostradamus' care probably did not hold the same opinion as they awaited judgment day in a shroud, alongside Catholic corpses in a mass grave.

Nostradamus worked around the clock for the next 270 days administering his "medicaments." These consisted of a recipe of rose pills, prescribed to hundreds of patients, along with his usual Hippocratic regimen of clean water, clean air and other strategies used successfully in the past to arrest the plague. One might picture the diminutive, energetic doctor appearing in the fields outside town near sunrise in the summer months, overseeing the harvest of rose petals, to be carried back to his makeshift pharmacy. He would press a team of assistants to grind and pestle the rose petals into a fine powder, mixing them in the following recipe:

Take 1 ounce of sawdust from the branch of cypress wood, the most green that you can find. Of Iris of Florence: 6 ounces. Of Cloves: 3 ounces. Of Odorated calamus (sweet flag): 3 drams. Lign-aloes: 6 drams.

Reduce all of these into a powder that does not blow away from being overly evaporated. Then take three to four hundred incarnated red roses – which must be very fresh and gathered before dawn and the advent of the morning dew – and then pound them vigorously in a mortar of marble with a pestle of wood. When the roses have been pounded thoroughly blend them together with the aforementioned powder, and repeat grounding it strongly while adding a little bit of sugar of roses.

When the whole will be well mixed, then make small pats [pills] in the manner of *trocisques* [a small cone-shaped cake or lozenge] and make them dry in the shade. In addition to the good fragrance this prescription affords ... [to] make the composition even more excellent, add to it some musk and gray amber according to your preference. I have no doubt that you then will have composed a sovereign fragrance. Take the said pulverized musk and gray amber and dissolve it with the sugar of roses then mix together and dry in the shade.[23]

With the assistance of Joseph Turel Mercurin, whom he cites as a "pure and sincere" apothecary, they packed this concoction tightly into lozenges he called "rose pills." He admonished his patients to keep these pills under their tongues at all times without swallowing them. Not only are we told that these "rose pills" successfully prevented the spread of the plague in Aix but they had other beneficial effects:

Besides the goodness and the good fragrance this [rose pill] composition gives to the elements and the aforesaid compositions, if you would put a little portion in the mouth it will make a wonderful breath freshener that will last all day, [even if] the mouth was stinking either from corrupted teeth or from bad vapors coming out of the stomach … Moreover, if it was necessary for one to be in the company of people, [one only need] keep [the rose pill] in the mouth without chewing it. It will give a fragrance in the air so good that we will not be able to say where it is coming from. In times of pestilence, put it in the mouth often. You cannot find an odor which sooner takes away the bad and pestilential air …[24]

Can what is essentially a breath freshener stop the bubonic plague? Nostradamus' own statements about his rose pill medicaments reveal how blind he was about the plague's cause. In the beginning of the battle, when the outbreak was at its peak, neither bleedings, stimulants, nor hymns to God had "any more effect than doing nothing at all." The reference to bleeding patients has Lemesurier criticizing a number of modern writers, including myself, for fostering yet another new myth: that Nostradamus avoided bleeding his patients. But a close reading of surviving fragments of his medical instructions, such as those statements recorded in his *Almanac of 1559*,[25] proves that he was most reluctant to bleed plague victims unless the time of year and the strength of his patients could stand it. In most cases, it is safe to assume that by the time he saw them, they were too weak anyway. He seems to have been progressive at least in not applying leaches or lances to drain his patients of their blood and strength to fight the plague – in contradiction to the popular belief that this would drain the imbalance of fiery sanguine humors in the body that caused the plague victim's fever. However, beyond that, he stated that nothing could be done in the opening months when the plague spread "like a wild fire" through the people of Aix. His work therefore followed two courses: a systemic approach (applying his rose lozenges under the tongues of the yet uninfected citizens); and a diligent public hygiene program, including the removal of bodies, the burning of refuse, the flushing of the streets with ample clean water, and a quarantine of plague sufferers either in their homes or outside the city walls.

Beyond propagating a powerful belief in getting well (or not getting sick) by using his rose lozenges, Nostradamus, staggering in the darkness of his ignorance of the plague's causes, did far more to improve his patients' chances to survive by doing what people had done for centuries. Since the times of Galen the population of an afflicted city, believing that bad smells were the home of the pestilence's foul humors, became motivated by the pestilence to clear away or burn their flea-infested clothing, bedding and garbage. Burning rubbish and plague-infested structures seemed to work, but they did not know why. You could say that they threw the baby bacteria of bubonic plague out with the bath water, the house, the corpses, the rubbish, the rats, *et al.*, when applying the torch to the whole pile. People chased and killed rats as far back as biblical plague infestations described in the Book of Samuel;[26] but they did not make the connection to their filth attracting the rats, nor did they know that the rodents carried plague-infested fleas. It seemed that rats always liked to congregate wherever the invisible plague demons gathered, so if you killed them, it seemed to make the demons go away. Knut Boeser theorizes that the strong aroma of Nostradamus' rose pills shriveled the nostrils of the rodents.[27] Perhaps a pungent rose pill a day kept the rats away.

Nostradamus believed his rose pills saved the healthy and all but arrested the contagion towards the end of its visitation for one month. That would put his "success" sometime either in chilly December of 1546 or frigid January of 1547. Perhaps he is making the same mistake other doctors of the day made, believing his remedies had an impact, but it appears that this success coincided with the decimation of rat populations as a result of civic house-cleaning, prompt burials of infected humans, and the passing of the hot days of spring and summer into the colder autumn and winter months, when both rats and humans tended to take shelter rather than mingle their infections.

All pseudoscientific conundrums aside, Nostradamus was sincere and courageous in his efforts to save the people of Aix. Highborn and lowly citizens, Catholics and Calvinists, watched this man fearlessly enter their houses and attend to their loved ones. They witnessed him spend most of his waking hours from the late spring of 1546 to January of the following year, ever among the sick, administering to hundreds of victims, while himself untouched and healthy, and always confident of a positive out-come. Whether as a vision of Anubis in bird-beaked leather mask and overgarments, or dressed in the four-cornered hat and black robes of a physician, the doctor proceeded into a feverish reality with a delightful and soothing breeze of flowers and roses, as if he had brought Heaven's holy gardens into a private hell. He may not have known what caused the disease, but in his vigorous manner, he helped them as best he could, celebrated with them his often-accidental successes and sorrowed with them when his remedies inexplicably failed.

Beyond the satisfaction of healing so many people, he would forever carry the shadow of an emotional trauma that any doctor experiences when faced with their powerlessness to succor those in suffering. Nostradamus closes his account of his fight with the plague at Aix with an incident that haunted him for the rest of his days:

Among the unforgettable experiences that I actually lived through, one especially stayed in my memory. One day I went to a woman. I called in the window for her and she responded to me ... When she took a step back from the window, she covered herself with a death shroud and started sewing it together, starting with the feet. When the undertakers entered the house, they found the woman dead lying in the middle of the house next to her sister. She was just able to sew and cover half of herself in the shroud ...[28]

The people of Aix did not judge this doctor with the imperious arrogance of those living in more medically enlightened centuries to come. The people of Aix witnessed him risking his life for nine months, until either by his efforts or God's mysterious ways, the danger of the pestilence had passed.

The grateful citizens rewarded the doctor with money and gifts, and it seems that from 1547 onwards Nostradamus was financially secure. In the 19th century, Eugene Bareste concluded (upon records lost to us today) that financial security came from the Parliament of Aix awarding Nostradamus a pension for life. Moreover, we are told he was showered with gifts and money from the wealthier citizens but gave much away to the poor, and to the families and dependents of those he could not save. If any rewards had been collected, they might have found themselves shipped temporarily by wagon either to Marseilles or to his brother Jehan's house in St.-Rémy.

Nostradamus had no sooner finished his work in Aix-en-Provence than a summons came for his services from the town magistrates of Salon de Crau. On some mistral-whipped winter day, he passed beyond the city walls of Aix and rode west past the now empty and mute hospitals outside of town, arriving at Salon within a day.

The Battle of the Physicians

No one can say exactly when Nostradamus fell in love with the little town of Salon. We know that the winter winds blow markedly drier on the approaches to this former ancient Roman outpost, which might have spelled relief to the 42-year-old doctor's tender joints. We can reconstruct his first pleasing glimpse of the town from 16th-century historical accounts. Salon was a cozy walled town built at the edge of a desolate gravel desert known as the Crau. Its 3,000 to 4,000 souls lived under red-tiled roofs and behind sunburnt yellow and ochre plaster walls and limestone masonry, built around a rock outcrop topped by the rough rectangular walls and four squared towers of the 13th-century Château de l'Empéri. This castle squatted over the foundations of the original Roman fortress and hamlet on the last limestone promontory in an archipelago of limestone hills dipping into Crau plains from the northeast. He, like many wayfarers of those days, might have described Salon de Crau and its environs – with its hard chalky soil, olive groves, and pastures dotted with large flocks of sheep – as resembling a corner of the Peloponnesian peninsula of Greece. At that time, almond and olive trees and vineyards spread across the surrounding countryside. Perhaps he thought about staying there as long as November; God willing, he might see the dry and pleasing winds of autumn push the spiral of sails of the town's five windmills to press a bountiful harvest of almond dough and wine.

Any delicate threads of idle dreams that may have decorated his mind were soon brushed aside by the serious concern of healing the sick of the town. There is little information to reconstruct his ministrations to those suffering from plague in Salon. One can safely speculate that the outbreak was far less serious than it had been at Aix, and that Nostradamus applied the same systemic and hygienic strategies to preserve those still uninfected until the summer heat, and the plague, ran its course. He most likely lodged in the house of his brother Bertrand de Nostredame.[29] Possibly he was introduced to his brother's associate and friend Jean Beaulme, a wealthy lawyer, and his new bride, Anne Ponsarde. It is also possible to fancy that their meeting had taken place under tragic circumstances. Jean Beaulme soon died, most likely a victim of the plague. Nostradamus may have been summoned to what was only recently the newlywed's nuptial bed, where the feverish Beaulme lay too far gone to save.

Word of the famous plague doctor spread up and down the trade routes of the Rhône valley faster than the pestilence. The hero of Aix had no sooner accepted responsibility for ridding the Salonnais of the plague when he received an urgent call from the distant city of Lyon, a whole month's mule ride to the north, to fight an outbreak of whooping cough.

Imagine the scene that faced Nostradamus, tired from his long month's journey, when he introduced himself to doctors at the city's hospital, the Hôtel-Dieu, packed with hundreds of men, women and children laid low with the gasping hack. At the time Lyon was France's second-largest city with a population of 40,000. It was second only to Marseilles as the pestilence capital of France. The citizens of Lyon frequently suffered from colds and pleurisy, thanks to the town's heavy, humid atmosphere – oppressive in the summer, dank and clammy in the winter. Lyon, like Paris and other major cities, paid the price of the Renaissance boom in economic prosperity that brought rapid and poorly planned urban growth, which in turn paved the way for disease.

Before he could wrestle with whooping cough, Dr. Nostradamus found himself in a skirmish with the town's most prominent physician, Dr. Philippe Sarrazin. In later years he would preface his side of the encounter with his flair for flinging all due respect in the form of inflated praise, listing Sarrazin in *Traité des Fardemens* as:

A notable personage of incomparable knowledge ... *Phil. Saracenus,* whom I provoked in my later years with my basic [medical] principles ... I hold him no grudge, but it seems to me ... [he] had no wish to see his not-too-durable doctrine ... [collapse in an argument with me].[30]

The aged Sarrazin was quite territorial, and, if his name is any indication (a *Saracen*), he may have promoted Arabic and Jewish medical theories and even disparaged the younger, Hippocratic revisionist behind his back to the city council. Sarrazin obviously took Nostradamus' invitation by the city council of Lyon as a personal affront to his reputation. Perhaps the patients, fellow physicians and apothecaries in the oppressive wards of the Hôtel-Dieu at last witnessed a public outburst from Sarrazin, causing a retaliatory and "Hippocratically" Greek-fired salvo of Nostradamian temper.

Bareste says Sarrazin became a jealous colleague who rejected Nostradamus' good advice. After the encounter our hero apparently retreated to his temporary lodgings, whereupon a delegation came to his door, begging him not to abandon Lyon in anger. Nostradamus, his temper cooler, concluded that Sarrazin's fundamental disagreement with his medical practices required the people of Lyon to choose which doctor stayed. To which, Bareste writes, they enthusiastically replied, "We choose Dr. Nostradamus, liberator of the town of Aix!"[31] Sarrazin was dismissed, and he left Lyon in a temper to stay in nearby Villefranche, just a few miles north of the city. Soon after his departure, Nostradamus eradicated the plague of whooping cough through mass prescriptions filled by pharmacist René le Pillierverd.

Bareste bases his story on "Astruc [and] Bouche ... the historians of Lyon and the Provençal chronicles." In 1919, Parker's skeptical perusal through the archives of Lyon found not one mention of the incident by Astruc or Bouche. If Parker was another historian victimized by time's inexorable depreciation and misplacement of documents, then some future historian will have to find Bareste's lost sock of a fact in that mysterious place where all lost socks and dubious historical sources go. Parker did confirm via the *Revue du Lyonnais pour 1835* that an epidemic of whooping cough visited the city in 1547. This matches Nostradamus' own mention and praise for the apothecary Pillierverd in *Traité des fardemens* for services rendered there in "1547."

CHAPTER FIVE

The Renaissance of Nostradamus

✢

A Patient Lost is a Lover Earned

Dr. Nostradamus returned to Salon de Crau no later than the "second spring" – which is what the Provençal natives call the second growing season beyond the autumnal equinox, when the lingering warmth of the low-angled sun suckles one last bountiful harvest before the arrival of the frosts of late November. He was approaching his forty-fourth birthday and it seems he was growing physically weary of the rootless and strenuous life of a vagabond physician. Perhaps there was more than a wayfaring widower's loneliness and desire for stability and security motivating his return to Salon. He already had a "mistress." His true and secret love walked and pined through the shadowed halls of his subconscious mind – her name was "prophecy." Perhaps he had delayed remarrying for so long because he sensed how difficult it would be for an ordinary woman to wed a man who would serve two mistresses in one home: one, a mother of his children and a homemaker of flesh and blood; the other, a "muse" of pure and sometimes frightening prescience.

What *Le Charbon*, the Lord of the Rats, had taken away nine years before, it gave back to Nostradamus upon his return to Salon. The fateful hand of the pestilence that carried off his first wife in Agen in 1538 had perhaps made a widow out of the young and wealthy Anne Ponsarde *Gemelle* ("the twin"),[1] in the spring of 1547. Thus, the wife of the man who could have been Nostradamus' unfortunate patient, the late Jean Beaulme of Salon, was free to bestow to him her hand in marriage in the autumnal Provençal "spring" of that year. They were married on 11 November 1547.

No painting or woodcut of Anne Ponsarde survives. A facsimile of her appearance might be derived from salvaging some presumed impression out of an angular, almost grotesque, self-portrait of her firstborn son, César de Nostredame.[2] The cheeks are sunken, the cheekbones prominent. Most striking is César's long Roman nose, the kind one expects from the beauties of Provence. There is an angularity of the jaw, a straight yet delicate mouth, thin in lip, earnestly set. The skin is firm, the face generally wolfish. If these are genetic attributes of his mother, one might hope that the visage of an aquiline Provençal beauty with high cheekbones had given birth to the testosterone-sharpened reflection of herself in her son.

Given the average marrying age of well-to-do bourgeoisie at this time, we might infer that Anne was between 23 and 25 years of age – old enough to be the good doctor's daughter. Their marriage might have raised a few eyebrows in town, second marriages not being the accepted norm of the 16th century. Canon law officially forbade them in medieval times; later on, in the early Renaissance, the priests and justices of the church relented somewhat as the harshness of daily life made for many lonely and unfruitful young widows and widowers.

In his writings, Nostradamus betrays a long and simmering disgust for members of the urban lower classes and agrarian day laborers of Salon. The seed of this ire may have come early on from the taunting and snickering he and his new wife suffered behind their backs. Perhaps they were the objects of the era's mock serenade to newlyweds, called *Charivartis*. This ritual sometimes included a public lampooning by the townsfolk. If this ritual was true to form, it might have involved parading effigies of the newlyweds alongside a straw-stuffed facsimile of the deceased first husband. This would have most likely taken place either during the Christmas festivals of 1547 or early in the following year during Mardis Gras.

Nostradamus' rich and well-connected bride saw to it that her new husband was well received by the Salonnais bourgeoisie. Leoni refers to Anne Ponsarde as "that always-useful person, a rich widow,"[3] thus feeding the myth that Nostradamus was a gold digger. Lemesurier sides with those scholars who believe it likely that Nostradamus had obtained a pension for life from the parliament of Aix, as well as many private financial rewards for his healing work in Aix, Lyon, and even Salon itself. If so, then this was a marriage between two wealthy and consenting adults.

They purchased a solid limestone house on a narrow impasse off the Place de la Poissonnerie (the fishmonger's square) in the Ferreiroux quarter, situated at an equal distance from the northeastern curve of the town's wall and the base of the limestone promontory, topped by the Château de l'Empéri. The house exists to this day, but the interior has undergone numerous changes. The façade has also had its share of facelifts and, like the rest of the town's old quarter, suffered damage from the great Vernègues earthquake of 1909. As a result, the Ferreiroux quarter (including Nostradamus' house) is a patchwork of smoothed-out, modern Mediterranean houses and updated façades propping up the crumbling charm of masonry and stone casements from medieval times.

The newlyweds most likely purchased the house in the late autumn of 1547. At the time the house had two arched second-story windows, there was a good chance that their delicately carved stone casements were still intact. There would be a large and imposing hardwood double door, symmetrically centered in the façade. The interior of a typical Salonnais Renaissance house consisted of a ground floor providing space to receive guests and set up business by day, and an upper floor(s) relegated to private and service quarters by night. The newlyweds would find their house had a good cellar (which has since been filled in) along with a modest inner courtyard filtering warm light throughout the lower levels. A distinctive spiral stone staircase twirled up the side of the little stone courtyard to the private rooms of the second floor.

Every dream house has its faults. Although their home was roomy enough to satisfy business needs, it lacked sufficient space to provide an inner sanctum – or the space for the many children they were planning to have. The fresher layers of masonry give indisputable evidence that Nostradamus ordered the construction of a third floor.

The first workers had barely begun erecting the platforms for the construction of the new floor when Nostradamus, in the early spring of 1548, bade farewell to his bride and rode off to Italy. While he was away, it is likely that Anne lived with her relations in town while overseeing the remodeling of their new home.

Searching for Secrets in the Heartland of the Renaissance

Anne Ponsarde might have received the first long-awaited letter from her husband sometime in late spring, or perhaps even in the summer when, we might surmise, the laborers had finished laying down the wooden beams of the floor for the new third story and the hot sun burned the necks of the masons as they began framing and raising the stone walls. Letters written in her husband's straight, methodical handwriting arrived infrequently, by way of wagoners or merchants. These transient documents might have marked his passing through magnificent cities, such as Turin, Genoa, Savona, Venice, Rome, or Florence. Along with caressing words of tenderness, he might have mentioned details of his crystallizing knowledge of herbal medicine, and his ever-sharpening skills in the manufacture of cosmetics and preservatives. We can only guess that one of the occasional letters coming late that year contained florid apologies and reasons why his return would be delayed until sometime in the coming year. Anne Ponsarde Gemelle seems to have been a patient, stoic, perhaps even submissive, wife. She either faithfully supported or tolerated the ambitions of her second – and somewhat eccentric – husband, and she must have surrendered to his timetable for achieving them. Upon the specu-lation of biographers, we can infer that Nostradamus finally passed back into her glad embrace sometime in the first half of 1549.

The sparing mention of the cities and regions of Italy in his later writings are the few threads of a surviving tapestry upon which the historian must reconstruct Nostradamus' 18-month search for secrets in this heartland of the Renaissance. His prophecies con-tain 107 geographic references to Italy and adjacent islands such as Capua, Sardinia, and Sicily. This is second only to the number of place-names logged for his native France. If we combine the mul-titude of geographic locales from the prophecies with the rare mentions of locales found in his medical journals and recipes, we can attempt to map his route east from Salon into Italy via the mountainous coastline alongside the azure waters of the French Riviera. His view from the saddle, cantering out of the western approaches to Genoa, would have brought him in contact with the great lighthouse rising from the rocky western horn of the thriv-ing port's sprawling half-moon harbor. While in Genoa he studied how to perfect the making of aromatic mothballs out of unadul-terated labdanum imported from Arabia. He brought back a half-pound of this rare and expensive substance because of its benefi-cial properties. "For in Arabia," he wrote in *Traité des fardemens et confitures,* "it is collected from the stomachs of goats and sheep ... Nothing is better for protecting one against infection in times of pestilence or during outbreaks of dangerous illnesses."[4]

He mentioned Savona, a coastal center west of Genoa, where he met and took lessons from the renowned apothecary Antonio

Vigerchio, adding to his medical recipes two remedies for constipation.[5] At some point he passed north as far as Milan and translated an ancient account of a feast of gastronomical excess from classical Latin archives there.

West of Milan, in Turin, a villa bears an inscription over a doorway that implies that Dante Alighieri and Nostradamus had slept there – the former in the early 14th century, the latter in 1556. Nostradamus would certainly pass through the capital of French Savoy either at the beginning or at the end of his Italian journey because it was a key eastward overland route to Provence. The inscribed date, however, is out by at least seven years, and probably chronicles the year the inscription (and perhaps the myth) was hammered on the plaque.[6]

He did sleep in Venice more than once. "Incomparable" Venice was mentioned as Nostradamus' source for candies and confectionery recipes, and because it was a center for some of the finest makers of bitter black-cherry preserves. Also of interest to Nostradamus, Venice was the center of the Italian book-printing industry and a chief source of Europe's classical tomes, magical or otherwise, printed in Greek.

After Venice, there is strong circumstantial evidence pointing to a mule ride south along the Adriatic coast to Ancona, because it had the second largest colony of Jews in the Italian peninsula (exceeded only by Rome). Nostradamus was obliged to visit both cities and gather more experience in (and literature from) the Jewish mystical arts. Ancona often appears as a synecdoche[7] for the Papal States in later prophetic works. Nostradamus names Ancona five times in his prophecies, and he would also write about the nearby fiefdom of Senegalia and the Duchy of Urbino with an implied firsthand intimacy of their history.[8] He might have had letters of introduction in his possession permitting travel to Ancona and its environs signed by Bishop Leonardo della Rovere of Agen, for he and Pope Julius II's family had ruled that Adriatic region of Italy since 1474. Nostradamus' predictions of death and destruction for future scions of the House of the della Rovere did not materialize; yet one prophecy envisioned a "great track" built over the Mark (or province) of Ancona, possibly indicating that Nostradamus correctly foresaw the railways and bullet trains that would span that region in the 20th century.[9]

One of the most famous, and disputed, legends of his awakening prophetic genius concerns the Mark of Ancona. As Nostradamus rode down a muddy road to or from the city, he stopped his mule and baggage train to allow a group of Franciscan friars trudging on foot to pass without being splattered by his animals. The story goes that he took notice of Brother Felice Peretti, dismounted his mule, and immediately bowed, kneeling in the mud. The other friars were puzzled. Peretti was of low birth and, the story goes, had only recently come up in rank from a swine-herder to a full-fledged friar.

They asked the French physician to explain his odd behavior, to which he replied, apparently in Latin (not having been fluent in the Tuscan dialect most travelers used in Italy in those days), "I must yield myself and bend a knee before his Holiness."

The friars must have thought him a queer foreigner as they slogged on. You do not salute swine-herding monks, or for that matter anyone, with the title only reserved for a pope! Thirty-seven years after the incident, lowly-born Brother Peretti had become Pope Sixtus V.

Here is what we know as fact. Peretti was a native of the Mark of Ancona. He was a Franciscan novice from the age of 12 and was ordained a full priest in 1547, at the age of 27 – one year before Nostradamus visited Italy. He did indeed become Pope in 1585. Modern skeptics question that he could have been a swine herder at age 12, but they may be forgetting that child labor practices of the Renaissance era were not what they are today. Indeed, stout-hearted children of poor, illiterate farm laborers of the 16th century commonly practiced swine herding. Skeptics are right, though, to question the belief that Peretti, in 1548, had "recently" been a swineherd. In fact, he had been taken into the order as a novice sometime in 1533–4. However, it cannot be ruled out that Nostradamus might have traveled to Italy more than once. If we put him back there during his lost years of wandering (1538–44), Peretti's removal from the pigsties of Grottammare, near Ancona, was indeed far more "recent," and the stickler of "chronological weakness," as Lemesurier puts it,[10] does not necessarily undermine the efficacy of this story.

After perhaps passing through Ancona, Nostradamus reached Rome, the capital of Western Christendom. Its future and its succession of pontiffs would occupy his prophetic attention in hundreds of prophecies yet unwritten. We can assume that the skills of augury he would later master came in part from perusing papal archives in Rome's vast and scattered storehouses (which future popes would consolidate into one vast Vatican library). He may have toured and marveled at the construction site of St. Peter's Basilica; predictions written in the next decade would mark this sacred edifice for destruction by fire and water in a future apocalypse.[11] Might he have had a chance encounter on the construction site with St. Peter's newly appointed architect, Michelangelo? In the view of some modern Nostradamian students, there is another, more likely (though uncorroborated) contact: like many French expatriates passing through Rome, he might have called on Cardinal Jean du Bellay, the French Ambassador, and in so doing he might have reconnected with a former schoolmate from Montpellier, the cardinal's scruffy, keen-eyed secretary, Rabelais.

In Rome, Nostradamus would imbibe the frequent sacred ceremonies and refresh his universal faith, but a greater Mecca beckoned to him. Like so many greater and lesser thinkers of the Renaissance from a Europe awakening from an intellectual sleep of many centuries, Nostradamus was drawn to Florence. He ventured there to gain illumination from its resident thinkers and artists, while circling about the Kaaba of grand libraries and galleries that its rulers, the House of Medici, glorified and sheltered in the navel of the Renaissance. The passionate homily Nostradamus showers on Florence in some editions of *Traité des fardemens et confitures* is not rivaled by any other foreign location mentioned in his travelogues or prophecies. In essence, he implies that he uncovered in Florence those classical sources and teachers that would later crystallize his professed abilities to forecast the future. He tarried there many months, perhaps even a year, seeking the counsel of the learned, walking the same halls that master artists, political scientists, poets, philosophers (such as Thomas More), and physicians (such as Paracelsus) roamed in their search for intellectual absolution. While in Florence, it could be that his future prophecy of a "secret" to be rediscovered in the future by a man named "Pasteur" was inspired by his coming into contact with the hypothesis of a contemporary, Dr. Girolamo Fracastroro. This might have occurred through discovering his book *De contagione et contagiosis morbis*, published just a few years earlier in 1546, while Nostradamus was in Aix; or it may be that he heard of Fracastroro's theories firsthand in Florence. Perhaps this sparked his muse of inspiration to augur a new "secret" vector for the plague: fantastically small particles, too tiny to see with the naked eye, passing contagion through the air or by the touch of the infected – the same vector Pasteur would call a "germ" over three centuries later.[12]

All abstract musing aside, once Florence satiated Nostradamus' quest for arcane knowledge, he carefully copied those works he could not bind and carry away in stuffed saddlebags for the long ride home.

Forbidden Ceremonies

Nostradamus was open for business by the first spring of the new decade. Before long, the previously empty cellar and workrooms facing the tight little courtyard of the renovated house were stacked with shelves of jars containing all kinds of steeping and curing concoctions. With implements arrayed on long tables and newly hired apprentices on hand, he labored over the myriad medicinal and sweet-tasting, health-enhancing and youth-sustaining remedies and preservatives that posterity would later read about in *Traité des fardemens et confitures*. Armed with spatulas, clay pots and slow flames, he would conjure rejuvenation creams, hair and beard dyes, herbal and rose bath oils, rose-scented mothballs, astrological birth-sign perfumes, cherry elixirs for the skin, blueberry compresses for the eyes, and so forth. Anne might have been at his side helping, but a 16th-century merchant's wife's responsibilities usually focused on selling the goods and keeping an accurate ledger of purchases and accounts. She would specifically have had the role of marketer and promoter. Perhaps Nostradamus delighted her feminine vanity by making his wife the walking advertisement of his beauty products. With forearm or face anointed with moistening lotions, Anne would invite women friends and relations of the wealthy gentry to touch them and marvel. She would be the first, but certainly not the last woman of Salon and its environs, to delight in the way Master Nostradamus could make a woman's skin fresh and unblemished. Perhaps the fashion-conscious ladies with deep purses who so admired Anne's gold-tinted tresses (courtesy of her husband's hair dyes) soon were infected with the craze.

The new business flourished, and Nostradamus all but retired from practicing medicine. Biographers tell us that many women of the local gentry beat a path to his door. A customer walked, rode, or was carried through the aromatic obstacle course of the fish-monger's square, then ventured through Nostradamus' door into a perfumed oasis of rose balls – rosewater perfumes floating in a background of aromas wafting from boiling pots in the walk-in stone fireplace in the kitchen-turned-workshop beyond. Each new day Madame Nostradamus might introduce customers to new delights and wonders. They might sample the delightful aerosol of any number of citrus or berry fruits steeping in honey or boiled in white or red wine. There would be samples of new and expensive desserts, such as marzipan, next to items advertised as both medicinal and pleasurable for the palate, such as boiled pumpkin slices drenched in sugar syrup. There would be arrayed vessels containing quince jellies, bitter black cherries, green ginger pastes, sugared preservatives for almond pastes, sweet muscatel grapes, pears, confections made of pine nut kernels, Venetian candies, Arabian penide sugar and purgatives of rose water.

Women might be directed by the Master, or by Madame Nostradamus, to the many jars of herbal and fruit pastes, pomades, sublimates, and beauty powders, and be invited to savor the aroma of vials of benzoin oil-based perfumes, the musk mothballs of aromatic room fresheners and Florentine violets. They would hear the confident master of cosmetics promise that his various fantastic ointments would whiten the teeth and face, color the hair or enhance youthfulness. His concoctions would rekindle sexual desire, cool fevers, clean and perfume rotten teeth, erase blemishes, aid pregnancies, rosy the cheeks, or moisten and preserve the skin of any respectable Salonnaise lady from the harmful effects of the blast-furnace winds of Provençal high summer. We might imagine that rapid success in the business, with profits to spare, would warrant the purchase of a small farming plot on expensive land just outside the town walls. Nostradamus might have planted the seeds of numerous species of herbs for his cosmetic and herbal remedies, along with vegetables and seeds of the leafy vegetable he brought back from Italy called "lettuce," which was said to augment pleasurably the diet in a novel dish called "salad."

Each working day when the sun departed Salon over the horizon, the town fastened its shutters. The shops closed with the setting sun. Indeed some municipal officials fined artisans and merchants for keeping their shops open after dusk. Candles were expensive and, as night fell, one might peek out into the shadowed townscape to distinguish the wealthy from the poor by the candles flickering in the few tinted-glass windows.

Once the customers had fled the streets, supper was usually served, and the master of the house held court with friends or extended family and servants. Meals were laid, family issues discussed, work chores for the coming day delegated, and by the time the afterglow of dusk had faded into night, the household settled for sleep. The servants retreated to their crowded, storehouse rooms, often several to a makeshift bed.

At some point in the evening, Nostradamus would steal away from the hubbub and the boiling tubs of herbs and confections, up the spiral staircase. But this was usually not the end of his working day. On a few occasions when the urge to breathe the lamp of occult scholarship did not so compel him, he might lay down for the night with his young wife behind the curtains of the four-poster master bed, and engage in activities possibly enhanced by his own elixir-of-life concoctions. More often than not he might climb the staircase to his study for the night. After daytimes spent playing the roles of part-time physician and fulltime cosmetics designer, dedicated Catholic, and husband (and later family patriarch), the advent of nocturnal hours left for him just one more role to play. Now, as the curious and nosy neighbors had fallen mute and unseeing, Nostradamus was wide awake and primed to play sorcerer.

Sleep, we are told by Chavigny, never came easy to Nostradamus, nor, apparently, was much of it needed – perhaps three or four hours a day. By day he may have been all outward smiles and flattering diplomacy, but inside he was waiting impatiently for the cacophony and pretense of the outer world to vanish in night's silence and darkness. Let the night's psychic quietude fill the void and sooth and sharpen the mind of Nostradamus, who at last could climb the newly built segment of the spiral staircase to reach a special room in the third-floor addition. There he would unlock the heavy door to his inner sanctum.

His candle would glide planes of light and darkness across chests that contained the occult treasures and instruments he had collected on his far-flung journeys. The flickering light might have revealed an astrolabe, magic mirror and graven brass bowls, and perhaps illuminated the parchment of scrolls and the titles of forbidden books. When Nostradamus shut and bolted the door, he would leave behind the false illumination of broad daylight, which cast this famous wayfarer in the form of a domesticated man. The night knew better. The traveler had not stopped traveling; only the direction of his path had changed. Now the roads he trod would be of time, and the geography encountered would be that of the undiscovered lands of the future.

For centuries scholars have wrestled with and fought over the rare and often nebulous confessions as to the actions taken behind this door closed darkly. By the onset of the 1550s, the nocturnal retreats made into the one room off limits to daily life were evermore frequent. The grist for this occult debate comes primarily from a long stream of clause-encumbered, loosely punctuated sentences in the *Preface* that Nostradamus would compose in 1554 for the first edition of his work of prophecies. These often cloudy and coy confessions serve up too little to nourish the ambitions of dilettante magicians, and they strive to make ecclesiastically bland any descriptions of his study of biblical astrology or classical magic techniques that might in any way contradict the Church and the justices of the Inquisition. The few pearls of revelation pitched by Nostradamus before the swine of sympathetic and unsympathetic biographers give them a good idea what books and tools Nostradamus used, even if they still dispute whether he used them for a divine calling, or a charlatan's folly.

Armed with enough confessions and circumstantial clues, anyone can fashion their own speculative narrative of Nostradamus' secret life beyond the locked door and conjure up an elemental facsimile of how that secret study may have looked. We will go there now, but I caution you to remember that a "rogue" scholar like myself, as well as the more respectable scholars who suppress the temptation to take you there, possess enough fertile imagination to project their own occult interpretations and myths, rather than shine a small candle of factual illumination into Nostradamus' inner sanctum.

Thus warned, pass with me now on wings of speculative reverie, through the locked door into that chamber, on some night in the early 1550s.

∝

There is a star-like cluster of golden candles on a large writing table. The "teeth" on the grill of a small box-shaped iron stove in the walk-in fireplace cast a warm, rectangular and russet-colored grin across the room. The contents of the wooden chests are now carefully placed on tables and propped against the walls of the room. What a tale they could tell if the collector of these tools of magic knew how to command them to speak for us tonight and recount how and when they were created, and how and where their new master found them during his years of wandering. But, alas, the magical sword, the ritual knife, the brass tripod chair, the vials of mercury, the incense and special herbs, the charcoal brazier, and the pentagrams are patiently mute, awaiting the practiced administrations of their master. The voice of the water in the brass bowl is still as the night, and the leaden mirror chooses to reflect a melancholy projection of the soft candlelight on its dark and inscrutable surface. At this moment no one else is in the room, but the master's presence nearby, at the apex of the limestone steps that ascend through the slanted lean-to beams of the roof. He is up in his astronomical turret, meditating. Nostradamus is hidden in darkness, paroled by night's deep silence from the need to mingle with the daylight denizens of Salon, whom he would later define as "brute beasts, barbarous people, mortal enemies of learning and letters."[13] The buzz of nutmeg or other stimulants keeps sharp his contemplation and helps him resist a temptation to sleep. Contemplating the array of planets and their configurations, Nostradamus plots and calculates in his mind what ritual passage inward into magical realms is best supported by tonight's celestial influences.

For now we leave him in his open-air observatory and return to the secret study. The magnification of candle-power coming from behind the high back of a finely carved hardwood chair, which sits before a large writing desk, draws our curiosity to sit down in it. The desk is cluttered with manuscripts, an ephemeris or two, a celestial sphere in the corner, and a pile of parchment with astronomical calculations and notes, beneath a pair of calipers used temporarily as a paperweight. In front of the chair is an angled platform holding open a volume apparently taken from a weathered set of precious books, each tome of which reveals a broken-in spine and a leather binding softened and buffed by frequent study.

Spread before our eyes is a copy of Marsilio Ficino's 1479 Latin translation of *De mysteriis Aegyptiorum,* the famous book on Egyptian, Chaldaean, Greek, and Assyrian magic rituals by the celebrated neo-Platonist magician Iamblichus (died c. 330 C.E.).[14]

✣

Let us briefly move out of speculation's astral projection into Nostradamus' secret study to consider what was objective fact concerning the message of Nostradamus' bible on magic. When and how Nostradamus came to possess his chief manual for his instruction in the classical arts of ritual theurgy (conjuring divine media) is not known. The bookstores of Marseilles in 1544 and Florence in 1549 suggest themselves as possibilities.

The book is written as a long and comprehensive reply to questions and statements of Iamblichus' master, Porphyry. One could distill the occult philosophy of this Greco-Syrian mystic as follows: Humankind lives in the visible or physical world. Above this exists the higher vibratory dimension of the invisible and eternal world of the gods. The former is changeable, whereas the latter dimension is ever constant and perfect. Between the worlds of Eternity and Mortality is an astral dimension that one can access to link the divine with the physical. Iamblichus describes an elaborate hierarchy of astral messengers that Nostradamus must incant and recognize to aid him in this task. If he is successful he will achieve direct contact with a god; if not, Nostradamus may still attain the magical concentration and skills to conjure the more frequently encountered messengers Iamblichus categorizes as the archangelic, angelic, heroic, and daemonic astral emissaries. If one looks beyond the marble ruins of classically antiquated terms, a modern explorer of the astral and inter-dimensional realms would recognize Iamblichus' hierarchy of spirits as those discarnate souls in various stages of evolution one can encounter through journeys out of the physical body to the five higher and subtler psychic dimensions beyond the physical plane. Beyond the sixth plane lies the divine seventh level wherein all identities are merged and annihilated and one obtains ultimate godliness itself.

Aided by Iamblichus' book, Nostradamus intends to become his own Orpheus entering the subconscious underworld of his mind, and whatever the motivations, the dangers to Nostradamus' sanity will be great. He will also risk heresy, and the shattering of his understanding of mortal reality. In that state of ever-*now*-ness, Nostradamus will endeavor to grasp and decipher the dark shadows of portentous future events.

A large piece of the conjuror's puzzle of occult understanding would be missing if the theoretical magic of *De mysteriis Aegyptiorum* was all Nostradamus learned. Though rich in its description of the greater world and the eternal powers of the grand emissaries of spirit, it gives the reader no direct incantations or instructions, nor does it list the many magical tools needed to trigger the states necessary for incantation. These keys must come to the disciple from direct initiation by a master, yet Iamblichus was dead for over 1,200 years and Nostradamus never divulged whether he had a teacher. In any case, it is certain that within Nostradamus' secret study he had within arm's reach two Latin *grimores* (grammars) of far more ancient textbooks of ritual magic than *De mysteriis Aegyptiorum* – without which no serious mage would practice his art. His own writings indicate he had a copy of the *Clavicus Salomonis* (Key of Solomon) and *Sigillum Salomonis* (Seal of Solomon). The story goes that King Solomon (c. 973–33 B.C.E.) set down in Hebrew one of history's most famous and notorious works on incantation after an angel sent by Jehovah presented Solomon with a magic ring which granted him powers to enslave Satan's fallen angels (demons) to do his bidding. The Key of Solomon recorded the names, categories, and functions of each hierarchy of demons. As far back as the 1st century C.E., Josephus mentioned in his histories of the Jewish people a version of these spirit-conjuring keys under Solomon's authorship. They resurfaced again after a thousand years, and were translated into Latin, becoming a genre-redefining influence on medieval magical literature.

Sandwiched between these textbooks in the stack of volumes on Nostradamus' desk would be an infamous work on demonology: *De Daemonibus* ("Of Daemons ...") by the neo-Platonist Byzantine scholar Michael Constantine Psellos (1018–80?). It could be from Psellos' critique of demonic conjuring that Nostradamus was tempted to explore the forbidden and spurious techniques of what church inquisitors called "perfidious" biblical and pagan magical practice. A hint of just how much white magic Nostradamus blended with the black in his occult interests is implied by the grimores of King Solomon. One could imagine that Nostradamus saw himself in a similar light to Solomon who risked accepting the ring of power as a gift of God. In Nostradamus' case his "ring" or "key" from God was the knowledge forged by his own exploration in mystical arts by blending the best disciplines of Hebraic, Hermetic, Greek, and neo-Platonist sources to bring down a "divine" – not daemonic – power. *Soli Deo!* (Only God) was the family motto of Nostradamus. Ultimately, it implies a belief that God would aid his conjuring and control of higher and lower astral entities and elementals for magical incantations. He might have imagined in *fact* what Dante imagined in fiction for his epic *The Divine Comedy*. He might have believed he could use the shades of departed pagan heroes or figures of classical history, plucked out of their more respectable outer rims of Hell, as his spiritual guides in the aid of his magical inquiries as long as his power to summon them came from God and a pure heart.

Devout prayers to the almighty for illumination and protection would preface every preliminary reading and practice of the occult arts. Moreover, Nostradamus would invoke God in his magical practices in a way similar to what Richard Cavendish described in his foreword to S. Liddel MacGregor Mathers' 20th-century translation of the *Key of Solomon*:

It is a fundamental principle of European magic that magical power works automatically and regardless of the magician's motives, like an electric light switch, and that divine energy can be tapped through prayers and incantations, and by the use of the "names of power" which volley and thunder through the Key's processes. The most potent of them are names or epithets of the God of the Old Testament, believed to contain his identity and force.

ⅆ

But soft. The master stirs in his observatory. He descends the stairs into the candlelit room. It is time. He moves to a corner of the room, standing beside a large bathing dish and begins slowly, carefully, removing his clothes. Returned from the darkness of the night, his gray eyes have a transparency of one who has prayed and fasted for three days in an effort to disconnect from the corporeal energies of the body. The preliminary steps for conjuration, as specified by Solomon, would also see him abstain from sex to build his psychic energies and direct them upwards towards the ethereal plane. Now he must divest himself of the last link to his daylight life and strip himself naked. He chants a prayer in Latin, raising an earthen jar to pour a sharp cold stream of pure consecrated water over his head and body to wash himself clean of the psychic energies of the daytime. In place of his street clothes, he throws over his head and shoulders a flowing gray-hooded robe of rough woven cotton resembling the ancient garb of a neo-Platonist, or Hermetic priest.

One should imagine that it is a still and peaceful night because these are the conditions preferable for the conjuration of spirits. The weather is soft, the winds have paused with the coming of a clear evening, and when the moon later rises, no cloud will come to disturb him from his concentration on the ebb and flow of light and shadow through the courtyard window, or breathe light and exhale darkness down the observatory stairs.

It is time to begin. Great care has already been taken to plot astrologically the right hour for conjuring each specific class of spirit messenger. Now our attention, like his own, is directed to the magic circle at the center of the room drawn upon the floor to protect himself from the divine emissaries about to be conjured. A short distance away there is a triangle drawn on the floor where it is expected they will manifest. Words of power and seals of Solomon decorate the edge of the circle and triangle to magnify the protection of the conjuror, and the imprisonment of the "astral emissary," until service in the physical realm is complete and a command dematerializes the spirit to its place of origin.

When he steps into the circle, taking with him the magical tools deemed necessary for the night's incantation, he will whisper the sacred rites quietly, as he lights the candles surrounding the circle. It will be hard to hear what language he uses. Perhaps it is Latin, Greek, or even Hebrew, depending on his intent that night. His grudging confessions in later writings about just what *exterior* (nonphysical) beings visited his magic triangle indicate that he saw and heard (or projected in his imagination) the signature aural lights and clairaudient sounds of angelic and daemonic messengers of fire, water, earth, air, and ether described in the convocation of spirits by Iamblichus and King Solomon. However, Nostradamus' specific emphasis on the "fiery missives brought by [God's] angels of fire"[15] indicates he had more magical empathy and success conjuring elementals in harmony with his own passion for the hot and dry climate of his native Provence.

The rites of Theurgy would dominate this and other nocturnal vigils, but further magical tools in his study awaited their use as self-hypnotic totems and talismans to suggest to Nostradamus' mind a state of trance. But on this night, the tripod brass chair is folded to one side, next to a large metal pot. The latter will be used for boiling sulfur and herbs into a stench sufficiently intoxicating and foul to replicate the fumes inhaled by the Delphic oracles when preparing for their own prescient ecstasies while sitting on the brass tripod seat placed over a volcanic fissure. In nights to come, he would gaze into the *mirouer ardent* (a conclave metal mirror used to magnify the sun's rays by day). Perhaps on some future vigil and with the aid of a steady, unblinking gaze, the mirror might burn with ardent images of the future issuing from its dark unlit surface.

Other vessels, used for ritual hydromancy, are set aside tonight. There will be another time to experiment with forbidden ceremonies of Assyrian magic, catalogued by Psellos. If prayers and self-hypnotic suggestions can bolster his courage and strengthen his faith in the grace (and protection) of God, then Nostradamus will prophesy by means of a basin filled with water, resting over the water's surface a litany of secret words that attract the spirits creeping stealthily in its depths. He will put to practice what he has just read in the accounts of Psellos:

The basin then full of water (to the brim) seems ... to breathe as with sounds; it seems to me that the water was agitated with circular ripples as from some sound emitted below.

Now this water diffused through the basin differs but little in kind from water out of the basin, but yet it much excels it from a virtue imparted on it by the incantations which have rendered it more apt to receive the spirit of prophecy. For this description of spirit is peevish and earth-bound and much under the influence of composite spells.

When the water begins to lend itself as the vehicle of sound, the spirit also presently gives out a thin, reedy note but devoid of meaning; and close upon that, while the water is undulating, certain weak and peeping sounds whisper forth predictions of the future.[16]

The cock is crowing. It is now time to leave our speculative reverie.

∝

After each night in nocturnal vigil passed, Nostradamus steadily gained confidence in his mastery of sacred and forbidden arts. Thus at sunrise the electrified yet physically spent inner explorer sat before his writing table, replacing books of magic with rare books or scrolls he admits had been "hidden for many centuries."[17]

Are they the angular arched and flame-licked figures of Hebrew script on theomancy, the Cabala, or perhaps ancient treatises on Jewish astronomical augury? We do not know. His writings imply that they included works of Hebrew judicial astrology[18] exempted by canon law and Holy Scripture from the judgment of heresy. It seems they gave Nostradamus, in his mind at least, a way to test and disseminate his magical and subjective communications with spirits through the testing regimen of a marriage of objective astronomical calculations with astrological interpretation. Yet he admits these ancient scriptures burdened him. Perhaps by night in secret study, troubling thoughts about his wife sleeping in the bedroom below his secret study invaded his meditations. At last, Anne carried in her womb the first of what would be six children.[19] Perhaps he dreaded what might happen to them if today's Canon seal of acceptance became tomorrow's heresy. Events in the family of Christian life in France were growing ever darker. The children of Christ were taking sides between Calvinist and Catholic beliefs. Worse was to come. Perhaps he saw shadows of this in the parabolic distortion of his burning mirror, or, in a trance, he thought he heard warnings from ephemeral lights and figures brought into his triangle through the magic sword of Solomon or the laurel branch of neo-Platonist magic. Or perhaps he extrapolated present-day signs of coming religious discord with nothing more than an educated guess cloaked in the gray and hooded robes of someone playing magician. Whatever the motivation, the scrolls sat in their slots or on shelves with the silence of the condemned, waiting for some future night in which their admiring master could no longer stay his hand. That night came at last, perhaps in the winter of 1553–4, a short time before he expressed dread for what use might be made of these scriptures and consigned them to the flames:

[Then] shooting forth into the atmosphere, there came an unusual brightness, clearer than that of natural flame – bright as lightning – suddenly illuminating the house as if in a sudden conflagration.[20]

Nostradamus watched what could have been priceless heirlooms of his Jewish ancestors sacrificed to the flames in the secret study's large fireplace. He confessed he did it to protect his second-born child, César, addressing him later in writing:

Thus, so that in the future you might not be led astray in a search for the perfect transformation of silver, or of gold, or of incorruptible metals under the earth, or hidden in the waves, I have reduced [these books] to ashes.[21]

The Prognosticator

The chroniclers of prophetic cycles of time will tell you that human evolution peaks roughly every 500 years. History accelerates the birth of new technological, artistic and social growth in tandem with an increased travail of wars, social strife, and natural catastrophes that arise from collective human resistance to the changing of the status quo. Four 500-year evolutionary "steps" ago, when "B.C.E." switched to "C.E." (the common era), Rome attained its golden age of the Pax Romana, but the seeds of its fall were sewn by a purported immaculate conception and the advent of Jesus Christ and Christianity. By the 5th and 6th centuries, Rome fell and the Dark Ages in Europe began. Islam appeared and its spiritual revolution rapidly spread across Arabia, Persia, North Africa and westward to Spain, and a golden era of Arab arts and sciences flourished. The next 500-year acceleration of history began around the 9th and 10th centuries, heralded by a wave of Viking invasions and general hysteria across Europe's Christian realms. Both Christians and Vikings anticipated their own versions of a Doomsday/Ragnarök myth that never manifested. The new cycle saw the first of several Christian Crusades break out of the isolation and backwardness of Medieval Europe into the Holy Land. Humanity suffered a new level of violent holy war; yet the crusaders experienced the advanced culture of the Muslim world and eventually carried home many of the fruits of its mathematical, medical, and social enlightenment, all of which would help Europeans snap out of their cultural backwardness. Five hundred years passed and history quickened once again with the birth in the East of the new religion of Sikhism, in the midst of the golden era of art, music, and literature that was Mogul India. Intellectual and artistic insight also thrived in Europe, for this 500-year peak in history gave birth to the Renaissance, and the discovery of the New World of the Americas. Human civilization experienced the first pangs of globalism with Magellan circumnavigating the world and Vasco da Gama opening up trade routes to India. Even far-off Japan would know its first permanent colony of Western traders and priests preaching Christianity in the black Jesuit cloak.

In the Renaissance, scholars sought to redeem and resurrect the classical enlightenment of earlier 500-year surges in history, such as the Hellenic enlightenment of the 6th and 5th centuries B.C.E., and the Pax Romana's neo-Platonist renovation of astronomy, science and the occult in the 1st century C.E., without which Nostradamus could not conjure his magic and mark his stars. However, this is also the new turn of a 500-year cycle that gave birth to modern times with a bloody travail of devastated New World civilizations and the painful contractions in the religious status quo of Europe. The birth pangs of modern times killed an estimated 50 million North and South Americans from the plagues and diseases carried by European conquerors. Back in Europe, the Protestant Reformation and the Counter-Reformation ripped apart the fabric of European society and soon led to the apocalyptic religious wars in France, the Netherlands, and Central Europe – culminating in the latter losing half its population in the Thirty Years War in the early 17th century.

To an outsider, the foreboding of many French people living at the eve of the 1550s might appear similar to American concerns at the present onset of a new 500-year cycle and a new millennium. Under the surface of 50 years of the greatest increase in economic prosperity and political expansion ever seen in the country's history, there were unsettling signs of political and social instability ready to hatch out sometime in the new decade. The cost of living outstripped the means of living and the nation was divided over religious and social values. The division of the French in 1550 was not between rich and poor, like that dividing the Americans of today. However, the new king of France, Henry II, and his court seemed to be just as insulated to the warning signs as a new American president and his "Bush team" 500 years later. France in the early 1550s, like America in the early 2000s, was about to embark on strategically ill-defined and prohibitively expensive military adventures when the economic gains of the past half-century were clearly declining rapidly. Inflation was denied or ignored by the new king and his ministers while ominous changes in the weather and economic signs only cast a pall of foreboding that increased the leadership's will to distraction with foreign adventures.

The travails of nature, God, and the economy, born at the resumption of every 500-year cycle, present and past, create a demand in people to seek unorthodox rationalizations and answers. It is a lingering habit of human nature that when people face a new era of wonders and danger, they often reach out helplessly to those who claim to see into the future. They hope that a sooth-sayer's advice will help them take back some control of their lives, or at least help them understand and weather the coming blow.

In the mid-16th century, the book-printing and literacy revolu-tion paralleled the late 20th and early 21st century's internet infor-mation revolution. The people who could read, and the greater number of illiterates who liked to be read to, turned to an increas-ing selection of popular almanacs for augured answers. Chavigny indicates that, by 1549, Nostradamus was already at work on the first experiment in a new career – one that he had considered long ago when students at Avignon named him the "little astrologer." He would try his hand at writing almanacs. His manuscripts would have the usual medical remedies, farming information, a combination religious/secular calendar, a lunar ephemeris marking the best times for planting and harvesting, and so on. There would be the usual astronomical and prophetic essays for chief political and social events for the coming year, but Nostradamus obviously believed he could provide new angles in this overwritten genre by pouring forth the rich mental storehouse of a man widely traveled through the outer, as well as the inner, world. He would produce a test installment of what he hoped would be an annual opus that closed with entertaining and sometimes terrifying stream-of-consciousness prose prognostications and four-line quatrain prophecies for the coming year.

No original manuscript or published volume survives of Nostradamus' first literary opus, but based on the evidence of later efforts, his quest to be published must have taken him northward by mule or boat, along the meandering Rhône valley to Lyon, the scene of one of Nostradamus' past medical successes. Lyon had become one of France's premier and oldest printing and publishing centers since the final decades of the previous century when Gutenberg (as one might call him, a former-day Guten-"Bill"-Gates) found a way to use the hardware of wood and iron presses to print on the software of paper. Nostradamus readily found a Lyonnais publisher for his first almanac. No record survives to tell us in whose charge he left his manuscript before returning home: perhaps it was the journeymen of a publisher named Chaussard, or Bertot, or Brotot, with or without Volant,[22] preparing typeface for an almanac we can only guess was called *Almanach* or *Les Presages* or *Les Prognostications* of M. Michel Nostradamus, for the year 1550.[23] Once the stamp of Royal *privelège* marked the fore page (granting the king's approval via his court representatives), the publisher's journeymen and printers began producing hundreds if not thousands of copies. They soon lined the book dealers' tables of Lyon and trundled down the rutted roads in the late autumn of 1549, making their slow progress to book dealers across the kingdom.

Highest in the pecking order of readership were those in the printing and publishing business, apothecaries, and surgeons. A slightly smaller procession of potential buyers came from the ranks of musicians, painters, metalworkers, taverners, courtiers, and members of the royalty. The books would be held avidly in the refined hands of educated ladies of royal families and upper-class bourgeoisie, but few women below their station could read. Up to half the laymen furriers, leatherworkers, and artisans in the textile and clothing trades of that day could read and might have purchased a copy of Nostradamus' first almanac. Hardly any representatives of the construction, provision, or transport trades would be present in the bookstore – nor gardeners or unskilled day workers – but that does not mean they did not "hear" the book read to them after work, by gathering around those who could read aloud. The same was the case in the far less literate rural society which generally had a far more burning interest in almanacs because they provided calendars and advice on when to plant, and predictions of what to prepare for in the coming year's meteorological fortunes. Many a well-to-do peasant farmer was literate, as were many lords and ladies of country manors and their retainers and servants; and on occasion they would read their almanacs aloud to their peasant laborers and families. Thus the prognostications of Nostradamus for the year 1550 became known throughout France as Christmas and the author's 47th birthday approached.

His prognostications were an immediate success.[24] The wide-ranging interest in what he had to say, and the financial reward coming in its wake,[25] greatly encouraged him to pursue his writing career further. He would endeavor to produce a new almanac for each year as long as he lived.

CHAPTER SIX

A History of the Future

⊱⊰

The Inner and Outer Watercourse Way

No element better represents the patient power of surrender than water. It finds the easiest way around an obstacle to reach the sea. It will acquiesce to limits imposed upon it by the river banks unless a harsher injunction of earth and rock should obstruct its path. Water is not responsible for the resultant flood that breaks boundaries, because it cannot forever be held in abeyance. It will wait. It will lie down against resistance until it buckles, or relax towards the weakest point of defiant earth until the weight of its surrender to gravity excavates a new pathway to its inexorable, oceanic destiny.

In addition to Nostradamus' love of the spirits of fire and of dry, hot climates, he was also in love with water. He poured pure aqua quicksilver to clean the contours of skin over the hollows and hills of the body of a patient. He bade those in his care to consume copious amounts of spring water to purge illnesses. Practitioners of his medical advice knew they must never be too far from the fount of a natural spring if they were to reproduce faithfully the intended medicament or confection. To be healed, Nostradamus believed one must seek the diamond purity of the spring and avoid the dull water of city fountains blemished by algae and the grope of filthy human hands. Later, when he retired from active medical practice to study magic, he anointed his own body with pure water before the sacred rites held in his secret study.

Nostradamus' desire for pure water was made more intense in response to the tyranny of the dry and unyielding earth of Salon and its parched environs. In 1553, he had an opportunity to comment publicly about the local water, and for posterity, when the municipal consuls, Paul Antoine and Nostradamus' good friend Palamède Marc, invited him to compose a dedication for a new public fountain in the center of Salon. After Nostradamus regarded what was apparently a shoddy piece of finished public work, and tasted the chalky bite of its product, he went home to compose a Latin dedication, later chiseled on a marble slab. The gathering of citizens at the christening ceremony looked on and listened with awe as Nostradamus recited his dedication:

SI HVMANO INGENIO PERPETVO
SALLONAE CIVIB. PARARI VINA POTVISSET
NON AMOENVM QVEM CERNITIS
FONTEM AQVARVM. S. P. Q. SALON. MAGNA
IMPENSA NON ADDVXISSET
DVCTA. N. PALAMEDE MARCO.
ET ANTON. PAVLO CONSS
M. NOSTRADAMVS
OB SALONENSES
M.D.LIII

One can imagine Nostradamus afterwards, looking on impassively as those few other learned citizens in the large throng who understood Latin stifled their laughs. The inscription, loosely translated here to capture its *lingua* in *bucca* content, if not its exact syntax, reads:

If perpetual human ingenuity
Could have provided the citizens of Salon with a constant supply
of wine,
This unlovely fountain, that you see before you,
Erected by the Senate and Magistrates of Salon, at great expense,
Under the consulship of Palamède Marc,
And Paul Antoine,
Would not have been necessary.
M. Nostradamus
On behalf of the people of Salon,
1553

As a present-day local historian of Salon wrote in a popular tourist booklet, "Certainly humor is not missing to indicate that the water did not taste good and that nothing is as valuable as the rosé of Provence."[1] The fountain has survived the water-stained trickle of time, but the original marble slab with Nostradamus' inscription no longer exists. It has been replaced and re-chiseled into new marble by latter-day consuls a little wiser to the translation made *per iocum.*[2]

The new fountain tittered and bubbled its watery laughter into the pond, perpetually and mindlessly innocent to the drought of love and tolerance growing in the hearts of those who dipped their thirsty hands and plunged their vessels into its waters. Hope was drying out for a miracle that could end the growing rift between Salon's Catholic majority and those citizens who conspicuously abandoned their pews and went to pray in secret meetings in safe houses or gathered at night outside the town walls to pray together as members of the new cult referred to as John Calvin's Reformed Church. Soon Protestant and Catholic Salonnais alike, taking their turns at the fountain, began hearing and spreading rumors about Protestant vandals across France breaking into cathedrals and desecrating sacred statues and altars. There came news of more frequent and violent street riots in reprisal. Catholics of Salon drawing their water and daily ration of gossip at the fountain began to use a new and derogatory name for these Protestants whose faith was spreading across the kingdom. Now they called a Calvinist a *Huguenot.* The label came from *le roi Huguet,* a character taken from a popular folk tale from Tours. He was the ghost of a wicked king who chose not to pass his nocturnal penance in Purgatory, but instead haunted the night, waylaying lonely travelers on country roads and rattling the shutters and doors of decent people's homes, disturbing their sleep. It so happened that the Calvinists of Tours gathered at night to pray at a city gate known as Roi-*Hugon.* Priests and parishioners across France reveled in the pun that identified Protestants shuffling off after dark to pray and hobnob with the unrepentant shade of King Huguet. The Huguenots (freely translated as the "followers of Huguet") were soon compared to the mythological ghouls and ghosts who once a year, on All Soul's Day, ventured out from their tombs for a night of unholy Halloween mischief before settling back into their graves.

One can only guess that the serving girls gathering water for their respected and learned master residing in the Ferreireux quarter gossiped with other laborers about the most pressing issue of the day: Whose side was Monsieur Nostradamus *really* on when it came to God and the Church? It was well known in town that he publicly denounced the Huguenots, attended mass regularly, and appeared to be a devout Catholic, but people of the unlettered serving classes were ever suspicious of those possessing the intimidating aura of scholarship and learning. Over time, village wags and ne'er-do-wells began spreading rumors about Monsieur Nostradamus' eccentricities. By 1553, his hired help must have let it slip that after the sun had set, Monsieur would bid his wife good morrow and ascend the stairs to his study, stringently demanding that no one disturb him, and then lock himself away for all the unholy hours of night. Just what was a God-fearing Christian doing up all night? Were not the darkest hours between midnight and three o'clock the dominion of unforgiven spirits and demons?

Moreover, what unholy power did this man have over sleep? By day in his shop he was ever alert, polite, and courteous. He was regularly seen walking the short distance out the northern gate to attend daily mass held at the Franciscan Church of the Cordeliers just outside the city walls. Just what did Dr. Nostradamus reveal to the priest when he took his confession?

Let idle and unlettered tongues wag. Few people (even his intimates) likely knew the true nature of the occult watercourse that pressed against the dam of his public and religious façade until he proffered a confession to history, a few years later. Some inkling of his years of inner soul-searching, during the early 1550s, can be garnered in excerpts from the stream of oddly written prose he fashioned for the Preface to his prophecies, finished in March 1555, and addressed to his newborn son César:

Although for a long time and often, I have predicted that which has come to pass, and in the particular regions [meaning France in his annual publications of the now popular Prognostications], acknowledging all to have been accomplished through the virtue of divine power and inspiration and [to have foreseen] other joyous and sinister events which have come to pass with increasing promptness, which have later come to pass throughout other climates and regions of the world, I was willing to keep silent by reason of the injury – and not only to the present time, but also for the future time as well – and refrain from writing because the [present day] kingdoms, sects and religions will make changes so diametrically opposite to the present view, that if I came to reveal what will happen in the future, those present kingdoms, sects, religions and faiths would find [the future] so little in accord with [their] fantasies they would like articulated that they would damn that which future centuries will know and have seen to be true.[3]

Much is implied in the river of words in Nostradamus' long and meandering sentences. One could assume that he had been making predictions regularly, perhaps for all of his life, but had only recently reserved this eccentricity for pen and paper. He takes a moment to give us some background on his earlier prophetic experiments and successes. A mounting pressure of revelations leaked out in regular and highly successful attempts at prognostications and almanacs for the years 1551, 1552 and 1553. By 1554, his annual predictions for the coming year were widely read across France. This reality caused him more anguish than joy. The success of his early experiments in prophecy made him meditate long and hard over what harm he might do to himself, his family, and the future at large if he should publish a work of prophecies that dipped deep into the fathomless distant future and stretched the limits of perception and tolerance of his own society and its religion. Nostradamus, it seems, was well enough aware of the fragility of human expectations. A majority of his readers would want the future to conform to their beliefs. Yet, if he dared write down events as they appeared to him, would he not insult and disappoint their fantasies? Would they not then damn their own future? Moreover, who would be responsible for this curse? Would enough people, seeing their hopes dashed, effect by their collective reactions a worse future than the one he published? Would future kings and governments use his work to bring more darkness to the world?

Nostradamus must have suppressed the impulse to soothsay behind the same smiling yet guarded expression he showed when receiving a special visit from Adam de Craponne, his young friend, who after returning to Salon in early 1554 from adventures abroad was now a celebrated hydraulic engineer and architect. Craponne learned his trade at the local Franciscan Collège des Cordeliers. He distinguished himself as a brilliant military architect, providing France with a fine defensive fortification around Metz to resist the Imperial Hapsburg forces of Charles V, before returning home to Salon at age 28. Craponne had come to ask Nostradamus for financial aid to fulfill his life's dream. He had returned home with the intention to dedicate most of his inheritance – and seek additional funding from others in town – to excavate a watercourse that could draw water off the distant Durance river, quenching the thirst of Salon and irrigating the arid plains of the Crau.

Salon "of Crau" as the town was called in the 16th century, was built on the edge of a gravel and shale wasteland, among the most barren areas in all of Europe.[4] This flat and arid plain is divided into the "Petite" and "Grande" Crau. If we could travel back in time to the 16th century when the northwestern tower of the Château de l'Empéri still stood, it would have provided us with sweeping views of the marginal lands of the "small" and the graveled wasteland of the "great" expanses of the Crau. If Nostradamus and Craponne ever stood together on this tower, this highest vantage point on the windswept plains around Salon would have provided them a fine vista to dream about a future time when canals could stretch all the way from Arles to Salon and turn much of the Petite Crau into a garden. Adam de Craponne, the down-to-earth and practical engineer and visionary, found a kindred spirit in the more potently subjective – and deep-pocketed – Dr. Nostradamus. The latter was among the first notables of Salon to donate money and much-needed encouragement for the project. Perhaps in Craponne, Nostradamus saw the builder of a bridge to Nostradamus' utopian dream of the desert-like landscape of the Crau surrounding Salon transformed into fertile grazing lands and farmlands. The archives of Salon record Nostradamus' first donation of 200 gold crowns to the project, witnessed and dated 27 July 1554 by a lawyer named Laurent.[5] The Provençal Parliament at Aix granted permission for the project on 17 August. Most likely the pick-and-shovel work began sometime shortly after a groundbreaking ceremony was held with much pomp and circumstance at the end of August. No doubt Nostradamus, like other benefactors, stood alongside Adam, his older brother Frédéric de Craponne, and their team of architects and surveyors. The flat plain stretched northward as far as they could see to the distant Durance river through which an army of laborers would soon begin working on stage one of the grand plan: digging a trench that would cradle a watercourse to the foot of the city walls of Salon.

Omens and Nocturnal Vigils

When a new era is entered, with its ensuing loss of certainty, people seek to assuage their anxiety through embracing the irrational. In times perceived as dark and dire they will be predisposed to mark the signs and omens that seem to come fast and furious, while blithely ignoring the same signs when times are more mellifluous. In France, the year 1554 opened with a bevy of serious problems – enough to tempt many to seek paranormal indications of what next would come. The economy and weather worsened. The Huguenots converted members of the upper classes and other figures of nobility and authority at an alarming rate and France's majority population of lay Catholics began to fear that John Calvin ("the Antichrist") might overtake the kingdom and court in a *coup d'Eglise* (through an overthrow of the Catholic church). In the mid-16th century, France saw the illiterate and the literate alike on the lookout for portents and astrological clues to reveal what would come next. The sale of almanacs containing prognostications soared.

Nostradamus' Almanac and prognostications for the year 1554 (published by "Bertot," Lyon)[6] became another bestseller, and the initial royalties reflected this. His satisfaction and happiness doubled in early 1554 with the birth of his second child, a son. He and Anne named him César. To this day, parents of Provence often follow the custom of naming children after those famous classical Roman leaders who shaped the region's culture and history, such as Julius Caesar. Then again, Nostradamus might have chosen the name as a link to his estranged mentor, Julius Caesar Scaliger.

The child may have been present (perhaps cradled in his mother's arms) one afternoon in early 1554 when a procession of townspeople from Sénas gathered before their front door, and presented for Nostradamus' examination a hideously deformed human creature, considered to be of portentous significance. Sixty years later, the grown César de Nostredame set down a record of what followed, as it was later told to him:

The year 1554 ... I do not know what sad and unhappy events begin and follow creatures hideously deformed and prodigious. Scarcely had January ended when one saw born at Sénas a monstrous child, having two heads, which the eye could not look upon without some sort of horror: he had been predicted some time previously by those who had knowledge of the course of future events ... He was carried to my father and seen by several persons.[7]

On seeing the twin-headed child at his threshold, Nostradamus had the impulse to have the creature carried into the presence of his good friend, the First Consul of Salon, Palamède Marc. As it happened, that day Marc was host to the Governor of Provence, Duc de Tende, and the Admiral of the French Eastern Fleet, Baron de la Garde, and also Commandeur de Beynes. All three men, by coincidence, had made a stopover in Salon while on their way to an important society baptism at St.-Rémy. Afterwards, Nostradamus returned home near sundown to have supper with family and friends and recount to those assembled what reactions and statements the Consul and his notable guests had made. César continues:

Little was spoken of during almost the whole of supper apart from these hideous monsters and the disasters and divisions that they always seem infallibly to presage; namely, the bloody schism and the Wars of Religion that would follow shortly afterwards, always manifesting themselves contrary to the laws and customs of nature – not, indeed, as causes, but as the true signs and extraordinary yet certain portents of unhappy and baleful events.[8]

Nostradamus was well versed in the classical divination technique of apantomancy (the divination of omens – particularly the appearance of monstrous newborn children and animals). One might imagine the supper conversation was an echo of what he must have declared earlier to Marc and his important guests who, it is imagined, came out to meet Nostradamus and the child in the courtyard of the Château de l'Empéri, as the townspeople of Sénas and Salon looked on. Nostradamus would have said that true omens of the future always come in twos, and that he anticipated the imminent news of a second horribly deformed creature (animal or man). If the second two-headed omen appeared he would be convinced beyond all doubt that a malevolent division of the French people was soon at hand, and that there would be a civil war fought over religion.

Forty-five days after the encounter with the two-headed child, César reported that news reached Nostradamus of a two-headed horse born in Aurens, near Salon.[9] In Nostradamus' mind, the second omen sealed not only France's destiny, but his own. King and country were now in imminent danger of some defining event that would take destiny's path into the chaos of religious civil war. The second omen at last compelled Nostradamus to action. He resolved to set in motion the dissemination of his prophetic findings, to forewarn his countrymen and his king of tomorrow's gestating events.

Nostradamus would publish a history of that future. It would have a straightforward enough title, *Les Propheties de M. Nostradamus* (The Prophecies of M. Nostradamus). He had it in mind to disseminate his visions in 1,000 four-line poems (called quatrains) divided into 10 volumes – a "century" of 100 quatrains apiece.

Later on, when Chavigny arrived in Salon and became a purported intimate of Nostradamus' creative process, he recorded the following conclusions:

Foreseeing the signal mutations and changes which were to occur universally throughout Europe, and also the bloody civil wars, and the pernicious troubles fatally approaching the Gallic Realm, full of enthusiasm, and as if maddened by a furor entirely new, he set himself to write his centuries, and other presages, which he kept a long time without wishing to publish them, feeling that the novelty of the matter could not fail to cause infinite detractions, calumnies and backbiting more than venomous, as indeed happened. Finally, overcome by the desire that he had to be of service to the public, he brought them to light, with the result that their fame and renown ran quite incontinently through the mouths of Frenchmen and of foreigners with the greatest admiration.

It is believed Nostradamus stole away into his secret study to begin writing his book the next auspicious Holy Day, favorably blessed by the stars: the evening of Good Friday (Friday the 13th!) in April 1554. Aided either by a divinely blessed window in time, or a self-seduced belief in such by psychic suggestion, Nostradamus made his way home, bathed in the afterglow of his own private meditations and prayers from the Good Friday evening Mass at the Franciscan Church of Cordeliers. He mounted the circular stairs to his secret study, sat before his desk, and under the glow of wick and candle wax took up his pen, said a final prayer, and wrote the opening set of four-line poems:

> *Estant assis de nuict secret estude,*
> *Seul reposé sus la selle d'ærain:*
> *Flambe exigue sortant de solitude,*
> *Faict prosperer qui n'est à croire vain ...* [10]

Being seated at night – secret abstraction,
Alone in repose on the tripod of brass:
A very small flame sallies forth from seclusion,
That success not in vain faith should come to pass. [11]

La verge en main mise au milieu de branches,
De l'onde il moulle & le limbe & le pied:
Un peur & voix tremissent par les mâches
Splendeur diuine. Le diuin pres s'assied.[12]

The wand in hand in the middle of Branchus its place
    to be,
With water, he moistens the hem and the foot upon
    the ground:
A fear! And a voice quivering down through the
    magician's sleeves,
Splendor Divine! The divine one sits nearby, perchance
    to sound.[13]

He began the book with a description of his first Theurgic experiments. These were a variation on the classical oracular techniques
that one might suppose had now dominated his nightly vigils for
over a year – techniques that could well have been the modus
operandi for accessing the future with help from a discarnate
divine source. The techniques were an amalgamation of those
practiced by priestess oracles at Delphi and in particular the
Brachidae, the legendary descendants of Branchus, son of Apollo,
the sun god. (Branchus was said to have entered mortal life
through his mother's mouth and later met his divine father in a
forest. A grateful son's kiss upon his father's cheek empowered
Branchus with the gift of prophetic sight. His descendants were
the priests and priestesses at the temple of Apollo at Didyma near
Mitetus in Asia Minor.)

Nostradamus, ever sympathetic to prophetic lineages, took on
the passive and receptive role of the descendants of Apollo. Over
the preceding year, dressed in a simple white-hooded robe, he had
spent many nights sitting in silent meditation upon his brass
tripod chair. (Assuming he could afford to fashion a chair that was
sufficiently elevated, he would have suspended either a brass or

clay bowl over a small charcoal brazier underneath his chair, centered between the three legs. If his chair had been more modest, he would have placed the bowl before his feet). Prior to sitting down he would ceremoniously fill the bowl near to the brim with consecrated water, mixed with powerfully pungent (if not somewhat hallucinogenic) herbs, and keep enough glowing charcoal beneath it to sustain a slow and steady boil so that he and his chair would be embraced in a column of steam. The recipe of herbs used by Nostradamus was never divulged, but one can imagine it stank and had a sulfuric back-note to its blue-flamed Vulcan stench. The bowl and herbs were designed to resemble fumes out of the volcanic vent the Oracle of Delphi sat over and inhaled to bring on a prophetic trance. The Brachidae, like Nostradamus, did not have the luxury of volcanic vents and had to fashion the next-best thing.

Nostradamus lifted and modified phrases from a passage in Iamblichus' *De mysteriis Aegyptiorum* (see the underlined words below) and inserted them into the first two quatrains describing his magical ritual. Clearly, he intended to assume the role of the prophetess – a composite of the Oracles of Delphi and the Brachidae. He believed that his Christian God, via a classical personification, would possess his mind and body according to the directions written over a thousand years before by the neo-Platonist pagan Iamblichus:

The prophetess of Delphi, whether she gives oracles to mankind through an attenuated and fiery spirit, bursting from the mouth [or sulfuric vent] of the cavern, or whether being seated in the adytum on a brass tripod ... becomes sacred to the God ... she entirely gives herself up to a divine spirit, and is illuminated with a ray of divine fire. And when ... fire ascending from the mouth of the cavern circularly invests her in collected abundance, she becomes filled from it with a divine splendor. But when she places herself on the seat of the God [i.e., the brass tripod], she becomes co-adapted to his stable prophetic power: and from both these preparatory operations she becomes wholly possessed by the God. And then … he is present with and illuminates her in a separate manner, and is different from the fire, the spirit, the proper seat, and, in short, from all the visible apparatus of the place, whether physical or sacred.

The prophetic woman too in <u>Brachidae,</u> whether <u>she holds in her hand a wand</u>, which was at first received from some God, and becomes filled with a <u>divine splendor</u>, or whether <u>seated on an axis</u>, she predicts future events, or <u>dips her feet or the border of her garment in the water</u>, or receives the God by imbibing the vapor of the water; by all these she becomes adapted to partake of a metaphysical illumination of the God.[14]

Once the bowl of fumes was brought to the boil, Nostradamus would climb into the pillar of steam, sit on his brass tripod, and begin a secret incantation to empty his soul, mind, and heart of all care, solicitude, and vexation until he attained a state of tranquility and stillness of mind and spirit. At the right moment, upon the incantation's final reinforcing suggestion and blessing, he would take his laurel branch and dip it into the boiling water. He would shake hot droplets upon the hem of his robe, stinging his bare feet. The sharp heat of the water on his skin might have triggered a mysterious state of ecstasy bringing an initial terror as the conjured god began to sound in whispers down his robe. (Or, Nostradamus, now sufficiently auto-hypnotized and giddy from deep drafts of his possibly narcotic fumes, might have obtained a state of altered consciousness that projected the voice of another upon his own murmurings.)

How did this state of consciousness look to Nostradamus? We can only conjecture as to the shape of the ecstatic trance that he underwent. In the final analysis, only those who have undergone the sacred rite of ecstatic trance themselves are fit to write about it – and even then, how inadequate the description!

With these limitations in mind, let us imagine a "scene" in which he is "taken over" by divine ecstasy.

✂

His many days of purification, fasting, and magical preparation have not been endured in vain. A yawning gap spreads aside normal consciousness to let flicker the slender flame of divine witness that only burns in the smallest of candelabras – this atomically small yet eternal moment known as the present. It comes to him! He sinks into the state of "nowhere" …

He has become "now here"…!

He can comprehend the angelic and divine one, sitting nearby in the triangle beside his magic circle.

The emissary's words bring on the divine fire of prophecy descending upon the seer's stilled mind and heart with the brilliance of the sun. Thus, a guide, a spectral emissary [either hallucinated or authentic] supplies the mortal medium upon his brass tripod the power to be, or believe he is, a medium that can prophesy.

✂

Hidden in the flood of quatrains to come are two more that hint at how Nostradamus experienced his possession by "divine" ecstasy:

Le diuin verbe donra à la substance,
Côprins ciel terre, or occult au laict mystique:
Corps, ame, esprit ayant toute puissance,
Tant soubz ses pieds comme au siege Celique.

The divine word will give to the essence,
Containing heaven, earth, the hidden gold in the mystic deed:
Form, soul, spirit [have] all power's presence,
All is beneath his feet as at the feet of heaven [perceived.][15]

Corps sublimes sans fin à l'œil visibles:
Obnubiler viendront par ses raisons:
Corps, front comprins, sens chef & inuisibles.
Diminuant les sacrees oraisons.

Essences sublime forever visible to the eye,
Come to overcloud by their own reason-wish:
The form, brow comprised, sense and head, vanish by and by,
As sacred prayers begin to diminish.[16]

Nostradamus never directly described the nature of his visions, but a comprehensive study of the written prophecies hints that they often came cloaked in shadows with different times, events, and personalities overlaid. He could sometimes hear as well as smell the future. He occasionally interjected a brief reaction to what he saw – more often he expressed horror, bewilderment, but on rare occasions, hope for the future.

In a long and generally unpunctuated passage from the Preface to his son,[17] composed in the year after writing the first 353 quatrains of his planned 1,000, Nostradamus gives a sweeping if somewhat vague overview of what it is to be a prophet. He tries guardedly to convey by what means a mortal man becomes a vessel for divine sight and by what disciplines he can thereby translate his divine ecstasy into words:

As for ourselves who are but human, we can discover nothing by our own natural notions of our ingenuity about the obscure secrets of God the Creator ... However, in the present or in the future there may be persons to whom God the Creator might wish to reveal through fanciful impressions, some secrets of the future, according to judicial astrology, in much the same manner that in the past a certain power and voluntary faculty came over them like a flame, inspiring them to judge human and divine inspirations alike.

Next we read Nostradamus combining Iamblichus' neo-Platonist and pagan definition of the hierarchy of divine and elemental spirits one conjures in a theurgic ceremony with his own Christianized definition:

For the divine works, those which are totally absolute, God accomplishes; those which are medial, the angels; and the third kind, by the evil [spirits] ... The hidden prophecies [can either] come to one by the subtle spirit of fire, [or] sometimes [manifest] through the [mind's] judgment being disturbed in contemplating the remotest of stars; [in either case] while remaining alert and watchful, we, surprisingly, can take the pronouncements down in writing. We [thereby can] pronounce them without fear or shame and with the minimum of verbiage ... Because all these things did proceed from the divine power of the great eternal God, from whom all goodness flows.

What, then, is Nostradamus? Is he a prophet, equal to the biblical prophets of old? He diplomatically defers the term "prophet" to others, even though he intimately describes the challenges a prophet encounters as if they are his own.

Furthermore, my son, though I have inferred the name of "prophet," I do not wish to attribute for myself a title so sublime for the present ... A prophet – strictly speaking, my son – is one who sees things remote from the natural perception of all creatures and men. And, for instance, it can happen that the prophet, by means of the perfect light of the prophecy manifestly appearing before him, [can see] things which are divine, as well as human; which he cannot yet understand, for the effects of future prediction extend far. For the incomprehensible mysteries of God and their efficient virtue belong to a dimension very remote from natural human knowledge, taking their immediate origin from the free will. They bring about the appearance of causes which of themselves could not acquire enough attention to be known, neither by human augury, nor by any other hidden knowledge or virtue comprised under the concavity of heaven, even from the present fact of all eternity, which comes in itself to embrace all time but through some indivisible eternity and by means of Heraclian agitation, the causes are made known by celestial movements.

He admits to the pitfalls of a mortal mind quickened by magic and meditation to behold the rarified nature of reality as it is seen in God's perfect and eternal vision. Catching a glimpse of Eternity's harmony as it is, is like encountering the full moon, not its many reflections. The mortal cannot explain in his own limited terms the source of Eternity's reflection. Eternity's unified clarity becomes like a million boiling and bobbing reflections of a rising moon in the water. Eternity is not time and the message of events seen in a continuum of the "ever now" will invariably be misread as it is reflected in infinite ways in the waters of time.

Nostradamus claims that divine nature transcends all time and all illusions of natural human perception. He returns to Iamblichus' view that our lives in mortality and time are embraced by the divine Eternity, which is the invisible source of the cause of phenomena and time in the physical world. Notice that he says the state of Eternity embraces "all" time, not just time in general. This implies that many alternative, or quantum, futures are available to us depending on our individual or collective actions in the present moment.

Star calculations anchor, as best he can, the glimpses that a mortal man conjures of a divine trans-temporal eternity through what Nostradamus defines as a trance state of "Heraclean agitation" – in other words, by some epileptic state – hence the descriptions in his first quatrains of shaking and quivering when possessed by the prophetic state. A deeper meaning is implied if by "Heraclean" Nostradamus is hinting that time and eternity become a circle wherein all opposites have neither a beginning nor an end, as defined by the Greek mystic Herakleitos (Heraclitis c. 540–c. 480 B.C.E.). In Herakleitos, Nostradamus had a kindred spirit, for he too was labeled "the dark" or "the obscure" because his philosophy was non-dualistic. He called this philosophy the Hidden Harmony. If we take the words of Herakleitos as a guide, someone in a "Heraclean agitation" would experience a state of transcendent consciousness in which "God is day and night, winter and summer, war and peace, satiety and want … the way up and the way down are one and the same. Even sleepers (the unconscious and sinful ones) are workers and collaborators in what goes on in the universe. In the circle the beginning and the end are common."[18]

In his Preface, Nostradamus continues his confession to his son:

I do not say, my son, that the knowledge of this matter cannot yet impress itself upon your tender mind, nor do I say that very distant events are not within the understanding of reasoning man, notwithstanding those which are simply the mere creation of the intellectual person out of current events. They are not by any means too greatly hidden from him, nor, on the other hand, can they be said to be revealed at all. Nevertheless, the perfect knowledge of events cannot be acquired without divine inspiration, since all prophetic inspiration receives its principal motivating force from God the Creator, then from good fortune and nature. Thus for this reason, the presage is fulfilled in part or has been correctly predicted in proportion to the extent to which similar events have manifested themselves similarly or have failed to manifest themselves. For human understanding, being intellectually created, cannot see hidden things unless aided by a voice coming from limbo by means of the slender flame showing in what direction future events will incline.

Nostradamus is not saying that the non-dual dance of opposites is beyond his son's – or others' – grasp. Nor is the shape and quality of distant future events beyond the understanding of a reasoning man. But he is adamant that authentic prophetic vision comes from accomplishing the awakening of the correct psychic instincts, the achievement of union with and direct experience of one's God-source, and, last but not least, encountering a bit of good luck along the divinatory way. Moreover, one does this by conjuring "the voice coming from limbo" – namely, the conjured divine, angelic or daemonic spirits – and by unlocking the powers of the *exigue flâme*. The latter, beyond what has already been described as a thin flame of heightened perception, could also stand for a key letter unlocking the Cabalistic arcana. Thus, the initiate can climb, as it were, the stations of the tree of life, using it as a road map to the divine godhead. He implies indirectly here that the accuracy of his prophecies will depend in part on his ability to suspend his psychic, mental, and emotional projections and limitations to capture what direction the events of tomorrow will take. Nostradamus' use of the verb "incline" makes it clear that he at best can predict the apparent rather than the actual directions or outcomes of a given present-day action. Nothing in his history of the future is written in stone.

In another passage from the Preface,[19] Nostradamus comes closest to admitting to his son how a pure and inspired vision of the future passes the gauntlet of the mortal mind and its dialectical limitations to become a written account:

Although the eternal God alone knows the eternity of the light proceeding from himself, I say frankly to all those to whom he wishes to reveal his immense magnitude – immeasurable and unknowable as it is – after long and melancholic ecstasy, that it is a hidden thing divinely manifested to the prophet by two means, which are contained in the understanding of the inspired one who prophesies: One comes by infusion which clarifies the supernatural light in him who predicts by the doctrine of astronomy, making possible to predict by divine revelation; the other comes by means of an authentic participation with the divine eternity; by which means the prophet can judge what is given to him from his own divine spirit through God the Creator and his genuine initiation; so that what is predicted is true, and has an ethereal origin. This light and the slender flame [presumed to be one's inner spark of God] are altogether efficacious, and of exalted origin no less than natural clarity and the natural light that renders philosophers so sure of themselves that by means of the principles of the first cause they have attained to the innermost cores of the most exalted doctrines.

In the 16th century, if one dared ponder into the realm of the abstract, the supernatural, the mathematical, one was guided by a *melancholic* humor. Nostradamus enters his work with fiery spirits as cold, dry, brooding, indeed as emotionally Saturnian and aloof from passion as his incantations and meditations can make him. His gray eyes are freeze-dried with dispassion as they gaze into water or upon the concave mirror, or interpret the positioning of stars. He makes himself a dark vessel for the oracular possession by a supernatural presence. Though ecstasy floods over him, and his body might tremble like an epileptic upon the first entry of fiery missives and presences either from God or from his overwrought imagination, he is telling us that his point of witnessing such fantasies or authentic paranormal phenomena is as cold and dispassionate as a Zen monk gazing at a winter rock garden.

Once he attains the meditative distance derived from a "long and melancholic ecstasy," he is then capable of perceiving and later translating a divine prophetic vision into words by following two principles, which he defines as "infusion" and "authentic participation." Infusion is the principle of becoming an empty vessel or, as the Eastern mystics say, becoming the "hollow bamboo" upon which God plays his own tune. By obtaining the melancholic state of no mind, no emotion, negation of personality and time – the ultimate state of being "cool" and dry – he attains the second principle of "authentic participation" with the divine.

Later this disidentification would help Nostradamus to accomplish the recording of divine messages aided by the abstract language of mathematics and astronomical calculations. Exactly what those calculations were is withheld from us. One might expect a detailed accounting of just how he used such calculations to make sense of his visions as objective proof of his powers.[20] They might have gone up into the same unearthly light as the forbidden books laid to flame in his secret study. Why he did not divulge any of this is a mystery. Perhaps he kept it secret because it is in his mathematical calculations that one finds the true "code" to unlock how and what Nostradamus, in his own mind, believed were divine messages about future events.

Some scholars have stretched the angle of their astrolabe to the extremely suggesting that most of Nostradamus' prophecies were not a work of Theurgy and divination but were essentially astronomical in nature. Lemesurier is the staunchest champion of this theory to date. According to him, Nostradamus used his ephemeris to calculate the latitude and placement of stars as they appeared over the skies of significant events of the past. Then he calculated planetary, lunar, solar, and stellar positions that either approximated or paralleled those configurations of the past in the future – the idea being that similar aspects over similar geographic locales and latitudes in the future could repeat similar historical events. Thus, the past repeats itself in the future.

Lemesurier may be onto something significant here, but if he has grasped hold of some of the details of Nostradamus' calculations for time windows, the daemon in the details is still a creature of divination, rather than math. You still have to interpret the signs, mathematical or otherwise. Nostradamus may have structured his historical account of the future upon some variation of the Nietzschean theory of eternal recurrence, as calculated by the stars, but Lemesurier, in his bold test of this theory, last published in 1998, passed a philosopher's stone of failed prophetic conclusions. For example, according to Lemesurier, the following events should have happened recently in Nostradamus' astrologically reoccurring time windows:

- By 1998, Asiatic armies occupy Iran, then attack the city of Trebizond, then Turkey.

- By 1999, Islamic and Asiatic armies and navies overrun Israel, Cyprus, Turkey, Greece, Egypt and Libya.
- By 2000, violent sea battles on the Mediterranean! Islamic armies invade and conquer Italy by land and sea and Eastern Europe falls to Islamic and Asiatic armies all the way up to the River Danube. The pope evacuates Rome and sets up shop in the Papal palaces of Avignon.
- By 2002, a horde of Islamic marines hit the beaches of Provence ...[21]

By the end of 2002, according to Lemesurier's reading of Nostradamus' stars, Islamic land and sea forces should be gathering for an offensive against European and US forces in southern France. The fighting by 2007 will lead to the first use of weapons of mass destruction on the battlefields along the Rhône valley. In reality, the end of 2002 saw US and some European forces preparing for an invasion of Iraq, deep inside the Islamic world; it would seem that such weapons of mass destruction would be used far sooner than 2007. Rather than European and US forces retreating from the juggernaut of millions of troops commanded by a new Islamic Hitler, 2002 ended with European and US coalition forces occupying Afghanistan, firing cruise missiles down the mountain rat holes of isolated survivors of Usama bin Laden's al-Qaeda terrorist organization.

If prophecy were merely a mathematical problem, or the stuff of star charts, we could all play Nostradamus. But we can only glean from his few confessions that he believed he had the power to take the subjective visions of each nocturnal vigil, and use his secret slide-rule of arcane Hebrew astronomical calculation to make sense of what had been "infused" and directly participated in while in audience with "God." On Good Friday the 13th, 1554, he began solidifying the belief in his own ethereal reveries into the objective evidence of pen and ink that would be used by others for centuries to come to measure his state of sincerity, and his sanity.

The Apostle from Beaune

Four months before the first picks and shovels of Adam de Craponne's construction gangs began breaking the hard sunbaked surface of the Crau, another young man, 30 years of age, presented himself and his letters of reference at Nostradamus' door sometime in early April 1554. His name was Jean-Aymes (Aimé) de Chavigny of Beaune. He had a doctor's degree in law and theology, and had been the mayor of Beaune in Burgundy in 1548, at the tender age of 24. Chavigny abandoned what was shaping up to be a brilliant political career to tread the path of mystic knowledge. He was particularly interested in finding a master who could teach him how to prophesy via the celestial science of Judicial Astrology.

According to his own written accounts, his path to Nostradamus' door began in Paris, around 1549, when he became close friends with Jean Dorat, the principal of the Collège de Coqueret. Dorat had been in the forefront of a movement to organize the grammar of the French language and enrich its vocabulary with classical Latin and Greek. Since his days in Agen, learning alongside Nostradamus under the tutelage of Scaliger, Dorat had risen in stature as a poet and grammarian and gathered around him a coterie of young students who would soon become France's most brilliant literary stars. These would include Pierre de Ronsard (1524–85), Joachim du Bellay (1522–60), Jean-Antoine de Baïf (1532–89), and Étienne Jodelle (1532–88). Dorat's "poetic brigade" (as they called themselves) would soon be honored across France and beyond, as that star cluster of literati known as the Pléiade. Their work would influence literary giants of the high Renaissance such as Sir Francis Bacon and William Shakespeare.

Chavigny insinuates that he had acquitted himself sufficiently to rub shoulders with Dorat's prodigies as one of his students, but may have been exaggerating when he said he was a close friend – he may have read more into Jean Dorat's habit of being ever a force of optimism and encouragement to talented young writers. Dorat, it seems, had remained a dedicated supporter of Nostradamus ever since their days in Agen. There is little doubt that he had in his possession a mounting stack of Nostradamus' highly successful annual almanacs. Inside these, Dorat discovered praiseworthy originality in the way Nostradamus injected classical Greek and Latin terms into the French vernacular of his quatrains and prophetic narratives. It is safe to speculate that Dorat's students were subjected to readings and held discussions about Nostradamus' unique brand of nebulous-yet-lurid writing. Chavigny obviously caught Dorat's infatuation with the seer of Salon. However, not all of Dorat's most promising pupils were so enthused. A few years hence, Ronsard would offer cautious praise while Jodelle would acidly condemn Nostradamus' writings as turgid claptrap.

Jean Dorat, it seems, was still in contact with Nostradamus, and he was obviously well aware of Chavigny's interest in Judicial Astrology and mysticism, but the set and sequence of hurdles that brought the former young mayor of Beaune, via Dorat's introduction, into Nostradamus' presence are not detailed by Chavigny. All that can be told is that Chavigny resolved to leave the company of Dorat and his poets in Paris, with or without letters of introduction, and risk the two-month journey south from Paris to Salon to offer his services to Nostradamus. He intended to become his secretary and student in mystic arts.

The prospective mentor Chavigny met in 1554 was now a half-century old. If Chavigny were of average height, he would be looking downward at Nostradamus, who began to resemble the majority of woodcut studies and paintings based on César's portrait of him, age 63. He wore the black robes and four-cornered hat of a scholar atop his high, flat forehead. The neatly groomed beard falling in two forks touching his broad chest gave length to what Chavigny described as his "straight and even nose" and flat moon face. Chavigny definitely did not see the myth of bony angularity painted and sketched in latter-day renditions that are

based more on clichés of the generic fictional sorcerer than historical fact. There were few frown wrinkles on his brow, nor did his
face appear weather-beaten, notwithstanding the years spent in the
elements on the rough-hewn 16th-century road. Moreover, this 50-
year-old had remarkably smooth skin with a peaches-and-cream
complexion highlighted by two dollops of ruddy cheeks. Perhaps
this face enjoyed the results of countless applications of his youth
creams? Then again, the smooth and youthful visage painted from
memory by César could be fading memory's flattery replacing fact.

Chavigny would write that Nostradamus was a vigorous man
up until the last few years of his life. Thirteen years later, his hair,
as per César's lingering memory, was short-cropped and the long
beard had paled to solid gray. It is possible that Chavigny first
found the hair and beard of 50-year-old Nostradamus ruddy black,
thanks to the application of one of his own hair-dye treatments.

If we take Chavigny's own detailed character study as the basis
for speculation one might reconstruct their first interview in the
following way. The polite and reverent young man presented his
credentials and while describing his background fell under the
quiet yet complex gaze of Nostradamus. Chavigny would note
that the master's expression was "generally pleasant" yet set in a
face "both severe and smiling," as (he thought) would be expected
of a man whose face was overshadowed with direct and long experience of the cruelty of the world (and, perhaps, of the world to
come). Yet this was not a grim, world-weary man. The fruits of
compassion that such trials of life can harvest in a man equally
softened his stern countenance. Clearly, Chavigny did most of the
talking, while Nostradamus looked on, measuring the young man,
silently – perhaps only answering him carefully and clearly after
long and contemplative pauses.

Chavigny got a job as Nostradamus' secretary; this fact is without question – whether it was full-time or part-time is unclear. To
what extent he became an ever-present fixture in the household, or
an eager shadow following Nostradamus around for the rest of his

life, is dependent upon one objective record – Chavigny's. Strangely, the accounts of Nostradamus' other significant eyewitness biographers, his son César, and his brother Jehan, are more ambiguous. This could be the result of pique playing history's censor in the memoirs of blood relatives confronted with an upstart disciple, greedily taking much of Nostradamus' attention and energy away from the family. Alternatively, Chavigny could have been a fixture to them no more remarkable than the family's deferential and mostly invisible house help and serving women who are absent from César's accounts. He was just a secretary.

Chavigny would beg to differ. Decades later he would present himself as part of Nostradamus' intimate household when he set out to compose one of the first of many interpretive studies of Nostradamus' prophecies to come. In his mind he is not just the hired literary help, but Nostradamus' intimate friend, dedicated editor, secretary and disciple up to his master's death. If Chavigny had lived in Salon for the next 12 years without a break, evidence in the archives of Salon presents next to nothing that substantiates this. Then again his claim cannot be completely dismissed until a forensic record of business deals, legal writs, tax lists, the census ledgers of other towns, and such like, points to Chavigny living elsewhere.

∞

Chavigny, with quill and wits sharpened, was ready to go to work by Good Friday of 1554, when it is believed that Nostradamus began setting down into rough draft his magnum opus of prophecy. It can be imagined that the months passed for him in a mix of creative excitement and the repetitive drudgery of tedious hours of copying and editing. Chavigny would come to know his master's bad temper and see what he later described as his usually pleasant gray eyes suddenly blaze with anger. He admits his master was often prone to rage, but does not allude to why. Perhaps he was a difficult and demanding author, or maybe

Chavigny was often too slow to pick up his master's editorial intentions. It seems these frequent outbursts were short and sharp, and they left few, if any, lingering emotional scars on either man. He admits that Nostradamus had a "good and lively" mind "understanding easily what [it] wanted to."

Chavigny certainly attended church with his master and his growing family, because his reflections reveal at least Nostradamus' public attitudes and views on religion and the worsening state of spiritual life in France:

He approved of the ceremonies of the Roman Church and held to the Catholic faith and religion, outside of which, he was convinced, there was no salvation. He reproved grievously those who, withdrawn from its bosom, abandoned themselves to eating and drinking of the sweetness and liberties of the foreign damned doctrines, affirming that they would come to a bad and pernicious end.

I do not want to forget to say that he engaged willingly in fasts, prayers, alms and patience; he abhorred vice and chastised it severely; I can remember his giving to the poor, towards whom he was very liberal and charitable, often making use of these words, drawn from the Holy Scriptures: *Make friends of the riches of iniquity.*[22]

Chavigny would come to know his master as one "maddened by a furor entirely new" as he produced a stream of hundreds of quatrains for him to copy over the next year. We might imagine the drafts of these four-line poems coming before Chavigny's eyes each morning after his master, flushed with the excitement of what was beheld of the future, descended the circular stairs from his nocturnal vigils. Unfortunately, there is next to no corroborating evidence indicating just how privy Chavigny was to the secret ceremonies. It might be argued that Chavigny's attempt decades later in the 1590s to interpret and decipher Nostradamus' prophecies proves that he was a relative outsider to their secrets when they were composed.

The Importance of Being Earnestly Obscure

Scholars from the Renaissance to modern times have woven fascinating and elaborate theories in an effort to answer a lingering riddle: Why did Nostradamus write his important revelations about the future so obscurely? Perhaps we can quickly cut through the root of this bramble-bush of speculation by seizing on key passages in Nostradamus' Preface to his son, and the prophecies. As we have already learned, Nostradamus dreaded what harm he might do if he recounted too clearly the future changes in political, social and religious attitudes that were "so diametrically opposite to the present view" that his contemporaries would "damn that which future centuries will know and have seen to be true."

Finally, when faced with a pair of monstrous omens which he believed marked the advent of a religious civil war between his countrymen, he could no longer suppress his visions. He might have reasoned that the French people had to know enough of what he saw coming so that they could make positive changes – but not reveal enough to aid those who would make the future worse than he had foreseen. He had to think of a way to simultaneously share *and* shroud his revelations:

Later, [I] decided to relinquish withholding my tongue, and pen from paper because of foreseeing the advent of the common [vulgar] people.[23] [Therefore I wrote] in dark and cryptic sentences the causes of the future evolution of human kind, especially the most urgent causes, and the ones I perceived, [and, doing so] without scandalizing and upsetting fragile sentiments [in the present or the future] by clouding my writing in obscure but, above all, prophetic language.[24]

Few in literary history took more pains to mar the measure and ruin the rhyme of their poetry than Nostradamus. He extensively used anagrams and created enigmatic names for people and places,[25] or hid important clues in classical metaphors so subtle that none but a handful of his readers steeped in classical history and geography might decipher them correctly. Using a turgid application of Latin grammar games,[26] he dropped enough words out of many a poetic line to force the reader to plant their own projections in the gaps of unclear syntax and meaning. With his heavily Latinized vernacular French as the base, he decorated his poems with a polyglot spicing of several languages – including Latin, Greek, Italian (Tuscan and Piedmontese dialects), Dutch, Basque, Spanish – and many a word picked up from French dialects learned on the road, such as Occitan and Breton, along with many from his native dialect of Provençal. His poems were all in rhyme, but he would often – and awkwardly – break the rules of rhyme and meter if the beclouded content required it. Later he would define his verses as creatures born from a coupling of his nocturnal calculations composed out of his "natural instinct" (his gift of sight) with a "poetic frenzy."[27] His prose in prophetic language seen in the first Preface (and a second, entitled *Epistle to Henry II of France*, written as an introduction to the final three centuries) is a maze of rarely punctuated sentences with clauses often a half-page long. It is a classic example of an occult narrative – namely, a literary device that intends the existential impact of reading the words to be more significant than the content. In short, he must be read between the lines.[28] Even if, for argument's sake, his intentions to use a ruse-filled narrative or cloudy poetic language were noble, such devices will ever mark his work with that stigma of a "con," given the human habit to judge fast and investigate little.

Nostradamus' device of obscurity has cast a shadow of charlatanism on his legacy. I believe he knew this would be the case. There are enough passages from the Preface and future Epistle letters to prove that he anticipated such "calumny" from the learned, and especially from the greater numbers who are less learned and dim in wit. The price was worth it, as passages from his Preface have already implied. Years had passed before Nostradamus could find just the right obfuscating literary voice that would allow him to embark on writing his magnum opus. Let the ignorant and prejudiced soon tire of his calculatedly cloudy prophecies. Let them deem him a fool and leave him alone. Let cynics believe he was establishing a con that would live beyond the grave. The more open-minded might pass beyond the verbal road-blocks to glimpse future human potential for good and evil.

In the Preface to the prophecies, Nostradamus tries to explain to his son how God uses him to prophesy in mystifying ways while helping him ground his work of nebulous devices in solid cosmic calculations:

Inasmuch as: *Thou hast hidden these things from the wise and the prudent, that is, from the powerful and from kings, and hast revealed them to the small and the weak* [Matthew 11:25 – misquoted from memory by Nostradamus] and also to the Prophets, by means of the Immortal God, and his good Angels, they receive the spirit of prophecy, by which they behold distant things and future events; for nothing can be accomplished without Him whose great power and kindness to his creatures is so great that as long as these dwell in them, much as they may be exposed to other influences, on account of their good genius this prophetic heat and power approaches us: it comes to us like rays of the sun casting influences on bodies both elementary and non-elementary[29] ... For it is by means of this inspiration [Judicial Astrology] with divine revelation, and continual nightly watches and calculations, that we have drafted our prophecies into written words ...[30] But [beyond this] it is that judgment which is coming by means of the discernment obtained through calculation of the heavens that I want to reveal to you. By this [insight] one has knowledge of future events while rejecting completely the fanciful imaginations, which will occur. By limiting the circumstances of the locations by means of harmonizing divine and supernatural inspiration with astronomical computations, one can accurately name places and periods of time, with an occult property by virtue, authority, and a divine faculty.

By the appearance of this [faculty], the cycles of time and the past, present and future become one eternity: *For all things are naked and open.* (Hebrews 4:13)[31]

He possibly is self-delusional, but he is not a charlatan. He believes he has something to share beyond obscurity's barrier. He admits to being an all-too-mortal explorer of God's prophetic messages for humankind.

Thus, my son, notwithstanding your tender mind, you can easily understand that the lights of the sky can prophesy things that are bound to happen at night, which are natural, coupled with the spirit of prophecy. Not that I would assume the name or quality of a prophet but by revealed inspiration, is like a mortal man, no less distant by fame and sense from Heaven than his feet from the ground. *I cannot fail, err or be deceived* although I am the greatest sinner in the world, subject to all human afflictions. But many times a week I am overtaken by a prophetic ecstasy – and by exhaustive calculation, having rendered my nocturnal studies out of an agreeable fragrance – I have composed books of prophecies, each containing one hundred astronomical quatrains composed of prophecies which I have required to polish a little obscurely. They are perpetual prophecies, for they extend from now to the year 3797.[32]

All human failings aside, he presses us to believe that God has inspired his prophecies, and he implicitly invites us to untangle these visions, which he found necessary to pass through his beclouding poetic devices, in a history of the future that stretches insight and credulity 2,242 years beyond the year 1555!

It is possible, that some will raise their brow at seeing such a far-reaching extent of time and a treatment of everything under the vault of the moon that will happen and [will be] universally perceived all over the earth, my son. But if you attain the natural span of human life, you will come to see, under your own native skies, the surprising future events [I have] foreseen.[33]

Upon signing off on this prefaced promise on 1 March 1555, Nostradamus sent a written record of his prophecies to a publisher, trusting that time and the fulfillment of events would be his judge.

CHAPTER SEVEN

The Queen's Oracle

⌀

The First Nostradamian

The blackened fingers of typesetters at Macé Bonhomme picked metal cubes of type containing Nostradamus' prophetic thoughts and placed them in rows on two-page plates for the presses. The compositors kept a feverish pace, feeding the inkers' new arrangements of typeface while recycling the old letters – always in short supply. They hastily wiped them clean of the oily ink, putting back the letters into their appropriate boxes from where others would pull the typeface out again for new page plates. The surviving product in museums indicates that Macé Bonhomme ran an unusually efficient publishing house for that day. Inspecting the binding process, he must have sifted through sets of diminutive unbound manuscripts, cut in demi-octavo, satisfied that he had convinced his new client, Nostradamus, that a serialization of his planned book of 10 "centuries" of 1,000 quatrains was too ambitious. A much smaller and more mass-marketable volume – containing a Preface to 353 quatrains – was in the best interests of all. Publishers present and past are ever desirous of shortening the wordage of books, thus lowering the cost of paper and maximizing their earnings.

The author, in far-removed Salon de Crau, must have glared in horror at the errors in his specially bound author's copy. Wide geographic spaces traversable by hard months of travel protected Bonhomme from hearing face-to-face the author's outbursts hurled at the many typographical errors, frequent spaces dropped to meld lines, and words combined to save space. Distance also insulated Bonhomme from the author's undoubted rage at the frequent consolidating of verses to save paper at the cost of poetry. Overall, Bonhomme was confident that the virtues of the compact little book would outweigh these editorial deficiencies. Nostradamus could at least admire the fine leather cover and the decoration of his manuscript with the publishing house's signature woodcut illustrations and ornamental designs on the front page. Indeed, they were considered some of the finest of the age. Fine illustration elevated the stature, if not the content, of every author lucky enough to have their words branded by ink on paper under the famous imprint. *Les Propheties de M. Nostradamus* ("The Prophecies of M. Nostradamus") might see itself bound in fine leather covers for local distribution in and around Lyon, but Bonhomme most certainly shipped thousands of unbound copies via pack horses for distribution in distant provinces of France. Not only did this save his mailing costs and increase profits, but the extra labor and material costs were passed on to the retailers or book purchasers, who would commission their own leather covers and bindings.

The process of printing and distributing books retains today the measured and methodical pace virtually unchanged since the 16th century. Nostradamus could count himself lucky that Bonhomme and his team were unusually efficient and prompt for their day. The Preface and 353 quatrains from Centuries (Volumes) 1, 2, 3, and over half of 4 were completed by Nostradamus on 1 March 1555 and sent to Lyon shortly thereafter, most likely by expensive special courier. They might have reached Lyon in a month. Bonhomme received the *imprimateur* of royal privilege[1] sanctioning the production of the book on the final day of April 1555. It was signed by Hugues de Puis, Seigneur de la Mothe, Counselor of the King and Seneschal (Lord Lieutenant Governor) of Lyon. Copies were in print from 4 May onwards. That means the completion of manuscript, mailing, and the approval process by royal censors in Lyon leading at last to printed copies for sale, took only nine weeks!

Next, Bonhomme would send one of the first finely bound copies straight to the Royal Library in Paris. The rapid spread of the information revolution of the printed book and free ideas across France compelled François I, in 1522, to decree that all publishers in the realm were obligated to send a copy of every newly printed book, post-haste, to the Royal Library where it was indexed and scrutinized. There, too, a new book would pass through another process of royal scrutiny and approval for the coveted right to be published in the French capital, the intellectual center of the French Renaissance. A volume of *Les Propheties de M. Nostradamus*, pungent in its gleaming leather cover and new ink, found its way to the Royal Library, and not long afterwards, perhaps in early June 1555, a librarian or a courtier in the library – possibly an avid reader of Nostradamus' earlier *Prognostications*, or someone appointed especially to be on the lookout for the newest occult, magical or astrologically oriented books – made his mistress aware of this exceptionally ambitious stab at divination. Thus it came to pass that one of the first persons to lay her laced and richly bejeweled hand across the opened pages of quatrains was none other than the Queen of France, Catherine de Medici.

Since coming (quite accidentally) to the throne in 1547, Catherine quietly endured a number of physical, emotional and political impediments to her ambitions and happiness. It seemed that fortune had dealt her a hard hand in this life, yet like any unlucky and unchastened gambler, she believed fate's future held a change for the better. You could say she wantonly used occult arts to gain advantage in the high-risk game of court politics by second-guessing the cards before they were dealt out. Her husband,

King Henry II, loved another – the charismatic Grand Sénéchalle and the Duchess de Valentinois, Diane de Poitiers – and so he could only give her the respect she warranted but not the caresses and tenderness she desired. The queen was not pretty. Her eyes were large and fishy, resting on a set of bags. Her face was an oval ending in a weak chin that only accentuated the tyranny of a long nose. No court painter dared portray her true equine profile while she lived.

"She is a fine woman, when her face is veiled," explained Giovanni Capello, an Italian at the French court. "I say this because she is tall, her figure is elegant, and her skin is fine. As for her face, it is not beautiful, the mouth is too large and the eyes large and pale."

Catherine tried her best to distract the visage-obsessed court from her plain face by dressing herself in immaculate attire that strategically drew attention to those charms she did have. All agreed she had an admirable set of legs – a custom-designed saddle was made to expose as much leg as decently possible when her skirts flew while she tried to keep pace with her athletic husband on hunting excursions. Postmortem vanity preserves their memory in her sensuous, naked statue reclining on the royal tomb at St. Denis. Her youthful body in repose alongside Henry's is draped loosely in a marble funeral shroud with one of her handsome long legs completely exposed for posterity.

Fate's fortune had made her the Italian Duchessina d'Urbino, a child of an upstart lesser noble. She was the object of a political marriage the Medici pope, Clement VII, made with François I in 1533, for the latter's younger son, Henry Duc de Orléans. The thin, plain yet quietly strong-willed 14-year-old girl understood and endured her fate as the instrument sealing an allegiance of the papacy, the Medici, with the French Valois in a Franco-Italian alliance against the Hapsburgs in François' interminable wars to dominate Italy. She was borne on a litter to a new and alien life at French court, but she anticipated the intellectual solace she would gain from bringing along the magnificent Library of Lorenzo de' Medici. In order to secure an heir, Prince Henry dutifully obeyed his mistress's commands to enter his wife's bedchamber on nights deemed most astrologically well starred for fertility, yet years passed and there was concern at French court that Catherine was barren. This was none too serious a problem, for Henry was not at the time the heir of the Valois throne; that fell upon Henry's older brother, and the king's favorite son, François. However, François suddenly fell ill and died in 1536, while on campaign alongside his brother and father in Italy. Some say he was poisoned by iced water tainted by a Medici agent employed by that cunning family to make their unsuspecting niece the Queen of France.

When Henry ascended the throne in 1547, Catherine eventually produced ten children, including four sons – all potential heirs. His Highness, her husband, was ever respectful. He admired her once or twice for trying her best to keep up with him on horseback. He was ever solicitous, discrete in his affair with Poitiers, but a pall of perfunctory duty and a little pity surrounded his intimate liaisons with the queen. Henry was Catherine's first intimate liaison with a man, and he awakened and quickened in her an ever stronger desire – but a desire unrequited and frustrated – to be first in his heart. She loved him as those who desire what they can never have, and with suppressed desperation she centered her life completely on his needs and his schedule. She was a dedicated mother to his children. She wore black to mourn his absence, and ordered the court ladies to wear the same whenever the king was away at military camp.

Diane de Poitiers was over two decades his senior, yet she was a maturing woman of legendary and lingering youthfulness, a fine horsewoman, and one to make the most of identifying herself (in her fair complexion and athletic form) with Diana, the classical Goddess of the Moon and the Hunt, from whom she took her name. Henry was 12 years old when, attired in Diane's family colors of black and white, he rode up to the royal stands on the day of his first public tournament to dedicate his martial feat of arms to the 30-year-old de Poitiers. A platonic, boyish crush and mutual friendship over the coming years yielded eventually to a consummated romance. Once the appropriate period of mourning the death of his father was complete, Henry redesigned the consecration ornaments and livery of his predecessors. Along with his regal finery of rich embroidery with pearls four fingers wide, he decorated his doublet with three crescents intertwined and carrying the cipher of the double D (for Diane) linked with the letter H (for Henry). This was his official homage to his Moon mistress, his "goddess-huntress," Diane, his truest love, above and beyond his plain-faced queen.

Catherine never avoided or publicly insulted her rival in public; rather, she included the Duchess de Valentinois intimately into her life. Poitiers likewise rendered dedicated and respectful service to her queen.

"With Madame de Valentinois," wrote Catherine to Henry de Béarn, "everything was in all honor. But those who were so stupid as to make a scandal about it, the king would have been highly annoyed if I had kept them with me."

As Catherine's children were born and de Poitiers moved from fertility counselor to choosing their wet nurses – and eventually receiving much of their love, as is indicated in their written dedications to her – Catherine would always guard her hurt and jealousy behind a mask of proper deportment. After all, she was the queen. Time was on Catherine's side, even if it had been kind to the charms of Diane de Poitiers. Nevertheless, her husband's Moon mistress was old enough to be his mother. Catherine was a Medici. Her family was known for its formidable political intrigues ever fomented in polite patience. A Medici bestowed smiles to targets of assassination. The Medici no doubt inspired Shakespeare's Iago.

"Always caress your enemies," Catherine once confided to an intimate. *Odiate et asperate* (hate and wait) was her motto.

She had learned well the art of sublimating disappointment to feed her plans and her patience. From the courtier Brantôme comes a story perhaps more existential than factual. It has Catherine, spying through a peep-hole drilled through the floor above Diane's bedchamber so she could watch her husband cavort in amorous passion and tenderness – first on the bed, then consummating his desire as he rolled with Diane across the grand throw rug. Catherine then rose to her feet weeping and sobbing – steadied in the arms of her lady in attendance – and crying out, "Why does not my husband love me like that, and treat me tenderly with the same wanton games!"

Her lady consoled her as best she could, reminding the queen that her current vexation and anguish were the price of curiosity, and that she could not expect less from the king and his mistress. "Alas, yes! I desired to see a thing I ought not to have desired to see, since the sight of it torments me."

Brantôme finishes his tale saying, "However, having been consoled and taken heart she ceased to brood over it and continued as much as she could with this pastime of watching, and turned it to laughter and perhaps something besides."

While Diane's area of mastery was in dominating the king, Catherine became the mistress of disguising, or feigning, her intentions and feelings. This gave her a trained eye and a crystallized instinct to recognize another's attempt to mask his true intentions when the librarian presented the queen with a newly printed book in early summer of 1555.

Catherine was wont to collect books, astrologers, necromancers, and magicians in her private apartments at the Louvre, or sequester her soothsayers and their magical and scrying tools for secret ceremonies at Chaumont, her private château along the Loire. Inside her private apartments in Paris, at the Louvre, or at the summer residence of St.-Germain-en-Laye, she would lay aside the pretense of being the most Catholic Queen of the realm. The defender of the Holy Church practiced the occult arts because she believed it was her royal right to use them – sometimes as a window of insight, at other times as a weapon to preserve her reign and protect her children. On secret sessions held in her apartments she would enter the proceedings by ceremoniously reversing her crucifix so that Christ was against her breast, and revealing on the reverse side to all assembled an effigy of naked Apollo, god of divination, founder of the prophetic line of Brachidae.

In the company of her young priestesses and brooding astrologers she would consult her gods beyond the magic mirror or read the signs hidden in a wide variety of forbidden arts, which could help her map a future course, put hexes on her enemies, and further her ambitions. Behind the mask of a submissive and tolerant queen, there lay coiled and primed a great will and expectation that her four sons and three daughters would follow the Medici tradition, and bring greater influence of the Medici/Valois upon the kingdoms of Europe through strategically arranged marriages into dominant royal bloodlines.

Lately the signs were not good. The portents showed a threat to the continued good fortune of her husband, the king. His cloudy fate could endanger the future of the French throne and that of their children. Consequently, her captivation with Nostradamus and his new book of prophecies was instantaneous. A number of spine-chilling clues in the hypnotically wild and cryptic quatrains must have caught her eye. Modern scholars often take for granted certain key contemporary statements and descriptions that the first Nostradamian would never overlook.

She only needed to turn the first few pages to fix her attention on Quatrain 10 of Century 1, where the author appeared to be speaking about her, the future of the House Valois, and her children:

Serpens transmis dans la caige de fer,
Ou les enfans septains du Roy sont pris:
Les vieux & peres sortiront bas de l'enfer,
Ains mourir voir de fruict mort & crys.

The serpent's coffin in a vault of iron to dwell,
Where the children – the seven – from the King are spread:
Their ancestors will rise to behold them from hell,
Before dying, see! The fruits of their line are dead.[2]

She might take note of the prophecy launching off with a complex double entendre on the words *serpens/septains*. The "serpent" could stand as a symbol or an emblem of a person laid to rest in a *sarpos* (Greek for coffin) in a vault of iron, along with the *septeni* (Latin for "the seven"). Records do not exist indicating exactly when Catherine became interested in the magical symbol of a serpent ring of power, but being in her own right an expert student of occult symbols, she might already have sensed that Nostradamus was applying the serpent symbol to her. Indeed, by presenting this message in the first edition in 1555, he may have induced Catherine to adopt later as her personal emblem the symbol of a serpent arching in a circle, clasping its own tail. An occultist would recognize in this symbol a secret yet perilous will to power. The wise serpent holds its tail in its clenched teeth, but if balance is lost, the serpent devours itself. By choosing such an emblem, Catherine showed her keen awareness of the dangers risked if she dare invoke dark occult powers to aid her monarch, country, and her children. One false move and all could be devoured by the serpent power evoked.

The seven children mentioned in line two were her own: François, Elizabeth, Claude, Charles, Eduard-Alexandre (Henry), Marguerite, and Hercules. The final two lines threaten extinction of the Valois bloodline. These feverish words of melancholic fury would not see the book slammed shut, or a call for Nostradamus' arrest, but would pull Catherine's attention deeper, inured as she was by a life filled with Saturnian disappointments, restrictions, and delays. As she read further, a desire was born for a discreet interview with Nostradamus – if they could speak in private, perhaps he could put aside feigned words and speak directly about the dangers set before her children and their bloodline. Perhaps she could compel him to come to court and join her circle of soothsayers.

She would read on and soon come across Quatrain 35, Century 1. Perhaps her own initial and unguarded reactions later gave rise to gossip whispered through the court that a fellow named Nostradamus dared publish a prophecy of mortal danger for the king:

Le lyon ieune le vieux surmontera,
En champ bellique par singulier duelle:
Dans caige d'or les yeux luy creuera:
Deux classes une, puis mourir, mort cruelle.

The young lion, he will surmount the old one,
On the field of combat in single battle told:
He will pierce his eyes through a cage all golden:
Two wounds become one, then dying in cruel death's cold.[3]

The queen, like many of her courtiers, believed the older lion mentioned was the king. Henry had a passion for ritual combat, and he usually thundered down the lists leaning on his steed with lowered lance behind a shield displaying a lion. Even though Nostradamus beclouds specifics in the cryptic riddles of lines three and four, a hint of malevolent destiny came through clear. If the older lion was Henry, he faced a cruel death from a double wound of some kind, delivered by a younger combatant, either through war or, nearly as dangerous, a clash of weapons in ritual combat.

Surviving correspondences dated from the following year clearly indicate that Nostradamus' quatrain rekindled Catherine's interest in a similar prediction delivered years earlier by one of her occult counselors back in Florence, the celebrated astrologer and mathematician Luc Gauricus, the Bishop of Civitate. Before Henry's accession to the throne in 1547, Catherine had ordered Gauricus to draw up their horoscopes. Because the future king and queen were born a mere 10 days apart, Gauricus wrote that they had similar malefic aspects of Mars and Saturn which made them prone to illness affecting the head or violent death from a head wound. If two two-headed omens could inspire Nostradamus with the temerity to publish his prophecies, two similar portents from two seers of Florence and Provence resolved Catherine to bring this issue before Henry even though he was loath to indulge her infatuation with the occult.

Before the Court and Public Opinion

It is not known when Nostradamus was introduced to Claude of Savoy, Comte de Tende, the Governor and Grand Seneschal of Provence – whether it was before or after his presentation of the infant two-headed freak of nature – but Nostradamus could count the governor as the first of many influential friends at court. It is likely the governor's courier paid him a visit in early July 1555, at which time Nostradamus must have risen happily from his labors over cosmetics to make him welcome, and to eagerly ask what tidings he had brought from the governor. Clairvoyant as he seemed to be, Nostradamus could not have expected what happened next. The courier presented him with a royal summons to appear before the King of France. The Comte de Tende had sent this courier from Aix to see that all necessary arrangements be made for Nostradamus to make ready to leave for Paris as soon as possible. So urgently was his attendance required at court that the governor of Provence had been instructed by the queen herself to provide M. Michel Nostradamus with the finest horses of the royal post to hasten his journey; she was arranging for him to reduce the time of his journey to Paris by half – from two months to one. It seems that Catherine had shown Nostradamus' quatrain to Henry II. Henry's first impressions are unknown, but it is safe to say that he remained skeptical, yet intrigued enough by the serendipitous parallel forecasts of two noted astrologers from distant quarters that he humored Catherine's desire to have this Dr. Nostradamus summoned from Salon to explain himself.

Most biographies of Nostradamus' Paris adventures rely on the guarded and gushing accounts of César de Nostredame and Chavigny. Both men place the date of Nostradamus' departure from Salon the following year, on 14 July 1556. A closer examination of public records and correspondence make that time frame impossible. Nostradamus signed a document before a lawyer named Laurent, releasing 200 crowns for Craponne's canal project, on 27 July 1556 – that is around the time one might expect he was on the road, half way to Paris. A surviving letter written in 1556 by occult scholar Gabriel Simeoni, an intellectual acquaintance Nostradamus perhaps made during his visit to Florence before the former became a member of Queen Catherine's occult team at the French court, states his hope that Nostradamus' visit to Paris in "the previous year" had brought him success. Lemesurier makes a good educated guess that no copy of the "1556" Almanac survives because Nostradamus had never written it. If he had been in Paris in the summer of 1555, he would have forfeited the usual time in which he composed his almanacs for the coming year. Hence, a proper revision of his life story would have our doctor leaving Salon with pensive relations and some public fanfare on 14 July 1555. This would precipitate the demise of another popular myth. It was not the momentum of public interest in his work that eventually brought him to the attention of Catherine de' Medici and the court the following summer. Indeed, the spread of his fame and reputation might have come to the rest of France starting from the top down instead. The queen was one of the first people to read *Les Propheties* and spread the news around court; a few months later, the tome would arrive at bookstalls across the kingdom in the first sizable numbers.

New evidence does not color Nostradamus' mood very brightly after receiving his summons to Paris. We might consider with a little irony that our 51-year-old wayfarer, lurching with difficulty back into the saddle after too many pleasurably sedentary years, marked the onset of his first harrowing relay from post to royal post on 14 July – the date on which future Frenchmen would celebrate "Bastille Day," the overthrow of the Bastille keep and dungeons that ignited the French Revolution in 1789. When Nostradamus rode through Lyon on 27 July, he expressed a pre-monition of foreboding to an associate that one might expect from a condemned man on his way to the Bastille prison. Nostradamus confessed a fear that his trip to Paris would end with ill treatment, imprisonment, and the chopping block before 25 August.

Paris at last stretched out before the weary and anxious rider on 15 August 1555. The date of Nostradamus' arrival happened to coincide with the Assumption Day of the Blessed Virgin Mary. Either by intent or chance good omen, Nostradamus reached the southwestern approaches of Europe's second-largest metropolis (of 160,000 souls)[4] on the feast day of his sacred namesake *Notre Dame*. Following the lead of other self-fulfilling omens he lodged himself in the Inn of Saint-Michel near Notre Dame Cathedral.

César wrote that his father was worn out by the journey and had taken little money with him. Somewhere between the time of say-ing a prayer of thanksgiving at Notre Dame Cathedral for his safe arrival and dragging himself through a labyrinth of congested streets back to the inn, he had made the acquaintance of a trusting stranger, Jean Morel, who lent him two rose nobles and twelve crowns.

It can be imagined that Nostradamus turned in early, seeking a goose down, pillowed passage to temporary oblivion. A rest would nourish the façade of calm that he would require to hide his nerves during the forthcoming royal audience at court. He must have his wits about him if he were successfully to touch, parry, and explain his prophecies face to face with those people who had the means to alter the future history of France that he dared foretell, for bet-ter or for worse. As night came on, and Nostradamus let sink his mind into sleep's cessation of thought, occult Paris awoke.

The capital numbered her magicians and necromancers in the thousands.[5] They had a patron in Queen Catherine de' Medici. Decades later, when a young Sir Francis Bacon returned to Elizabethan England from the French court, he remarked that the Queen of France was quite "superstitious" and "was given to curious arts."[6] Perhaps one of her frequent nocturnal occult reveries was in session in her apartments at St.-Germain-en-Laye, just outside of Paris, on that very same night as Nostradamus slept. Indeed, there is a good chance that Nostradamus was the subject of that evening's explorations into hidden realms. The evidence is clear from incidents in her long and controversial life that Catherine was not only true to her family bloodline's passion for second-guessing "La Fortuna" through black and white arts, but that she herself possessed the gift of second sight – if not always the reasonable mind to interpret the signs properly. She would pass along her "insights" (uncovered with the aid of magic mirrors) or conjuration about Nostradamus to her assembly of sorcerers and astrologers, chief among whom were the notorious Florentine necromancer Cosimo Ruggieri and the celestial scientist Gabriel Simeoni. A whispered feminine opinion might also come from one or two sycophants – particularly the chosen young princesses ever in attendance as her magical assistants. Sitting in her large oak chair, pale eyes wide, face brooding, whenever her paranormal attentions were trained on the subject of Nostradamus, her team of soothsayers fed her eager and impatient anticipation of their meeting with favorable omens (either because conjurors and astrologers such as Ruggieri and Simeoni actually saw good fortune, or because they understood the need to offer a politically and occultly "correct" portent to satisfy their intensely obsessed monarch).

⚮

Early the next morning none other than Anne de Montmorency, the Grand Constable of France, summoned the exhausted

Nostradamus from his hotel room. Such was the queen's urgent desire to see the prophet that she had summoned the Commander-in-Chief of all French forces to escort Nostradamus for a prompt royal audience outside of Paris at St. Germain-en-Laye.

The entire French court awaited his arrival. The Constable and his charge dismounted and made a path to the royal apartments through a gathering crowd of immaculately dressed and bejeweled nobles and ladies, pressing close over a forest of lace and plumes for a peek at the little scholar in his plain four-cornered cap – the "prophet," the "humbug" from the Midi. It is safe to assume that Nostradamus was assailed from all sides by questions (as well as the aroma of perfume). He accepted their queries and jokes in polite silence. It was three months since printers began lifting copies of *Les Propheties* off their presses, and by now the prophecies had been devoured and discussed by many in court; and certainly many others who had not read his book nevertheless offered their unqualified opinions for and against the prophet. *Les Prophecies of M. Nostradamus* was all the rage among the upper classes and nobility thanks to a readership Nostradamus had already cultivated from the success of his almanacs. The peasants and the unlettered gave vent to their seemingly inbred suspicion of him as a conjuror of the devil. The response from the French Renaissance intelligentsia was mixed. Great thinkers either praised or cursed the Preface's occult rambling narrative followed by 353 queerly rhymed and metered poems, and even his supporters in Dorat's brigade of poetic stars, such as Ronsard, could not well defend him against detractors, such as Jodelle, who could not abide Nostradamus' crabbed and wild verses. Leoni cites a passage in LaCroix du Maine's *Bibliothèque* of 1594 in which he summarizes the rewards and perils of publishing popular bestsellers: "He wrote an infinite number of Almanacs and Prognostications, which were very well received and sold so well that several imitations of them were made … under his name (which were composed by ignorant people and were consequently full of lies …)."

History does not leave a record of those who were in the throng of France's highest nobility as he followed in the wake of the Constable (with the oddly effeminate first name, Anne) making a path to the royal reception room. At least some of them, even as they murmured their initial impressions of Nostradamus to individuals in the crowd, might have already had their destinies published, albeit obscurely masked, in the first serialization of his book. The fates of members of the greater noble (and Protestant) house of Bourbon-Navarre, and the lesser noble (and Catholic) House of Guise, the Montmorencys, as well as other power brokers – such as Gaspard de Coligny, Prince d'Andelot and many others – were hiding in the pages they read and scarce understood. Some sympathetic biographers would say that their coded names and inferred plots and counterplots – yet to be dreamed and undertaken – to seize influence over the weak Valois heirs had already found their history forewarned in these cryptic verses.

Nothing but a most dry and matter-of-fact account by César begins to address a biographer's interest in knowing intimate details of what transpired or was discussed at Nostradamus' royal audience. We know that Henry excused himself early, and that Nostradamus and Catherine, once alone, spoke without break for two hours. When Nostradamus left the audience, he was not ushered away to the dungeons by dark-humored guards. Instead, a bank of pages in festive Royal livery politely directed him to fine guest apartments at the neighboring palace of the Archbishop of Sens in St.-Germain-en-Laye.

Beyond these dry facts, there are a number of themes for discussion that we can assume transpired between a reverent (yet secretly nervous) royal subject, a moderately interested (yet intellectually lightweight) king, and a queen suppressing her excitement sufficiently to sustain the proper regal airs. It was said that Catherine de' Medici had the ability to adapt herself to whoever she met and place herself on their level at once. By putting Nostradamus at ease, she could begin the process of unmasking the secrets this inscrutable yet kindly eyed and deferential Provençal held about her husband and her children's future. Beside her, Henry was a model in studied French boredom. If Nostradamus had written a book about tennis, or a treatise on jousting and hunting – now that would have conjured more than a passing interest.

The monarch was essentially a handsome and virile man of easy charm and magnificent athleticism, a natural warrior; and yet he turned out to be a weak and ineffectual ruler, relegating most of his responsibilities to a cabinet beset by powerful egos from lesser noble families vying to influence and dominate the throne. Cabinet feuds further complicated and confused royal policy when advisors gave their ruler counsel that was ever more poisoned and motivated by the intense religious differences among them. Catherine already fathomed that her lord and his realm were just a single blow to her husband's head away from catastrophe. Years ago, she had sought horoscopes for herself and Henry from Gauricus back in Florence, after the sudden and unexpected death of the heir apparent had suddenly catapulted her husband, the Duc d'Orleans, out of a genial yet aimless and carefree life to the French throne. She knew that the unsteady suppression of ambitious usurper princes in her husband's cabinet could erupt with the unexpected and fatal blow to his head that Gauricus forewarned, unless some new details augured from the future could reveal a way to forestall that destiny. Then comes Nostradamus, a prophecy lurking in his new book paralleling Gauricus' warnings of a head injury with fresh clues. Look for a mortal head wound on a field of combat; perhaps in a future war, or maybe elsewhere; perhaps from an unexpected blow received during the king's favorite pursuit – ritual combat in tournament. Whatever way this danger might manifest, Catherine knew and dreaded what Henry was too cavalier to confront – just one blow to his head and their sickly adolescent son, the *Dauphin* François, might take the throne several long years before attaining his majority – an immature child at the mercy of a cabinet of political wolves.

Henry most likely excused himself as soon as Nostradamus had diplomatically explained quatrain 35 of Century 1 to his satisfaction. What could Nostradamus have said to please the king and send him happily off to the tennis courts or out riding in the royal hunting reserve? Nostradamus' future dedication of the final three centuries of *Les Propheties* reveals that he knew how to stroke Henry's vanity with the turgid, syrupy eloquence of his words. He was also aided by Henry's often-recorded sense of fair play with fate. Henry could serenely face any outcome of a test of arms, be it victory or death, as long as he carried himself into the fog and violence of war with honor and nobility; the rest would be for God to decide. The fulfillment of prophecies from astrologers such as Gauricus or Nostradamus was rendered unto God. Because God alone controlled his destiny, the king found it easy to shrug off the words of soothsayers.

Nostradamus' first serialization of his prophecies contains circumstantial evidence to piece together a more detailed explanation that would have belayed Henry's concerns, if he had any. Nostradamus may have told him that death in some military or ritual combat was but one of two destinies he predicted for Henry. The alternative destiny had him rise to greater glory as *Chyren Selin*, Nostradamus' anagram code name for Henry in the prophecies. He may not have needed to explain the anagram *Chyren Selin*, for it was well known that upon taking the crown Henry designed a monogram for the new royal livery that hung the crescent of his mistress, Diane de Poitiers, on the horizontal bar of his letter "H." Therefore, *Chyren* is an obvious anagram for "Henryc," the old French spelling for "Henry," and *Selin* – for *seline*, the Greek word for "moon" or "crescent" – stands for Poitiers. If Nostradamus, standing before the King of France on that most significant day of his life and prophetic career, was disposed to take this unique opportunity to influence the future course of events, he could have directed his lord to examine two of the planned eight quatrains referring to that alternative future.[7]

Firstly, Nostradamus could have recited Century 2, Quatrain 79:

La barbe crespe & noire par engin,
Subiuguera la gent cruelle & fiere:
Le grand CHYREN ostera du longin,
Tous les captifs par Seline baniere.[8]

The beard all curly and black – through ingenuity,
Will subjugate a people both cruel and proud in manner:
The great HENRY will take from distant locality,
All of those captives imprisoned by the crescent moon's banner.[9]

The prophecy promises Christendom's defeat of the Ottoman Turks in a great battle, and Henry II would lead that crusade, delivering Christian prisoners from their captivity under the Islamic banner. The inference of a multitude of liberated captives implies that these are thousands of galley slaves released after a great "naval" battle. Future Nostradamians would attribute this prophecy to the curly-black-bearded commander of the Christian armada at the battle of Lepanto in 1571, Don Juan of Austria – not Henry II of France. As it turned out, when Don Juan's galleys smashed those of the Ottoman fleet, he (and not Henry) earned the glory and achieved the honor of freeing 15,000 Christian galley slaves from captured Moslem ships.

Next, Nostradamus might have recited Century 4, Quatrain 34, promising the king that Italy would finally become a conquest of France (that is, if Henry II had no accidents and lived to see it):

Le grand mené captif d'estrange terre,
D'or enchainé au Roy CHYREN offert:
Qui dans Ausonne, Millan perdra la guerre,
Et tout son ost mis à feu & à fer.[10]

The great one led captive from a foreign land,
By gold-enchained offered to King HENRY's hand:
He who in Ausonia, Milan in war will not stand,
And all of his army put to the sword and firebrand.[II]

It seems Nostradamus consoled himself and Henry with a prophecy of French revenge for their defeat at Pavia in 1525, with a crushing defeat in the near future of Hapsburg and Spanish arms near Milan. Though at Pavia, Henry, his late brother François, and father, Francis I, would suffer capture, so too would the enemy lords, if not Emperor Charles V himself, and suffer the destruction of their army as well as capture. Perhaps even Charles V would be led back to Paris, where he would be led before Henry II in a victory parade, his hands chained with gold. The principalities of northern Italy and Ausonia (the Kingdom of Naples) would at last fall into mighty Chyren's hands. That is, if Henry chose the right destiny. In this case, prophecies forming in Nostradamus' theurgic vigils to come would find themselves in quatrain serializations, defining Henry as France's second Herculean Charlemagne. He would unify the breach between French Catholic and Huguenot and establish a new French Empire, which would finally wrest Italy from Charles V, repel the Islamic hordes by sea and bring widespread peace to Europe at last.

Once the flattered monarch had made his excuses and left, perhaps Catherine and Nostradamus warmed up to each other, discoursing on a wide range of topics leading at last to astrology and prophecy. It is safe to say, based on the following historical events, that Catherine was deeply impressed by Dr. Nostradamus; indeed, she might have been the royal who arranged to move his lodging to the magnificent palace of the Archbishop of Sens. Once ensconced in his luxurious surroundings, all the excitement and strain of the audience brought on illness. The following day a page presented the bedridden soothsayer with a velvet purse from the king and queen containing a financial reward to compensate for his long journey from the south of France. Once alone, he poured out the contents of the purse, and it can be surmised that he flared up into one of his short but powerful rages.

Years later in 1561, Nostradamus relates his own reaction to this paltry sum to Jean Morel in one of his few authenticated correspondences:

As a fine reward for having gone to court, I became sick, whereupon His Majesty and King sent me one hundred crowns. The Queen sent me thirty. There you have a fine sum for having come two hundred leagues: having spent a hundred crowns, I made thirty crowns out of it.[12]

Astrological Diplomacy

Nostradamus soon rectified his financial woes with a steady flow of courtiers and nobles paying for astrological readings. However, the upset and workload, added to the strain of the long journey, and the heat-inducing wines and heavy northern French cooking, landed the aging 52-year-old in bed for 10 days with his first serious recorded attack of gout.[13]

This sets the stage for another Nostradamus legend. One night, while he lay in bed in the archbishop's palace, a page belonging to the eminent Beauveau family was searching the nearby streets for his lost charge, his Lord's prized hunting dog. In desperation, the boy sought the prophet's help at that late hour, knocking on his door with all the persistence of royalty. "What troubles you, king's page?!" exclaimed an angry voice behind the door. "You are making a lot of noise over a lost dog. Go along the road of Orléans. There you will find the dog led on a leash."

The boy rushed as fast as he could down the aforementioned road where he found the dog being led back to St.-Germain-en-Laye by a servant on a leash. After collecting his wits, the page was left wondering how Nostradamus knew he was a king's page as well as the whereabouts of the dog, from behind a bolted door.

The boy spread the story throughout the court in the following days, catapulting the prophet's reputation to mythic proportions.[14] When Nostradamus had sufficiently recovered from his illness, Catherine sent him (either by litter or carriage) down the picturesque Loire valley to the royal Château Blois to draw up the horoscopes for her seven children. The king's father and grandfather, Francis I and Louis XII, had poured a sizable portion of their royal coffers into the glorification of Blois, which was the seat of the royal court during their reigns. It contained the best innovations of Italian Renaissance architecture, including Italian loggias in the style of Bramante's Vatican and its famous octagonal staircase. There, within its fabulous interiors – or in the grand garden designed by Pacello da Mercoliano, with alleys wide and long enough to ride horses at a full gallop – Nostradamus was introduced to Catherine's seven children. He was in a delicate position, for his pen had already written prophecies foretelling a tragic fate for every child.[15]

In the following excerpt, James Laver surpasses all other interesting stretches of speculation as to what Nostradamus might have felt or suppressed when introduced to each child:

For, in the cloudy language of the Centuries, were not their fates already written? That boy of thirteen who shall one day be Francis II, who shall be married while still a child to that other unhappy child Mary Stuart, and who shall die miserably after one year of reign; that girl of eleven [Elizabeth], destined also to die young, the child-wife of gloomy old Philip of Spain; that girl of nine [Claude] who will die in her twenties as Duchess of Lorraine; that melancholy little boy of six [Charles] in whose staring eyes shall one day be reflected the fires of St. Bartholomew; that boy of five [Henry] who shall be twice a king, but in both kingdoms unhappy, and whose body will be pierced by the assassin's dagger; and that other boy of two, François, Duc d'Alençon, the perpetual *Malcontent*, titular sovereign of the Netherlands, suitor of Queen Elizabeth, laughing stock of Europe – what a nursery to prophesy for! The only child with any soundness and sweetness in the whole brood was the tempestuous Marguerite, then a girl of four, who was to be married to the enemy, Henry of Navarre, to be repudiated by him for her adulteries, to outlive them all and to go down to history as the raffish, ragtaggle but not unlovable Reine Margot.[16]

When Nostradamus settled down to work on the horoscopes of the royal heirs, he must have paused to ponder this situation. Could he have ever imagined that the first installment of his prophecies, published just a short few months before, would catapult him to the highest circles of power to give prescient council to the French monarchs, plot charts for high notables of the court – and now this! Finding the right words to soften the blow that his astrological conclusions must have struck at the heart of the very great lady, his queen, whom he much admired and perhaps secretly feared. She was not someone to take lightly, or to disturb with dreadful news, for he had already written and hid dreadful tales in his quatrains, and he must now stir the stars and awaken the dire monsters (the now-arcane word for "omens") of the last kings and princesses of the dying Valois bloodline – and contemplate this task while sitting in the inner sanctum of the Valois! Modern history can draw a parallel to only one other soothsayer whose counsel held sway on a queen and thereby influenced the future destiny of her kingdom – Grigory Rasputin (1871?–1916) the occult counsel to Alexandria, the last Czarina of all the Russias.[17]

As Nostradamus plotted the horoscopes for Catherine's children, he calculated the future in the same measure as he calculated the danger to himself as the messenger of ill omens. Perhaps he carefully considered shadows of their dark lives that colored his previous conjuring of other "shadows" of the future, haunting these very halls and private chambers of the Château Blois and down in the graveled courtyard below his windows. Did he already see the long shadows of conspirators hanging on pikes below his window? Did the floors above already creak in his reverie with the fleet foot of assassins, and groan with the heavy fall of bodies? Did the thick wooden beams stifle muffled cries from the midnight hours of a future night? Did Nostradamus gaze darkly beyond the astrological figures on parchment to mark the murders by that smiling five-year-old when he grew into manhood, the Duc d'Anjou, who became Henry III, a physical and moral degenerate – the last Valois King? Did he already see the child in the garden slaughter one of his princeling playmates, the Duc de Guise, 33 years hence, and thereby drag France into a three-way civil war between the Catholic armies of the king, those of the Catholic League (made leaderless by the murder of Guise), and the Huguenot armies of Henry of Navarre? Some believe Nostradamus had already written details of the murder of Guise in Quatrain 1 of Century 85, the year before. Now in his apartment at Blois, did he hear the sounds of a stormy night in far-off December 1588, when Henry III's *Mignons* – a dozen of his best male friends, male sexual partners, and bodyguards – pounced on Henry de Guise with swords bared – his cries of "my friends!" drowned out by the steady drumbeat of a downpour? Would Nostradamus know that in a bedroom immediately below the murder scene, Catherine de' Medici would lie, 70 years old, spent and ailing from a severe head cold, sleeping through the tumult upstairs? The morning after the murder, her son the king, all flushed with the exhilaration of revenge, came to her bedside and triumphantly declared he had killed his rival. The news broke her will to live and soon afterwards her head cold developed into a fatal case of pneumonia. Catherine knew then that Henry III was doomed, and with him would come the end of the Valois line, just as Nostradamus had predicted so long ago when she first opened his book of prophecies.

We know nothing of the details of his written report to Catherine, for it no longer survives, except that whatever he finally wrote down, his report must have been a work of the finest astrological diplomacy. We know she was at least satisfied with his astrological finding assuring her that all her sons would become kings. Actually, as it turned out, the irritating buffoon Duc de Alençon reached for, but never gained, the British crown as consort to Elizabeth Tudor of England before he caught a cold and died in 1584. Perhaps Nostradamus had made an educated guess of four crowns for four boys, not yet divining, as some believe, that the little Duc d'Anjou would be crowned twice – a king of Poland and later France.

If Sir Thomas Bacon was speaking about Nostradamus as the unnamed astrologer in the following passage, then perhaps Catherine might have intrigued something more out of him than horoscopes for her children at Blois:

When I was in France, I heard from one Doctor Pena, that the Queen Mother [Catherine] … caused her husband's nativity to be calculated, under a false name; and the astrologer gave a judgment, that he would be killed in a duel; at which the Queen laughed, thinking her husband to be above challenges and duels …[18]

A mysterious visitor awaited Nostradamus on his return to Paris. He described her in a letter to Jean Morel[19] dated several years later, in 1561:

After I returned to Paris from Saint-Germain[-en-Laye],[20] a very striking, great lady – whose identity I do not know, but who [I reckoned] by her appearance seemed to be a very honest and honorable lady – came to see me the night I returned and spoke to me for some time – I could not [reveal publicly about] what – and took leave quite late.

The next morning she came to see me again. After her Ladyship had conversed with me about her affairs with more intimacy than before, she finally told me that the Gentlemen from the Justice of Paris intended to find me in order to interrogate me about the science of which I made use and how I predicted what I did. I told her by way of reply that they need not take the trouble to come on such a mission, that I would save them the trouble and that I had planned to leave the next morning for return to Provence, which indeed I did.[21]

There may have been another motivation for Nostradamus making a rapid exit from Paris. Some Nostradamians, including Arthur Prieditis, speculate that Henry (coached by the queen) offered Nostradamus a post as a court astrologer.[22] Lemesurier makes a good educated guess that Nostradamus left before Catherine could deliver a hard-to-reject royal invitation to add himself to her "permanent menagerie of leading magicians and astrologers."[23] Rather than become her occult master in the queen disciple's gilded cage, he found life more appealing, and likely longer-lived, in the sunny (and relatively safe) backwater of Provence, far removed from the intrigues at court.

Sometime that autumn, after Nostradamus had returned safely to honors and a life of celebrity at home, Catherine received Henry's permission to send Luc Gauricus a letter asking him to re-examine the king's horoscope. In a reply dated 5 February 1556, Gauricus told Henry "to avoid all single combat in an enclosed place, especially near his 41st year [1559], for in that period of his life he was menaced by a wound in the head which might rapidly result in blindness or even in death."

Henry remained serenely noncommittal about dire fortune awaiting him with lances and lists. He told the captain of his Scottish Guards, Gabriel de Lorge, Comte de Montgomery: "I care not if my death be in that manner more than in any other. I would even prefer it, to die by the hand of whoever he might be, so long as he was brave and valiant and that I kept my honor."[24]

CHAPTER EIGHT

Notorious Success

ᕲ

A Military Disaster Presaged?

Nostradamus returned to Salon sometime in the autumn of 1555. When presenting himself to the glad arms of his wife, his head was still firmly affixed to his shoulders and not the ripe and fallen fruit of a headsman's axe on a Parisian street as he had feared. It is not known to what extent that graying head had swollen with royal importance, but we do know that mingling with the royals brought to Nostradamus a spike in his local celebrity – not an entirely welcome event – but he certainly appreciated the increase in business that attention to his prophetic works brought to his door in those economically strapped times. The curb next to his house off the Place de la Poissonnerie was ever more congested with idle litter bearers and the coaches of highborn families from across France on a quest for expensive cosmetics and astrological advice. Archival records and published works for the next two years indicate he was not disposed to rest on his new-found fame; rather, he withdrew further from public attention, as if celebrity had laid siege to his time and energies. Nostradamus returned from court eager to plunge fully and methodically into his literary projects – chief among these the urgent need to finish conjuring and then write down the visions for the remaining 647 quatrains of the planned 1,000 needed to complete *Les Propheties*.

Although he recognized the power of abstinence to draw down the power to prophesy, nevertheless Anne Ponsarde soon became pregnant with their third child, Charles, born in 1556. It seems her husband's overabundance of creative energy would also hasten the birth of André and Anne in quick succession: André was born on 17 November 1557, Anne the following year. By the end of 1556, he had also brought a completed Century 4 and Century 5 into the world, and composed 99 quatrains for Century 6 and at least the first 40 quatrains for Century 7. All of these found their way to the printing presses as early as December 1556.[1]

Even with these activities, Nostradamus still had time to produce an almanac "for the year 1557" which was ready for imprint by Kerver, Paris, and a 69-page booklet called *Paraphrase de C. Galen*, finished by 17 February 1557 and scheduled for publication later that year by du Rosne, Lyon.[2] The booklet was a loose translation of a paraphrase on the medical philosophies of Galen by Menodotus, the 2nd-century Alexandrian Empiricist. Lemesurier, in his fine critique of the work,[3] suggests that this queer little booklet might be one of Nostradamus' first attempts at writing. Maybe the manuscript had been tucked away in one of his saddlebags for years on the road until 1557, when he quickly recopied and submitted it for publication. Lemesurier puzzles why Nostradamus would dig up old material in defense of Galen so late in life, especially when his intellectual passions dwelled elsewhere. By 1557, Galen's ancient dogmas had been put into serious doubt. Nevertheless, Nostradamus might have used Menodotus and Galen as an excuse to interject his own philosophies about medicine and thereby make this booklet a kind of final testament to a career in medicine now ending. Essentially, Nostradamus said in this booklet that human beings are given a superior artifice and consciousness that transcend the brutish behavior of animals;

and that we are thus obligated to use our transcendent gift of reason, expressed by human art and science, to heal and improve the world. The vehicle in which Nostradamus delivers this final testimony on medicine is a substandard translation of the Menodotus paraphrase – endorsed, he declares, by scholars – despite, it seems, his liberal interjection of spontaneous editorial comments.

The year 1557 may mark the birth of a whimsical legend of Nostradamus' prescient powers. We are told that one languorous summer afternoon found him sitting in the shade in front of his house enjoying the first cool breeze after a hot day. The neighbor's blossoming young daughter was passing by on her way outside the city gates to gather firewood for supper. "Good day, Monsieur de Nostredame," she said with a curtsey. "Good day, little girl," he nodded. More than an hour had passed before he saw her balancing wood on her shoulder. "Good day, Monsieur de Nostredame," she said. "Good day … little *woman*."

The story over time has gone through as many factual permutations as Nostradamus translating Menodotus. Various versions had the incident taking place either in 1557 or just a few years before his death in 1566. One version has him watching the maiden go to the woods; another has him notice her meeting friends at a place well-known in the town for secret liaisons between young men and women – and so on. Regardless of the scenario, Nostradamus' change in salutation from virgin "girl" to deflowered "woman" could be construed as merely a wily educated guess.

Around the time Salonnais citizens began projecting Nostradamus upon this story of "maiden scrying" (and not ancient Hippocrates to whom the tale is usually attributed), they were indeed seeing something far more ominous in the surrounding countryside. Henry II had denuded his frontier garrisons, amassing most of France's legions under the command of François de Guise for one last push to dominate Northern Italy. Thousands of soldiers wound their way east across Provence in great columns with banners waving following a drumbeat into the Po Valley seeking to pit blade and shot with Hapsburg imperials. It is doubtful that the king back in Paris or his generals on the march, burdened and exhilarated with thoughts of maneuver and counter-maneuver, had the time or inclination to read prophecies written in 1554 and published a little over two years before this Italian campaign. Hindsight might have guided the surviving soldier's hand over its pages to search again for the name of the military disaster which ensued when the armies of France encountered little resistance in Italy because their enemy was elsewhere, descending on the fortress town of St.-Quentin that Nostradamus had named two years before.

Hindsight is the ugly flipside of a prophecy's intention, if its seer augurs a warning to be heeded rather than ignored. Then follows repentance – the regret that elevates a prophet's stature at the cost of his failure to change dire actions that hasten dark times. After the smoke of battle and a town in flames had dispersed in the glare of August sunshine, thousands of readers across France gave way to hindsight, referring to the page in Nostradamus' book that warned France too late about the battle of St.-Quentin.

A string of fortress cities stretched in a line across Flanders and Picardy. Key to this defense line was St.-Quentin on the Somme river. Once seized, the door to Paris would be flung wide open, and the very heart of the French kingdom there for the taking. It is at St.-Quentin that the main force of the Hapsburg armies appeared in rank upon rank of crack Spanish infantry, English pike men and archers, and legions of Savoyard cavalry and infantry under Philip II of Spain, the successor to Charles V. At the onset of August 1557, Philip, with the assistance of the brilliant general Emmanuel-Philibert, Duke of Savoy, suddenly bore down on St.-Quentin from Belgium with an army of 64,000 men. The bulwarks of St.-Quentin could have held the Hapsburg tide if the garrison numbered its usual quota of 8,000 men. Unfortunately, the French king had stripped his frontiers of soldiers, reducing the garrison to only a few hundred men so that Guise, his finest commander, could march through Italy on a fool's errand. On hearing news of the surprise invasion, French Admiral Gaspard de Coligny put together whatever mercenaries and soldiers he could muster and rushed north from Paris to reinforce the garrison with a meager 3,200 men and a handful of artillery pieces.

Soon after Coligny arrived, the Hapsburg horde invested St.-Quentin and a siege began. The marshlands of the Somme narrowed the Spanish infantry's line of attack against the city walls, allowing Coligny to put up a heroically mismatched defense. Back in Paris, Henry II and his Grand Constable, Anne de Montmorency, frantically gathered a makeshift relief force of 20,000 – most of the infantry being second-rate, low-paid, disgruntled German mercenaries. On 10 August, Coligny and his beleaguered garrison peered over the half-broken parapets scoured by days of Hapsburg shot and shell to spot the gathering shadow of Montmorency's relief army moving up from Paris. The Duke of Savoy's brilliant flanking maneuver, aided by Montmorency's blundering advance, saw two-thirds of his force either killed or captured, with Montmorency among the prisoners. Only Coligny's brother, the intrepid François d'Andelot, managed to bring a few hundred survivors of the relief force over the marshes to aid the besieged city. The brothers held St.-Quentin for another 17 days. On 27 August, a furious Spanish sortie poured through seven breaches in the city walls. The French garrison fought hand-to-hand in the flaming streets of the heavily shelled town. Coligny was captured, but his brother swam back through the marshes of the Somme to safety.

The fall of St.-Quentin was a national catastrophe. Rumors spread across France of an imminent march of Spanish forces on Paris, and it was even whispered that the kingdom would cease to be and the king would lose his throne. The general perception of imminent doom was not dispelled by the appearance of Guise directing the main French army in rapid forced marches out of Italy to save Paris and the king. Nevertheless, Paris and the Valois king were spared. Some would later say that God, rather than

Philip II's military ineptitude, made him hold back the exasperated Duke of Savoy long enough for Guise to bring up his forces to block the road to Paris.

The hunt for scapegoats and prophetic antidotes began after the immediate danger had passed. For a time, the Grand Constable was dishonored for his blundering into Savoy's ambushes. Even the king was made to account for his own oversights, and it is said that news of the military debacle at St.-Quentin had a maturing effect on him. Nostradamus and his prophecies rose in stature as others fell, thanks to two quatrains that many in court and around France believed had foretold and detailed the military disaster two years before it happened.

The first prophecy discussed and argued over was Century 1, Quatrain 19, which reads:

> Lors que serpens viendront circuir l'are,
> Le sang Troien vexé par les Hespaignes:
> Par eux grand nombre en sera faicte tare:
> Chef fruyct, caché aux mares dans les saignes.[4]

> When serpents will come to encircle the altar,
> The Trojan blood is vexed by the Spanish:
> By them a great number will be made to suffer.
> Chief flees, in marsh within marsh to vanish.[5]

Those trying to pin this poem on St.-Quentin might argue that in the summer of 1557 France was the metaphorical sacred "altar" surrounded by the armies of Spain, England, and the Hapsburgs on five fronts. Sang Troien (Trojan blood) stands for the French. Jodelle, Nostradamus, Ronsard, and other French poets of the day enjoyed promoting the popular classical myth that their kings were descendants of Trojan royalty. Thus their king would see his blood curdle in anguish at being caught by a surprise attack along his northern front by the vaunted "Spanish" pike men and conquistadors who made a bloody ruin out of the French relief army. As the details of the disaster became better known at court, many began to see Andelot as the fleeing "chief" of Nostradamus' "marsh within marsh" riddle. Andelot came to St.-Quentin's garrison through the marshes with the survivors of his relief force, and he later vanished "within [the] marsh" to make his successful escape when the city fell.

Those who searched for a direct mention of St.-Quentin in the little volume of prophecies would find it under Century 4, Quatrain 8. Indeed the following words, printed two years before the battle, might appear as a presage of the slaughter and fall of the garrison city:

> La grand cité d'assaut prompt & repentin
> Surprins de nuict, gardes interrompus:
> Les excubies & vielle sainct Quintin,
> Trucidés gardes & les pourtrails rompus.[6]

> The great city by assault prompt and sudden,
> Breaking in upon them at night – guards surprised:
> The watchmen and guardians of Saint Quentin,
> Slaughtered sentries and the front gates compromised.[7]

If this prophecy is the work of a fortunate coincidence then it is quite remarkable in accidental detail. St.-Quentin is named; the final overwhelming attack of the Spanish on 27 August was indeed "prompt and sudden," taking Coligny's exhausted company by surprise with its speed and ferocity. The front gates were opened after other parts of the wall were compromised. For two days, the Spanish commanders let their troops run riot over the town, pillaging and cutting the throats of any French troops deemed too lowly born to earn a decent ransom.

No doubt prophecies such as these inspired the era's best French poet, Pierre de Ronsard, to write the following verses and hear a draft of them read at court by those who would make a cautious defense for Nostradamus. A literal translation of Ronsard's rhyme would read:

Thou mockests also the prophets that God chooses amongst thy
    children, and places in the midst of thy bosom, in order to
    predict to thee thy future misfortune.
But thou dost but laugh at them.
Perhaps it is the immense eternity of the great God that has
    aroused the fervor of Nostradamus.
Or perhaps a good or bad demon kindles it.
Or perhaps his spirit is moved by nature, and climbs to the
    heavens, beyond mortals, and from there repeats to us
    prodigious facts.
Or perhaps his somber and melancholy spirit is filled with crass
    humors, making him fanciful.
In brief, he is what he is; so it is that always with the doubtful
    words of his prophetic voice, like that of an ancient oracle,
    he has for many a year predicted the greater part of our
    destiny. I would not have believed him, had not Heaven
    which assigns good and evil to mankind, been his inspiration.

"Monsterdamus"

It could be said that, when confronted with a concept such as prophecy, a concept that cannot be rationalized, tamed, or categorized to satisfy our ideals, we tend to contract emotionally and intellectually. Perhaps our will to power cannot tolerate the neutrality of our ignorance; our minds need to cloak the nakedness of a void with an opinion. More often than not, that opinion is negative, even fearful. Fans of Nostradamus who are sympathetic to the idea that he foretold the future must eventually collide with those individuals predisposed to disbelieve. A dispute ensues – one that has continued, often raucously, for more than 450 years. One

side, it seems, cannot exist without the other. The argument officially found itself in print after St.-Quentin. Believers and
debunkers of Nostradamus began feeding off each other – needing
each other. Pierre de Ronsard started the debate rolling with his
poem. He was not completely forgiving of Nostradamus' nebulous
and seemingly shady prophetic delivery, yet he felt compelled to
defend him in print against idle and offhand dismissal – especially
when the brush-off came from fellow members of the poetic intelligentsia, the clique of court poet laureates known as the *Pléiade*.

Ronsard's defense of Nostradamus suffered when a new edition
of *Les Propheties* appeared throughout France at the close of 1557,
published by du Rosne of Lyon. Nostradamus had intended that
his next edition would include the completed 1,000 quatrains;
however, the apparent success of his St.-Quentin prophecies put
pressure on him and his new publisher to rush through publication a new and still incomplete volume. This included the original
Preface to César, Centuries 1–3, with the addition of complete
Centuries 4, 5, 6, and the first 40 quatrains of Century 7. Scholars
presume that Nostradamus sent the complete Century 7 to du
Rosne. It seems that 60 quatrains were left out in the final printing because if published they would draw too deeply into the
paper stock and the planned profit margins of the publisher. The
final product was also rife with editorial and typographical errors,
and the general mediocrity of the printing quality only hastened
to undermine Nostradamus' fragile credibility.

Jodelle[8] was the first among the *Pléiade* to counter-attack
Ronsard's poem with the now-famous Latin distich:

Nostra damus cum falsa damus, nam fallere nostrum est;
Et cum falsa damus, nil nisi nostra damus.

The Latin pun-ishment is mostly lost in the translation, which in
bland English fare reads:

We give that which is our own when we give false things;
    for it is in our nature to deceive;
And when we give false things, we give but our own things.

A free translation that attempts to return the spirit of Jodelle's
Nostradamus punt could read:

Nostradamus comes false – Ah, damn us!
When he "noses up" to damn us with his deceptions;
For it is our nature-damn-us to note-a-damn falsehood!

Chavigny may have entered the fray issuing the following poetic
retort:

Vera damus cum verba damus quae Nostradamus dat;
Sed cum nostra damus, nil nisi falsa damus.

[Loosely translated:]

It is truth we give with words that Nostradamus begat:
For it is useless words given otherwise that falsify this fact.

A new rendition of the above may have come from Nostradamus
himself:

Nostra damus cum verba damus quae Nostradamus dat:
Nam quaecumque dedit nil nisi vera dat.

[Loosely translated:]

We give with our words that which Nostradamus said
For, no better rendered is the truth in whatever way he said.

Printed attacks on Nostradamus were particularly harsh from the Protestants at court and abroad. The Calvinist Théodore de Bèze, in Geneva, apparently hid himself behind the fictional university rector Jan de la Daguenière (or Jan "of the Dagger-makers"), author of *Monstre d'Abus ... in Nostradamum*. His "Monster of Abuse" begins with a belittling stab at Nostradamus' occult poetic style, cutting down anyone who professes magical powers but who cannot properly splice two sentences together in his own mother tongue. Barbe Regnault printed the pamphlet – the same Parisian publishing house that printed editions of Nostradamus' writings. Next came *La Première invective du Seigneur Hercules le François contre Monstradamus*.[9] This nasty pamphlet's author hid under the pseudonym "Sir Hercules of the French." He made a wicked pun out of the name of his victim, blending *Monstra* (the Latin-to-French word for "significant omen," "portent," or "monster") with the Latin *monstro* (to show, point out, teach). His derogatory name *Monsradamus* became a popular rallying call thrown at Nostradamus by a growing number of detractors.

Essentially the pamphlet characterizes Nostradamus as a "24-carat liar" hiding his deceptions and mockery of God's providence with contrary, doom-laden verses of calculated obscurity that he brazenly chose to change in new editions of his prophecies and almanacs when they failed to foretell the future. (In the case of the quatrains in new editions of *Les Propheties*, this accusation is patently false. The content of the quatrains was never altered; only minor typographic and editorial errors were changed in later editions. Perhaps the author of this "prime invective" against Nostradamus relied on a fraudulent edition – and there were many out there.) The pamphlet demands the extermination of Nostradamus unless he returned to the path of truth and salvation, calling him among other things a slippery sorcerer, mountebank, and purveyor of darkness. Certainly, this "Sir Hercules" harbors an expectation not unlike that of most Nostradamus cynics, past and present, that the future should be rigid – that a true prophet must make clear and detailed predictions that must come true 100 percent of the time. Christians and Jews who were suspicious of Nostradamus, yet were believers in Old and New Testament biblical prophets, would demand that the prophecies follow the supreme litmus test of full accuracy defined in Deuteronomy, where Moses proclaimed that Jewish prophets could never be wrong about the future if they were true. Of course, we can only take the word of Moses, Jeremiah, Isaiah, and Zechariah (or their biblical interpreters) that they never got their predictions wrong, since no corroborating evidence from a non-Jewish contemporary source survives to back or refute their claims.

Nostradamus had already admitted why he felt it necessary to cloud his vision. He accepted the consequences and accurately predicted how that would undermine his credibility. However, beyond this, his confessions in print indicate his belief in a future that cannot exist entirely fixed and rigid. The future is dynamic, alive; it is fluid. He said, among other things, that his ability to forecast accurately depended on the way future events "inclined." That means he saw the river of destiny ever changing its flow because of actions taken in the present, in which case Nostradamus is implying that there is much gray area in our destiny. That is not an observation that simplistic minds seeking black-and-white absolutes like to hear. Nor can cynical and suspicious minds believe there is any other use for a cryptic literary device than to hedge one's prescient bets while deceiving gullible people.

Debunkers and believers alike have fallen into the misty dale of Nostradamus' enigmatic poems, tripping over their own interpretations. Every generation, from those obsessed and overwhelmed with the national tragedy of St.-Quentin in 1557 to those in America obsessed and overwhelmed with the national tragedy of 11 September 2001, will seek and find clues and details in his prophecies about portentous events of their particular century. Those who only look into Nostradamus to dismiss him will always be able to refute such findings. It takes no power of clairvoyance to predict that expectations past, present, and future will remain the same. Nostradamus' writing style will never completely satisfy either camp. Just when his esoteric prattle goads the skeptic to dismiss and condemn him as a charlatan, up comes an open mention of St.-Quentin, and what appears to be intimate details of a battle fought there. The believers cry "triumph!" – the debunkers cry "coincidence!" – and none are objectively the wiser. In the end, all frustration and blame is heaped upon Nostradamus. He is suddenly a sincere yet delusional figure, and one's own delusions are never noticed.

Whatever his motivations, Nostradamus was pushing the envelope of the prognostication genre, and he was bound to run headlong into controversy. Innovation is an eccentric phenomenon. Innovation is another word for mutation from the norm. The unknown and the new always bring an all-too-predictable resistance from those who wish to uphold the status quo. Contemporary French intellectuals, hiding behind their pseudonyms when writing their condemnatory pamphlets against Nostradamus, generally demanded he should satisfy himself with being a mere mathematician, a simple astrologer contemplating the movements of stars, or a philosopher, but should keep his more abstract ideas to himself. In short, he should not make waves or claim to soothsay like some un-Christian heathen of Delphi, and then wrap up what he has said in riddles, and he deserved the wide suspicion and ridicule that he suffered.[10] Conversely, what skeptics of Nostradamus often selectively overlook are the surviving references to another gallery of angry critics that came forth from 1557 onwards who demanded severe punishment or even death for Nostradamus because he *was* accurate – *too* accurate!

Nostradamus' nightly vigils continued and work on the final Centuries 8 through 10 progressed quickly. He started composing a new dedication letter to Henry II sometime before 15 March 1557 – a date mentioned in the opening pages of what eventually became a 2,500-word epistle it seems he intended to include with the final set of 300 quatrains.[11] What started as a dedication to his king soon rambled off into an overview of a future history seemingly unfixed in time. Events described in mid-sentence often jumped centuries forward or backwards. Over the last several centuries there has been much discussion about this most obscure rush of predictions. The Epistle's rant is sticky enough to trap each generation's projections on its dangling literary flypaper participles and the nebulous noun and vaporous verb constructions. With that said, there is one passage that is not easy to misinterpret, because Nostradamus takes the rare risk of mentioning a date punctuating a 235-year cycle of persecution of the Christian church in France and Europe up to the year 1792:

... & sera le commencement comprenant ce de ce que durera & commençant icelle annee sera faicte plus grande persecution à l'eglise Chrestienne que n'a esté faicte en Affrique, & durera ceste icy iusques l'an mil sept cens nonante deux que lon cuydera estre une renouation de siecle ...

And then will be the commencement of what will long endure and beginning with this year [1558] will experience greater persecution of the Christian Church than it had ever experienced in Africa and this will last till the year 1792, which they will believe [marks] a renewal of time ...[12]

This could be Nostradamus' attempt to forewarn his king of the imminent split of the Christian faith in Europe between warring Catholic and Protestant camps, beginning in 1558, leading to an era of Christian civil wars and persecutions that would last until the year 1792. Indeed a collapse of religious tolerance began in France by the latter half of 1559, leading by 1562 to the first of nine religious civil wars, which would not cease until 1598. After the firestorm of religious wars were ignited in France, they would spread over the Spanish Netherlands (1568–1648) and move yet farther east, consuming half of central Europe's population in the

Thirty Years' War (1618–48). Across the Channel, Puritans and Catholic-leaning Royalists braced pikes and clashed swords in the English Civil War (1642–6). After 1648, armed combat over religion abated, but one could argue that the next 144 years saw Christianity's hold on the European mind challenged by a more subtle, secular, and scientific enemy known as the Age of Reason and Enlightenment. The spread of Secularism led to open war with the Christian Church in the French Revolution, starting in 1789. In the year 1792, the new French Republic was born. It overthrew its king and abolished the Catholic Church, replacing Christianity with a state religion called the "Cult of Reason." Persecution of the Church would continue in France, but not end in 1792, as Nostradamus believed. It was not until Napoleon Bonaparte put the brakes on the revolution with his dictatorship in 1799 that churches were once again open in France. Nostradamus, however, did accurately date 1792 as the year French revolutionaries created a new calendar to mark the dawn of what they believed to be a new age.

A year and three months passed before Nostradamus completed his *Epistle*, signing off on 27 June 1558. It is assumed that he worked on it in spurts while composing the last 300 quatrains, only finishing the Epistle after the 1,000th quatrain was composed and copied, presumably by Chavigny.

Outside of this busy time, becoming a veritable factory of predictions and almanacs, little else is known about his life during 1557 and 1558. Despite the mounting bad publicity (or perhaps because of it), reprints of his prophecies and Almanacs began to spread throughout Europe. His translated almanac for 1558 found a publisher in London and it was also read in Italy and Holland. So successful were his foreign editions that preparations were underway in 1558 for two more English translations of his up and coming Almanac for 1559. Throgmorton, Queen Elizabeth of England's ambassador in Paris, had already alerted the Queen to the French Court's growing interest in Century 1, Quatrain 35.

The translated prognostications for that year were widely read throughout England, since it was the first year of Queen Elizabeth's reign. For once, Nostradamus seemed to agree with John Calvin, who saw nothing good in a kingdom's destiny if a woman were to sit on a king's throne. Calvin, in a letter to Sir William Cecil, wrote that the English Queen (even if she was sympathetic to the Protestant cause) was a perversion of nature that "ought to be held as a judgment on man for his dereliction of his rights."[13] From Nostradamus' side, English copies of his prophecies for Elizabeth for that year predicted "diverse calamities, weepings and mournings" and "civil sedition" that would result in "the lowest rising up in rebellion against the highest." Indeed, the concerns that were spread across England by Nostradamus' prophecies may have influenced Elisabeth's famous court astrologer and necromancer, John Dee, in his effort to find the most favorable astrological date on which both God and secular authority might bless her ordination.[14] John Dee's biographer, Benjamin Woolley, portrays him as a mathematically based astrologer opposed to "the divination practiced by Nostradamus." In France, a second press run of the sloppy du Rosne edition of *Les Propheties* (including everything up to Century 7, Quatrain 40) appeared after 13 November 1558. This, along with the ever-widening readership of the almanacs, steadily increased the prophet's profit margin.

Modern climatologists in their study of the "Little Ice Age" – an intensification of cold and inclement weather that was occurring during the 16th century – depend heavily on the rare yet meticulous meteorological records of a certain French farmer, Gilles de Goubeville. This "quasi-peasant," lord of a small manor at Le Mesnil-en-Val, inland from Cherbourg in Normandy, kept a 20-year journal of observations about the worsening weather that was the grist of an almanac writer's bread-and-butter prognostications. Goubeville's journal reveals that he was an ardent fan of Nostradamus' advice about timing the planting of crops according to the cycles of the moon. Goubeville read Nostradamus' meteorological prognostications and experimented with his planting times, reporting a good crop for 1557, but as a result of only average success for 1558, his copies of Nostradamus collected dust on his shelf from then onwards.[15]

Nostradamus' almanacs were translated into German by 1560. A translation of *Traité des fardemens* in 1572 includes an anecdote in a new preface written by the German translator. If the dating is accurate, it describes Nostradamus walking through Montpellier in the summer of 1558 bent on saddling up his horse and rushing to complete some important mission. The errand and destination were unspecified, but it appears that he was detained for days by a number of sick people needing his care and advice, not only about medicine but also about other matters, which we might assume concerned forecasts about what dire days lay ahead. According to the translator, Dr. Hierimias Martius (Mertz), the crowd of people seeking medical and prophetic advice from him became so large that he could not ride on, and he retreated behind the bolted door of a special apartment.

"What he prophesied about King Francis, the first of this name of most praiseworthy memory, before he set off towards Pavia, was amply borne out by the pitiful outcome of the expedition and the dismal dungeon,"[16] says Dr. Martius, making him the surviving source of a myth that has Nostradamus in 1525 attending medical school at Montpellier, making one of his first – and successful – prophecies: Francis I marching off to military disaster and imprisonment after the battle of Pavia.

Anne gave birth to their fourth child, André, on 3 November 1558. This happy event paralleled the publication of a third edition of *Les Propheties* by one of Lyon's most prestigious publishing houses, de Tornay. It included Century 8, Quatrain 1 through Century 10, Quatrain 100, at last finishing the millenary of auguries. Clearly, the move to de Tornay came as a consequence of the sloppy work of de Rosne, who it is assumed retaliated by withholding the draft copies of the final 60 quatrains of Century 7.

There is no surviving copy of this edition; however, it is recorded that the final 300 quatrains did not include the new Epistle to Henry II. Until 1989, when Chomarat and others had published references to the existence of de Tornay and Benoist Rigaud editions published in 1558 and 1561 respectively,[17] it was believed that Nostradamus had decided against publishing the last three centuries while he was alive. The myth reasons that he had a sense of foreboding concerning the king, who in 1559 would be entering his forty-first and most perilous year. As suggested earlier, it may be that it was something Nostradamus confided to Catherine de' Medici in their discussions in Paris in the summer of 1555, that spurred her to ask for more specific astrological findings from Luc Gauricus the following year.

Even though the date of its completion was 27 June 1558, Nostradamus' dedication to Henry II did not find itself printed with the final three centuries in the de Tornay edition of 1558 but later in the Rigaud edition in 1560–61. Why the letter and its rambling prophecies did not receive public dissemination until after the king's death is one of the Nostradamian world's lingering mysteries. Perhaps there was something in the letter, and not the final 300 quatrains that Nostradamus decided was better published posthumously. It is safe to say that Henry and Catherine did read a copy of the letter, as fast as the postman could carry it to them in Paris, which was probably at the end of August 1558. The rumored revelations, if not the letter itself, might have circled throughout the court when the year 1559 dawned – the most important life-changing year for its royal recipient *and* its author.

"Cursed be the divine who predicted it, so evilly and so well!"

The people of Salon might have marked 20 April 1559 with a special celebration. Adam de Craponne's army of laborers had completed their five-year excavation of a wide, 40-kilometer

(25-mile) trench ranging out of the east, all the way from the Durance river to a spot on the northern approaches to Salon de Crau. Notables and citizens might well have thronged out of the town's north gate to gather on the freshly cut lip of the trench and watch with hope and satisfaction as the priests blessed the sudden flood of life-giving water. The great ditch became the watery road to the Petite Crau's resurrection into agricultural prosperity. Everyone knew that before long Salon and its environs would sprout windmill pumps for irrigating the fields, doubling the region's harvests and wealth. Certainly, Nostradamus and his extended family would witness this moment. He was investing a thirteenth share of the necessary capital and a lion's share of encouragement to aid Craponne. The first stage was complete and on schedule. From Salon the picks and shovels would try their strength on the gravel wastes of the Grand Crau. If Nostradamus was indeed a prophet, he could already foresee (or at least fantasize) the result of their accomplishments, long after he had departed this earth: a network of canals crossing the desert westward all the way to the sea.

April 1559 also brought hope for the future of France. A little over a fortnight before the people of Salon cheered the flood of water down their new canal, Henry II of France and Philip II of Spain signed the Peace of Cateau-Cambrésis, effectively bringing a positive political and financial end to the interminable Hapsburg–Valois Wars. Henry II had summoned hitherto unsuspected resources of military and political brilliance in the year following the military disaster of St. Quentin. By the spring of 1558, he had rallied his forces in a bold counterstroke, dividing Philip from his English allies and capturing their key continental strongholds of Calais, Dunkirk, and Thionville. Next, Henry moved boldly on the political front. He successfully pressed Scotland's Royal House of Stewart to bestow the hand of Princess Mary Stuart to his heir apparent, the *Dauphin* François, thus checking any political gain Philip achieved in the British Isles through his marriage/alliance with Queen Mary Tudor of England. Good fortune smiled once again on France when Philip's Anglo-Spanish alliance evaporated with the sudden and unexpected death, on 17 November 1558, of Queen Mary Tudor, bringing to the throne her Protestant half-sister, Elizabeth. Stripped of a key alliance and strapped for cash, any further prosecution of his war with France was sure to bankrupt the Spanish empire. Thus, it became incumbent on Philip to acquiesce to Henry's invitation for formal peace negotiations.

The Treaty of Cateau-Cambrésis was signed on 2/3 April 1559. France ceded Savoy, Corsica, and its Italian holdings to the Spanish-Hapsburg sphere of influence while retaining the fortress towns of Metz and Verdun, and a lease on the strategically important port of Calais. St.-Quentin was also restored to the French. Henry had ceded continental dominance to Spain, yet the Valois' loss in the half-century-long Franco-Spanish struggle for European hegemony was considered a small price to pay. French territories had actually increased. The injurious drain of war on the economy was over. Two years earlier, the fall of St.-Quentin appeared to have rung the death knell for Henry's reign and for the continued existence of the French kingdom. The meeting of minds with his Spanish adversary at Cateau-Cambrésis led to a development far more significant than the inky promises of peace treaties that history in time ever rips asunder. Blood alliances were proposed. Couriers and merchants passing through Salon in early May were probably the first to spread the happy news that Philip planned to marry Elizabeth de Valois, the king's daughter. A French princess was destined to be a Spanish Queen, securing France's southwestern frontiers. In addition, it became known that Henry had matched Emmanuel-Philibert, the Duke of Savoy, in a blood tie with another Valois, bringing security to France's eastern frontiers. It would seem that the vanquisher of French forces at St.-Quentin – the same fire-breathing general so eager to march on Paris and end the Valois rule – would no longer draw French blood on the battlefield but mix his own with royal Valois in a marriage to Henry II's sister, Marguerite de Valois.

The Franco-Spanish peace now solidified by blood alliances brought celebration across Western Europe. In France, and in Salon in particular, discussions about a better future might have ensued, even at the supper table of Nostradamus. If topics might occasionally dwell on any negative impact of the peace, they would concern what to do for the tens of thousands of unemployed soldiers returning home from the wars. There was sure to be increased brigandage on the roads of France, because few jobs were to be had in the European economic depression that began in 1557. Craponne's labor gangs might profit though from this influx of able-bodied men as he was about to continue excavating his canal trench westward into the more inhospitable gravel plains of the Grande Crau. Certainly, the Catholics were thankful to see the German mercenaries make for their homes beyond the frontiers. The bulk of the Catholic king's "French" armies was made up of these predominantly Lutheran mercenaries, and while their weapons stood idle between infrequent battles, the proselytizing across France of their Protestant "heresy" did not. Now with them gone, Catholics held renewed hope that the rapid spread of the Huguenot cult would also end.

Discussion in the market squares in the spring of 1559, and whispers in the Catholic cathedral pews and Calvinist safe-prayer houses across France, must have turned on the hopeful signs that their king was at last maturing into his responsibilities. Now that Henry refrained from being distracted with the blood sport of war, like his father before him, maybe now his Protestant and Catholic subjects might harbor a hope that he would at last train his renewed energies on the kingdom's long-neglected religious, social, and economic problems. The expectations placed upon him from the two religious factions were quite different: Catholics prayed for Henry's suppression and expulsion of the Protestants; the

Protestants prayed that Henry negotiate some equitable truce or edict of tolerance.

The king was not in the latter's camp. Marriages planned for his daughter to King Philip and a sister to the Duke of Savoy brought him under the influence of those fanatic Catholic princes who willed the extermination of the "Lutheran" plague in France. Cardinal Trivulzio happily observed the king's renewed and evangelical fervor at the French Court when addressing the "Lutheran" question: "The King displays a very genuine desire to cure the disorders of the realm, and almost every day he speaks of this in his council."[18]

Lucien Romier reflected on the change in the king's attitude in terms more ominous: "The truth is that the religion of the men of this time did not answer to the picture with which we are familiar. Far from hysterical, their beliefs had grown hardened under the weight of reasons of State, and reasons of monarchy. Heresy in their eyes was not reformation but rebellion."[19]

The celebrations of peace and the dual royal marriages would commence in Paris by mid-June. Young 14-year-old Elisabeth de Valois would marry the somber, middle-aged Spanish monarch (by proxy) on 22 June. On 28 June Marguerite de Valois and the Duke of Savoy would ceremoniously sign their own marriage contract, launching a three-day-long ritual contest of arms, pitting Henry II against his finest captains of the guard, after which a long series of banquets and festivities would climax with the marriage of Savoy and Marguerite on 9 July. Invitations were sent to notable personages across France and Europe. It would seem likely that if Nostradamus had been invited, some record of the invitation would have existed – some comment at least – even if he had declined. Perhaps it was not good form to invite one who was believed by many at court to be an augur of ill tidings for kingly jousts. Perhaps some wags on the streets of Salon openly ribbed Nostradamus and members of his family that this fountain of good news was bad business for doomsayers.

His specific opinions about the planned festivities are unknown, but the astrological predictions recorded in August 1558 for publication in a booklet in Paris (published by le Noir) clearly indicate that he expected some great catastrophe would befall France. The essential prophetic warning of his paper entitled *Les Significations de l'Eclipse qui sera le 16. Septembre 1559* ... is that malevolent aspects of the planets Mars and Jupiter would magnify the effect of a lunar eclipse on 16 September 1559. The evil influence of the stars and moon would begin manifesting in March and show their first powerful and destabilizing impact on the French community by June. The effect would last all the way through 1560, with the potential to foster civil and religious discord a further two years. In short, Nostradamus warned that by June 1559, and until 1563, France would suffer great doubt, enormous social and religious fracture, violence, conspiracies, and great profanities against God committed by the "Jovialists" (his name for the Huguenots). Starting in June a shadow of great fear and doubt would cover and darken the land, clouding over the reasoning of Christian monarchs of the true (Catholic) religion.

Already the first inclinations of that gathering shadow had arrived when on 2 June Henry set in motion his long-anticipated purge of Protestant "heretics." Some members of Parliament resisting his edict publicly denounced it in Parliamentary session, in the presence of the King and Charles de Guide, Cardinal de Lorraine. They were arrested. One of the councilors, de Bourg, was condemned to death by the King in person for heresy after he had compared the monarch to the evil king Ahab. "It is thou that troubles Israel!" said de Bourg, standing before the King in Parliament. Execution by hanging and burning would take place sometime after the festivities had ended. Thus at the onset of state celebration of the Peace of Cateau-Cambrésis and the dual weddings, some at Court were already whispering that the first influence of malefic stars for June was already in effect. As festive fluttering banners, pavilions and magnificently dressed gentlemen, ladies, and the princes of Europe converged on the city, Paris was already divided over religion. Many believed Henry's persecution of the parliamentarians was the first step taken towards a religious civil war.

∝

The three-day tournament in celebration of the dual marriages was held in an enclosed and fancifully decorated temporary arena constructed in the eastern suburbs of Paris on a stretch of the broad rue St. Antoine before the Palais de Tournelles. Sunny June weather blessed the three-day test of arms. Queen Catherine de' Medici sat in the place of honor on the festooned platform in front of the tournament lists. The Duc de Guise and Cardinal of Lorraine, the key cabinet members preaching a hard line against the Protestants, took their seats beside the Queen and the Dauphin (some would say hemming them in), their political influence made ever more intimate as blood guardians to the fair and flame-haired *Dauphine*, Mary of Scots, their niece and future queen of France. The Grand Constable, Montmorency, was forced to sit farther away, rehabilitated into royal favor though he was after the debacle at St.-Quentin, but subservient for now to the smothering encroachment of the fanatic Catholic Duke and Cardinal who had the king's ear. Among those notables taking in the tournament, leaning on the bright tapestry-draped rails of royal boxes, was the grim, skeleton-faced General de Alva representing the Spanish delegation. The delegation's dress was so shabby looking compared to the French nobles that some believed Philip II had sent these royal ragamuffins to make a sleight-of-fashion statement against their hosts. Actually the lack of luster in the jewels and threads of the austere Spanish princes and ambassadors belied how serious was the financial drain Spain suffered from successfully waging their war against France. Beside the Spanish sat the imperious Duke of Savoy alongside his eager yet homely new bride, Marguerite de Valois. The marriage signed that morning on the first day of the tourney was a necessary strategic move by Emmanuel-Philibert even if the matronly vessel for his heirs was not that sexually appealing. Old "Ironhead," as his soldiers nicknamed him, was resigned to his lot. Unlucky in romance, the Duke had come to the festivities not expecting the sincere warmth kindled in his stalwart heart for Marguerite's debonair brother the king, who now charged below his seat in a flash of plumes and armor to carry through one successful tilt after another, to the delight of all. Savoy looked on approvingly – there was a manly friendship worth the anticipated and tedious nuptials planned for 9 July.

Somewhere, too, on that rampart of princes and ambassadors of Spanish and German Hapsburg and French royalty sat the King's lover, a fair and remarkably fetching 60-year-old, Diane de Poitiers. She most likely sat in a prominent place, yet as far removed from the Queen's presence as etiquette required. It was on this very street nearly 30 years before, in front of the Palais de Tournelles, that her champion, the King, aged 12, rode out to wage his first public joust bedecked in the same black and white colors of her coat of arms. That day on the rue St.-Antoine marked the beginning of their famous love affair. She might have privately prayed that the sunshine-soaked festive banners and costumes and the rays glinting off the polished and gilded armament of her lover on these festive, heady days should ever represent in her memory the celebration of their abiding love – their great open secret.

For the next three days a fine array of hundreds of gentlemen and gentlewomen from across France and Europe crowded on the square of pillared and ribbon-wrapped platforms, cheering on the resplendently armored figure of Henry II, who wielded a jousting lance and a lion-decorated shield as he surged down the lists on his gray charger, Compère, unseating his opponents in victory after victory. His eldest son, the pale and slight 15-year-old François, yearned to join his father, but his adolescent body was maturing slowly and reluctantly. Although he and Mary of Scotland were mutually in love, their marriage remained unconsummated as the onset of his puberty was delayed. Desire as he might to test himself in martial arms, he was not yet sturdy enough to carry a lance. Yet on these days he was happy, standing in his father's close proximity, taking his turn holding the lists each day along with Prince Alphonso of Ferrara, Duke Charles III of Lorraine, and, from time to time, the Duc de Guise.

Sunset on the third day drew long shadows over yet another successful set of jousts. Henry prepared for his final bout against the younger and formidable Gabriel de Lorge, the Comte de Montgomery, the captain of the King's own Scottish Guards. Henry's blood was up. Never before had he unseated so many fine adversaries in ritual combat or in the view of a more distinguished gallery of princes. There was just enough light remaining to topple one last challenger – then let the sun set and all cheering guests flood the dining halls of the Palais de Tournelles to celebrate long into the night this most triumphant of days with festivities and feasting.

The King's bout with Montgomery ended in a draw. If Queen Catherine ever was pondering the words of her Florentine astrologer, Luc Gauricus, or turning the verses of Nostradamus' 35th quatrain of Century 1 around in her mind, the fall of lances on the ground from mutually missed thrusts might have brought a sigh of relief. This was the last scheduled bout of the final day. Her husband, now four-and-a-half months into his forty-first year when dire head blows were threatened, had finished his last joust for the day, and perhaps for the year. The prophecies of Gauricus and Nostradamus had seen their moment pass. Chyren Selin, the present and future second Charlemagne that Nostradamus promised in his alternative future, yet lived and thrived.

Catherine did not hear the horns blaring the fanfare signal closing the tournament. We might fancy that she and hundreds of others searched the flurry of pages and grooms attending to the King and Montgomery who sat spur to spur having a heated discussion.

The King looked annoyed and gestured dismissively at something Montgomery had said. The King had lifted and loosened what many recall was his gilded visor to speak more emphatically. It is said that Montgomery's manner betrayed nervousness when the King asked for a second and unscheduled bout. Montgomery joined in by Duc de Guise and Montmorency reminded the King that it was already late and a second run of the course would throw the festivities off schedule. Henry bushed their concerns aside. He would unseat worthy Montgomery in another bout, period! To which Montgomery bowed his head and drew up his own lion-embossed shield heading for the opposite end of the course. Whether Montgomery at this interchange cautioned the King not to tempt fate because of prophecies made by Gauricus or Nostradamus is unknown, yet the possibility that he had annoyed the King by mentioning them is a hope held close to the heart of those who perpetuate Nostradamian lore.

The drums rolled. Both adversaries reached for new lances. Catherine – with François and his wife Mary of Scotland sitting at her side – had stoically endured the terrible suspense of the last three days. Now she must endure a few moments more.

The ritual warriors circled around the lists pressing their chargers forward for the collision. Twice they missed one another, orbiting again the sawdust course and finding their range to hurl themselves at each other a third time. The crowd fell silent. Suddenly, there was a loud crack letting fly an explosion of tumbling wooden shards from Montgomery's shattered lance. A cry of horror rose from the crowd. The King, reeling in his saddle, rode out of the explosion of wood with a gnarled and bloody splinter protruding from where no shard of wood should be. Catherine de' Medici let out a blood-curdling shriek and fainted, as did François and Mary beside her. Diane de Poitiers, sitting farther down the dais of honor, also screamed – her face paling, eyes disbelieving.

A splinter from Montgomery's broken lance had either pierced or slipped under the King's visor, which an attendant in haste of his impetuous master had fastened too loosely.

The King swayed on his slowing horse, grasping the pummel, slipping into the arms of his grooms. They opened up his visor and were bathed in his blood. The splinter in the impact had shattered, impaling his forehead and plunging a number of spines deep into his eye socket behind his destroyed left eye. It was left to the Duke de Guise and Cardinal de Lorraine and their political rival Montmorency (together at last, some would remark) to hold the King by his arms while others lifted his legs to carry him rapidly through the pandemonium towards his bedchamber at the Palais de Tournelles.

Upon reaching the foot of the stairs to his bedchamber Henry stirred from his state of shock and demanded they set him down. He walked up the staircase under his own power, to the amazement of many. Henry reached the bed, collapsing from the effort, finding one last ounce of strength to pull the bedcovers over himself, fold his hands and begin to pray. Physicians were summoned to begin their necessary torture – they were the noted anatomist Andreas Versalius (Philip II's personal physician) and Ambroise Paré (the father of modern surgery). Once the physicians could wipe the gory face and neck free of blood, it became clear that beyond minor abrasions there were two serious wounds, most likely mortal. They counted five splinters impaling the bone of his brow and planting themselves deep into his head, most sprouting from the corner of his lifeless left eye. The King showed his measure of physical strength and toughness when Paré and Versalius began extracting the shards. Only once did he let out an agonized scream, when they removed the longest splinter piercing his brain. Paré pressed Versalius hard that they should use his trephine to remove some bone plate to relieve pressure on the brain and make sure they had cleared all splinters from the deep wound. Versalius decided against it. Paré instead lightly wrapped the left half of the

King's head in a cloth bandage. He did not believe the King would outlive the night.

Thus began the vigil of Queen and cabinet members taking turns sitting or standing pensively before the bed. Henry survived the night and by the third day showed signs that he might yet recover. He asked for Montgomery but was told the captain of his Scottish guards had ridden out of Paris immediately after the disaster.

"What has he to fear?" puzzled the King. "I know that this accident happened not through his fault but by an unlucky chance." The King then cleared him of all blame and demanded Montgomery be returned to his presence at all costs. The King then closed his surviving right eye and asked for music.

Later that day the King once again became feverish, passing in and out of consciousness. When the dressings were replaced, the wound, which the physicians had not yet cleaned, displayed a large abscess swelling against the King's brain. Yet the King lingered day after interminable day, and an oppressive and suspenseful atmosphere fell over Tournelles and across Paris. Across from the rue St. Antoine, where somber laborers could be seen clearing the street of lists and pretty banners, stood the guest apartments of Diane de Poitiers. She could only look at Tournelles from across the street. Catherine had made it clear that the King's mistress was barred from coming inside.

For days now Poitiers had challenged all who came into her presence, asking "Is the King dead?" She surely was pained at the irony that the same stretch of street where her love affair had began with a tournament might soon end because of a tournament. "As long as the King lives, I have no fear of my enemies," she was oft heard to say.

Montmorency had at first taken turns at the bedside watch, but a week into the vigil he was missing when his chief rivals, François de Guise and his brother, the Cardinal de Lorraine, perched like vultures over the King's fever-ravaged form and began fomenting calls for Montmorency's impeachment. "Was it not he who poorly fastened the King's visor?" was their false presumption. At the time, Montmorency was seen wandering the halls of Tournelles; grief for his dying master had cast a stunned trance over the aging warrior and, it seemed to some, would likely hasten signs of senility. Courtiers heard him mumbling about evil predictions, of unheeded warnings delivered by astrologers and prophets to the Queen. It is not known whether he remembered now that four years earlier he had guided one of these astrologers of doom to an audience with the King.

If he did not remember, there was time enough for others at court to recall the words of Nostradamus during the King's agonizingly painful and slow passage into twilight:

> The young lion, he will surmount the old one,
> On the field of combat in single battle told:
> He will pierce his eyes through a cage all golden:
> Two wounds become one, then dying in cruel death's cold.

Many concluded Nostradamus' words had foreseen this unhappy end over five years before in Quatrain 35 of Century 1. The King and Queen had called him all the way from far-off Provence to explain the prophecy. Now the future's course, as Nostradamus would say, "inclined" towards that end Catherine and her occultists had tried so hard to forestall. Catherine, like many others, would probe Nostradamus' cloudy words, and be predisposed to consider them in the clearer light of Luc Gauricus' warnings that the King should not participate in ritual combat in his forty-first year.

The young lion, he will surmount the old one ...

Henry was 41. His challenger Montgomery was 35.

On the field of combat in single battle told ...

The tournament on the rue St. Antoine is that field of single combat.

He will pierce his eyes through a cage all golden ...

During the final pass, Montgomery failed to drop his lance in time. A rumor spread amongst Catholics at court that Montgomery let his sympathies for the "Lutheran" cause keep his lance held high on purpose. Whatever the motivation (or perhaps through mere oversight), a moment later shards of his shattered lance pierced the gilded cage of the King's visor.

Now all those at Court who were believers in this interpretation of Nostradamus' quatrain held their breath for the fulfillment of the final line of the prophecy:

Two wounds become one, then dying in cruel death's cold.

Indeed the splinters had penetrated the King's forehead and eye in two wounds. Now infection spread from the unclean wooden splinter fragments in his two wounds, making them "one."

By the end of the eighth day, the King's hands began to swell from the rapid spread of peritonitis throughout his body. The end was near, and his drifting mind could scarcely pick up the vengeful threads of the conspiring Guise brothers. The issue of Montmorency's impeachment was ignored as irrelevant. His fading mind aided by the Guise hovered between expressing an obsession to purge his kingdom of heretics one moment, then slipping into a stupor of regret. Now that life was ending, he pondered how little happiness he had enjoyed despite its favors of wealth, power and a true love.

On the morning of the ninth day, the Dauphin was summoned one last time to his bedside by Catherine to receive his father's final benediction. The sickly future king of France had already fainted twice before the deathbed. "My God! How can I live if my father dies!" he was often heard to cry. The fitful adolescent was so overwrought with nervous collapse that for a time Catherine had to shift her vigil to his bedside. On this day, she brought forward the pallid heir who listened to his father's fading voice murmuring out from underneath a turban of heavy bandages, "My son, you are about to lose your father but not his blessing. I pray God that he make you happier than I have been."

That night the marriage of Emmanuel-Philibert to Marguerite de Valois went ahead with all the joy and hopefulness of a funeral. Catherine de' Medici did not attend. She had retreated to her bed, a victim of nervous fatigue. The following morning, on 10 July, a courier from the Spanish king delivered a message to Henry, which seemed to help him to relinquish his life at last. Philip in his message promised to protect the Dauphin if any danger should beset the throne. Spain had pledged its assistance to uphold the Catholic Valois heir against any enemies gathering in the coming dark days ahead. The Protestants would see their bloody day!

A few hours later, Henry's long and cruel ten-day deathwatch ended. Montmorency, stabbed with grief, was heard to cry, "Cursed be the divine who predicted it, so evilly and so well!"

That night, César tells us that an angry mob was seen in the suburbs burning Nostradamus in effigy, calling upon the Church Inquisitors to burn him as a heretic.

CHAPTER NINE

Fame and Infamy

∽

In the Year of the One-Eyed King

If we could see what lies ahead of us on history's path, it might be as if standing in the high branches of a tree to see far beyond the horizon observed from ground level. From this tree of "pre-science," we can wave to those far below on the path of the present as they pass by, taking the road to a future topography that they cannot yet see. From far up in our rarified vantage point of prescience we might call down a warning of an abyss lurking around the bend, but those we love, our friends and countrymen, cannot understand our words. They ignore our cries and blithely wander toward disasters. We may watch powerlessly at what will inevitably come, but are only able to look on in anguish as they wander blindly down the present's pathway.

Whether imagined or authentically foreseen, dark premonitions bring a sense of dread to the seer and to believers of the prophecy. And in either case a public prediction will engender reactions of misunderstanding and ridicule. It does not matter whether a message is given in cryptic verse or clear words. The forewarning of any unborn event remains only an abstract reality until hindsight gives it a flesh-and-blood presence. For example, American seer Jeane Dixon clearly predicted and documented in *Parade* magazine in 1956 her vision that the next US president elected in 1960 would be a young and physically handsome man, a Democrat, who would die violently while in office. The impact of the prediction only hit home to many in hindsight, after President Kennedy, who had been elected in 1960, was assassinated by Lee Harvey Oswald in late 1963. What America endured of this tragedy from 1963, Jeane Dixon had endured since 1956.

After President Kennedy came to office, Dixon wrestled with the intensified foreboding that the president might be assassinated. She even spelled out in a new vision part of the assassin's name: "os" and "d" – (OS)wal(D). In late November 1963, when it became known that Kennedy planned to fly down to Dallas, Texas, she sensed that the attack was imminent. It is known that Dixon made calls and sent telegrams to her contacts in the White House begging that they warn the president not to go to Dallas. There were no riddles or anagrams open to interpretation in her prediction. It is said that even the president himself had a premonition that he might be shot at in Dallas. Nevertheless, his premonition, like Dixon's, was too abstract and irrational to heed.

However, if a prophecy is heeded, then a dire event foreseen yet avoided remains an abstract possibility, ephemeral, and unsubstantiated. There is also a human weakness to test fate. Henry II of France had it; so did President Kennedy. Henry jousted in his forty-first year, and Kennedy went to Dallas where he would travel in an open motorcade with premonitions of death. The prophecies of Nostradamus and Jeane Dixon became hindsight's reality. Both would henceforth become the most famous seers of their day upon the merits of failed warnings.[1]

Only a failed prophet becomes famous. The death of Henry II catapulted Nostradamus to international celebrity. Too late came the wide-ranging interest in cryptic warnings – too late to forestall the King's blinding and death. Phrases such as "he will pierce his eyes through a cage all golden" became afterthoughts for dark entertainment and titillation after the fact of his death. Yet, soon after the King's funeral procession to his interment at St. Denis, Nostradamus had more readers than ever, spread across the French kingdom, and at last they began seeing the "blinding-and-death" link of Century 1, Quatrain 35 with another quatrain foretelling the long-term results for France. In Century 3, Quatrain 55, Nostradamus' warning was heeded five years too late:

En l'an qu'un œil en France regnera,
La court sera à un bien facheux trouble:
Le grand de Bloys son ami tuera:
Le regne mis en mal & doute double.[2]

In the year that France has a one-eyed ruler,
The court will be in very great trouble.
The great one from Blois his friend will he murder,
The reign – evil placed – and in doubt double.[3]

The people of France living in the dark and uncertain days of late 1559 who read and heard of this prophecy would certainly have been tempted to mark this quatrain for that year when Henry II drew the covers of his deathbed over himself, his left eye destroyed by the splintered shaft of Comte de Montgomery. They would understand and regret what Nostradamus may have secretly regretted five years before it happened – that the "one-eyed" king's premature death would leave the French court in chaos. However, believers of this interpretation would face an escalation of ridicule.

Nothing unnerves and angers the cynics more than a seemingly clear detail of the future foreseen. Up to Henry's reign there had never been a one-eyed king sitting on the French throne. The doubters of Nostradamus in 1559 would be at pains to dig deep into the toolbox of cynical brush-offs and pull out a new reason to cool the ardor of believers in Nostradamus' prophetic powers.

They might theorize that a fake prophet such as Nostradamus might seek the glorification of his name for centuries to come by making a generalized prediction about the coming centuries, counting on there being another half-blinded king reigning at some time, and future courts of France suffering "double doubt." Why not trust your post-mortem legacy to history's repetitive nature and count on future generations of fools and dreamers calling you a prophet?

What could a believer of Nostradamus say in response? Nothing too convincing. The people arguing for or against Nostradamus in the year 1559 could not know that there were another 233 years remaining in the royal succession of French Valois and Bourbon kings. They couldn't know that France would never again see a one-eyed monarch. Nor could they imagine that despite all tribulations to come for French courts in the next two-and-a-third centuries, never would there be another as grievously divided as theirs starting in 1559.

The one-eyed king of the year 1559 was dead. Long live the runaway inflation, social turmoil, mounting religious divisions, and the governmental corruption Henry delayed facing for 13 years until a wooden lance and peritonitis unexpectedly cut short all further time to procrastinate. He left the French kingdom with an estimated national debt of 40 million livres, with repayment on loans due for 19 million from European lenders and creditors. The government was bankrupt, and the Crown had not paid the armed forces, most members of the army of civil administrators and magistrates, or even the provincial Seneschals for four years. When gangs of taxmen could manage to catch the fleeing citizens, they collected annual gross revenues of 12 million livres, most of which evaporated on debt interest payments alone. In this climate of economic instability social disorder increased. Naturally, people turned to religion. France's religious divisions were by far the worst of any kingdom in mid-16th-century Europe. A cycle of half-hearted attempts to repress the spread of Protestantism in the

1540s had failed. By the late 1550s, verbal abuse and threats from one Christian community against the other were primed to boil over into open kingdom-wide violence. The year of the one-eyed king was marked by Protestantism's sudden and rapid spread throughout France, primarily in the middle and upper classes. Nearly half the nobility and a third of the French bourgeoisie were vernacular bible-carrying "Huguenots" by the time the King expired.

The King's eldest son, François, being 15 years old, was by law already in his majority, yet signs of his immaturity of mind and body were sufficiently apparent that Huguenot ministers seriously challenged his full claim to the throne by stretching obscure clauses in Salic law (the ancient rules and qualifications set down for French kings) postponing his majority until he turned 25. François de Guise and his brother the Cardinal de Lorraine won the civil trial, aided by the lawyer Jean du Tillet, and the sullen and stunted Dauphin was recognized as King François II. Nonetheless, it was soon clear to both sides of the dispute that François was far from ready to take on the full responsibilities of the crown. It was therefore incumbent upon the Duc de Guise and the Cardinal to shoulder temporarily the adolescent's political, religious, and military burdens and direct his education assisted by the late king's wife (now his unofficial regent) and France's "Queen Mother," Catherine de' Medici. From 1557 up to Henry II's death, the Guise clan had already exerted great political influence over the throne, thanks to Montmorency's capture and dishonor for losing the French relief forces before St.-Quentin. They furthered this claim of influence as uncles of the new Queen of France, Mary Stuart (the daughter of the Queen of Scotland, Mary of Guise). Once the grief-stricken Catherine had stirred from the shock of losing her husband, she was a wallflower no longer. She stepped with both feet into the struggle for power, asserting her influence over her son. Thus, she began crystallizing her decades-long role as the unofficial mothering (and some would say smothering) "power behind the throne" of sons François, then Charles, and finally Henry, Duc d'Anjou.[4]

The "great trouble" within the French Court foreseen by Nostradamus came from its division after the King's death into four contentious factions, each competing for the favor and chance to influence a self-consumed, slow-learning, late-pubescent teenage king. The Guise faction, which was pro-Spanish and fanatically anti-Protestant, tried to make François hawkish against heretics. The Montmorency faction grew to check the ambitions of the upstart Guise with desires of their own to dominate the young king. A third faction supported the Queen Mother as a tempering force wedged against the Guise and the Montmorencys. All of these predominantly Catholic factions at Court (except for Admiral Coligny of the Montmorencys) might gather for mutual as well as individual advantage to confront the fourth and largest faction, the Protestants led by King Antoine de Bourbon of Navarre and his brother, Louis I, the Prince de Condé.

No one at Court believed the tenuous arrangements pledged by Protestant and Catholic princes in the aftermath of the national tragedy could survive for long – maybe months, maybe a year. Those reading for an answer in the last two lines of Nostradamus' prophecy for the year of a "one-eyed" king might have puzzled over this riddle:

The great one from Blois his friend will he murder,
The reign – evil placed – and in doubt double.

The court nobles of 1559 were about to begin mixing religion with politics in a long and bloody decimation of their generation and that of their sons and grandsons in 40 years wracked by nine civil wars. The survivors might look back to Nostradamus' final two lines and believe (perhaps rightly) that they described the coming power struggle for the French throne after the death of Henry II. It would come to pass that hindsight marked his third successor and son, Henry III, as Nostradamus' "great man of" the Château "Blois," the place where the prophet first met him as a child and plotted his stars for his mother. Nearly three decades after the year of the one-eyed king, Henry III would convene a meeting of the Estates-General in 1588 at Blois. There he would lure the grown son of the present Duc de Guise to his murder by first feigning reconciliation with his old friend. The assassination would split the Catholic alliance in two ("doubt double"), launching a three-way civil war between Huguenots, the Catholic royalists, and the Catholic League.

Prophecy, true or imagined, tends to make our story stray ahead of itself. Twenty-nine years earlier, as the captains and the kings-to-be might have marveled over the first lines and puzzled over the last, Nostradamus was about to be paid in full for either the trouble or the truth his prophecies evoked.

Quack Baiters and Powerful Friends

Nostradamus had become the Jeane Dixon of his age.[5] Like Dixon, Nostradamus became the darling of his era's version of yellow journalism and tabloid half-truths. Yet, in contrast to Dixon's circumstance, the long, lonely and brigand-infested roads of 16th-century France kept Nostradamus for the most part peacefully removed from his ever more demanding public, hungry for predictions and astrological charts. The controversy surrounding his prophecies would grow at a lazy, old-world pace. Salon was far from the hotbed of Paris, the center of France's troubles, and Nostradamus in Provence was forced to confront relatively few stalking fans or skeptical predators – notably the church Justices in Paris who were lobbied by a mob to have him burned alive.

In 1560, literary forces contrary to Nostradamus flooded the book and pamphlet market because the fulfillment of his dire prediction of national catastrophe created an "attack-the-messenger" mentality. His astrological forecasts for 1559, added to the apparent realization of his somewhat shadowy prediction for the death of the king, rubbed raw the national psyche. His 1558 forecast that a general drift towards darkness and civil and religious disruption would manifest itself from June 1559 onwards only threw oil on the fire in those predisposed to malign, even threaten death, to the messenger rather than accept the message. The obscurity of Nostradamus' prophecies was clearly part of the problem. His literary "steam" of beclouded words cooked up a varied recipe of threats and editorials from all sides of the civil and religious divide. Indeed, it appears that many of the critiques and downright slanderous attacks were not even based on the authentic writings of their victim.

The habit of tabloid hacks composing prophecies in his name is not solely a fixture of the Nostradamian controversy in our own times. The 16th century had its own versions of the loud pictures and sensationalized headlines that we are accustomed to seeing on the 21st-century tabloid magazine rack. Readers in a French Renaissance bookshop could take their pick of pamphlet or bound volume variations of today's supermarket silliness. The title pages might display some grotesque cartoon woodcut of Nostradamus predicting all and everything fantastic (and patently false) about the near future. Since the first serialized edition of his prophecies appeared, the yellow shadow of hack journalism over Nostradamus' legacy has waxed and waned along with the fluctuations of interest in his prophecies. The peak in national attention after the king's death in 1559 brought out a number of flagrantly outrageous books and pamphlets falsely attributed to him. Then as today, the attempts to deceive and profit from Nostradamus' fame increased public attention for and against his prophecies.

He may indeed have used nebulous literary devices to protect people of the future from making events less dire than foreseen, but fuzzy poetry has always been the bread and butter of parlor magicians and con artists, seeking a new "trick" after their stage careers wind down. Unfortunately, intentional cloudiness also feeds the urge to debunk on the part of rigid-minded (though sincere) professional skeptics who cannot think outside of their own intellectual boxes. Thus, the staunchly Catholic authors saw in the shapes of his clouds of verse the form of a sorcerer. Protestants saw an agent of the Pope propagating their destruction. The unlettered and mostly Catholic French peasantry and urban labor classes thought Nostradamus an agent of the Huguenots who hated their Catholic king enough to use black arts to predict and even influence his death. The more progressive Renaissance minds blamed him for feeding the era's fearful superstitions with yet more vaporous prophetic fuel. The cynics saw in his cryptic cloudiness a prophet making a profit from public hysteria and fear. Influential foreign politicians, such as Queen Elizabeth's Secretary of State, Sir William Cecil, cast him as a propagandist and subversive. Astrologers wrote pamphlets denouncing him as an ignorant quack. Apparently, there were phony pamphlets printed shortly after his work on the significance of the lunar eclipse of 16 September 1559, which had astrologers dismissing his fuzzy math for placing the sun twice in the same sky, or derailing his planetary transits completely off the stellar map; or for not knowing the first degree of how to calculate ascendants.

In his own defense, Nostradamus declared his astrological work to be of divine inspiration, yet in the Preface and his Epistle to Henry II he paints himself as one who grounds his divine inspiration in cold and hard celestial calculation. If Nostradamus can be faulted for a calculated deception (beyond that of sincere self-deception, as some past and present critics pose), it was that he sometimes tried to clothe in the objectively mathematical garb of a celestial science what was a truly subjective gift: psychic premonition.[6]

His cloudy writing style may be more than just an occult device. In fact, he may have tried to conceal in words of mysteriousness a severe case of dyslexia. His own natal chart revealed aspects astrologers recognize as signs of learning disabilities.[7] Any astrologers, past or present, worth their witchcraft would see Nostradamus' thin emotional skin on the subject – what with his natal Scorpio Moon in a grand water (emotional) trine. Throughout his life, he would not take criticism lightly – warranted or unwarranted. The Scorpio Moon would mask the face in inscrutability, but any competent astrologer would know that behind the aloof and mystical mask was someone oversensitive to hard compassion or calumny. Inside Nostradamus was a wounded animal that liked to play the martyr, although his astrological aspects made him guard his wounds close to his heart. He might have wept and hissed at the walls in the privacy of his secret study, but he dared not let slip in public his legendary politeness and diplomacy. However, no one can successfully repress something in their subconscious forever without it sneaking out elsewhere in their behavior. He took and suppressed the sting of the "slap" delivered to his impassively polite façade by good critics and bad, only later passing it along in rages directed at those in his household service. Whether such rages also befell family members is not recorded.

There is no doubt that his authentic astrological rant dominating the pamphlet *Les Significations de l'Eclipse qui sera le 16. Septembre 1559* ... could nonplus any mainstream contemporary astrologer's understanding with his odd crystal ball celestial mathematics. And yet, the intuition hiding behind Nostradamus' chaotic astrology appears to have been accurate. The stars turned malicious in June with a controversial arrest of Protestant French parliamentarians followed by the death of the king. The subsequent total eclipse of the moon on 16 September seemed to cast more than a momentary dark shadow over the throne of the Valois. By September, it became clear that François II was a mediocre teen monarch, easily overwhelmed by the "advice" of a four-way fractured cabinet and court. France *was* falling into a period of "deceptions, abuses, secret factions," and "rumors" of Protestant conspiracies to "overthrow" the kingdom were indeed manifesting.[8]

The year 1560 opened with detractors lining up to take stabs at the thin skin of Nostradamus. Already the Protestant debunkers were especially vulgar and violent of pen. In 1558, an author purporting to be the "Catholic" Laurens Videl, who later became secretary to Huguenot leaders such as Duc de Lesdiguières, wrote a vicious pamphlet called *Declaration des Arbus, Ignorances et Seditions de Michel Nostradamus*. He called Nostradamus every insult in the book of Old French gutter-slang which can be translated into "intolerable pest ... poor fool ... lunatic ... brainless fool ... a big beast ... a bigger ass ..." – ad nauseum. Videl could have been the Calvinist Pierre Viret, Minister of Lausanne, who reveals himself a jealous fellow astrologer denouncing Nostradamus as a black magician, heretic, and a drunk. (And we should not forget to add that Videl called Nostradamus a "scabbed and mangy blockhead" who "needed his brain fumigated.") Periodicals appeared condemning him as a charlatan and a heretic, with less whipping than witty prose such as Charles Languois' *The Contradictions of Nostradamus* published in 1560, and the Latin attacks of the first English debunker, William Fulke, who based his assaults on the first fraudulent almanac copies.

After achieving success, Nostradamus equally cultivated condemnation from authors and townspeople across France who read cheap and heretically provocative pirate almanacs and false centuries attributed to him but actually written by fanatic Huguenots or Catholics trying to use his obscure verses to foretell the success of their diametrically opposed religious world views. In fairer times, an imprimatur of *Privalege* for publishing one's prognostications would come easily from a provincial governor and his priestly advisors, but after 1559 – when the dire forecasts began to resemble too closely the dire present – such privileges became scarcer. The governors of whole provinces began censuring the publication of these prognostications in a sweeping purge of books. For example an ordinance from the Seneschal of Orléans issued on 31 January 1560 declared, "And because those who prognosticate things that are to come, publishing their Almanacs and Prognostications, using the terms of astrology, against the express commandment of God – a thing which ought not to be tolerated by any Christian Prince – we prohibit all publishers and libraries of publishing, from exposing for sale any Almanacs or Prognostications that first have not been seen by the Archbishop, the Bishop, or such as they may appoint. And against him who will have composed such Almanacs will be prosecution by our extraordinary judges and corporeal punishment."

Whether aware of these edicts or not, he began to curtail his travels. He was thus saved from entering Orléans in the New Year, or a half dozen other provinces where he could be arrested, and not solely for his own prognostications, but for anything fell and rabid written by a fraud under his name.

Over a year before the king died and before Nostradamus entered an altogether new chapter of fame and infamy, the prophet may have already recorded his hypothetical reply to unfair criticism, or outright slanderer – private or official – when he wrote:

Although there are some who would attribute to me that which is as much mine as that which is not mine at all, Eternal God alone – who is the thorough searcher of human hearts, pious, just and merciful – is the judge of the matter, and it is to him I pray to defend me from the calumny of evil men.[9]

The victor of the battle of St.-Quentin rode into Salon de Crau in October 1559. Emmanuel-Philibert, the Duke of Savoy, was on his way home to Nice with his entourage. News came to him there of an outbreak of the plague across Savoy, and he decided to reside at the Château de l'Empéri for several months until the danger had passed. By December, the Duke found Salon so agreeable that he summoned his new wife, the Princess Marguerite de Valois, to share the enjoyable dry winter climate with him there. Plans were made to provide much pomp and ceremony for her arrival. Salon's most notable citizens were summoned to arrange for the festivities. Either at that time or weeks before, the Duke was probably introduced to Nostradamus. The Duke, still wearing funeral black, sitting in the audience hall of the Empéri, might have been curious to meet the man who had already foreseen the glory of his victory at St.-Quentin.

The city consuls had garlanded arches constructed, and Savoy called upon Nostradamus to compose a suitable inscription. Later that December the new Princess of Savoy, dressed in fine mourning weeds in memory of her dead brother, the King of France, was carried in a litter, leading the way before equally finely (and somberly) dressed members of her entourage and the traveling Savoyard court as they passed into Salon under the arches with Nostradamus' poetic Latin salutation:

SANGUINE TROIANNO, TRIANA STIRPE CREATA
ET REGINA CYPRI

Marguerite had no difficulty understanding and being flattered by the salutation. She was eager to meet the man who welcomed her as one French princess "of Trojan blood, created out of Trojan stock and queen of Cyprus." He had honored her with a coded device used in some of his prophecies to represent French royalty after one of their favorite myths – that ancient Frankish kings were the descendants of Francus, son of Hector of Troy. The reference to "queen of Cyprus" indicates Nostradamus was proud to show the visiting duke that he knew Savoyard hereditary history. After the death of the last Luignan king in 1475, one of the two female pretenders married the Duke's ancestor, bequeathing her rights to her son. Venice (which possessed exotic Cyprus at the time), supporting her rival, won out.

The whole town gathered before the scarlet-draped dais, where Princess Marguerite received town dignitaries and celebrities. Not

only was Nostradamus introduced to her, but he might have edited and written the speeches delivered by the town consuls, before
she was carried through the garland-decorated narrow streets of
Salon up the promontory steps into the Château de l'Empéri.
Meeting the man who so many believed had foretold her brother's
tragic death did not appear to cause her any ill ease. César later
reported that Princess Marguerite found Nostradamus' Latin
inscription in fine taste and added, "a gentleman who was present
at all of these events assured me that this Princess entertained [my
father] a long time and did him much honor."[10]

If some governors were banning the works of prognosticators,
the Duc de Tende and Grand Seneschal of Provence, who was
present at the festivities, was happy to greet Nostradamus publicly
as his friend and receive astrological consultations. It is related that
Nostradamus also read the stars of Comte de Crussol and the
horoscopes of other powerful friends and nobles of Provence, such
as Commandeur de Beynes and Baron de la Garde, the Admiral of
France's Eastern Fleet.

It is clear from her documented comments that the Queen
Mother, Catherine de' Medici, was aware of these consultations
and looked increasingly to the prophet for guidance. This may
have even led to a secret summons in 1560 for Nostradamus to
divine the future fates of her children.

Hot Mountain Smoke and Mirrors

Down the Loire valley, in the deep gloom of the hours after midnight when the white stone battlements and towers of the Château
de Chaumont are as pale as bones in the anemic light of the moon,
a hooded and white-robed priest of the magical rite laid out his
tools in the occult observatory of Catherine de' Medici. Within
the spare stone-built room, illuminated by candles with the green
ambience of the moonlit night soaking through one window, he
drew his magic circle and placed skull, pentagrams and a drugged

cat in their appropriate places. On his table were arranged his magical dagger, sword, and vials and jars holding ingredients sweet and noisome for the incantation of spells. Standing before his magic circle was a large mirror, made of lead. Whispering softly, the hooded priest dabbed a finger into a vial of pigeon's blood and began drawing on the four corners of the mirror in Hebrew the names of God – Yahweh, Elohim, Mitratron, and Adonai. Candles were lit. All was ready. The great lady of the Château was summoned.

The shadow of the Queen Mother entered, a vision of widow's black. A face pale as the full moon, her eyes grim with dark intent, she offered her hand to the hooded priest and together under the caress of his soft and encouraging incantations they entered the circle. Vowels sighed and consonants chafed Hebrew verses of invitation for the invisible Angel Anael to breathe life into the mirror.

They both stared intently into the dark and polished metal surface. Through the dim light the queen and the wizard saw a vision of the room's reflection float farther away as if they were seeing the walls of another room beyond the laboratory. As their hypnotic contemplation deepened, they perceived a youth in royal finery move out of reflected shadow. Young François II stepped forward, his eyes fixed on his mother. Upon the priest's Hebrew invitation the reflection of the king orbited the "other" room like a sleepwalker. After one orbit he was made by ill omen to vanish. This signified his death was at hand. After François came the apparition of his younger brother, Prince Charles, who when bidden to stroll the reflected room made 14 turns before vanishing. Alas, this signified Charles would only live to reign for 14 years. Catherine's favorite child, the future Henry III, next appeared. He circled the room 15 times.

The hand of the Queen Mother tensed in the hooded priest's grasp. She gathered her long frame up, preparing herself. All but one of her sons remained to enter the circle, Hercules Duc d'Alençon. This was the least loved of them all, yet perhaps he would grow with maturity, live long, and prosper upon the French throne when better-favored sons had ruled too briefly. The mirrored specter of the Alençon appeared, yet the child's image suddenly clouded over and faded. In his place another child appeared – an image of a young heretic, the Huguenot prince, Henri of Navarre. She let go of the hooded priest's hand and stepped back. "No! Oh no!" she cried, biting the palm of her hand in despair. The priest lunged forward and blew on the mirror to banish the image of the Huguenot prince.

This would be the final magical rite held at Chaumont before the late king's mistress, Diane de Poitiers, would spend her forced retirement there until the end of her days. "Chaumont" means "hot mount," which implies it once was an ancient hot spring, and, at least metaphysically speaking, a psychically charged location for oracular vigils. After the ceremony, the Queen asked the hooded man if the mirror's image might have deceived them. He insisted that it could not lie. It is said that upon the merits – some would say the narcotically induced and hypnotically suggested visions – of the hooded man's magic mirror Catherine de' Medici would contemplate a union of her youngest daughter, Marguerite, to the Bourbon Henry of Navarre, the chief contender for the Valois throne. Haunted by the vision, she chose to wage marriage as a strategic weapon to ensure the survival of the Valois through its female bloodline. This occultist influenced the future of French history, yet historians and scholars still dispute exactly who the mystery wizard was hiding under the hood.

Detractors and debunkers of this now famous "Magic Mirror Séance" protest vehemently that Nostradamus could not have been the medium. After all, Catherine's other famous astrologer, Cosimo Ruggieri, was living at Chaumont at the time. He must have been the one under the hood who unlocked the flaming visions of the mirror in her newly constructed occult laboratory. Perhaps, but skeptics rest this assumption on only one historical biographer's account of the life of Catherine de' Medici, that of Nicholas Pasquier. In addition, the assumption ignores the well-documented fact that Chaumont was a "base" of operations where Catherine sent many of her magicians and astrologers to practice their arts. It is possible that, given her great love for using the metallic magic mirror to see into the future, not only Ruggieri but also Nostradamus was invited to apply his skill at Chaumont in 1560. J.R. Jochmans in *Nostradamus Now*, speculates that such a secret, and therefore hard-to-document, meeting at Chaumont could have taken place between Catherine and Nostradamus as early as the year he had his royal audience at St.-Germain-en-Laye and fulfilled his errand to draw up the horoscopes of her children, who at the time resided at the Château Blois, just upstream from Chaumont. One need only examine a few pieces of surviving correspondence from late 1559 between Nostradamus and his business clients, reproduced in Jean Dupèbe's *Nostradamus – Lettres Inédites*, to see that the subject of a second visit to Paris was being considered by the prophet for 1560, but it then was cancelled.

In his letter to Jean Morel, signed on 31 October 1561, Nostradamus states his hope to visit Paris and go to Court both to set his son César at his studies and to "satisfy several personages who beg me to come there, which I will do." As stated earlier, the Morel letter does not mention Nostradamus' trip to the Loire Valley from St.-Germain-en-Laye to plot the charts of the Valois children, perhaps because the mission was secret. We might assume that if the Queen Mother had summoned Nostradamus for a second journey to the Loire valley to conjure images on a magic mirror in a ceremonial hooded robe, he would also have kept this secret. Those who believe Cosimo Ruggieri was the man under the hood might draw comfort (if not objective confirmation) for their case from Manly P. Hall's observation that at age 57, Nostradamus' constitution was no longer hardy enough to withstand long journeys by horseback or unsprung coach. Indeed, there is no indication from the steady flow of almanac publications in 1560–61 that months of travel interrupted his writing schedule, as they had in 1555–6. Also, the source of the story of the magic mirror does not come from an eyewitness or a historian, but from one of France's finest 19th-century novelists, Honoré de Balzac – even though Balzac, like his contemporary, Alexandre Dumas, was quite scrupulous in his research.

If Balzac's account is true, then the actions of the mystery magician himself may best cast doubt on his being Nostradamus. The fiery Ruggieri was known for being blunt and undiplomatic. At the last, he lost favor with Catherine and ended his career on the rack. If it were Nostradamus blowing off the offending image of little Henry of Navarre on the mirror and if the Queen Mother had asked him whether the Angel of the mirror had deceived them, it would seem out of character for Nostradamus to stubbornly insist that the mirror could not lie. He was ever deferential to a royal personage and wary of royal retribution.

Prescient Vindication

Ralph Roeder, in his biography of Catherine de' Medici, described the first half-year of the young king's reign as a "prolonged hunting-party." François was all too happy to "seek relief from the long agony of his father's passing in the violent exercise which, for a Valois, was the only antidote for the vicissitudes of living."[11] The king's handlers, the Guise, and the Ambassador of Spain, had encouraged his obsession to ride down game to distract him from most of his duties – some would say, all the better for the Guise to draft and control royal policy according to their designs. They could, however, take honest satisfaction in the effect the grueling tour of royal hunting forests from Meudon, Dampierre, Saint-Germain, Viller-Cotterêts, Nateuil, Longport, Fère-en-Tardenois, and Fismes had had on the king's body. As he turned 16, François, energized by his exertions, began a dramatic phase of catching up on his earlier stunted growth. The future flower of a vital man in the seed of the sullen boy was beginning to sprout at last in a lanky physique.

As spring approached in 1560, other things were blooming early on the fringes of royal hunting properties – a Protestant coup d'état. Since the death of Henry, the Protestant faction at Court had swelled with power and influence through the conversion of Gaspard de Coligny and the Bourbon Prince de Condé to the Reformed Church. In early 1560, François resumed his marathon hunting tour after briefly attending to his royal business. His wanderlust for blood sports took him through Bar, Fontainebleau, Marchenoir, and Châteaudun, and he finally directed his reduced Court of carefree hunters to pitch camp in the forests of the Loire valley surrounding the Château Amboise, near the fortified town of Amboise. Coligny and Condé masterminded a plot to overtake the king's hunting party in the château's surrounding forests and dales with a band of several hundred Huguenot horsemen personally led by Condé. Their intention was not to harm the king, as all sides viewed him as a political and sacred figurehead of France. Instead, Coligny and Condé intended to "liberate" François from the clutches and council of the Guise – by pistol shot or rapier thrust if necessary. The conspirators intended to bear down on the king's hunting party, grasp his horse's reins and lead his young Highness off to neighboring provinces south of Amboise sympathetic to the Huguenot cause. Condé would then present the king with a petition for the convocation of the Estates-General. It was hoped that in this rare assembly – akin to a constitutional convention where the king discussed reforming law with representatives of the aristocratic, clerical, and bourgeois classes of French society – that some edict of tolerance and promised security could be agreed upon that would safeguard the civil rights of the Protestant French community.

The outcome of their scheme may have been recorded five years before it happened. Not long after Duc de Guise had decorated the crenellations of the Château Amboise with the rotting, decapitated bodies of dozens of captured and executed Huguenot horsemen, courtiers hunted for references in Nostradamus. Soon eyewitnesses at Court to the public beheadings staining the court-yard gravel of Amboise, along with readers throughout France, quoted Century 1, Quatrain 13 as a successful prophecy for what had come to be known as the Conspiracy of Amboise:

Les exilez par ire, haine intestine,
Feront au Roy grand coniuration:
Secret mettront ennemis par la mine,
Et ses vieux siens contre eux sedition.[12]

The exiles because of ire and intestinal hatred,
Will bring against the King a great machination:
Secretly they will place enemies as a threat [bated],
And to his own old ones, against them sedition.[13]

To those sympathetic to the Catholic cause, and the Queen Mother's regency over her son, the "exiles" who had returned to France from their capture at St.-Quentin were recognized as Coligny and Montmorency. The former had converted to the Protestant faith while in a Spanish dungeon. Coligny and Montmorency were implicated along with the Bourbons as those with enough "intestinal hatred" of the Guise to be accused of a conspiracy to send an army of selected horsemen to seize the Château Amboise, capture François II, and murder the Guise. An informant in their camp leaked the plot, allowing François de Guise, the Lieutenant General of France, time to summon French military forces to protect the king from "seditionists."

The Presage for April 1560 from the new Almanac for the current year might have come to Catherine's attention. If Nostradamus intended it for the conspiracy, he only missed his timing by a fortnight. The bloody day of the failed ambush came in mid-March, not in April. But the rest of the details, presciently gathered in his secret study the summer before, seem to describe details of the conspiracy:

Du lieu esleu Razes n'estre contens,
Du lac Leman conduite non prouuée,
Renouueller on fera le vieil temps;
Espeüillera la trame tant couuée.[14]

With the place chosen, the Shaved Ones discontented,
From Lake Geneva, led – proof's test yet to see,
They will cause the old times to be resurrected:
They will expose the well-hatched plot, frightened [they] flee.[15]

Hindsighted Nostradamians would later energize their interpretations when it was discovered that the preliminary secret meetings between the yet untested (*non prouuée* literally means "unproven") French Protestant plotters did take place in Geneva with John Calvin. Amboise was the "place chosen" at the meeting in Geneva for the ambush. Nostradamus states the obvious in line 1: a kidnapping of the Catholic French king would not go down well with the Catholic priests (code named "Shaved Ones" after their shaved pates). The riddle about "old times to be resurrected" plays with the Nostradamian comparison of Protestantism to a neo-pagan cult of Jupiter (i.e., the "Jovialists" mentioned elsewhere in the previous year's pamphlet predicting the malefic influence of these seditionists emerging around the time of the lunar eclipse of 16 September 1559). The last line, if Catherine and her court sympathizers applied it to events at Amboise, accurately foresaw François de Guise exposing and frightening off Condé and his host of Protestant plotters.

Courtiers might have turned to Century 8, Quatrain 52, where it seems the locations of the conspiracy are mentioned directly, in a prediction Nostradamus documented for publication as far back as November 1558 – too directly it seems. The censors responsible for granting the publisher privilege to print dismembered line 4:

Le Roy de Bloys dans Auignon regner,
D'Amboise & seme viendra le long de Lyndre:
Ongle à Poytiers sainctes æsles ruyner,
Deuant Bony.[16]

The King of Blois, in Avignon, to hold sway,
From Amboise and weak [Paris], he will come the length
   of the Indre:
Talon at Poitiers, sacred wings to decay,
Before Boni ...[17]

Amboise is 25 miles down the Loire from Blois. The Indre flows into the Loire another 25 miles downstream from Amboise, below Tours. Poitiers is 75 miles to the south. These geographical clues allude to the Conspiracy of Amboise. On 4 March, the Comte de Sancerre was patrolling the Loire outside of Tours when he came across a band of armed Huguenots led by Baron de Castelnau. Sancerre tried to arrest the brigands but they were too numerous, and he fled. After acquiring reinforcements, he traced the Huguenots' trail to the Château de Noizay, just a few miles out-side of Amboise, and arrested the band. This incident was one of many that exposed the Protestant plot and led to its ignominious and bloody end. *Seme* could be a double-pun for the Old French *seme* ("weak") blended with an erratum for the *Seine* river (repre-senting Paris, the seat of the Valois). In other words, *seme* could mean "weak Paris" alluding to the weakness of François on the throne. Line 3 implies the ruination of the hunt through a metaphor of spoiled falconry – one of the pursuits of French royalty. The ruination of wings might further imply the thwarted escape or "flight" of those conspirators from Tours, a hotbed of Huguenot activity, soon found hanging and rotting on the crenel-lations of the Château at Amboise.

   Thanks to the Protestant debacle, the Queen Regent made her first significant entry into the political arena. She became

Nostradamus' foretold *Vers. Serpens* mentioned first in Century 1, Quatrain 10. At last she was ready to play the dangerous bite-but-not-too-tight game of the serpent's ring of power (her new occult totem). The metaphorical message was: wisely clasp and control your own tail of dangerous powers, without hunger for more domination seeing you eat up all your power. Catherine the political "serpent" would use her new power to sink her teeth into the "tail" of the Bourbons and Montmorencys, not letting her enemies escape, but keeping them held close in her ring of influence. She needed them at court, not hanging from a gallows, otherwise who could counterbalance the equally consuming ambitions of the swaggering Guise? She used her influence over her son to have Montmorency and Coligny forgiven and pardoned, and had the king pardon other key perpetrators, such as Antoine de Bourbon and Condé. Grasped in the balance of her serpent power, the latter two owed their lives to her, and she would grip the powerful allegiance of these most dangerous enemies to offset the threat of the Guise. In the future, enemies such as Coligny and Condé would break this alliance with new acts of treachery. Her totem of power would finally lose its poise. Teeth, so to speak, would sink in revenge, and the serpent power she wielded would devour herself and her sons to the ruin of the Valois, as foretold.

But that was to be the final act, fomented by her third son, decades down destiny's twisted road. The tragedy of the first son was at hand. As the winter of 1560 approached, the king's tenuous health forced him frequently to cancel appointments and retreat to his bedchamber. Courtiers consulted their copies of *Les Propheties* and began quoting Century 10, Quatrain 39 under their breath.

Premier fils vesue malheureux mariage,
Sans nuls enfans deux Isles en discord,
Auant dixhuict incompetant eage,
De l'autre pres plus bas sera l'accord.[18]

First son, widow, unfortunate marriage,
Without any children the two isles in discord,
Before eighteen years, incompetent age,
For the other, while younger, betrothal's accord.[19]

Many believed line 1 must describe in terse and loaded detail
Catherine's first son, the young heir, François II, who after
Amboise lost his fledgling vigor. He moved the Court to Orléans
and returned to the responsibilities of government a timid and
sickly figure. The widow was his mother, the regent. He also
returned to Mary Stewart's bedchamber and remained the impotent husband of a childless and therefore "unfortunate" marriage.
On 17 November, François had a fit of convulsions and fainted.
Three days later the Venetian ambassador, Michele Suriano, posted a letter to the Doge of Venice from Orléans: "Every courtier
recalls now the 39th quatrain of Century 10 of Nostradamus and
comments on it under his breath."[20] As November passed the
health of the king worsened. On 3 December, the Tuscan ambassador, Niccolo Tornabuoni, informed the Duke of Florence by letter
that "the health of the King is very uncertain, and Nostradamus, in
his predictions for this month, says that the royal house will lose
two young members from some unforeseen malady."[21]

Conventional wisdom would tell us that Tornabuoni refers to
the Presage for December in the Almanac for the year 1560. In fact,
the prediction has nothing to do with this subject,[22] but
Nostradamus' allusion to the wedding of François and Mary
Stuart as being a "funeral song" begins back in the January Presage
for the Almanac of 1558, and it must have been widely quoted in
court by the end of 1560.[23] Nostradamus again ties their "nuptials"
together with "death" in a Presage set for December of 1558.[24]
Perhaps this is the prophecy the Tuscan ambassador and so many
at Court were applying to December 1560. Nevertheless, François
did die on 5 December, two days after the letter was posted to
Florence, just a few weeks short of his seventeenth birthday, and

certainly before his eigtheenth, just as Century 10, Quatrain 39 foretold.

Other elements of this famous quatrain would continue to reveal themselves in the following years. Mary Stuart, "without any children," would return to Scotland and become Mary Queen of Scots. This would throw the two island kingdoms (alluding to England and Scotland) into "discord" over a power struggle between Mary and the "childless" Queen Elizabeth I of England. If Elizabeth Tudor remained a virgin queen she would have to surrender the English throne to Mary. Charles IX, the next heir to the French throne, is the "other" mentioned in line 4. He was betrothed to Elizabeth of Austria at age 11 – an even earlier age than his dead brother was to Mary Stuart (age 14).

Another prince did die before the end of December 1560. He was the young heir of Roche-sur-Yon, the most junior branch of the Carpetian royal house, whose father was Governor of the future Charles IX. I cannot find the slightest hint that this Court rumor of a second foretold death can be derived from even the wildest stretch of Nostradamus' Almanac prognostications for 1558 through 1560. It was a dubious prophecy, immortalized by a coincidence. Yet the chance death of Roche-sur-Yon combined with the king's foretold demise incited Chantonnay, the Spanish Ambassador, to complain bitterly about Nostradamus in a letter to Philip II, posted on 12 January 1561: "It has been remarked that in one month the first and last members of the royal house have died. These catastrophes have struck the court with stupor, together with the warning of Nostradamus, who it would be better to punish than to allow to sell his prophecies, which lead to vain and superstitious beliefs."[25]

The new decade dawned with Nostradamus becoming famous throughout the courts of Europe. In May 1561, the Venetian ambassador Suriano wrote to the Doge of Venice, saying, "There is another prediction very widely spread in France, emanating from this famous divine astrologer named Nostradamus, and which threatens the three brothers, saying that the queen mother will see them all kings."[26]

The prophecy mentioned by Suriano can be found in three quatrains. French courtiers of the next two generations would have many opportunities to apply them all to Catherine's sons who indeed did become kings: the three Valois brothers, François II, Charles IX, and Henry III. The first "three-brother" prophecy is Century 8, Quatrain 17:

Les bien aisez subit seront desmis
Par les trois freres le monde mis en trouble,
Cité marine saisiront ennemis,
Faim, feu, sang, peste & de tous maux le double.[27]

Suddenly cast down will [be] those [once] at ease.
By the three brothers, the world put in trouble,
Marine city will be seized by enemies,
Famine, fire, blood, plague and all evils doubled.[28]

Lines 1 and 2 were easy enough for readers of Nostradamus in 1560 to apply to the topsy-turvydom following the accidental death of Henry II, though it is unknown how Catherine and the Catholic factions felt about Nostradamus' dire warning to the world about her sons. The English, aided by the Huguenots, did seize France's chief "marine city," Le Havre, in 1563, during the First War of Religion. All the apocalyptic elements of line 4 could be applied to the nine wars French Protestants and Catholics fought from 1562 to 1598.

However, beware the ease to which the obscurity of Nostradamus' quatrains can shape themselves to events of one's own time. Skeptics are right in countering that such a quatrain is general enough to be applied to any number of turbulent periods. For instance, if "three brothers" is taken metaphorically, then this could be applied to a purported 21st-century alliance of three terrorist-sanctioning "brother" nations such as those identified by American President George W. Bush as an "Axis of Evil" – Iraq, Iran, and North Korea. Likewise, one could move backwards into the 20th century to another axis of evil and suggest that the prophecy stands for three brothers (leaders) of Fascism – a "world put in trouble" by the Axis Alliance of Adolf Hitler, Benito Mussolini, and Emperor Hirohito. In this case, the "marine city" could once again be Le Havre, seized by the Nazi invaders in 1940.

A more specific "three brothers" prediction pops up in Century 8, Quatrain 46:

Pol mensolee mourra trois lieuës du Rosne,
Fuis les deux prochains tarasc destrois:
Car Mars fera le plus horrible throsne,
De coq & d'aigle de France freres trois.[29]

Paul the Celibate shall die three leagues from Rome,
The next two fled the oppressed Tarascque monster:
For Mars will set up the most horrible throne,
Of Cock and of Eagle of France three brothers.[30]

Three popes have ruled the Papacy under the name "Paul" since 1555: Paul IV (1555–9), Paul V (1605–21), and Paul VI (1963–78). Only the last one specifically died six leagues from Rome at the papal summer residence at Castel Gandolfo. Still, Nostradamus may have applied this to his own grim contemporary pontiff, Paul IV, the former head of the Roman Inquisition, who as a formidable celibate did indeed mercilessly purge his Cardinalate in Rome of its hedonistic ways (along with persecuting Rome's Jews and ordering the torture and burning of thousands of women convicted as witches across Europe). In this case, it could be assumed that "the next two" were his successors, Pius IV (1559–65) and St. Pius V (1565–72). They metaphorically fled the Protestant scourge, compared here to the Tarascque – a pagan Provençal version of the

Loch Ness monster legend. The Tarascque was a water dragon that
slithered out of the Rhône each May to devour a majority of the
youth from the town of Tarascon. One May, 2,000 years ago, it is
said that he was tamed by St. Martha. In the Nostradamus allego-
ry, the Huguenot cult is the "dragon," annually "devouring" the
youth of France by converting them to its heresy. He therefore
implies that the popes following Paul IV would flee from this
"dragon," rather than tame it – which indeed was to be the case.
The successors to Paul "the Celibate" did little or nothing to help
stem the spread of the Huguenots or render much financial or
military assistance to the French Catholics in the first four civil
wars fought during their reigns.

Alternatively, the courtiers of 1560 might link Nostradamus'
mention of Mars in line 3 to a similar warning he made in his widely read pamphlet about the malefic influence the lunar eclipse for
16 September 1559 would have with the martial planet. They could
expect that war was coming within the two-year window described
in the pamphlet (1560–62). Mars did "set up his horrible throne" of
war in 1562 with the first of nine civil conflicts. Courtiers of later
generations, guided by hindsight, would agree that this war "of the
Cock and of the Eagle" was specifically French, as these were
the kingdom's ancient symbols. Thus the "three brothers" would be
the three last Valois kings overshadowed by the "horrible throne"
of war. The Conspiracy of Amboise dominated the short rule of
François II; four civil wars and the St. Bartholomew's Day massacre
eclipsed his successor, Charles IX, and Henry III waged and was
finally consumed by four of the five remaining civil wars.[31]

The last clear reference to the "three brothers" prophetic theme
can be found in Quatrain 36 of Century 9:

Un grãd Roy prins entre les mains d'vn Loyne,
Non loing de Pasque confusion coup cultre:
Perpet. captifs temps que fouldre en la husne,
Lors que trois freres se blesseront & mutre.[32]

The great king captured by the hands of a youth,
Not far from Easter, confusion, thrust [of the] knife:
Ever captive times – what lightning on the roof,
When the three brothers will be wounded – murdered life.[33]

Many of its elements, though viewed as dire in 1560 for the coming reigns of the three Valois kings, would only take on airs of specific prophetic significance after the assassination of the last brother, Henry III, in 1589. People would later identify the "great king" as Henry III (although he was far from great). So disliked was he by his own Catholic forces that Henry had to ally himself with the Protestant military camp, and alongside Henry of Navarre he besieged Catholic Paris. In the end, a young priest who summoned him to within whispering range then stabbed him to death ("captured by the hands of a youth"). The deed was certainly far from Easter though: Brother Clément stabbed Henry III on 1 August 1589. Still, it seems Nostradamus identified the assassin's weapon correctly ("thrust of the knife"), and also identified the years of chaos and war that led to the ninth and final civil war ("ever captive times," "confusion"). However, the final line of the quatrain is wrong: Henry III was the only Valois brother murdered. François died of the fainting fever; Charles IX succumbed to pneumonia.

At the onset of 1561, French courtiers and foreign ambassadors in Paris were dressed once again in mourners' black after the death of a second Valois king in 18 months. They might have pondered the fate of the remaining Valois sons and the ominous days ahead. The "famous divine astrologer named Nostradamus," mentioned by Suriano in his letter to the Doge of Venice, had published a prophecy in May 1555 that many readers in centuries to come would believe described intimate details surrounding the assassination of Catherine's last son who was a king. Quatrain 97 of Century 1 reads:

Ce que fer, flamme n'a sceu paracheuer,
La douce langue au conseil viendra faire:
Par repos, songe, le Roy fera resuer,
Plus l'ennemy en feu, sang militaire.[34]

That which sword or fire did not know how to
    undertake,
A sweet, smooth-speaking tongue in council will make
    achievement [flood]:
While sleeping – a dream – the King will need
    to contemplate,
'Cus the enemy at the hearth fire, is in bellicose
    blood.[35]

The last king of the Valois, the five-year-old child to whom
Nostradamus was introduced at the Château Blois in August 1555,
was a morally and physically spent 38-year-old by August 1589. His
situation was precarious in the extreme. After conspiring to
murder Henry de Guise, Henry III was forced to flee with his
homosexual lovers/bodyguards to the camp of his enemy, Henry
de Navarre. Calls for his death issued from all sides of an eighth
civil war, yet Henry was neither cut down by iron sword nor the
flame of a matchlock shot. The instrument of revenge was to be
Brother Clément, a Dominican friar, who obtained a private audience in the king's bedchamber at St Cloud. Clément's mild manner and gentle speech threw the king off guard and, as he stood
near the cozy fire of his hearth to read a letter brought by the
young friar, he drew close as Clément sweetly motioned him to
receive a whispered message. No one had searched this man of
God to discover the dagger that Clément would thrust into
the king's abdomen. Loyal bodyguards hearing the king's cry
burst through the doors. It is said that Clément turned around
and met death on their swords with arms outstretched like a
crucified Christ.

Sympathetic translators believe the use of *feu* in line 4 is figurative for the Latin word *focus*, which can be defined as a fireplace, especially a hearth. Perhaps a specter of Nostradamus' inner occult mentation revealed to him the image of the hearth burning and the king reading the letter in its light when Clément struck with his dagger. It was well known that a few nights before Henry III had foreseen his own demise in a dream and related to his male lovers his nightmare vision of the crown and scepter of France being trampled by a monk-led mob ("a dream the king will need to [or be made to] contemplate").

For the year in which so many across France discussed the prophecy of the three brothers, Nostradamus opens his Almanac for 1561 with a presage ostensibly presented as a general prediction for that year. This quatrain, however, may be a secret coda to the end of the Valois kings, for in it may lurk details and names for a deed fulfilled in 1589 when Henry III, doubly a king of France and Poland, fell to an assassin's blade:

The King, King, not to be, destruction by the Clément one ...[36]

Christ versus Christ

They stalked Nostradamus down the narrow streets of Salon, pressing close enough that the old man with the Malaccan cane and the long beard (marking him as a Huguenot patriarch) could hear the young Catholic hooligans whispering amongst themselves about what they would do to him. A beating perhaps? Something worse maybe? The adolescent peasants and young bravos boldly hissed their debate down the old man's neck as they shadowed him, closer ... closer ... At any moment now would come the blow from a stone, some rotten refuse, or worse. Let him walk ahead, leaning on his cane, terror gripping his heart, unable to run. Their prey was well-shod and his scholar's robes and cap were made of the best fabrics. He must be one of the heretics and his street clothes betrayed the suspicious costume of a man of letters and learning.

Nostradamus swiveled around, swiping at the youths with his heavy cane. The sudden violence of his move, the spiked flame in his enraged eyes coming in close and threatening, took them by surprise. The Cabans scattered in all directions.

"Be gone, you clod-hopping scoundrels!" he roared after them, shaking his cane. "You will not step on my throat, while I'm yet alive, nor after I am dead!"[37]

The parents of those Catholic hooligans might have been dutifully polite in public dealings with him but in private they cursed and disparaged Nostradamus as one who must be in league with the Huguenots. Who else but a heretic would predict the deaths of good (and devoutly Catholic) King Henry and his son? Their children were fed this hearsay of hate and, as others across the realm, they became the active weapon of a community's building hatred for Protestant minorities.

Not to be left out of the mayhem, there also appeared roving gangs of a Protestant intifada wherever their communities were at parity with or held a majority over their Catholic neighbors. Though less predisposed to murder than the Catholic peasant gangs, they tended to ransack and disfigure churches, assault priests and destroy the property of suspected Papists. In Poitiers in 1559, Protestant boys and girls – some as young as 10 and 12 – overthrew the Cathedral altar, toppling statues of the Virgin Mary and the saints, calling them the stone spawn of Catholic idolaters. Protestant gangs were more inclined to indulge in demonstrations of their new-found piety, singing Psalms in the vernacular in street parades, and these usually ended in brawls with Catholic onlookers. Huguenot students disrupted universities whenever lessons of Catholic theology – of "the old religion" – took place. They all but shut down the University of Toulouse in 1562. The Catholics of that town, like many others across France, bided their time, took quiet note of the slights and who dispensed them – then, a decade later, they gathered across the kingdom in the hot summer nights following St. Bartholomew's Day in August 1572 to take their revenge. The killings began in Paris – some say prompted by Catherine de' Medici – and reluctantly approved by François' successor, Charles IX. Catholic bands broke into the bedchambers of their Huguenot tormentors, pulling both men and women out from their beds. Most of the victims were already in a state of nakedness because of the stifling summer heat; if not, the mob stripped off their nightshirts and shifts. The Catholics then took them down into the streets and massacred them by the thousands. The bodies were ceremoniously tossed into the rivers of France in a macabre rite of post-mortem baptism which, radical Catholics believed, purged and purified their victims so that they could repent their Huguenot heresy in Purgatory.

It is likely that the gang of Catholic youths bearing down on Nostradamus, perhaps sometime in the first half of 1561, wore the distinctive gray winter cloaks that gave them their name, the *Cabans*. They mostly were country peasants, directionless youth, idle and unemployed in the off-season between increasingly meager harvests, who adopted the religious hatred of their parents as an excuse to pillage, rob, and murder not only suspected Protestants, but anyone who was suspected of being rich, educated, or just "different." The Cabans presumed God was closest to the poor and humble-born, and all rich people or all those made abnormal by learning and letters were sinners and they deserved what they got.

The peasant hooliganism of the Cabans became so extreme that for a time Nostradamus could not venture out of his door. In the streets below his closed window, he heard the upwelling echo of violence and threats to him and his family. Salonnais extremists of both persuasions of Christian belief mixed fanaticism and jealousy into their bitter criticisms of their neighbor on the Place de la Poissonnerie. The intolerant Catholics denounced him as a Jewish sorcerer – his long and famous association with the publishing industry in Lyon, a center of the Huguenot rebellion, marking him as a fifth columnist. They saw his long scholar's beard and thought he wore it in Huguenot fashion to taunt them, hiding an evil Calvinist behind a heretic's beard and mask of piety; whereas his Protestant neighbors, be they highly born or low, denounced this "Monster-damus" specifically for his Catholic piety and his prophecies fomenting conspiracies in their name.

The climate of hate in Salon eventually became so onerous that he considered moving his family to another town. Records in Avignon dated 1561 reveal Nostradamus signing a lease for a house there. One might speculate that some of his paternal grandfather's kin still lived in the city of that Papal enclave and might have encouraged his move to that Catholic oasis surrounded by the desert of sectarian violence and famine now gathering over Provence. Apparently, he never moved to Avignon, and the archives there indicate he handed over the lease of his new house to another buyer. The street violence in Salon had spent itself by the autumn of 1561, when law and order was restored and most of the Cabans returned to the fields to bring in the first good harvest in years.

His private correspondences during the early 1560s reveal a neutral position on the subject of the Protestant–Catholic discord. If there was any heat in his words, it is directed towards the dogmatic in their faith, Huguenots and "Papists" alike. James Randi has theorized that Nostradamus was a closet Huguenot on the grounds of his use of the derogatory term "papist" to describe ultra-orthodox Catholics in three letters to a German horoscope client, L. Tubbe.[38] Certainly, the reference to "papists" was of enough concern for his son and apologist, César, in his latter years, to demand and receive the letters with the offending word back from the client's family. Weighing this one comment to one Lutheran client against a mountainous record of pro-Catholic statements and an objective record of avid support by Catholic royals – including the Queen Mother of France and Princess

Marguerite of Savoy – makes this supposition untenable. If Nostradamus was indeed a Protestant, one might imagine he would have singed the fingers of his pen hand on 17 March 1561, when upon finishing his manuscript for his Almanac for the year 1562, he signed off his flowery dedication letter to Pope Pius IV.[39] Manly P. Hall relates that this dedication earned Nostradamus great gratitude and respect from the Catholic hierarchy in France.

Randi's sensational theory prompts us to look for a more down-to-earth explanation for the father's three offhand statements, and for his son's concern. Nostradamus, it would seem, was caught in the human foible of trying to please everyone. It will be seen that none other than the Spanish Ambassador to Philip II exposed this habit, a few years hence. A lingering literary record of the father trying to please a client exasperated his son in his later years, especially when religious passions rose again for a renewed persecution of Huguenots in the early 17th century. No doubt César's fears were motivated by any number of surviving childhood memories of the persecution of his father and his family. When the Cabans tormented his father, a move of home might have threatened the child's sense of domestic security, and in the following year César would have endured another emotional wound when he saw his pregnant mother weeping and his father in a state of shock and trauma upon his return from Marseilles. Nostradamus had spent some days or weeks under arrest there. He had been swept up in a citywide dragnet crowding the city dungeons with anyone under suspicion of being a Huguenot. It is said Nostradamus was imprisoned in the Castle of Marignane, outside Marseilles, under a charge of spreading inflammatory literature. It seems some Catholic official reasoned that only a heretic could write dire forecasts about the throne. Prior to the disasters of 1559 and 1560, his predictions might have been dismissed as idle foolishness, but when they began matching real events, fame's infamy put him on a number of police lists as a subversive to be watched. It is not known why he was quickly released from jail, but it is most likely he obviously kept his wits about him and made his jailers aware of his powerful friends, such as the most-Catholic Governor of Provence, the Duke of Savoy, and the Queen Mother of France. Surely he reminded his jailers how displeased they would be if he remained chained to a wall, behind bars.

César, though he was ever a Catholic, rightly feared that he himself might repeat history in his twilight years and, like his father, see himself arrested under suspicion of being a heretic. Even though the Protestants enjoyed civil rights after the nine Wars of Religion had spent themselves in 1598, this was only a short-lived interlude. A second Catholic terror all but purged them from France during the 1620s when the son of Nostradamus sought to hide away any mention of "papists" in his father's letters.

Nostradamus could still count on powerful friends who kept him one step ahead of the Inquisition's flames or the rapier thrusts of Protestants. In December 1561 he received a summons to Nice from the Duke and Princess of Savoy.[40] There he could enjoy a peaceful and luxurious respite away from the mean streets of Salon, drawing a horoscope for an unborn child of his royal patrons. He correctly calculated that the child would be a son and went on to predict that his stars would see him become "the greatest captain of his age." The future Charles-Emmanuel was called "the Great." He would become Savoy's most significant ruler, if not the greatest king of his generation. He would marry a daughter of Philip II of Spain and wage long wars with the Huguenot boy in the magic mirror at Chaumont – Henry of Navarre, the future Henry IV of France – and later with Navarre's heir, Louis XIII. It is said that in one of Nostradamus' many astrological consultations with the Princess of Savoy, he predicted the year of her husband's death "when a nine precedes a seven." Emmanuel-Philibert would die in 1569, when a "9" did precede a "7" – the year 1570.

After 1560–61, when the waves of sectarian violence had passed over Salon, moving to other regions of Provence, Nostradamus was left with the luxury of presciently propagating a solution to a crime of religious bigotry, set 22 miles away from the relative peace his town now enjoyed. In December 1561, the Cathedral at Orange joined the long list of hundreds of Catholic places of worship across France vandalized by the Huguenots. Sometime after Nostradamus returned from Nice he received a letter from the venerable Lords of the Church Canons of Orange asking his prophetic help in returning the holy relics stolen. Nostradamus' reply was signed off on 4 February 1562, and soon after was mailed to Orange, more than two months after the attack. Some scholars, such as Leoni, were puzzled as to why the cycle of correspondences took so long, because Orange and Salon are but 35 kilometers (22 miles) apart. Perhaps Nostradamus stayed in Nice longer than expected. Most likely, the long delay might be circumstantial evidence supporting just how difficult and dangerous life on the roads of Provence had become for mail-carrying wagoners and couriers as civil strife and armed bands of Cabans and unemployed mercenaries filled the countryside.

In the letter,[41] Nostradamus supplied a horoscope in the rectangular Roman fashion. Aided by this star chart he went into great detail about the perpetrators being fellow Catholic brothers of the church – not Huguenots – who used the pandemonium of riots to steal Church silver and smuggle it away to Avignon as "booty to be divided among canons who are at present like soldiers." Nostradamus instructed that a meeting of all the Lords of the Church Canon of Orange should be convened. He believed two of them were the thieves and suggested that on hearing his letter read at the meeting, the prophecies of plague and catastrophe for the perpetrators and their city would engender a facial reaction that would expose the culprits to the other church lords. "The faces of those in collusion will change," promises Nostradamus, "with great shame and confusion that they will be unable to suppress."

If indeed the letter was read aloud in the meeting, and if these "wolves" that, according to Nostradamus, the sheep of Orange have been entrusted to were present, he promised the thieves would die a terrible death, or repent and secretly return the holy goods to the altar.

Rest assured my venerable Lords, if that which was stolen is not returned, one way or another, the perpetrators will die the most miserable death, more lingering and more violent and of more unbelievable intensity than ever before occurred – unless everything is restored and replaced in its ancient repository, and thus you will find it to be.

Unfortunately, there is no surviving record of whether this "propheganda" fear tactic persuaded the culprits to return the goods. Neither is there a record of anyone in Orange suffering a specifically apocalyptic strain of the plague as divine retribution. Perhaps if records existed they were lost after the onset of a 40-year era of religious civil wars – long warned against by Nostradamus – that began to overtake France the following year.

CHAPTER TEN

Twilight Triumph

༜

Scry Havoc and Dogs of War

For the year 1562, Nostradamus predicts the "season of winter" would be "good," the spring "sound." Evil weather (both in climate and perhaps in the humors of men) comes by summer. The autumn will be "pernicious, dry" and wheat crops "rare." The wine harvest will be "enough," but the latter half of the year has "evil eyes, deeds" and other molestations in store. There will be "war, mutiny" and "seditious waste."[1] The first civil war was coming.[2]

The Presage for January[3] gives goodness one last chance, for in the first month of the new year a "hidden desire for the good" would succeed with "religion" in "peace, love, and concord." This last effort for a peaceful resolution between Protestant and Catholic factions did indeed take place in January 1562, when Catherine de' Medici enjoyed her highest moment of diplomatic success, drafting the Edict of January. It was Catherine's "hidden desire" to bring peace by legalizing the coexistence of two religions in one state. However, the hopefulness of Nostradamus' poetry reaches a snag by the third line when he says, "The wedding nuptial song will not be completely in accord." This might be a perverse euphemism for Catherine's marriage of religions putting an edict's paper-thin seal over a powder keg ready to explode.

∽

Church bells called the faithful of the town of Vassy to worship on Sunday, the first of March. The chiming caught the attention of François de Guise, who, followed on horseback by his family and an armed troop of 200 men, was riding through the town. He was informed that a congregation of Huguenots was assembling for worship at the nearby Grange, which had become their makeshift temple. Thanks to Catherine's Edict of January, they could gather in broad daylight on the Christian Sabbath to sing and pray. Guise was curious, and considered observing their service, but remembered it was Sunday and decided to attend mass instead. As it turned out, the Catholic church was next to the local Grange. Guise and his family began their devotions but it seemed to the Lieutenant General of France that the vernacular hallelujahs coming from the Huguenots in the neighboring place of worship were purposefully too loud and strident. Guise ordered some of his armed guards to hasten next door and admonish the Huguenots to quiet down. He once again began his devotions to *his* Christ when a new and louder chorus of angered voices disturbed his prayers. He emerged from the Catholic church to see his soldiers engaged in a pushing and shoving match with Huguenots at the Grange barn door. Some Protestants, probably children, recognized Guise and threw stones at him. His escort unsheathed their swords and charged the barn and its occupants. In the ensuing slaughter, 30 Protestants were killed and 130 wounded.

It is a peculiar irony that the long-dreaded religious civil war would come at last on a Sunday, and that the first blood spilt should stain the muddy earth separating two embattled neighboring churches. A Presage from an earlier Almanac intended for August 1561 reads more fittingly for the bloodshed inflicted at

Vassy in March 1562.[4] It mentions "the nonchalant ones of the change" soon "dead and seized" at the "Grange." They could have been the Huguenots, singing purposely loud, made bold by the "change" brought on by the Edict of January. Equally, Guise and his party were too nonchalant in turn to see how praying next door was an act of provocation; thus flowed the blood of innocents worshiping different beliefs about the blood of Christ.

The Presage ends predicting "the united ones locked up in the ruin[ed] Grange; through long help the strongest one astonished." It would seem that it implicates Guise, who was seen staggering through the heaped bodies of the dead and wounded in the massacre's aftermath. He could be the "astonished one" who beheld the wreckage of human life on the Christian Sabbath. It shocked him how quickly the incident had escalated from pushing and shoving to thrusts with halberds and swords. When faced with the grim harvest that he had "long helped" to foment over the years, he could not bring himself to comprehend it, now that the fruits of his hatred lay at his feet. Once he had collected his wits, he angrily summoned the justice of the peace of Vassy and rebuked him for allowing Huguenots to assemble openly. The magistrate reminded him of the Edict of January, at which Guise nonchalantly dismissed him, saying, "the sword will soon cut the knot of the edict."

Some might suggest that Nostradamus conjured a vision of François de Guise waxing metaphorical in his statement about the edict, which could be construed as tantamount to cutting the tangled safety rope to peace. The final line of his Presage for January in the year of the Vassy Massacre – the year of the first civil war – said, "The high ones who are low, and [the] high, put to the rope." The "high" François de Guise would be laid "low" in the coming war, a victim of an assassin's bullet at the siege of Orléans. On the opposing side, the "high" Antoine de Bourbon would follow, also felled by an assassin at the siege of Rouen. Beyond these, all the other "high ones" – Catholic and Protestant nobles and leaders

Nostradamus, a student doctor at Montpellier University, c. 1529–1532, attended anatomy sessions similar to that depicted in Bartolomeo Passarotti's "An Anatomy Lesson for Artists" (Galleria Borghese, Rome, Italy).

Speculative 18th-century portrait of Nostradamus in his thirties, during the Agen years (1533–1538).

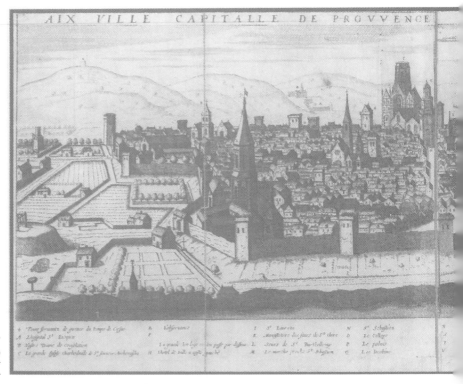

AIX VILLE CAPITALLE DE PROVVENCE

A mannequin of Nostradamus writing down his prophecies at his writing table
in a hypothetical reconstruction of his secret study as displayed in his restored
house-turned-museum in Salon de Provence (Maison de Nostradamus).

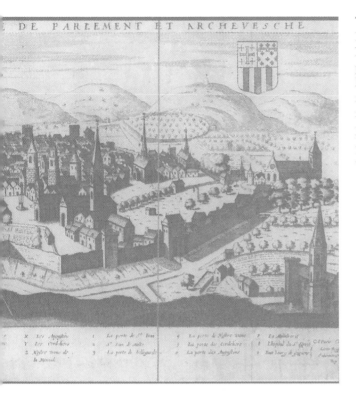

The city of Aix-en-Provence, where Nostradamus the physician single-handedly fought his most famous nine-month battle with the plague beginning in May 1546 (Civic Museum of Arbaud).

Nostradamus adopted some of the tools used by classical Greek oracles (depicted here) to conjure a divine emissary, such as sitting on a brass tripod and breathing in hallucinogenic incense – excluding the serpents (engraving by A. Poirauy).

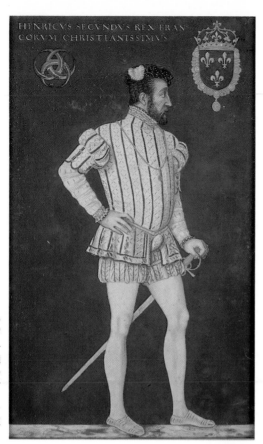

Portrait of King Henry II of France by Francois Clouet. (Musee Conde, Chantilly, France.)

Miniature of Catherine de' Medici, by François Clouet, around the time Nostradamus and the Queen of France first met in the mid-1550s (Victoria & Albert Museum, London).

TOVRNELLES

A· La Royne pleurant.
B. Le Cardinal de Lorraine.
C. M.le Connestable.
D. Postes courant & des medecins & Cirur-

giens bien expers, enuoyés de Flandres par le
Roy d'Espaigne.
E. Gardes de la chambre du Roy.
F. Medecins & Cirurgiens.

The death watch for Henry II of France, engraved by eye witness, Ambroise Paré. The surgeon Andreas Versalius walks to the bed with sponge and bandages while surgeon Ambroise Paré with his back turned grimly works at the table crowded with surgical tools and medicines. A gesticulating Anne de Montmorency stands at the head of the table to Paré's left. Standing along the far bedside (from left to right) are Cardinal Charles de Guise, François de Guise, Queen Catherine de' Medici and perhaps Princess Marguerite. On the extreme right of the bed is the distraught heir-apparent, François, with hands outstretched. At his side steadying François with her arm is his wife, soon to be the Queen of France, Mary of Scotland.

François II by François Clouet
(Bibliothéque Nationale, Paris,
France).

The house of Nostradamus in Salon-de-Provence. Note the
opened front doors revealing the inner courtyard (Maison de
Nostradamus).

A 60-year-old Nostradamus in October 1564 reading the moles of 10-year-old Henry of Navarre, pronouncing him a future king of France. That Nostradamus made this prophecy is a documented fact, even if the attendance of a seated Queen Regent Catherine de' Medici, hunting dogs, courtiers, and Charles IX was a myth. (Painting by L. Denis-Valverane, Musée de Salon de la Crau.)

LES
PROPHETIES
DE M. MICHEL
NOSTRADAMVS.

Centuries VIII. IX. X.

Qui n'ont encores iamais esté imprimees.

A LYON,
PAR BENOIST RIGAVD.

A horoscope composed by the hand of Nostradamus in July 1552 for a German client named Rodolphus Maximilianus (Editions Eric Visier, Verna).

Frontispiece to "The Prophecies of M. Michel Nostradamus" published by Benoist Rigaud, 1568. (Private collection.)

Right: Cesar Nostradamus, self-portrait. (Private collection.)

Below: Nostradamus becomes more angular in appearance in illustrations from later centuries (such as this one from the early 17th century) as he falls prey to the urban legend that occultists and conjurers somehow must have large feline eyes, long bony faces, sunken cheeks and hooked noses.

MICHEL NOSTRADAMUS.
Médecin,
Né à St Remy, en Provence, le 14 Décemb. 1503.
Mort le 2 juillet 1566.

A Paris chez C. lieuure Mr d'Estamy es rue d'Anjou la derniere P. Cochers a gauche entrant par larue Dauphine. C.P.R.

responsible for initiating general civil hostilities – would be laid low by death within a few years.

Nostradamus might have met them all when he visited Paris in 1555. With the onset of the civil wars, many contemporary readers of Nostradamus would search for, and perhaps find, cryptic references to their own demise in Almanac presages and in quatrains from *Les Propheties.*[5] Anne de Montmorency, the Grand Constable of France, and the stiff martinet who guided Nostradamus to his royal audience with the king in 1555 (and who famously cursed the prophet in 1559 for his success in predicting the king's death), would be killed less than a decade later leading a desperate cavalry charge at the Battle of St.-Denis in a second civil war. His chief adversary, Louis I, Duc de Condé, would follow in the third civil war, shot in the back as he lay pinned under his horse at the battle of Jarnac (13 March 1569). Gaspard de Coligny's brother, D'Andelot, fell a few months later. Coligny's turn came on the oppressively hot summer's night of the St. Bartholomew's Day Massacre of 1572. He had been wounded earlier in an assassination attempt and had taken to his bed. Later that night, Catholic troops broke into his bedchamber, disemboweled him, and threw the still living man through window onto the street below, uncoiling his entrails as he fell. Only Charles de Guise, the Cardinal de Lorraine, avoided a violent fate. He died from a cold in 1574, caught while walking barefoot in the driving rain leading a procession of penitents. The cleric who along with his late brother, François, had worked so hard to bring about a violent purge of the Protestants, lived to see the fifth of the nine civil wars that his propagation of religious intolerance wrought upon France.

All but one of the major players who had witnessed Nostradamus' arrival at St.-Germain-en-Laye in 1555 were now dead. All, that is, except the one royal who cared most about what Nostradamus had to say. And to that royal lady, Catherine de' Medici, Nostradamus picked his words carefully when predicting her fate in Century 6, Quatrain 63:

La dame seule au regne demeuree,
L'vnic estaint premier au lict d'honneur:
Sept ans sera de douleur eploree,
Puis longue vie au regne par grand heur.[6]

The Dame alone in the realm to remain,
Her "unique" extinguished first on the bed of honor:
For seven years will she weep with grief's pain,
Then long life for the kingdom and fortune far fonder.[7]

Catherine de' Medici persevered as regent of a war-torn France through the reigns of her sons Francis II and Charles IX, at last losing power during the reign of her son Henry III. In the decades to come, she buried her husband (her "unique" one) in a false memory. She had craved and never captured his love; now she clothed her memory of Henry II in a myth of his uniqueness and glory that her sons were expected to match. In the end, they disappointed her, being far more truthful shadows of her husband's mediocrity as a ruler. Perhaps Nostradamus' prophecy had inspired her to extend the official mourning time to his preordained allotment of seven years. She would continue to wear her famous black widow's attire for the rest of her long and courageous, if checkered, life. Before dying in 1589 at the age of 70, she might have taken some comfort in the carefully ambiguous placing of phrases in the final line's message, taking it to mean long life for her and eventually good fortune for her "and" the kingdom. However, the coda for her life could also read that good fortune comes for France *after* her long life had ended. Seven months after she died in January 1589, Henry III followed. After his death, Henry of Navarre, son of Antoine de Bourbon, would eventually reconvert to Catholicism and take his place on the throne, becoming Henry IV. He would bring to an end the Wars of Religion in 1598, ushering in peace and prosperity for France.

Everything Coming Out "Sixians" and Sevens

For the bulk of the 1550s, Nostradamus' controversial literary crusade to write a history of the future had been for the most part conjured into the open by an ever-deepening foreboding about the coming religious civil war. Yet, when the storm finally broke over France it spared most of fair Provence, especially the town of Salon. Huguenot bands in the first civil war might ransack Orange, seize Beaucaire, and desecrate Catholic churches and tombs high up in the limestone fastness of the fortified town and château of nearby Les Baux, but no armies raided Salon to make refugees out of Nostradamus and his family. Only old age had escalated its attack on Nostradamus. At the onset of the first civil war in 1562 he was 58 years old. From then onwards, the raids and ravages of time could be seen in his ever more labored and unsteady handwriting, his hands now enfeebled with arthritis. His once legendary sources of energy were in their twilight through the onset of kidney trouble and what can now be surmised as progressive heart disease. Some biographers, projecting their modern view of aging on the 16th century, say that Nostradamus was "burned out" and prematurely old, forgetting that average life expectancy was between 35 and 45. Viewed from a 16th-century perspective, Nostradamus had already beaten the Grim Reaper by a few decades.

Despite the terror of the Cabans followed by the turmoil of civil war and the sudden press of old age, Nostradamus continued to produce a steady flow of literary work from 1560 to 1563. His manuscript (composed in 1560) for the 1561 Almanac peacefully found its way to the Paris publishing house of Barbe Regnault. The courier was not ambushed by brigands, nor did this horseman or wagoner collide with Maligny's 4,500-strong Huguenot raiding party, which followed those same post roads down the Rhône valley in an unsuccessful bid to seize Lyon. The same luck followed the courier to the Paris publishing house of Nyverd, who carried the manuscript of a pamphlet predicting "Marvelous Prophecies for 1560–68."[8] Evidence shows Nostradamus finished the dedication letters for the Paris edition of the Almanac for 1562 by 17 March 1561, and for the Lyon edition by April 1561,[9] and that he produced a pamphlet for plague remedies[10] before the Cabans shadowed him, and any thoughts of pulling up roots and moving to Avignon could disrupt his emotional equilibrium. Although March 1562 began with a massacre at Vassy and calls to mobilization for the first civil war, the spring was bucolic enough for Nostradamus in far-off Salon to complete his Almanac for 1563 by 7 May, for the publisher Pierre Roux of Avignon and later for Regnault in Paris. He dashed off a dedication for the latter edition to none other than the noble who was a target of children's stones at Vassy and whose bodyguards avenged the slight with their swords: François Duc de Guise.[11]

The seizure of Le Havre by the English and Huguenots, the sieges of Rouen and Orléans by Catholic armies, and the incessant raids by bands of Catholic and Protestant soldiers across France had not prevented the safe transport of Nostradamus' manuscripts to his foreign translators and publishers in England (William Powell, London) and Italy (Allisandro Benaccio, Bologna) – despite the fact that they went ahead without a license to print them! Only an English edition of the Almanac for 1564 survives, but it is evidence enough that the French original was unhindered in its journey to Lyonnais or Parisian printing presses by the closing hostilities of the civil war in the first half of 1563. Nostradamus would also issue a *Treatise on Astrology*, published in Paris in that year by an unknown publisher. No copy survives; still it is safe to assume that the heavy criticisms by astrologers against Nostradamus' free-wielding mathematics inspired what could have been this rebuttal. Perhaps the fact that no copy of it survives might beg the skeptic in us to assume that his answer to the critics was too nebulous and labored, making his treatise on astrology too forgettable to preserve.

Despite the free flow of his lesser works in the first half of the 1560s, Nostradamus, seeing his mortality catching up with him, must have suffered a lingering frustration that his masterwork *Les Propheties* would remain incomplete in a single volume. Sixty quatrains from Century 7 were still missing. Two years after Nostradamus died, Benoist Rigaud, in 1568, no doubt with Nostradamus' instructions and blessings, posthumously produced *Les Propheties* in an excellent single volume that most scholars have ever since considered the principal edition from which they base their translations of the original French. Though it is true that some of the fragmentary earlier editions have resurfaced, thanks to the research of Chomarat and Brind'Amour, there are strong indications that Nostradamus intended many of the editorial and typographical errors in these to be cleaned up by his planned complete edition with Rigaud. With that said, the Rigaud edition contains the Preface to César, followed by Centuries 1 through 7 (still incomplete), the Epistle to Henry II, and Centuries 8 through 10.

There has been a lot of speculation by modern scholars about how certain quatrains for Century 7 came to be lost and partially recovered. One theory suggests that Nostradamus was a messy archivist of his own writings and somehow misplaced and/or threw away those pages of the original manuscript for Century 7. He discovered these were missing, sometime after Rosne's sloppy edition came out in 1557 with the last 60 quatrains for Century 7 dropped. Lemesurier speculates that there was some falling out between Nostradamus and Rosne. He surmises that when Nostradamus approached Benoist Rigaud for a new and better-printed edition, in a fit of pique Rosne did not return his copy of the original manuscript with the extra quatrains. The complete consolidation of *Les Propheties* in the 1568 Benoist Rigaud edition clearly lists extra quatrains 41 and 42. Probably Nostradamus and Chavigny rummaged through their papers sometime in the early 1560s and found two surviving pages with the two quatrains. However, during Nostradamus' final six years of life, he was either unsuccessful in pressuring Rosne to return the other 58 missing quatrains, or Rosne and his inattentive copy editor had already thrown the manuscript away once printed copies were coming off the presses.[12]

After the Benoist Rigaud publication of 1568, twenty years would pass before new editions of *Les Propheties*, such as those published by Pierre Ménier[13] (1588), would print four new and eight duplicate quatrains for Century 7, numbered 72 through 83. The 1605 "Seve/Troyes" edition[14] cleans out the duplicates, giving us four quatrains numbered 73, 80, 82 and 83, recovered from the 60 lost by Rosne's edition from 1557. As these four do seem authentic, we might conclude that either César or other relatives rummaging through Nostradamus' papers discovered them. Perhaps the randomness of the find supports the theory that Nostradamus drafted each prophecy on a separate piece of paper. This would support the apparent fact that a few individual page drafts of quatrains for Century 7 remained while the pages containing others had been scattered and lost over time. The Seve/Troyes edition also includes apparently authentic duplicate quatrains under the following index numbers: 6Q100, 8Q1–6, and 10Q100. It is puzzling why there should be new prophecies under duplicate indexing. Perhaps these are rejects, or quatrains mistakenly numbered, placed aside by Nostradamus and Chavigny to deal with later, but then lost and forgotten.

The Seve/Troyes edition also unearths two quatrains indexed for a planned Century 11, and 11 quatrains for a Century 12. They seem authentic enough. Apparently, the early 1560s brought a temptation in Nostradamus to break with his old goal of a complete 1,000 predictions in 10 centuries and venture writing more volumes. The indexing of the surviving fragments implies that a full 100 quatrains for Century 11 and at least 65 for Century 12 could have existed, but are now lost to us.[15] Leoni believes that some of the fragments of Centuries 11 and 12 may have surfaced in publications as early as Ménier in 1589. Buget says he found them in Chavigny's *Janus françois*, printed in 1594.[16] The quality of these

25 "rediscovered" quatrains shows heavy editing. Nostradamus' gradual debilitation by arthritis required ever more diligent copying and editing by Chavigny.

Unless a researching miracle should happen, the original 58 quatrains of Century 7 are lost forever. Nevertheless, a revelation in 1605 will not let lost documents peacefully lie. The Seve/Troyes edition of *Les Propheties*, published in 1605, displayed in its appendix an unearthed rediscovery: exactly 58 Sixians (six-lined prophecies) attributed to Nostradamus, completing his planned thousand "quatrains." This sizable assortment of prophecies, which could only have been composed in the early to mid-1560s, somehow escaped even Chavigny's attention. Indeed these Sixians resurfaced a year after Chavigny died. Notes in the Seve/Troyes edition explain that they were placed into the hands of Nostradamus' grandson, Vincent Seve de Beaucaire of Languedoc, by a certain "Henry" Nostradamus. The Sixians appear at the end of the Seve/Troyes 1605 edition under the title "Admirable Predictions for the years running in this century" followed by an explanation that Vincent Seve had presented them first to Henry IV on 19 March 1605, at the Château de Chantilly.

Seve's dedication letter to the king tells the tale of Henry, a nephew of the late prophet, handing over this precious manuscript to trustworthy Seve before his passing. Seve kept the Sixians secret for many years until some Sixians pertaining to the future of the king and the Bourbon heirs had already been fulfilled.[17] At last, concern for the king then compelled him to bring these prophecies to royal attention. After many literary stoops and bows, the dedication letter invites the king to read them, promising he will find some things "worthy of his admiration." Seve says the Sixians are "no less worthy and admirable" than his late uncle's better-known prophetic works. He then adds that the Sixians are specific prophecies for the 17th century written "not as obscurely as [Michel Nostradamus] had done in his [first quatrain prophecies];

but by enigmas, and the things so specified and clear that one can safely judge when something has happened."

Are the Sixians a flurry of six-lined poems Nostradamus wrote in his twilight years to plug the gap of the missing 58 quatrains of Century 7, thus completing his planned 1,000 prophecies? Why indeed would he plug the structural hole with a gaggle of less cryptic and more flourishing six-lined forecasts, rather than keep to the harmony of the stylistically cloudier and more modestly tailored four-line quatrains? If time and events can be a judge, then Seve's oracular perception that the Sixians foretell French Bourbon destiny in the 17th century must have come to him through the haze of one too many rounds of bourbon. These purportedly "clearer" renderings by Master Nostradamus are clear failures.

There is a paper trail proving that Vincent Seve was a grandson of Nostradamus, as letters written by César[18] imply. Seve was regarded as a son to him; however, there is hardly an archival footprint to the origins or existence of "Henry" Nostradamus. He was no son of Nostradamus, and if the seer's other three brothers seeded him into existence, no archive of Salon, St.-Rémy, or any other town in Provence logged a surviving baptismal record of a "Henry Nostradamus" in three generations.[19] It appears that Seve sent a *copy* of the prophecies to Henry IV, not the originals. Only Jaubert in his *Eclaircissement* (1656) claims to have seen the originals in the library of M. Barbotteal, Canon of Amiens. He also claims to have seen "132 Sixians," not 58.

The Sixians have had their apologists. Even modern and respected Nostradamians, such as Charles de Fontbrune and Peter Lemesurier, still present a few Sixians in the pages of their interpretations of Nostradamus. Lemesurier to date made the staunchest defense for them in his *Nostradamus Encyclopedia*. His sincere theories deserve a skeptical response. First, he argues that a forger tries hardest to emulate the victim of his forgery. Thus, he believes only Nostradamus himself would or could summon the creative desire and skill to break his own style rules, and therefore become his own forger. But Lemesurier does not explain *why* he would want to break from his own established style. Nostradamus showed no such predilection to change his other narrative prose or poetic voices in his almanacs or his major works as they appeared in print between 1555 and 1568. There is just no plausible reason evidenced for this sudden and drastic change in style of the Sixians unless they are a forgery. Lemesurier thinks a forger would boldly claim these 58 Sixians as an attempt to complete the 1,000 planned prophecies when the true author would not boast about it. However, he overlooks the need of a shifty forger to avoid stating the obvious, because the obvious brings more scrutiny.

Lemesurier leaps over the fact that the Sixians present symbolic and enigmatic characters not seen in *Les Propheties*, yet he believes the themes "mesh extraordinarily well with those of earlier work, and their respective dates largely coincide too." He bases this finding, as do all Nostradamians, on the merits of his own ability to decode the prophecies. That is a very subjective call. I must admit that I would have a far greater respect for Lemesurier's ability to decode Nostradamus, if his very captivating and detailed 1998 documentation that Nostradamus had foreseen Muslim armadas and military hosts invading Europe by the dawn of the new millennium had not been such an utter failure.[20]

Lemesurier admits that the style and format of the Sixians is a bit suspicious, yet he believes the style nonetheless compatible with the poetic cadence and word usage we see in the latter-day presages from 1565–6. Finally, Lemesurier concedes that if indeed the Sixians are the work of a forger, and written no later than 1605, then this forger is an authentic prophet in his own right. Lemesurier thereby finds it hard to imagine who in 1605 had the skill and gift of sight to write the Sixians, if they were not originals from the hand and mind of long-dead Nostradamus.

An answer to this challenge can be easily tendered.

Someone qualified enough to forge the Sixians was alive up to a year before their publication. The person was intimately close to Nostradamus, and spent years pouring over his rough manuscripts – especially those Presages published in his final years – copying and editing them while he was alive. This strong candidate for authorship of the Sixians is none other than Jean-Aymes de Chavigny. Remember his motivation for dropping a political career to become Nostradamus' secretary and disciple. Consider, too, that he also had ambitions to be a prophet in his own right. The written and published record shows Chavigny ever interested in increasing the light of his own importance by standing near the light of his master. Jean-Aymes de Chavigny was alive up to a year before the Sixians "appeared." Conventional wisdom would pose that a forger might not want to "discover" these prophecies while the master's secretary was around to refute them, but it could also be reasoned that if the forger *was* the secretary then he might not want to be around to see *his* forgery discovered by others. It is a long and often suppressed historic fact in the traditions of prophecy that disciples write their own predictions under the names of their famous masters. The writing style of biblical prophets such as Isaiah, Daniel, and Zecharaiah strongly indicate more than one author hidden under their famous prophetic bylines. Chavigny could be such a disciple.[21]

The Pacification of One's Enemies

An unsteady peace fell over France after the First War of Religion ended in the spring of 1563. Due to the murder of François de Guise, and the minority of the 13-year-old king, Charles IX, Catherine de' Medici filled the power vacuum, taking on full responsibility as Queen Regent. She tried her best to temporize with the simmering religious factions, but after a year of applying her best efforts to mother the people and lead her kingdom, she concluded that a great tour of pacification was needed as a last-ditch effort to forestall a second civil war. Catherine reasoned that if she could meet the people, and present before them their young king, then a face-to-face interaction might yet strengthen the efforts for peace. Key to the planned two-year tour was a scheduled meeting on the Spanish border near Bayonne, where Catherine planned to speak with her daughter Elizabeth, now the Spanish queen, and her advisers. They would discuss how Spanish and French Catholics might better unify against the growing Huguenot threat.

The Royal Progression gathered in Fontainebleau in the spring of 1564. Catherine oversaw the scaling down of a mobile court and Royal Council of 800 courtiers and nobles. They would abandon the softer sedentary life of châteaus and palaces for a 24-month expedition, riding by litter, coach, or horseback across the length and breadth of France. Litter-bearers and coaches would also carry Catherine's "Flying Squadron." They were 35 fetching and high-born ladies chosen from the finest families all over the kingdom. Catherine's intention was to inject an atmosphere of charm and debonair fashion – those qualities that the plain Queen Regent in widow's black felt she lacked. Four companies of several hundred "gentlemen of arms" would supply security, along with a company of light horse and a full regiment of French guards. The caravan headed off with a long baggage train including hundreds of pages, servants, grooms, retainers, cooks, carpenters, laundresses, and all and sundry camp followers. By autumn, the expedition made its leisurely process south, keeping ahead of winter, reaching the sunshine and soft warmth of Provence. It is said that the roving court may have swelled to a caravan of 20,000 souls, including over 10,000 horses and pack animals, when by the latter half of October the first heralds rode ahead to announce the Tour of Pacification's arrival at the town of Salon.

A visit to Salon was given top priority. The string of Nostradamus' accurately predicted misfortunes had only awakened greater respect in the Queen Regent for him. Perhaps she hoped he could show her a way out of the evil string of events the death of Henry II had set in motion.

The arrival of the Court in Salon made its indelible mark on the mind and young senses of 10-year-old César de Nostredame, who published a detailed account of the royal visit a half-century later on pages 801–2 of his *L'Histoire et chronique de Provence*:

Very soon afterwards there came to Provence the young King, who was making a tour of his kingdom, and arrived at this town of Salon on Tuesday, 17 October, at 3 p.m. The plague had already been declared in this little place, where it had been very suddenly caught by four or five persons: such that the town being empty and deserted by people who did not care to struggle against such a pitiless enemy ...

Annals of 1563 across Europe recorded a general and fierce out-break of the plague. It carried off 20,000 people in London alone. For months now the Court, compelled by the expedition into a self-imposed homelessness, often encountered thousands of authentically homeless French subjects along the way, who were not only fleeing the plague but also were made homeless by the crippled economy and the civil war. The young king, riding into Salon with his vanguard, saw the lingering effects of the fear of the disease. César relates that Charles IX, regarding the sad and lonely houses and streets, concluded that Salon was in too pitiable a state to receive a royal train. César adds:

This moved His Majesty to command through criers sent from there that all the absent were to return, along with their belongings, under pain of prompt and heavy penalties: upon which each returned to his hearth as much to obey the royal command as to see His Majesty and more princes than Salon had seen in its entire history.

For the entry of this monarch, according to the custom of the times, several simple arches had been prepared, covered with branches of box, from the gate of Avignon by which he made his entry to the gates of the château [de l'Empéri], a magnificent and pontifical mansion. The streets were covered with sand and strewn with rosemary branches, which gave a very agreeable and scent-filled odor.

Roeder described the 14-year-old king as a "tall, thin lad, constantly unwell, frail, high-strung, of a retiring nature, and, like his father, guileless, good, melancholy, and mentally backward."[22] However, to César's awestruck young eyes, the regal mount and glory of fine clothes worn by the Lord of France made the man:

He was seated on an African horse, with gray housing and a harness of black velvet with large trimmings and fringes of gold. His person was cloaked in a mantle of Tyrian crimson – vulgarly called purple – enriched with silver ribbons; his hat and plumage accorded with his clothing. Antoine de Cordova, an honorable and generous gentleman, who shortly afterwards was made a Knight of Saint-Michel, and Jacques Paul, one of the richest men of his time, who likewise was ennobled several years later, being Consuls [of Salon], they received him at the gate by which he made his entry, under a curtain of violet and white damask.

Although César does not describe it, we can imagine that Catherine de' Medici, carried in her litter and followed by her flock of ladies-in-waiting, was strolling behind the king on foot. They immediately followed the king and his resplendently mounted and attired ministers and guards. The procession made its way to the château on the hillock in the center of the town where preparations for a royal audience were being made. Chavigny, who was apparently also an eyewitness to the royal visit, boasted later in his writings that Nostradamus "was the only thing worth seeing in France." He is the hyperbolic source of some myths that might make it appear that Catherine's royal course to the south was made chiefly to see her cherished Divine Astrologer. Certainly, a visit with Nostradamus was a priority once the Court made its slow six- to seven-month progress through central and eastern French provinces, finally making its way from Lyon down the Rhône valley into Provence. Moreover, as Salon was a hub for many far more important cities and towns, it only made it easier for the motherly mentor of the king to suggest they take the route to Aix via the road leading through her prophet's picturesque little town. Chavigny might have more accurately said that Nostradamus was the only thing worth seeing in Salon. Indeed, it is alleged that on entering the town, the king impatiently cut into the magistrates' flowery salutations declaring, "I have only come to see Nostradamus." César's narrative does support this sentiment, as once the royal party had settled at the Empéri, de Cordova and Jacques Paul hastened their way to Nostradamus' house nearby.

These two Magistrates, honorably accompanied by more nobles and bourgeois of the town, at once begged Michel de Nostredame – whose name was quite sufficient to account for their desire to have him along – to speak to Her Majesty at the reception, guessing quite correctly that she would especially desire to see him. But he excused himself as graciously as he could to Antoine de Cordova, his very intimate friend, and his companions, informing them that he wanted to move about independently and greet Her Majesty away from the vulgar mob, and from this crowd of men, being quite well warned that he would be asked for and sought when she arrived.

The itinerant apothecary who had tracked countless miles in search of herbal knowledge, the vagabond physician who hunted the plague across the kingdoms of France, Spain, and Italy (and for a time wandered as the hunted of the religiously intolerant), lumbered forth from his doorstep on one of the shortest but most significant journeys of his life. The afternoon of 17 October 1564 drew long and cool shadows from the château's eastern walls to ease his progress, as Nostradamus (perhaps with the assistance of his wife, and with his entire family and relatives in his wake) goaded his road-weary and gout-inflamed legs and feet to make the short, painful ascent up the wide limestone steps to the golden stone courtyard of the Empéri. He made his way through its arches and into the château's hall of honor, then waited his turn to be received by Charles IX and the Queen Regent of France. Standing not far behind, his firstborn son remembered the following:

Thus, very decently covered, he awaited the moment to render this homage to his King. The Consuls pointed him out to His Majesty, to whom he made a very humble and suitable reverence with a free and philosophical liberty, pronouncing this verse of the poet: *Vir magnus bello, nulli pietate secondus* ("A man great in war, second to none in piety"). Thereafter, as if completely beside himself with an extraordinary ease that he felt at this instant of seeing himself so humanely acclaimed by such a great Monarch, of whom he was born a subject, and as if indignant against his own land, he proclaimed these words: *O ingrata patria, veluti Abdera Democrito* ("O native land, ungrateful as Democritus' Abdera"); as if he had wished to say: "O ungrateful land, to whom I have given such a name, see how much my King still deigns to make of me!"

Abdera was a classical Greek town in modern Thrace, notorious in history for the stupidity of its citizens, who ridiculed and persecuted its most brilliant native son, Democritus, the 5th-century B.C.E. philosopher, who was the first Western thinker to conceive the theory of the atom. This was Nostradamus' moment to publicly honor his king with a classical flourish as well as enjoy what some would call a moment of "right revenge" – that is, in his case, when the unprompted and unexpected actions of respected people appear to silence and shame those who dishonor you. Let the town's hooligan Cabans, and other so-called devoutly "Catholic" brutes and beasts – unlettered and dismissive of Nostradamus – see him now, honored by his most Catholic King. Let the Protestant "Jovialists" across France be jolly now. What will their derogatory pamphlets dare say after he bathes in the king's approval?

It is hard to imagine that behind Nostradamus' aging mask of diplomacy and charm, there was not a deep-seated and supreme thrill that only those with a long and lingering martyr complex, illusory or warranted, can feel when reward and respect at last come their way. His heart must have soared like that of the tortured saints delivered into paradise. For so long since had the calumny of some of his neighbors and many across France wounded him. Despite this exultation, Nostradamus well knew that this gift of royal attention was dispensed on him from the Power behind the adolescent king. It must be assumed that the king's mother – and Nostradamus' avid believer – sat a few paces behind the king, in the background, her large pale eyes fixed on her now quite elderly-looking Magus and occult mentor.

César's account anticipates the impact his father's classical jibe would have when it was explained later to the unlettered Salonnais, after Nostradamus and the king had strolled together on a tour of the town before returning again to the château:

[This declaration about Democritus] he doubtlessly said openly enough in these few words, against the rude and uncivilized treatment that certain seditious rogues, gallows-birds, bloody butchers and villainous Cabans had given to him, who gave such glory to his native land.

Then my father, for it is of him I speak, accompanied [the king], always at his side, with his velvet hat in one hand, and a very large and beautiful Malacca cane, with a silver handle, in the other, to support him on the road (because he was often tormented by that troublesome pain in the feet commonly called gout) up to the gates of the château, and again in his own chamber, where he entertained this young King for a very long time, as well as the Queen Regent, his mother, who had a very benevolent curiosity to see all his little family, even to a little baby girl in arms. I remember this very well, for I was of the party.

It may be forgivable that history obsesses on Catherine de' Medici's darker occult activities and some of the ruthless means she applied against ever-present and dangerous enemies to justify preserving her sons on the throne. The record of her darker actions creates the myth that she was a witch in widow's weeds, yet Catherine was a complex and intelligent human being – Nixonian in her moments of near greatness and catastrophic mistakes – ever a prime target for a Bushism or two of black-and-white oversimplification. Some may find it hard to believe that this Catherine, who cradled and cooed at little Diane de Nostredame and delighted in Nostradamus' children, was the same woman whose orders would massacre men, women, and children by the thousands less than a decade later. They might even compare her to another notorious leader who similarly appeared sincere and tender when playing with the children visiting the Berghoff. To his playmates "Uncle Dolf" seemed too obscenely contrary to the tyrant their parents called Adolf Hitler.

Catherine was no saint, but the observation of one of her ambassadors might describe the monarch whose company César, his father, and family enjoyed so easily that day. Catherine had "humanity" and "goodwill, and patience in meeting everyone at their own level." The ambassador added that she was one who faced the first four years of her regency with "indefatigable constancy in receiving all manner of people, listening to their speeches, and treating them with so much courtesy that it would be impossible to ask for more consideration."[23] Ralph Roeder, in his insightful overview of her character, wrote:

Her goodwill lagged only when she was baffled by opinionation and bias, and then she betrayed it only by a lassitude which was the sole lapse of courtesy that she ever allowed herself. Her sophisticated simplicity, her poise and her sympathy, her genial vivacity and subtle reserve and her conversational skill were great charms which everyone felt who associated with her ... but these charms were mature and, by reason of her position, impersonal.[24]

Charles IX and the royal caravanserai left the next morning heading for Aix, the capital of Provence. From there the royal procession ventured west on the road to Arles, where they remained for 15 days, but it was not the last time Nostradamus would pay homage and receive honors from the king and his benefactor, Catherine de' Medici.

The Protestant Mole in Queen Catherine's Court

Catherine de' Medici left Salon with her wish upon Nostradamus' calculated stars that her dream for her favorite son, Eduard duc d'Anjou (Henry III), would come true. The horoscope given to her, and tucked away in her papers in a place forever lost to us, promised that he would become a king.

Her immediate thoughts about the previous day's audience with Nostradamus are not known beyond the satisfactory report of the horoscope. Certain obvious speculation might be entertained, such as thoughts of Nostradamus' rapid physical decline since she had last seen him in 1555 (or at least what the surviving documented record confirms was the last time she saw him – and not under a hood in 1560 at Chaumont). It is not known whether she was yet aware of the incident that took place early the next morning between Nostradamus and the 10-year-old Henry Prince de Béarn and future heir of the Kingdom of Navarre. If gossip caught up with her that evening in Aix, it might have further fed the premonitions that made all the beneficial wished-upon stars fade in the horoscopes of her sons.

The evening before, Nostradamus passed out of the royal presence and mingled about the multitude of nobles and courtiers crowding the château and the town. He became so intrigued with the 10-year-old Prince of Béarn that he asked the boy's governor and tutor if he might draw his horoscope. He also begged permission to read his moles and divine the child's future. According to the Coudoulet manuscript, the prince bedded down for the night at the house of Pierre Tronc de Coudoulet. The next morning the boy awoke to find his governor and Nostradamus bending over his bed. The prophet gently explained the reason he was there and persistently coaxed him until he reluctantly slipped out from under the covers to stand naked on the floor. Nostradamus stretched out his hand and slowly turned him by the head in quiet study of the play and pattern of moles on his body.[25] Then, after long reflection he turned to his governor and said his charge would obtain to his entire heritage. Then he added, "and if God gives you grace to live till then, you will have as master a King of France and Navarre." It is said that word of his prediction circled around the royal encampment. Even his most avid defenders must have thought Nostradamus had become a bit senile. A Huguenot prince on the French throne?! It was not taken seriously.

Great prophecies rarely follow conventional wisdom. The boy with the interesting moles became King of Navarre in 1572 and later a King of France in 1589, twenty-five years after the prediction was cast in the dermal blemishes. The boy was destined to become Henry IV, France's most beloved monarch.

His contemporary, Pierre de l'Estoile, the noted French diarist and historian specializing in the reigns of Henry III and Henry IV, is the credible source of this mole prophecy story. He wrote:

That which seemed incredible then has occurred in our own days: which prophetic story the King has since recounted often even to the Queen [Marie de' Medici], adding jestfully that because they delayed in giving him his shirt, so that Nostradamus could contemplate him at ease, he feared that they intended to whip him.[26]

Henry thought the fierce old man had come to give him a whipping because he was a frequent victim of the switch. His mother, Jeanne d'Albret, a martinet Calvinist, carefully instructed Catherine that while Henry was at Court she must promise to make sure her boy was taught to be a Protestant and follow a strict regimen of physical exercise – including frequent beatings to strengthen his sense of discipline. It appears that such treatment did not dim the future king's natural gaiety or his legendary *joie de vivre*.

The 19th-century Salonnais artist L. Denis-Valverane added many more fine brushstrokes of mythological color and glory to this incident. His painting can be seen in the Museum of Old Salon. He crowds the Coudoulet bedroom on the morning of 18 October 1564 with a packed gallery of important personages and their hunting dogs, all leaning in for a peak at the fair skin and seemingly mole-less object of Nostradamus' augury. Beyond the little naked prince stood his governor, and an entranced and otherworldly facsimile of Nostradamus, turning him by the head. Charles IX is there; so are what appear to be Montmorency and other Grand Seigneurs of the Court, with Catherine de' Medici seated closest to the shy object of divination, her equine visage looking on intently.

This myth has a basis in fact. Her ever watchful and thoughtful regard of the Prince de Béarn was accurate, even if she was not present at the reading of his moles. In the days to come she certainly would regard little Henry as Denis-Valverane had painted her, for she could not have overlooked the buzz around the Court about the prophecy. Was he not the little prince who had appeared in the magic mirror, obscuring her youngest son, Hercules? An occultist, yet politically pragmatic, had she not already contemplated marrying her daughter to the future king of Navarre in order to preserve the feminine Valois bloodline, just in case *La Fortuna* were to take an ill course, once again? In his book on Henry of Navarre, Lord Russel of Liverpool perhaps summed up her attitude to the boy destined to become the next king after all her ambitions and the Valois heirs were extinct:

During the years when he was brought up in Paris under the critical eyes of Catherine de' Medici she cannot have seen him growing up without a feeling of disappointment and, perhaps, even of envy, for her three sons, Francis, Charles and Henry, who were to become three of the worst kings who ever sat on the throne of France, could not hold a candle to him.[27]

Once Salon was left behind, the traveling Court enjoyed a 15-day sightseeing tour of Provence, dressed in its pale blue skies and golden autumnal best. They passed through picturesque Aix, Marseilles, enjoying the limestone promontories and cliffs jutting out of azure seas at Hyères, then off to Toulon, and the purported final resting place of Mary Magdalene in the hermit caves of La Ste.-Baume. Finally, the Court passed into Arles where they could admire its marvelous ruins of antiquity; chief among their touring itinerary were the delicate Greek amphitheatre and the ostentatious Roman coliseum. As it was now November, the fair weather had given way to torrential rains along the Rhône valley, making the river impassable for a fortnight. With winter rains putting a damper on sightseeing, and with time on her hands to brood about destiny and perhaps a Protestant's moles, Catherine most likely compelled her son, the king, to summon Nostradamus for another astrological consultation. Inflammation in his feet and knees from gout most assuredly had put an end to Nostradamus' years in the saddle. The old prophet probably made the two-day journey in a litter, either hired at his own expense or provided for by the king.

César describes his father's second royal audience with the king and his thoughtful mother:

While there [in Arles], [the King] desired to see more of my father, so he expressly sent to ask for him, and after several discourses, knowing very well that the late King, Henry II, his father, of very heroic memory, had made much of him, and had honored him greatly during his trip to France,[28] he dispatched to him a present of 200 gold crowns, to which the Queen added half as much, and gave him his patents as Counselor and Physician-in-Ordinary, with all the customary wages, prerogatives and honors.[29]

The river relented, and Nostradamus prepared to return to Salon and, for the last time, bade farewell to Charles and his mother, two key subjects of his forecasts who would elevate his prophecies and the mythology surrounding them (and their giver) to even greater fame beyond his days. In the following months, as the Royal Pacification wound through southwestern France on its way to the Spanish border, diplomatic dispatches give us some idea of the impact, both pro and con, of the Queen Regent's final meeting with Nostradamus.

The new Spanish Ambassador, Don Francisco de Alava, viewed the soothsayer from Salon with even greater cynicism than had his predecessor, Chantonnay. His first dispatch to Philip II from Arles gives us an interesting slant on the king and Queen Regent's audiences with Nostradamus:

Tomorrow there leaves secretly a gentleman sent to the Queen of England [Elizabeth I]. I know that the Ambassador is jealous. The first day that the King and Queen [Regent] saw Nostradamus he declared to them that the King would marry the previously mentioned Queen.[30]

This was a failed prediction. When Elizabeth received the offer to marry the adolescent King Charles, she wrote back with tongue in cheek, "Charles IX is too great and too small to become my husband."

Alava sent another critique to Philip II posted from Toulouse several months later. If his memory had not failed him, then it would appear that Nostradamus had not been summoned to Arles 15 days after the Court departed Salon, as César relates, but had joined the Queen Regent and the King as their special guest on their 15-day tour of Provence, only parting with them at Arles:

In order that Your Majesty may see how light-minded people are here, I will say that the Queen [Regent], when she passed through the place where Nostradamus lives, summoned him and presented him with two hundred crowns. She ordered him to draw up the horoscope of the King and that of the Queen [Regent]. As he is the most diplomatic man in the world and never says anything to displease anyone, he resolved in the two horoscopes to flatter the King and the Queen [Regent], so that they ordered him to follow their court, treating him royally until they separated and left him at Arles. The Queen said to me today, when I told her that I hoped, with the aid of God, that a great good would result from the future interview [between her and Philip II at Bayonne, specifically about solving the Huguenot problem]: "Do you know," said she, "that Nostradamus had affirmed to me that in 1566 a great general peace would reign over the world, that France would be peaceful and that the situation would become stronger?" And saying that, she had as confident an air as if she had quoted St. John or St. Luke.[31]

Catherine in her own dispatches to the Constable of France, Anne de Montmorency, recorded another pie in the prophetic sky coming from the horoscopes Nostradamus calculated while at Arles. She wrote with faithful confidence that "[Nostradamus] promises a fine future to the King, my son, and that he will live as long as you, whom he says will see four score and ten years [90 years] before dying."

This could have happened if a second civil war had not rained blood on Nostradamus' prophecy of general peace, and if the old war horse Montmorency had not ordered a reckless cavalry attack at the Battle of St. Denis in 1567 and so been killed at the age of 74. If Charles IX had been less nervy and self-indulgent, especially while hunting, he might not have died from bronchitis at the age of 24. Montmorency's death in battle and Charles IX's premature death were both implied in other prophecies written before June 1558. It seems that in his final days as an influential forecaster, Nostradamus let his gratitude, his pride, and his desire to please his benefactors blindfold his oracle.

At the very least, these unsatisfactory and final prophetic bromides for Charles' long life and general peace for France might point to an elderly Nostradamus projecting his hopes for a better future, rather than wishing to recount the dire times already recorded in *Les Propheties* and even in his Almanac for that "peaceful" year of 1566. Yet if we look beyond the Spanish Ambassador's cynicism, Nostradamus to his credit did get his "peace in 1566" prophecy partially right. Christendom's greatest threat, the Turkish Sultan, Suleiman the Magnificent, would die while successfully campaigning in Eastern Europe in that year, halting the clear and present danger of the Ottoman Empire's Western expansion deeper into Christian central Europe. Moreover, the year 1566 would also see some peace descend on the world, because our prophet's pen would be stilled by his death in that year.

That "peace" was still 18 months away when Nostradamus returned to his family from Arles with his gifts and rewards in hand. About this triumph in the gathering twilight of his days, his son, César, later wrote:

Sweet and agreeable things if they had had more import that is durable for him and his family, which could hardly have failed to raise itself by them to the best fortune if he did not abandon them. These royal favors which lasted only a moment seemed to be the signs and certain advance-couriers that a King greater than the one of France would very soon send for him to ask him to reply to His tribunal, as we shall see shortly.[32]

CHAPTER ELEVEN

From Life to Afterlife

∝

Anno Domini Almanacs

The subtitle of the Almanac for the year 1567 states that "the *late* Master Michel de Nostradame" wrote it.[1] A note from the editor of Benoist Odo publishers, Lyon, follows an opening dedication that Nostradamus wrote on 15 June 1566, explaining that Nostradamus had "exchanged the pain and misery of this life for something finer and sweeter" after he died on 2 July of that year. The editor adds that because of this he apparently could not endeavor to transmit the end of the "present prediction" (meaning the almanac) that he had embarked on with diligence a few days before, "foreseeing that the hour of his passing had come."[2]

It would seem that premonitions of approaching death had warranted that he summon one last burst of energy from the dying candle of his creative powers to compose a brief dedication for his final almanac, 17 days before he died. It is often asked by students of Nostradamus whether he was a prophet to the last, knowing the time of his death. A scrutiny of his final two almanacs reveals some interesting yet circumstantial indications that he might have sensed two potential death dates.

A complete and readily available edition of his second-to-last Almanac, for the year 1566, survives.[3] The dedication letter to the Comte de Tande (Tende) for the Anthoine Volant/Pierre Brotot Lyon edition was signed on 16 October 1565. Nostradamus tended to compose his almanacs for the coming year in the spring and summer months of the preceding year. The late date of this dedication letter might have been due to delays caused by the progressive, crippling pain of arthritis, making it ever more difficult to grasp the quill and scratch out his reflections. Evidence of this can be found in the last surviving business letter written to Johannes Lobbetius, a German client, less than two months later, on 13 December 1565. It clearly recounts a serious attack of arthritis beginning several weeks after sending off his manuscript.

The day after Gaspar Felchamer's visit, the bourgeois patrician of Augsburg, I had, by what bad luck I do not know, such an attack of rheumatism in my hands, that I was not able to make his horoscope for the agreed-on day. After which the pains passed from my hands to my right knee, then into my foot. Here it is now 21 days that I have not slept. Today I'm breathing a bit easier ...[4]

The letter then describes what was likely to be one of many instances in which Chavigny would copy his master's letters, as Nostradamus' twisted and painful fingers made his handwriting more and more illegible:

Hieronymous Schorer had asked from me a lot of work, and I sent it to him at Lyon, written with my own hand. He sent it back to me with disdain, saying that it was barely readable. I had it copied out, and yet he did not appreciate it ...[5]

The difficulty with breathing, plus the sharp fire and ache in the limbs and extremities, allude to something more than rheumatism. These are also symptoms of the last stages of heart disease.

Still, Nostradamus could yet again sense correctly a future waiting beyond his own life. He finishes his letter to Lobbetius, saying:

All that you write to me about Germany interests me, but I see as [if] from a lookout [point], great catastrophes menacing our poor France and even Italy. The wars of religion are going to break out again. There was seen at Arles, at Lyon and in the Dauphiné, a meteor, which presages great misfortune. [The meteor] was predicted in our prognostication of 1564.[6]

By now he had abandoned his penchant for weaving diplomatic promises of world peace into his prognostications for the satisfaction of Catherine de' Medici. His final Almanac, covering 1567, would be chock-full of ominous and accurate warnings for a second civil war in that year.

It could be surmised, because of certain clues in the Almanac for 1566 that work on the 1567 Almanac started early in the preceding year. Nostradamus, slowed and debilitated by more frequent attacks of gout, arthritis, and heart problems, might have believed he had but a half-year at the most to complete it. In other words, he may have given himself a prediction for a real deadline – his own passage into eternity – for 1 July 1566. In the Almanac for that year, we can find Nostradamus' latter-day literary habit of listing additional one-line predictions for each day of the month following the general presage for that month. A prediction for 1 July 1566 augurs *estrange transmigration* (strange transmigration). The phrase does not appear anywhere else in the day-by-day predictions in this almanac. He was only a few hours off. Chavigny tells us he died just before sunrise on 2 July.

There are more clues that he might have sensed the end coming with the advent of another hot and dry summer in Salon. Something he set down in verse of an unusually personal-sounding nature about debilitation and death can be seen in the Presages for May and July 1566. The first three lines of the Presage for May[7] run along with the usual oracular overview of discord and brutal enmity, deaths of princes, plague and the like, but the final line makes an abrupt change in tone and could be taken as a personal observation. It says, "Times good and full, but very dry and exhausted." Apparently, his final days were emotionally peaceful, and it seems he still basked in the satisfaction of his royal honors. The spring and summer months around Salon are known to be some of the driest in the land. Perhaps also, by the time he enjoyed his last spring on Earth, Nostradamus was physically burned out and "exhausted" by his eventful life.

The Presage for July[8] predicts tree blight and a good olive oil harvest, and Muslim corsair raids on the Mediterranean shores of France. (This being an endemic problem, it was a pretty safe prophecy.) It also forecasts the death of "some great ones." Are these the "great princes" dying in the Presage for May? One great prince was about to die, Ottoman Sultan Suleiman the Magnificent, not in July but in September 1566. That prince's death forestalled the planned invasion of a vast Turkish army into the heart of Christian Central Europe – a prospect intimated by these two Presages. Still, one wonders if Nostradamus was temped to use his wry wit to cite himself as one of the "great ones" dying in July.

There is no clear indication of just when Nostradamus composed the elements of his Almanac with its 14 Presage quatrains for the coming year 1567. A number of phrases and whole lines throughout the body of this final set of quatrains could in fact be either prophecies about, or accounts of, his last days. Because the 14 Presages are dated – two general predictions for the beginning and end of the year, plus one for each of the 12 months, knowing exactly when he composed them would have helped us better distinguish the true predictions from those that are historical chronicles, since he seems to have inserted personal events about his final days that roughly correspond to the monthly predictions one might expect from the previous year. The prediction for November 1567 in particular is widely believed to be a detailed prognostication of his own death back in 1566. One can only guess whether the manuscript was mailed to his publishers either on or a short time after 15 June – a full 17 days before he died at dawn on 2 July 1566. Chavigny claimed Nostradamus composed his own death Presage for November 1567, plus two more promising the resolution of family issues, eight days before he expired.[9] Certainly there is a chance that his manuscript was not mailed until some-time after his death, in which case it is possible that Chavigny edit-ed these predictions heavily and inserted details to punctuate his master's final work with a detailed, and retroactive, prophecy about his own death – the kind that are the most accurate! Equally, it must be stressed that cynicism, not evidence, "supports" the the-ory that Chavigny made final editorial touches of "propheganda." Indeed, as we have seen, the final "death" quatrain was scheduled for November 1567; this is strong circumstantial evidence that Nostradamus wrote it before his final health crisis, perhaps think-ing that he might have 16 months longer to live than was the case. Moreover, if we paint Chavigny as the forger bringing greater glory to himself by elevating his master's final prophetic success, one might imagine he would have switched the death quatrain from November to July 1567 to make it look like he got the month correct if not the year.

Chavigny's *Janus François* (published in 1594) ends with the November entry, intimating that it was the last quatrain of an incomplete final Almanac. Yet it seems that a long-lost manuscript of an earlier 700-page tome completed in 1589, entitled *Recueil des Presages prosaiques de M. Michel de Nostradame* ("Collection of Prose Presages"), was discovered in the archives of Lyon by Michel Chomarat in 1990. It contains a far more complete selection of Nostradamus' almanac verse and prose prophecies, including the missing quatrains completing the presages for 1567: one for December, plus a verse "for the end of the year." Why Chavigny would leave these important verses out of his later work is puzzling, and a bit suspicious, mainly because this is the only time we see

Nostradamus writing a presage quatrain for the end of a year. In his secretary's defense, it must be added that Nostradamus may have broken from habit because he believed this last quatrain would truly be the *end* of his last year and his prophecies.

Chavigny's statements in his *Recueil des Presages* declare that Nostradamus composed the quatrains for his final almanac last. Beyond innuendo and speculation there is no clear evidence to dispute this claim. And with that in mind, it can be assumed that the final three presages stand as prophecies for his death and its aftermath for his family. Any other references to illness and approaching death before his "November" presage could stand as secret mementos (laced with general and dire forecasts for the coming civil war) of his final struggles with death while he attempted to tie together the lingering business of his life.

"Hic prope mors est."

At a time when Provence decorates itself with many flowers, and the bright blue vaulted days of mid-June usually herald the early arrival of another delightfully languorous summer, Nostradamus was stricken with a severe attack of gout – a malady brought on by a necessary if vexing journey (by litter or unsprung coach) across the Crau wasteland to Arles to fulfill his duties as a Royal Councilor to the King. It seems that the trip not only disrupted his efforts to finish his Almanac, but inflamed the joints in his hands, right knee and feet, laying him low with the most serious attack of pain and sleepless nights yet endured. His final presages concern some cryptic *gift* or *treasure* Nostradamus is charged to deposit at the royal embassy in Arles. Whether this treasure is worldly or occult is not made clear; we only know that he is obliged to do this deed as a royal representative of the young King Charles IX. His Presage for April 1567[10] declares the recipient in Arles is deemed "a worthless one."[11] The correspondence that survives indicates Nostradamus had still been making day-long business trips to towns as far away from Salon as Aix-en-Provence in the summer of the previous year, so it is not out of the question that he dragged himself to a rented litter or coach for necessary journeys up until his final physical crisis. Perhaps the dating implies that the trip took place in April, and the wear and tear of the journey, duty-bound to satisfy some worthless royal bureaucrat in Arles, is blamed as the source of his collapse in June.

The April Presage further implies that Nostradamus took tender pleasure in his infant child, Diane (5), and his other young children, Anne (8), André (9) and Charles (10). At 15, his daughter Madeleine was for all expectations of that day nearly a full-grown woman, and his firstborn son, César (12), had nearly reached the age Nostradamus had probably been when he began in studies in Avignon so many years ago. In this way the presage's cryptic reference to "goods of old fathers," alongside a litany of other phrases about nuptials, marriage, and "the heritage of the father" imply that Nostradamus' final worries dwelt less on his eternal passage. He concentrated his dwindling energies on making arrangements for the dowry of Madeleine and the safekeeping of ancestral heirlooms, perhaps magical Jewish scrolls ("goods of old fathers") and the like in the safekeeping of César or his other sons.

By mid-June, Nostradamus stoically suffered a new threshold of arthritic agony resulting in prolonged difficulty in breathing and sleeping. He sensed death approaching. On 17 June, he summoned the lawyer, Joseph Roche, to dictate his last will and testament.[12] This document illuminates for us some of Nostradamus' concerns and 16th-century values. To some extent, we can get a flavor of his life by the possessions he accumulated. The will stands as evidence of how concise and clear were his ledgers containing the accounts for his successful business and the royalties from his books, in stark contrast to the often deliberately fudged and foggy way he set down his accounts of the future.

His fortune was recorded to be 3,444 crowns – a substantial sum for his day. Expressed in terms of equivalent wealth in the early

21st century, the estate of Nostradamus was that of a flush bour-geois with between $400,000 and $500,000 in U.S. dollars (£350,000). Leoni gives us the best measure of value when he says that a room in a good house in Paris during Nostradamus' time "could be rented for four crowns a year."[13]

The listing of the first benefactors in his Last Will and Testament should silence any speculation that Nostradamus was an anti-papist Huguenot. After bequeathing a one-time-only dis-pensation of 6 sous to 13 beggars upon his death, the next in line are local Salonnais servants of the Roman Catholic Church: 1 crown bequeathed to the Friars of the Observance of Saint-Pierre-de-Canon; 1 crown to the Chapel of Nostre Dame des Pénitents-Blancs of Salon; and, finally, 2 crowns to the Friars Minor of the Convent of St. Francis. His confessor, Friar Vidal de Vidal, the Friar Superior of said Convent, stood as his legal witness for his will. It would seem that if Nostradamus had been a closet Calvinist, he would not have had a "papist" priest as his witness or dispensed a single *sou* to representatives of the Church of "Mammon" in Rome.

After making these sacrifices to God, his first cousin, Madeleine Besaudine, daughter of Louis Besaudine, was set to receive 10 gold pistolets upon her marriage (and not otherwise). However, if she died before marriage the bestowment would be nullified.

Next on Nostradamus' mind was settling an issue that caused the most marital and family strife during the Renaissance era: pro-viding dowries for daughters. Being a man of means (and being a man whose genetic makeup did not burden his estate with six daughters), this was relatively painless. The 15-year-old "Mademoiselle Madeleine," the eldest daughter (and, according to some biographers, his favorite), would receive the largest share of the inheritance: a full 600 crowns, payable as a dowry if and when she married. Other inheritance/dowries of 500 gold crown-pistolets each were laid down for little Anne and Diana de Nostredame with the caveat that said dowries would be shared by surviving heirs if any one or all three daughters should die while in their "pupilarity" (as still unmarried wards of the family) or not leave behind their own "legitimate and natural" heirs.

Next in his thoughts for Roche's transcription was his "beloved wife." Upon his death, "Madame Anne Ponsarde" would receive 400 gold crown-pistolets that she could enjoy as long as she lived and did not remarry; if she were to remarry, this account would be repaid to his heirs in full. To her was also bequeathed the distinctive robes, clothes, rings, and jewels Nostradamus had worn, to be rendered in whatever way she pleased. She was guaranteed all the furniture and a third of the house ("whatever third she chooses"), which Nostradamus bequeathed to his eldest son, César. The itemized furniture reveals that the house of Nostradamus was, like many upper-middle-class bourgeois dwellings of the day, built without shelves or cupboard space in the walls. Most items were stored in large chests. He gave his wife a particularly valued walnut chest known by family members as the "Great Chest," located in the hallway, along with a smaller one which must have been the typical Renaissance wife's richly carved and expensive dowry chest "next to the bed." The four-poster, canopied master bed was generally the most valuable piece of furniture for a Renaissance household, and Nostradamus is quite meticulous in listing its various elements – bed sheets, mattresses, mattress covers, bolster and tapestry covers, and drapes. He also itemized the many intimate objects for serving food they enjoyed together, such as his wife's cherished six winding sheets, four towels, twelve napkins, a half-dozen dishes, a half-dozen plates, a half-dozen porringers, two pitchers (large and small), and a valued pewter cup and a salt cellar. He left her all the movable furniture according to the needs of one of her station, which included three casks to hold her wine, and what must have been a particularly coveted little square bowl, because it is specifically described. The will made the usual caveat that all these belongings must be returned to Nostradamus' heirs if she should remarry. Anne Ponsarde never remarried, or ever wanted to, it would seem; thus, it is presumed she enjoyed possessing and using the 400 gold crown-pistolets, the furniture and valuables listed for the 16 years until she took her place next to her husband's tomb in the Church of the Cordeliers, in 1582.

After rendering donations to beggars and the Church, establishing dowries for his daughters, leaving a house and valuables to his wife, and giving away of the garments distinguishing his station and identity in life, Nostradamus turned to a listing of his scholarly and astrological tools. If he indeed possessed all manner of forbidden books and magical devices, brazen chairs, pentagrams and magic swords, you will not find them in any official ledger, for obvious reasons. However, under the blanket theme of general scholarship and study, he declared that all of his books be given "to that one of his sons who will profit most by study, and who will have drunk the most of the smoke of the lamp [of scholarship]." All assumed this would be his eldest son, César, which indeed was the case. Along with the books, he had Roche list the following general dispensation for his correspondence and archived papers, which possibly included original manuscripts of his writings:

These books, together with all the letters that will be found in the house of the said testator [Nostradamus] has willed not to be catalogued at all, nor placed by their description, but to be tied up in parcels and baskets, until the one who is to have them is of age to take them, and that they be placed and locked up in a room of the house of [Nostradamus].

Clearly, Nostradamus did not want to leave an itemized record of his own papers, which likely included forbidden books on astrology and magic that could expose his heirs to suspicion of heresy. Except for a few surviving letters and the resurfacing of the handwritten manuscript of *Orus Apollo*, the will leaves us with the last objectively recorded image of Nostradamus' original manuscripts. They would be stuffed and sealed into wicker baskets, placed in a storage room or perhaps the cellar, and locked away from the sunlight not long after his death by the trustees of this will; and they would not likely resurface until 13 years hence, on the day César reached his majority at age 25. After that, no one knows through whose hands the body of his handwritten papers might have passed, or whether any were misplaced or lost. It is important to note that Chavigny was not a witness to this will, so any speculation that he had wide-ranging access to his master's original papers after his death is implausible, but this does not rule out the possibility that Chavigny had copies of the prophecies written in his own hand.

That César was the intended benefactor we know for sure, for Nostradamus declares him heir to the house wherein his papers are stored. The list of special heirlooms given to his son tells us which possessions Nostradamus likely cherished the most: such as his expensive cape, double-gilded in silver; his favorite large iron and wooden sitting chair; perhaps the very same chair he sat in when contemplating and writing down his prophecies. The house would remain the common property of César and his younger brothers Charles and André until the younger two reached the age of 25, after which the house would be left to César – with a third of the dwelling set aside for his mother until either the end of her widowhood or the end of her days. In other words, Nostradamus followed the usual practice of the day, in which the house was left to the eldest son. The other sons were promised a single dispensation of 100 gold crown-pistolets each upon attaining to their "full heritage" at 25 – the time that it was expected they would flee the nest and seek their own lives, *livres*, and fortunes. And, the will stipulates that if any of these sons died before reaching 25, the heritage would be divided up in equal parts to the surviving sons. Nostradamus' wife would be their guardian; she would feed and clothe them by drawing sums from the executors of the will, who were two of Nostradamus' friends, Palamède Marc, Lord of Châteauneuf, and the Honorable Jacques Suffren, a burger of Salon.

The next proviso intimates that Nostradamus was sexually active into his 63rd (and last) year, that right up to his last illness in June he was successfully satisfying his amorous desires behind the canopy curtain of the bed he had bequeathed his wife. He dictated the following to Roche:

If the said Anne Ponsarde his wife should be pregnant, and give birth to one or two sons [twins], he has made them heirs equally with the others, with similar substitution; and if she gives birth to one or two daughters, he has bequeathed to each of them the sum of 500 crowns, with the same payment and substitution as the others.

Death is ever married to debt and taxes. Out of an estate of 3,444 crowns and 10 sous,[14] Nostradamus set aside 1,600 crowns in three locked coffers in his house, passing the keys to Marc and Suffren, to pay off his debts with the aid of his ledgers, obligations, and notes in hand.

The final words of the will show that Nostradamus did not fit the generic image of the man in his deathbed dictating to the notaries, with somber friends and witnesses crowding the bedroom.[15] These words state that the will was transcribed "in the study of the house of Master Nostradamus." (Whether or not this is his secret study upstairs is unclear). In addition, from what Chavigny later said about his final days, Nostradamus was loath to lie in his bed. It could be that reclining only exacerbated his difficulty in breathing. It might be close to the mark to imagine him propped up in that large oak and iron chair mentioned in his will, his gouty and swollen right leg bandaged and propped up, while he dictated his final testament.

It seems that as far back as the Presage written for March 1567[16] (although that proved to be the wrong year), Nostradamus inserted a relatively safe prediction about the able prosecution of his will and worldly affairs to come. Line 1 cites an instance of a recurring litany in his last Almanac prophecies about public enemies (most likely his detractors) and the accounting of nuptials and marriages. The latter could be his prediction that around the time of his death there would be important royal marriages, or maybe more mundane nuptials, such as marriages in his own extended family of brothers and sisters, and betrothals of their children. In either case, there is no clear record that his forecasts of death and marriages were successful. Chavigny, in the safe hindsight of his commentaries in far-off 1589, believed that most of the Presages of 1567 describing "marriage and nuptials" actually predicted the massacre of St. Bartholomew's Day (1572) and the rise of Henry of Navarre as a king of France. Where line 3 states "the great friends will show themselves in the passage" this could be meant for the friends who would later gather in the study while his will was transcribed. Line 2, perhaps written out of sequence to be obscure, adds that "Death [coming] after, he [has] grown rich through the deaths." The cryptic line might indicate Nostradamus' acknowledgement for posterity that he understood, and perhaps dubiously prospered from, the success of his forecasts for the deaths of Henry II and his son François II. The final line predicts that his detractors from either side of the religious debate will be remorseful after hearing of his death: "Two sects to talk jargon, from surprise remorse later." But wishful thinking does not a prophecy make.

During his final days, Nostradamus had a bed moved to his beloved upstairs study, and a special bench was built so he could maneuver his disabled body through the room and prop up his swollen leg. Chavigny reports in his *Recueil* that Nostradamus "hardly wanted to see or sleep in the bed." The pain had kept him alert and sleepless in Salon, perhaps for weeks on end. Moreover, it seems that, from his vantage point, whatever time was left could not be wasted by sleep. If the note inserted by the editor of his final almanac is any indication, this final spurt of sleepless diligence was spent in the work's preparation (although, alas, he was unable to complete it). Chavigny says he composed his final three prophecies eight days before he died (24 June). Perhaps, exhausted, he dipped his pen in the inkwell one last time, wrote down the final line of his last Presage, then reached over with difficulty to write the following comment on the front page of his copy of Stadius's Ephemeris for the Year 1566:

Hic prope mors est.

Death is close at hand.

Death in Need of a Legacy, a Bed, and a Bench

The following day Nostradamus diagnosed that his gout had deteriorated into dropsy. In modern terms, he was possibly suffering from a mixture of kidney failure and pulmonary edema causing the entire body to swell painfully. Chavigny reported that he remained alert and serene to the end in spite of his acute suffering. Near the end of June, this serenity was sorely tested by what might have been the sounds of raised young voices in argument choked with tears, wafting up the spiral staircase to further torment the dying man in his secret study. A session of tearful lobbying from his two favorite children, Madeleine and César, soon followed. They desired to possess certain cherished and coveted heirlooms long before the will allotted for their release. Nostradamus was once again compelled to summon the notary, Joseph Roche, to dictate a Codicil to the will on 30 June. He advanced permission to let César possess his astrolabe and large gold doctor's ring after Nostradamus' death rather than after his own 25th birthday (a wait of a little more than 48 hours rather than 13 years). Madeleine would receive two walnut chests with all the jewels, clothes, and ornaments they contained, for her immediate enjoyment, rather than wait the long years until the chests were opened on her wedding day.

Perhaps his serenity was supported by prophecy, if we take some of the statements written for the Presages for May through July as a premonition of this final family crisis and its resolution. Rather than predicting disputes for future royals, Nostradamus' account of marriages, troubles with enemies, the mayor and magistrates, inheritance squabbles, treasures recovered and suchlike, might well be about his family. The death of a "great one" would then be Nostradamus. The first line of the Presage for May[17] reads: "From the father it approaches the son." Perhaps this is about César pleading for his dying father to change his last will and testament and bequeath to him the cherished astrolabe. The final two lines read: "Concealed, put in front, through the faith of reproaches; the good friends and women against the grumblings." These lines, if written before 24 June, could stand for a vision of the treasured astrolabe and ring unlocked and handed over to César the day after his father's death by the friends and executors of the will. The 12-year-old César then becomes the one who annoyed his mother and older sister with his simpering pressure tactics.

The first line of the Presage for June[18] reads, "Through the treasure, found – the heritage of the father." It seems to continue the inheritance theme. The "treasure" could be Nostradamus' legacy to his son, or an intangible gift discovered through use of some occult tool, book, or instrument (such as his astrolabe) cryptically concealed as treasure. However, the next three lines apply themselves far better to the catastrophic events of August 1572 leading up to the St. Bartholomew's Day massacre.

The next Presage for July (being the right month though the wrong year) should hint much about Nostradamus' final days, and it does:

Encor la mort s'approche, don Royal & Legat,
On dressera ce qu'est, par viellesse en ruyne:
Les ieunes hoirs de soupçon nul legat,
Thresor trouué en plastres & cuisine.

Once more the death approaches, Royal gift and Legacy,
What is, through old age in ruins, he will prepare:
The young heirs in suspicion of having no legacy,
Treasure found in plasters and in the kitchenware.[19]

The first line refers to his being close to death more than once in his final months. The "Royal gift and Legacy" is once again a repetition of his greatest twilight triumph: being honored in 1564 by Charles IX and Queen Regent Catherine with royal titles and 300 gold crowns. Line 2 is self-explanatory: he is preparing himself for death. Line 3 returns us to the family crisis surrounding the distribution of his valuables. The young and suspicious heirs are 15-year-old Madeleine and 12-year-old César. The rest of the children were perhaps too young to understand and indeed were more emotionally distraught and confused at seeing their father suffering and dying. The aging prophet hid these valuables ("treasure") either in some plaster container, or in a nook hidden behind a plaster wall. Perhaps he alludes to occult magical treasures not mentioned in his will. *Cuisine* can mean "kitchenware" or the "kitchen." In this way, we have a layered pun indicating the general location in the house where these treasures are hidden, perhaps in some special cooking pot squirreled away behind many others used to make cosmetics and preservatives.

The Presage for October conjures more potentially intimate details of his final days, and it is deduced by Chavigny that he might have written it no later than 24 June at the onset of his final physical agonies:

Les roys Magistrats par les morts la main mettre,
Ieunes filles malades, & des grands corps enfle:
Tout par langeurs & nopces, ennemys serfs au maistre.
Les publicques douleurs, le composeur tout enflé.

The Kings, Magistrates through the deaths, the [power]
   to place [there],
Young girls sick, and of the Great Ones body swells up:
All through languors and nuptials, enemy serfs for
   the master.
The public sad, the Composer all swollen up.[20]

The prophecy begins with a general forecast of the deaths of great
magistrates and future kings of France then swoops into what
seems to be a personal account about his young daughters, Anne
and Diane, who apparently had fallen ill themselves, perhaps seriously, at the same time their father entered his final illness.
Pulmonary edema made Nostradamus' body swell. Despite the
suffering and debilitation, he managed to arrange his last will and
testament, but "nuptials" – a code perhaps for dowries for his three
daughters – still obsessed his mind. He dispensed one last
denouncement against his favorite enemies in line 3: Salon's clod-
hopping "serfs" who are peasant Cabans pestering "the master."
Perhaps even now, they taunt him from the streets as news spread
that Salon's royally honored celebrity was about to meet his God
(or devil). The last line contends that the majority of Salon's
citizens were sad to hear that fatal dropsy had overtaken their illustrious doctor and composer of prophecies.

    Friar Vidal, the Superior of the Franciscan monastery of Salon,
was called on 1 July to hear Nostradamus' final confession and per-
form the last rites. Just what did Nostradamus confess? Clearly
in his own writings he admitted that he possessed all the weaknesses and frailties of human nature, and it is safe to say Vidal
heard his fill of mundane sins of intemperance, gluttony, greed,
lust, anger, pride and so on. What about what many detractors
would cite as his greater sins? Did Vidal hear any apologies for a
lifetime of smoke and mirrors? Not likely, for Nostradamus was
working on his prognostications right up to his death. Clearly,
he took to his grave the belief that God gave him a gift of

prophetic sight. After long soul-searching and prayer, God (not his subconscious mind) showed him how to present the future in obscure language.

At the end of his life, did Nostradamus harbor any sting of consciousness felt for all the people he had upset and terrified with his prophecies? Did he hold and admit to any fear that his sins might magnify across the coming centuries as he continued to scare, and some would say deceive, people yet unborn? Is it a sin that his obscurity of verse would tempt people to color their own projections for good or evil in the innate falsifying danger of nebulous narratives and quatrains?

The answer to all three questions is, no. Let the self-deceived lose themselves in the foggy labyrinth of his verses. As for the others with a better grasp of his secret work, it seems that he understood this work as hard love directed to enlighten the living and those not yet born. He was at peace with the hard reality of the human mind that needs to be scared straight – scared into changing its behavior today in order to create a better future tomorrow. If there could be no change to what he foresaw, then at least his prophecies could scare readers enough to girdle their loins and muddle through the future's many blows.

Did he fear a prolonged incarceration in Purgatory for perhaps revealing too much of the future so that evil men would recognize themselves and use his prophecies to make the future worse? That is hard to say. Had he known that the propaganda minister of the greatest murderer of his race, Adolf Hitler, would use his prophecies, scattered in leaflets, to demoralize and defeat his own future countrymen, would he have written them? His sympathetic interpreters would answer that he did know and that he was warning his future countrymen and fellow Jews about Adolf Hitler. In their minds, interpreters cite a quatrain in *Les Propheties* describing a man of "Greater Germany"[21] as someone more than a contemporary emperor of the Holy Roman Empire, such as Charles V. He is the same person Nostradamus in five other quatrains code-named "Hister" after the ancient name of the River Danube.[22] Skeptics counter that a river cannot be a person. Believers reply that Hitler as a boy grew up upon the banks of the Danube – the "Hister." The double entendre of river and man is obvious, they would say: it is a prophetic metaphor, a poetic device. Believers also think Hister is the bearer of the "crooked cross of iron" in another quatrain.[23] Supporters of Nostradamus would like to imagine that he might have seen this symbol of Nazism during some dark magical ceremony in his secret study back in the mid-1550s, and had it explained to him by one of his astral emissaries trapped in the magic triangle set beyond his magic circle. They seem to harbor only awe for a man who – granted – is often cloudy enough to be taken any way one likes, but clear enough to be recognized in the late 1930s by Magda Goebbels. The wife of the Nazi Propaganda Minister was an avid Nostradamian who nagged her husband about the Hister/Hitler association. Josef Goebbels saw the opportunity to exploit this, and other prophecies about the fall of France from a future German invasion, to his own advantage.

Those who cannot see beyond the thrill of making and fulfilling predictions do not recognize the sin of too much self-fulfilling clarity. For instance, his supporters will tell you that Nostradamus correctly pinpointed the path of a surprise attack on France by the Germans in World War II "through the Ardennes Forest."[24] It is only after the tragedies of 1940 that interpreters began seeing France as the victim of Nazi Germany's conquest. They would have us believe that Nostradamus foresaw the unexpected path Nazi panzers took to overthrow France through the Ardennes forest, on the lightly defended border of Belgium and Luxembourg. The same prediction spoke of an empire falling "through the Ardennes forest." This, say the Nostradamians in hindsight, was the French colonial empire in 1940 *and* that Nazi empire in 1945. On Christmas Eve 1944, a surprise German attack launched once again "through the Ardennes" failed to defeat the Allied forces in the

Battle of the Bulge. The devastation of the Nazi forces in the Bulge hastened the collapse of the Third Reich by May 1945. The prophecy was indexed "Century 5, Quatrain 45". Some interpreters believe it stands for the dating of the end of the Second World War in Europe: May (the fifth month) of (19)45. If this is so, it is certainly fascinating, entertaining, and altogether impotent as prophecy.

What good are prophecies fulfilled in hindsight? A prophecy unheeded is no more help than the histories and analyses that review the mistakes of our past from which no one seems to learn. Perhaps writing beclouded prophecies that always play well in hindsight is Nostradamus' sin. They increase his stature at the expense of his failure to warn. But it is doubtful that Friar Vidal heard him ask for forgiveness for the sin of fame through hindsight. If there is a Purgatory, one might imagine his spirit looking down at such successes and becoming more sinfully prideful, thus lengthening his stay there.

In his defense, there would come those who understood his warnings before they arrived, but they were ignored. People other than the Nazi Propaganda Minister's wife were aware that "Hister" was Hitler. There were those in France in the late 1930s who understood that a prophecy describing the folly of a great and deep fortification ditch dug along the eastern frontiers of France "divided by water into fifteen parts"[25] was the Maginot Line. They understood and warned people, upon the merits of Nostradamus, that the vast array of gun turrets and underground fortresses built after the First World War along the frontiers with Germany would fail in the coming war. What the skeptics, then and now, cannot explain is how Nostradamus knew that the Maginot Line was indeed divided by 15 rivers, this being the only defense line in history to be so divided by water.

Unfortunately, any golden precognitive insight gleaned from Nostradamus before events transpire is discounted by almost everyone outside of passionate believers because it comes from a great slagheap legacy of obscure dross. Though debunkers and even many believers might blame Nostradamus for forever hamstringing his prophetic message by suspicious literary devices, it is clear that Nostradamus faced death and final confession believing that there was no better way to protect the future from itself than by sacrificing clarity.

After last rites were given and Friar Videl excused himself from the study, Nostradamus, at least in his mind, was prepared for what mystery awaited him after death. There were, however, two lingering worries he held in the face of his demise. These concerns were not about death and damnation – about his post-mortem destiny, he was confident and serene; God would forgive and take him home. He had once said, when describing his Elixir of Life potion, that: "The One who has taught us how we are born into the world, He also has taught us [how] to die."[26] It seems, however, that God had not taught Michel de Nostredame how to let go of his obsession with what might happen to his corporeal remains.

Had he seen something in his nocturnal vigils that horrified him? Some desecration of his bones? To guard against this potential he wrote Quatrain 7 of Century 9:

Qui ouurira le monument trouué,
Et ne viendra le serrer promptement:
Mal luy viendra & ne pourra prouué,
Si mieux doit estre Roy Breton ou Normand.

He who will break open the monument he discovered,
And will not come to strain, to close it tightly, and lock
    it up promptly:
Evil will come to him and proof will not be uncovered,
[Whether] it be better to be a King from Breton or
    Normandy.[27]

The last line speaks of pagan kings who protected their remains from desecration either by burying them under burial mounds or through immolation. Nostradamus, as a Christian, did not have such protection. His last will and testament gave instructions that his body should be carried the short distance through the north gate of town to a sepulture at the Church of the Convent of St. Francis (the little Chapel was also known as the Church of the Cordeliers). His tomb would be set against[28] the wall between the large door and the altar of St. Martha and marked by a monument. Some biographers believe Nostradamus had himself buried upright against the wall because he was heard to rail at the Cabans that they would not put their feet on his throat while alive or dead. Alas, no objective evidence can overthrow this possible urban legend because the church has since been destroyed (some two centuries ago). Many colorful legends about his tomb fly free in the twilight between fact and fantasy,[29] but there is one documented incident recorded from the French Revolution that bears witness to Nostradamus' need to invoke a Tutankhamen-like curse against those defiling his grave.

In 1791, during the turbulence of the French Revolution, a ragged and inebriated band of Gardes Nationales from either Marseilles or Vaucluse broke into that church, bent on looting crypts for valuables. They smashed the eight-foot marble slab concealing the prophet's coffin and began to ransack its contents. M. David, the mayor of Salon, hurried to investigate the commotion. He arrived at the church to find peasants exiting the front door carrying off someone's bones. Inside he found soldiers and more townspeople prancing about the ossuary-dancing floor they had made with Nostradamus' skeleton. In the center of this grisly scene, it is reported that a guardsman ignored all warnings of a curse and drank wine from Nostradamus' skull. Centuries of old wives' tales had evolved the curse of Quatrain 7 Century 9 into a dare: If you drink blood from the skull of Nostradamus you will attain the prophet's powers; however, his ghost will bring you to a violent death soon after as punishment for vandalizing his grave. Wine seemed an acceptable substitute for blood, and the guardsman may have been either too drunk to be scared or too cynical to believe in such fairy tales.

M. David had to think quickly or see Salon's most illustrious bag of bones carried off as souvenirs. So he conjured up his own Nostradamus myth. He explained to the soldiers that Nostradamus had predicted the French Revolution.[30] David sputtered that he was their hero and ordered them to recover what was left of Nostradamus' skeletal remains, and now the tipsy guards liberated the peasants of the leg bones or other souvenirs stuffed in their pockets, and groveled on the floor to pile the prophet's bones back into the broken wall from whence they came.[31] Someone had to be punished. The "sacrilegious" man who made a wine goblet out of Nostradamus' skull met a violent end. One story says he was shot the following morning in an ambush with Royalists outside of Lançon.[32] Another account says he was later caught with stolen objects and hanged. The objects in his possession were not bones of the prophet, just someone's silverware.

Beyond his body's defilement in the future, Nostradamus' second lingering worry concerned attacks of a more abstract nature – those coming from skeptics, debunkers, and critics who he expected would hound his legacy for centuries to come. For them he wrote the following incantationed curse in Century 6, Quatrain 100:

LEGIS CANTIO CONTRA INEPTOS CRITICOS.
Quos legent hosce versus maturè censunto,
Profanum vulgur, & inscium ne attrectato:
Omnesq; Astrologi Blenni, Barbari procul sunto,
Qui alter facit, is ritè, sacer esto.

INCANTATION OF THE LAW AGAINST INEPT CRITICS.
May those who peruse this verse consider profoundly [what
I say],
Let the profane [ones], the vulgar and ignorant herd
keep away:

And all Astrologers, blockheads, Barbarians stay far away,
May he who does otherwise, be subject to the sacred
rite['s sway].[33]

Thus Nostradamus was nettlesome about his critics to the last. It would seem that the nerves of steel that a gift of prophetic sight gave him to perceive his own death, and the death and transformation of all that he knew and loved, came at the price of a lack of nerve when it came to taking criticism. With that said, he is right to ask each of us to consider profoundly the message of this verse. If there is a curse hidden here, it is directed towards the lazy mind hiding in all of us that is quick to judge what we do not understand. Nostradamus, grown weary of a present world well-trodden, and perhaps eager to be released from the burden of visions of the world to come, pleads with us to look beyond the obvious – to forgive him for his obscurity, and to find half-hidden in the ample dross of his strange ramblings a few golden glimpses of tomorrow's potential.

Chavigny, in his *Janus François*, claims to be the last man who saw Nostradamus alive.

The day before he exchanged this life for a better, after I had spent many hours with him, and late at night was taking leave of him until the following morning, he said, "You will not see me alive at sunrise."

The door shut behind Chavigny. The prophet was alone, at last. Chavigny, the final well-wisher, the last in a long line of friends and relations who had said their goodbyes, shed their tears, fumbled with their bromides and platitudes, and finally exited this last scene in the play of his life. Now the peace of solitude descended on the dying man in the womb of his private study. The travail of death would increase, bringing a rebirth of what new reality only God knows. What revelations stirred in the remaining agony of sleepless hours before the dawn – before the death – will remain his secret.

He deemed his study as a good place to die, otherwise he would not have taken such patient pains to say his goodbyes so he could pass from life alone, surrounded by the books and tools that he knew had been used to give birth to his last and most important child – his legacy. Perhaps there was now time to say farewell to the midwives that assisted in this birthing: the magic mirrors, the brass tripod, the spirit of Iamblichus and his *De mysteriis Aegyptiorum*, and the keys of Solomon. All would have to step aside now, for "the Work" had been born, and for better or worse, its passage through the halls of coming centuries was assured.

When reaching the final moments of a life story, the temptation is to rehash and recap the past of the individual – but Nostradamus urges us in another direction. By his own devices, he forces us to review his future, his afterlife.

Notwithstanding those who cannot contain the malignity of evil spirit as time elapses after my earthly extinction, my writings will have more [impact] than during my lifetime.

About this prediction, made in the Epistle to Henry II, there can be no doubt. Nostradamus has rendered his case of prophecy and it is given to future times to be his judge and jury. Moreover, to each new generation he will deliver his evidence – in verses and prose – with a majority of each new jury of serious readers declaring him "not guilty" of quackery. All supporters and detractors will fall under the spell of his prophetic quatrains, with all their maddeningly obscure imagery, and hear something different. All will hear what they want to hear, changing the interpretations or refutations of the same quatrains century after century. While the verdict of those skeptics among the jurists remains virtually unchanged, those positively caught under Nostradamus' magical spell are aided by the power of his nebulous verses to entertain many wrong and perhaps a few right ways to conjure a future in his name. They will take up their many editions and translations of Nostradamus and think they can look back at things he foresaw long ago. They will see the wars, the plagues, the fascinating inventions of radio, of submarines, and the atom bomb. They will think he has foreseen the falling comet of the Columbia space shuttle presaging a great war in the Middle East and capture an image in their imagination of modern jet pilots in oxygen masks in his predictions of air fleets piloted by "half-pig men." They will use his verses to walk "on a corner of the moon." They will perceive many people of history named outright, and many more decoded from his anagrams and from the whims of their own times. The 17th-century reader recognized Oliver Cromwell from the English Civil War as "the colonel" usurper in a prophecy, while the 20th-century reader believed the "colonel" to be Libyan strongman Colonel Qaddafi. There will be those who will substantiate their fear of tyrants past and present by the whim of word play. They will see Hitler in "Hister," and Napoleon in "Napaulon." And 500 years after Nostradamus was born, they have now entered the 21st century arguing over whether his fearsome "Mabus," who it would seem is predicted to trigger a 27-year war of terrorism in their near future, is either an anagram for President George Bush of America, the terrorist Usama bin Laden, or a reverse-image anagram for "Saddam" Hussein.[34]

Sometimes the interpreters will be right; however, at no time will they ever be able to prove it objectively, and Nostradamus must have known that this would be the case. And perhaps as he spent his final hours of solitude, Nostradamus might have entertained the many right and wrong ways people would "prophagate" in his name. He knew that his literary devices would grant his prophecies the grace and immortality of an existential myth. A mystery that cannot be completely solved lives on and thrives. The writing style of the prophecies nourishes this anima of magnetic attraction. Facts once understood are now as dead as a tomb, and thus we move on to investigate other mysteries, but no one, once engaged, can move on from these prophecies, for their resolution is ever beyond our reach. To say they only attract those who are willing and open to be deceived is to overlook how they also attract and enliven the skeptic to rise up and deny them. They live because both sides of the debate cannot let the prophecies go. Wonder and bewilderment work alongside debunkery to keep alive the power of Nostradamus' prophetic mythos.

There is a need for each new generation to argue and discuss where their present actions are taking them in the future. Where such discourse is encouraged, better destinies can be captured. What better way to sustain such a debate for centuries than by composing a crossword puzzle of cryptic and bizarre prophecies? The device worked in his lifetime and it works today. It will go on working as it reinvigorates the perennial debate, over and over again, about what our future will – and should – bring, well into the new millennium. As the sun of 2 July 1566 peaked over the distant limestone promontory of Mt. Saint Victoire to the east of Salon, Nostradamus succumbed to heart failure confident that his prophetic legacy, his controversy, and his memory would obtain a certain immortality.

At sunrise, Chavigny carefully led Nostradamus' family and friends up the spiral stairs into the master's study. They found Nostradamus, a prophet to the last, his lifeless body lying on the edge of the bed, with his gout-inflamed leg propped across the bench built for it, just as he had written eight days earlier:

Du retour d'Ambassade, don de Roy; mis au lieu
Plus n'en fera: Sera allé à Dieu:
Parens plus proches, amis, freres du sang,
Trouué toutmortprez du lict & du banc.

On his return from the Embassy, King's gift put in place.
He will do nothing more. He will be gone to God['s grace].
Close relatives [kinsmen and women], friends, brothers of
　blood kin,
Completely dead near the bed and the bench [will they
　find him].[35]

A few days later, close relatives and friends carried his coffin past
the silent citizens of Salon. We may presume Friar Superior Videl
led the way, saying prayers while two Franciscans in his wake
carried the two large funerary candles purchased as per the instructions of the late seer's will. Behind them followed the coffin with
pallbearers, the family, and most of Salon's high-born and influential figures. They passed under the weathered arches of the northern gate toward the modest Chapel of the Cordeliers where, it is
believed, Nostradamus regularly and fervently prayed. After the
funeral ceremony ended, stone masons applied limestone and
mortar to seal the coffin into the wall. The family, friends, and citizens ventured out under the beautiful summer sunshine, making
their way back into their town, each self-contained with their own
grief or their own contemplation of eternity. They could not know
that none of them would be remembered beyond their association
with the man they had just left behind – the man who would
become Salon's most famous historical figure.

We can surmise that the day after Nostradamus was publicly
interred, the stone masons, along with the widow of Nostradamus,
César, perhaps Chavigny as well, and other close family relations
likely returned to stand before the new tomb. Standing solemnly
in the fading fragrance of funerary flowers and the smell of drying
mortar, they would have watched the masons erecting a marble
plaque with words, it is said, composed in French by Anne
Ponsarde, and later translated into Latin either by César de
Nostredame, or Chavigny:

D.O.M.

CLARISSIMI OSSA

MICHAELIS NOSTRADAMI

UNIUS OMNIUM MORTALIUM JUDICIO DIGNI,

CUIUS PENE DIVINO CALAMO TOTIUS ORBIS,

EX ASTRORUM INFLUXI, FUTURI EVENTUS

CONSCRIBERENTUR.

VIXIT ANNOS LXII. MENSES VI. DIES XVII.

ORBIT ALONE AN. MDLXVI.

QUIETUM POSTERI NE INVIDETE. ANNA PONTIA

GEMELLA

CONIUGI OPT. V. FELICIT.

[Here rest the bones of the illustrious Michel Nostradamus, alone of all mortals, judged worthy to record with his near divine pen, under the influence of the stars, the future events of the entire world. He lived sixty-two years, six months and seventeen days. He died at Salon in the year 1566. Let not posterity disturb his rest. Anne Ponsarde Gemelle wishes her husband true happiness.]

Nostradamus was dead, but his legacy, his *afterlife*, had only just begun.

Chronology: Life and Afterlife

This is a select chronology of the more significant events and publications surrounding the life and legacy of Nostradamus since his birth 500 years ago.

THE LIFE OF NOSTRADAMUS

1503 Nostradamus born at St.-Rémy, Provence.

1517 or 1519 Nostradamus, either at age 14 or 16, begins his secondary education studies at Avignon.

1520 Avignon closes its schools because of an outbreak of bubonic plague.

1520–29 Nostradamus begins a nine-year exploration of a number of lands and countries (France, and possibly Spain, Italy, and the German states). He is on a quest for knowledge and understanding of the sources and origins of medicinal herbs.

1525–9 Various scholars speculate that, by 1525, he was either a licensed apothecary or medic, openly applying his self-taught medical skills with some success fighting the plague in Narbonne, Nîmes, Carcassonne, Toulouse, Bordeaux, and Avignon.

3 October 1529 He registers in the *scolasticorum* (the ledger for professors and students) for the University of Montpellier. The procurator, Guillaume Rondelet, because of disparaging remarks made about doctors, then crosses out his name.

23 October 1529 Cooler heads prevail, and Nostradamus enrolls in the university with Dr. Antoine Romier as his patron.

1529–32 Receives his doctorate degree at the University of Montpellier and joins the faculty.

1532–3 Leaves Montpellier faculty because of disagreements over medical dogma and embarks on a second wave of travels which may have taken him westward through Bordeaux, La Rochelle, and Toulouse.

c. 1533 While practicing medicine in Toulouse, Nostradamus receives a letter from Julius-César Scaliger in Agen, inviting him to visit and share knowledge on botany and medicine. They become friends.

1533–8 Nostradamus resides in Agen, starts a medical practice, marries and the couple have two children.

c. 1538 Plague infects Agen; Nostradamus' wife and children die. Her family successfully sues him for wife's dowry. Scaliger breaks his friendship with Nostradamus. The Church Justices of the Inquisition in Toulouse summon Nostradamus to explain heretical remarks expressed a few years before.

1538–44 Nostradamus slips out of Agen and wanders for six years. Beyond staying briefly in Bordeaux, little is known about exactly where he passed.

c. 1542–4 Some scholars believe he stayed for a time in seclusion at the Cistercian Abbey of Orval, near the French–Luxembourg border, possibly in an attempt to heal himself from the grief of losing his wife and family. Others believe he sought peace and meditation to acquaint himself with an awakening second sight, triggered by the shock of personal tragedy.

1544–5 Practices medicine in Marseilles.

1546–7 Fights a particularly violent outbreak of the plague in Aix-en-Provence for 270 days (May 1546 to early 1547).

1547 Fights plague in Salon de Crau (known today as Salon-en-Provence), and whooping cough in Lyon. He returns to Salon.

11 November 1547 Marries Anne Ponsarde Gemelle and settles down in Salon. Construction begins on a third floor of their new home.

c. 1548–9 Nostradamus makes a protracted journey through Italy seeking to put final touches to his knowledge of herbal remedies and cosmetics. It is possible he visited Turin, Genoa, Savona, Venice, and Rome. It is also speculated that he stayed in Florence for several months gathering magical knowledge, books, and occult equipment.

c. 1549–50 By day Nostradamus establishes a cosmetics and fruit preservatives business with some success, and by night begins teaching himself occult and magical arts.

1550 First Almanac possibly published, details of which no longer survive.

1551 Birth of first child, Madeleine. The success of the first Almanac warranted the publication of a second – no publishing details survive.

c. 1552 Writes Almanac for the year 1553 published by Chaussard, Lyon. He may have published *Traité des fardemens et confitures* for the first time, publisher unknown.

1553 Writes a whimsical dedication to a new fountain in Salon.

November 1553 Finishes Almanac for the year 1554 (Bertot?, Lyon).

January 1554 Publishes an Almanac for the year 1555 with Brotot, Lyon.

Early 1554 Birth of second child César.

c. March 1554 Sees a two-headed child from Sénas. This, along with the birth of a two-headed horse a few weeks later convinces Nostradamus that these are further omens supporting his vision of a civil war. The omens may have prompted him to draft and publish *Les Propheties*.

19 March 1554 He attains first foreign publication of his almanacs in German.

13 April 1554 Jean-Aymes de Chavigny begins work as Nostradamus' secretary. His first task is to copy Nostradamus' mounting production of quatrains for *Les Propheties*.

27 July 1554 Nostradamus gives first donation of money for Adam de Craponne's canal project.

c. 1555 *Traité des fardemens et confitures* published by Antoine Volant, Lyon. Finishes and dedicates *Orus Apollo* (an eccentric and cryptic discourse on Egyptian hieroglyphs) to Princess Marguerite de Valois, Henry II's sister. He is unable to publish the manuscript.

May 1555 Nostradamus has the first edition of his planned 1,000 prophecies published. They are an immediate success. *Les Propheties de M. Michel Nostradamus* (Macé Bonhomme, Lyon) included the *Preface à César* (Preface to César) and 353 of the planned 1,000 quatrains in Centuries 1, 2, and 3, plus 53 quatrains for Century 4.

c. June 1555 Around this time *Les Propheties de M. Michel Nostradamus* was brought to the attention of Queen Catherine de' Medici, who then persuaded King Henry II to summon Nostradamus to Court. A popular interpretation of his prophecy (indexed Century 1, Quatrain 35) had the king blinded and dying in ritual combat from a head wound. This interpretation paralleled an earlier prediction from Catherine's Florentine astrologer, Luc Gauricus.

c. 14 July 1555 Nostradamus begins the harrowing, but for the time rapid, one-month journey to Paris. The queen instructed the governor of Provence to provide Nostradamus with the finest horses of the royal post to reduce the time of his journey to Paris by half – from two months to one.

27 July 1555 Nostradamus, passing through Lyon on his way to his royal audience in Paris, mentions a premonition that he would be jailed and executed by 25 August.

15 August 1555 He arrives in Paris on the Assumption day of the Virgin Mary (his namesake – *Nostre Dame*). Following the lead of further self-fulfilling omens he lodged himself in the Inn of Saint-Michel near Notre Dame Cathedral.

16 August 1555 The Grand Constable of France, Anne de Montmorency, conducts Nostradamus to St. Germain-en-Laye where he has a royal audience with King Henry II and Queen Catherine de' Medici of France.

Mid-August 1555 Nostradamus' potentially apocryphal pro-phecy of the king's page finding his lost dog, it is said, increases Nostradamus' fame at Court.

Late August 1555 After recovering from his first recorded attack of gout, the Queen sends him to Château Blois to plot the horoscopes of the royal children. Nostradamus later predicts that her four sons will "all become kings," which is partial-ly true. There were four crowns worn by three of her sons. Henry III would be a king of Poland and France.

c. September 1555 Soon after his return to Paris, he makes a hasty retreat to Salon upon hearing that the Justices of the Inquisition wish to talk with him about his magic practices.

1556 Roux, Avignon, and Denyse, Lyon reprint *Les Propheties de M. Michel Nostradamus*, first edition. De Harsy, Paris, reprints *Traité des fardemens*. Kerver, Paris publishes Almanac for the year 1557. Third child, Charles de Nostredame, born.

1557 *Paraphrase de C. Galen* (translated by Nostradamus) pub-lished by du Rosne, Lyon. Cicognera, Milan prints Italian edition of the Almanac for the year 1557. Plantin, Antwerp, reprints *Traité des fardemens*. Fourth child, André de Nostredame, born.

August 1557 The French military disaster of St. Quentin stirs greater interest in the prophecies of Nostradamus, as it is widely believed that he named the location and details of the disaster over two years earlier in his first edition of *Les Propheties de M. Michel Nostradamus*.

November 1557 Du Rosne, Lyon, publishes second edition of *Les Propheties de M. Michel Nostradamus*. It includes the *Preface à César*, 640 of the planned 1,000 quatrains in Centuries 1, 2, 3, 4, 5, and 6, and 40 quatrains for Century 7.

c. 1557–8 A draft of Ronsard's poem in praise of Nostradamus' prediction of St. Quentin triggers numerous counterattacks at Court. A wave of highly critical pamphlets appears throughout France denouncing Nostradamus as a sorcerer and second-rate astrologer. The controversy only increases interest in his prophecies.

1558 Nostradamus publishes an Almanac for the same year by Brotot & Volant (Lyon) and possibly in Holland (Antwerp?). He then composes an Almanac for the year 1559. A best-selling (pirated) English edition is published in London. Sir William Cecil (Queen Elizabeth's Secretary of State) makes her aware of the now famous Century 1, Quatrain 35, assumed to predict the death of the French king. *Paraphrase de C. Galen* reprinted by du Rosne, Lyon. Fifth child, Anne de Nostredame, probably born.

c. June 1558 Estimated date by which Nostradamus completes his planned 1,000 quatrains for *Les Propheties*.

27 June 1558 Completes his *Epistre* (Epistle) to Henry II a year and three months after beginning the letter. It was meant to be a dedication for a second edition of *Les Propheties de M. Michel Nostradamus,* but was not published until 1561, two years after the king's death.

c. August 1558 Nostradamus writes a pamphlet entitled *Les Significations de l'Eclipse qui sera le 16. Septembre 1559* ... It clearly indicates he expected some great catastrophe would befall France beginning in June 1559.

Autumn 1558 Third edition of *Les Propheties de M. Michel Nostradamus* published by de Tourne. It included the final 300 of the planned 1,000 quatrains in Centuries 8, 9, and 10.

1559 Writes an Almanac for the year 1560 published by le Noir, Paris, and later translated into English by two London publishers.

Early 1559 Le Noir, Paris, prints *Les Significations de l'Eclipse, qui sera le 16. Septembre 1559* ... Du Rosne, Lyon, reprints *Paraphrase de C. Galen.*

2–3 April 1559 Treaty of Cateau-Cambrésis signed by Henry II and Philip II of Spain ends the Hapsburg–Valois Wars, and perhaps rumors of peace put into question Nostradamus' doom-laden prophecies for June 1559 through 1562.

20 April 1559 Adam de Craponne completes the 40-kilometer (25-mile) canal trench ranging out of the east from the Durance River to a spot on the northern approaches to Salon de Crau. It is assumed Nostradamus attended the opening celebration of the first leg of the planned canal.

2 June 1559 The citizens of Paris are split over a notorious trial convened personally by the king against Parisian parliamentarians. It is the beginning of a long-planned royal purge of Protestants from French society and the show trial is considered by many historians to be the catalyst that would lead in 1562 to the first of nine French civil wars fought over religion.

22, 28 June 1559 Celebrations of peace and the anticipated royal marriages commence in Paris by mid-June. Fourteen-year-old Elisabeth de Valois marries Philip II of Spain (22 June). The French king's sister, Marguerite de Valois, signs marriage contract with the Duke of Savoy (28 June).

28 June 1559 A three-day-long ritual contest of arms commences, pitting Henry II against his finest captains of the guard.

30 June 1559 In a final bout, the shattering lance of the captain of his Scottish guard half-blinds and mortally wounds the king.

9 July 1559 The Duke of Savoy marries Marguerite de Valois.

10 July 1559 After 10 agonizing days, Henry II dies of peritonitis. It was Nostradamus' prediction of Century 1, Quatrain 35 that had brought him a royal audience in 1555. The apparent fulfillment of his prediction of the king's death from

ritual combat establishes Nostradamus' centuries-long legacy as a prophet. A crowd amasses before the offices of the
Justices of the Church to demand Nostradamus be burned
at the stake for making the prediction. At the time, he is
safely far away in peaceful Salon.

Late 1559–60 His prophecies are avidly read across France and
England. In their wake is a second wave of virulent criti-
cism, especially from Protestants. Sir William Cecil calls
Nostradamus a propagandist and subversive. Nostradamus'
English counterpart, astrologer John Dee, also rejects his
mathematically unsubstantiated sorcery.

October 1559 The Duke of Savoy visits Salon and meets
Nostradamus.

December 1559 The Duke of Savoy's new wife, Princess
Marguerite de Valois, joins the Duke. She becomes
Nostradamus' chief astrological client after Catherine de'
Medici.

c. 1560 *Prophetie Merveilleuse* (1560–68) published by de Nyverd,
Paris. Also an English edition of *Les Significations de
l'Eclipse, qui sera le 16. Septembre 1559* appears (Daye,
London). He writes an Almanac for the year 1561 published
by Regnault, Paris and translated into English by Hackett,
London. There is also an edition published in German.
Volant, Lyon, reprints *Traité des fardemens.*

Early 1560 Catherine de' Medici convenes her final occult session
at the Château de Chaumont before it is handed over as
a retirement home for the king's longtime mistress, Diane
de Poitiers. Whether Cosimo de Ruggieri or Nostradamus
directed the magic mirror ceremony is still disputed.

Mid-March 1560 Huguenots in the French Court launch
the Conspiracy of Amboise. Contemporaries believe
Nostradamus foresaw and named the location of the first
attempted Huguenot coup d'état. His fame and infamy
increases.

Latter half of 1560 Persecution reaches Nostradamus in the streets of Salon from gangs of Cabans (Catholic peasant fanatics who believe he is a Huguenot).

17 November 1560 The new heir to the throne, François II, collapses at Orléans.

20 November 1560 The ambassador to Venice writes to the Doge, commenting that everyone at Court mentions Nostradamus' prediction (Century 10, Quatrain 39) about François' coming death.

3 December 1560 The Tuscan Ambassador describes similar details in a letter to the Duke of Florence.

5 December 1560 François II dies just before his 17th birthday. He fulfills many of the expectations of the prophecy, making Nostradamus the talk of the courts of Europe. The adolescent Charles IX, age 11, becomes the new king, his mother Catherine the Queen Regent.

c. 1561 Despite persecution and the gathering clouds of civil war, Nostradamus has a prolific year. He releases a fourth edition of *Les Propheties de M. Michel Nostradamus* published by Barbe Regnault, Paris. It included the *Preface à César*, Centuries 1 through Century 7, Quatrain 42, the *Epistre* (Letter) to Henry II, and Centuries 8 through 10. He publishes an Almanac for the year 1562 with le Noir & Bonfons, in Paris, and Volant & Brotot of Lyon, then again in Paris with Barbe Regnault. *Le Remede tres utile contre la peste ...* by Nostradamus published by de Nyverd, Paris. Sixth and final child born to Anne and Nostradamus – Diane.

12 January 1561 The Spanish Ambassador issues a letter to Philip of Spain, confirming Nostradamus' prophetic success and adding, "it would be better to punish than to allow to sell his prophecies, which lead to vain and superstitious beliefs."

c. First half of 1561 Persecution becomes so severe that Nostradamus considers moving his family to the Papal

Enclave of Avignon. By autumn, he drops the idea as law and order are restored to Salon.

May 1561 The Venetian Ambassador comments to the Doge of Venice on the impact of the successful prediction of the young king's death.

December 1561 Summoned to Nice (or Turin) to plot the horoscope of Savoy and Marguerite de Valois' firstborn son. While there he accurately predicts the future glory of Charles-Emmanuel of Savoy and cryptically hints the date of his father's coming death "when a nine precedes a seven."

1562 Writes an Almanac for the year 1563, Roux, Avignon/Regnault, Paris, the French publishers, Powel, London, the English, and Benaccio, Bologna, the Italian.

4 February 1562 Back in Salon from Savoy, Nostradamus writes a letter to the Church fathers of Orange instructing them how to catch thieves who vandalized their church.

March 1562 The First War of Religion begins, as foreseen by Nostradamus in 1558.

1563 *Traité d'Astrologie* (*Treatise on Astrology*) published in Paris, and publishes an Almanac for the year 1564 in France and England.

Spring 1563 First War of Religion ends with contemporaries believing (or projecting) that a number of Presages and Quatrains foresaw details of the conflict including the assassinations of Antoine de Bourbon and François de Guise.

1564 Writes an Almanac for the year 1565 (Benoist Rigaud, Lyon), and in Italian (Genoa), and a reprint with Odo, Lyon.

Spring 1564 Queen Regent Catherine de' Medici's Royal Pacification begins.

17 October 1564 The Pacification reaches Salon specifically to visit Nostradamus. He is the honored guest of the young King Charles IX and the Queen Regent, Catherine de' Medici.

18 October 1564 Nostradamus studies the moles of the 10-year-old Prince of Bearn and predicts he will become a future King of Navarre "and" France. The Royal Pacification leaves Salon for Aix.

November 1564 Nostradamus is summoned before the King and Catherine de' Medici one more time at Arles. He is awarded the titles Counselor and Physician-in-Ordinary of the King of France. To Catherine he predicts a general peace for the world in 1566. The prophecy fails.

16 October 1565 Signs off dedication letter for the 1566 Almanac wherein there is a prediction set for 1 July 1566 for "strange transmigrations" (i.e., death).

December 1565 Completes his Almanac for the year 1566 for Volant & Brotot, Lyon and translated into English by Denham (London). A Genovese publisher prints an Italian compilation of Almanac prophecies for 1565 to 1570.

1566 *Lettre … A la Royne mere du Roy* published by Benoist Rigaud, Lyon. Publishers Gerard and Jove of Lyon print the almanac for the year 1566–7. Italian publishers in Florence, Bologna and possibly Venice print a translation of an Almanac for 1566.

c. April 1566 Nostradamus returns from a physically stressful journey to the Royal Embassy at Arles that will precipitate his most severe attack of gout – by the end of June it develops into a fatal case of "dropsy" (pulmonary edema).

17 June 1566 With death approaching, he makes his final will and testament. His estate is worth 3,444 crowns (£350,000, or $400,000 in modern terms).

24 June 1566 Rushes the partial completion of the 1567 Almanac. It is believed the final three presages predict details of his coming death.

30 June 1566 Has a codicil to the will written granting his favorite daughter and son (Madeleine and César) their wishes to possess certain valuables upon his death rather than at the end of their minority.

Early 2 July 1566 At sunrise Nostradamus is found dead "between the bed and the bench" as he foresaw eight days earlier. He missed experiencing his "strange transmigration" on 1 July by only a few hours.

c. 5 July 1566 Michel de Nostradamus is entombed in the interior wall of the Church of the Cordeliers.

THE AFTERLIFE OF NOSTRADAMUS

Death usually ends a biographical tale but Nostradamus is one of the few historical figures who, many contend, lives beyond the grave. For most Nostradamians this afterlife is metaphorical – he lives on in our memories and our debates about the future thanks to a carefully planned literary device of obscure prophecies that work as a Rorschach test for every new generation trying to plot the future through his words. To others, however, the afterlife of the prophet is taken literally. There are those who have claimed to conjure the conjuring prophet back to life through magical and psychic means. In other words, the man who claimed to bring forth his own spiritual emissaries from beyond their graves during his magic rituals now becomes a spirit in the service of others.

c. Summer 1566 Nostradamus' final Almanac for the year 1567 is published a short time after his death by Volant & Brotot and later Odo, of Lyon, as well as Nyverd, Paris. London publishers Denham and later Bynnyman print an English translation.

1567 *Traité des fardemens* reprinted by de Marnefz & Bouchetz, Poitiers.

1568 Fourth edition of *Les Propheties de M. Michel Nostradamus* reprinted (and most likely updated with editorial corrections by Nostradamus before his death) by Benoist Rigaud,

Lyon. Like the Regnault edition, Century 7 had only 42 quatrains, yet with time the Rigaud edition was regarded by most scholars as the standard principal edition of Nostradamus' major prophetic opus. In addition, Nyverd, Paris, reprinted *Traité des fardemens* edited by the teenage César de Nostredame.

A quack calling himself Michel Nostradamus le Jeune (the Younger) publishes his first collection of prophecies and an almanac, posing as the long-lost son of the famous prophet. He is the first of many who will claim – at least spiritually if not by blood – to be the "true" successor of Nostradamus.

Bertrand, Nostradamus' younger brother, who may have introduced him to his second wife Anne in 1547, becomes an armed retainer of Claude de Savoie, Comte de Tende and Governor of Provence. During the Wars of Religion, he becomes captain of one of St.-Rémy's four defense companies. Later he will marry and father four children with Tomyne Rousse of Lamanon.

1569 The year Emmanuel-Philibert Duke of Savoy dies and fulfills Nostradamus' prediction: when a "9" precedes a "7" – the year 1570.

1571 Michel (the Younger), the humbug "son" of Nostradamus publishes further collections of prophecies.

1572 Henry Prince of Bearn, the 10-year-old subject of Nostradamus' mole prophecy reading from 1564, is crowned King of Navarre as predicted eight years earlier. *Traité des fardemens* reprinted by Bonfons, Paris; Benoist Rigaud, Lyon; and a German edition appeared, published by Manger, Augsburg.

César de Nostredame studies mathematics in Paris and witnesses the slaughter of Huguenots during the St. Bartholomew's Day massacre, an event many Nostradamians believe his father foresaw.

1573 *Traité des fardemens*, German 2nd edition reprinted by Manger, Augsburg.

1573–4 Bertrand de Nostredame serves as 1st Consul of St.-Rémy.

1574 Michel Nostradamus (the Younger) participates in the siege of Le Poussin in the Ardèche, and is killed. An account by d'Aubigné records a certain Saint-Luc had asked the prognosticator what would happen to the town. Michel "the Younger" pronounced that Le Poussin would perish by fire. "This fellow," adds d'Aubigné, "was found, during the pillage of the town, starting fires everywhere." Saint-Luc rode up to him and asked "Now then ... master, is any accident to happen to you today?" "No," Michel the Younger replied, to which Saint-Luc ran his lance through his belly. As he sank to the ground, d'Aubigné adds, "The horse upon which he sat kicked him – payment for his mischief."[1]

1575 Nostradamus' younger brother, Jehan, publishes *Les Vies des plus celebres et anciens poetes provensaulx*.

1576 Adam de Craponne dies, a suspected victim of murder. After the first leg of the canal from the Durance river to Salon was finished, funding for further work on the canal ran into financial difficulties and became stalled. The Wars of Religion had tempted Craponne back into designing military defenses. He was purportedly poisoned in 1575 and died the following year. His brother, Frédéric (d. 1623), will oversee the resumption of work on the canal, completing a segment across the Crau to Arles.

1577 Jehan de Nostredame dies at age 55. He had distinguished himself as the Attorney General of Provence and historian of Provençal poets.

July 1582 Anne Ponsarde Gemelle dies and is buried in a tomb alongside her husband in the Church of the Cordeliers.

1587 André de Nostredame enters the Capuchin (Franciscan) Order, becoming Friar "Seraphim." He had been a courtier of the Governor of Provence and had killed a rival, a certain

Cornillon of Salon, in a duel. He was released from jail after promising to become a Franciscan friar.

1588 Fourth edition of *Les Propheties* reprinted by Roffet, Paris, and Ménier, Paris.

1589 Henry of Navarre, the 10-year-old subject of Nostradamus' mole prophecy reading from 1564, is crowned King of France as predicted 25 years earlier. Fourth edition of *Les Propheties de M. Michel Nostradamus* reprinted by Ménier, Paris and Roger, Paris. Manger, Augsburg, publishes a second German edition of *Traité des fardemens*. Chavigny finishes collecting and interpreting all surviving examples of Nostradamus' almanac prose and quatrain (Presage) prophecies in *Recueil des Presages prosaiques de M. Michel de Nostradame* (*Collection of Prose Presages*).

1590 Fourth edition of *Les Propheties de M. Michel Nostradamus* reprinted by Roux, Avignon and Rouseau, Cahors.

Charles de Nostredame had earlier married Louis Becq and lived in Alleins. In this year, his firstborn, Anne, is baptized.

1594 Charles de Nostredame is described by Pierre d'Hozier as "Captain of the city of Salon." Chavigny publishes *La Première Face du Janus François ...* (*The First Face of the French Janus ...*) Along with printing the first biography, it sets the stage as the first of many future stabs at interpreting Nostradamus' obscure prophecies by others. The censors demand he expunge the book of any reference to Nostradamus as a "prophet." Chavigny sabotages their intent by telling the readers about their demand in the opening of the book. Using Nostradamus' prophecies, Chavigny correctly predicts that Henry of Navarre will become a great king of France, at a time when Henry has another long civil war to fight before securing the throne for himself. Chavigny inaccurately forecasts Henry seizing Italy, conquering the Ottoman Empire and becoming the Emperor of the world.

1594–6 Fourth edition of *Les Propheties* reprinted by Benoist Rigaud, Lyon.

1596 Anne (Nostradamus' second daughter) dies. She had married Pierre de Seva (Seve), co-Lord of Pierrefeu. Her son was Melchoir de Seva.

1597 Fourth edition of *Les Propheties de M. Michel Nostradamus* reprinted by the heirs of Benoist Rigaud, Lyon.

1598 César de Nostredame, already attaining the distinction of a historian, painter, and noted citizen in the town, becomes First Consul of Salon.

The Ninth and final War of Religion ends.

1600 César as First Consul hosts a visit to Salon of a second Medici queen of France, Marie de' Medici. Fourth edition of *Les Propheties* reprinted by Poyet, Lyon.

1601 Friar Seraphim (André de Nostredame) dies in Brignoles.

1602 "Captain" Bertrand de Nostradamus dies. He had ended his days a wealthy agricultural businessman, and his donations helped remodel and expand one of Provence's better-known Mas farmhouses, which he transformed into a château, at Roussan.

1603 Chavigny publishes *Le Pleiades*. The book inserts quotes of Nostradamus and expands on the all-too-grand failure of a forecast that Henry IV would become a second Charlemagne.

1604 Chavigny dies. César de Nostredame marries Claire de Grignan, the grand-daughter of Adam de Craponne. Fourth edition of *Les Propheties* reprinted by Pierre Rigaud, Lyon.

1605 Fifth edition of *Les Propheties de M. Michel Nostradamus* published by Seve/Benoist Rigaud. It includes the *Preface à César*, Centuries 1 through 4, Quatrain 53, the *Epistre* (Letter) to Henry II, and Centuries 8 through 10. In addition, it contains 141 Presages collected from the Almanacs, 58 Sixians, 25 duplicate quatrains for Century 7, 8, and extra quatrains in an incomplete Century 11 and 12.

19 March 1605 A certain grandson of Nostradamus, named Seve, presents Henry IV with a special copy of the 58 Sixians falsely attributed to Nostradamus.

1610 Henry IV is assassinated. Afterwards many Nostradamians believed an account of his assassination could be found in Quatrain 11 of Century 3 and Presage 72. The former, it is believed, named Henry and the street neighboring the scene of the assassination.[2]

1614 César publishes his epic *Histoire et chronique de Provence* and adds the distinction of local historian to his accomplishments as a painter of miniatures and portraits.

1616 César de Nostredame serves a second time as First Consul of Salon.

1622 Louis XIII visits the tomb of Nostradamus.

1623 Nostradamus' eldest daughter, Madeleine, dies. She had married Claude de Perussis, Baron of Lauris and Oppède. She had one son, Claude, and César reports that she was an accomplished lute player.

1629 Charles de Nostredame dies. He was remembered as one of the top three Provençal poets of his day.

1630 César de Nostredame is carried off by the plague at St.-Rémy. He died childless, and apparently in some financial trouble as he had asked d'Hozier the year before to establish for him a modest royal pension.

c. 1630s? The spinster, Diane de Nostredame (Nostradamus' youngest daughter), dies some years after César. His will left Diane the house, its furniture, and 200 crowns. The will also leaves behind the barest words of perfunctory regard to the last surviving child of Nostradamus. It is possible that the seer's descendants endured into modern times through his feminine bloodline.

1656 Etienne Jaubert publishes his *Eclaircissement des Veritables Quatrains ... de Maistre Michel Nostradamus (Explanation of the True Quatrains ... of Nostradamus).*

1660 The future Louis XIV, with his mother, Anne of Austria, and Cardinal Mazarin, visit Nostradamus' tomb.

1672 Théophilus de Garencières publishes *The True Prophecies or Prognostications of ... Nostradamus*, the first serious commentary on *Les Propheties de M. Michel Nostradamus* in the English language, albeit filled with errors, as it was poorly translated from a false French edition from 1568.

1673 Chevalier de Jant uses Nostradamus' prophecies (especially the spurious Sixians) as a basis to propagate the greater glory of Louis XIV.

1689 W. Atwood writes *Wonderful Predictions of Nostradamus* forecasting the downfall of France and Rome.

1691 W. Cross in *Predictions of Nostradamus Before the Year 1558* submits the French seer to his unsuccessful propaganda forecast of the "humiliation" of Louis XIV, the reformation of his kingdom and the return of Protestants to France.

c. 1701 Palamèdes Tronc de Coudoulet writes his 12-page overview of the life of Nostradamus (*Abrégé de la Vie de Nostradamus*) and two other short and unpublished biographies. They are the first serious attempts at gathering further details of Nostradamus' life story since brief biographical efforts of Chavigny and César de Nostredame.

1711 Johann Jacob Held publishes the first German commentary on *Les Propheties de M. Michel Nostradamus* (*Prophezeuungen ... Nostradami*). In addition, Pierre-Joseph Haitze writes the first full-size biography (*La Vie de Nostradamus*). He relies heavily on the Coudoulet sources.

1712 Jean Le Roux publishes *La Clef de Nostradamus* (*The Key of Nostradamus*). It is considered the best commentary from the 18th century. Le Roux is quite critical of the high-handed and sloppy work of previous interpreters, but he also makes his own wild interpretations. For instance, he states that the Preface to César is not for Nostradamus' son, but addressed to a future initiate who will unlock its prophetic meaning and be able to interpret the quatrains correctly. Thus with Le Roux begins the long quest among the more eccentric scholars of Nostradamus to stake a claim to be that "enlightened" interpreter.

1715 An interpreter under the pseudonym "D.D." publishes his commentary *The Prophecies of Nostradamus concerning the fate of all the Kings and Queens of Great Britain since the Reformation*. It stands as one of the first examples of a future habit of non-French commentators applying most of Nostradamus' quatrains to their nation. By the 1980s and 1990s this habit will be stretched to extremes by about a half-dozen Japanese commentators who believe Nostradamus was only interested in the future of far-off Nippon.

1721 *Propheties de Michel Nostradamus* by François Geofroy proffered the failed interpretation upon Nostradamus' obscure verse that James III of Great Britain would return from exile.

August 1724 An unknown and skeptical scholar publishes a long letter in the *Mercure de France* establishing for the first time a popular theory amongst debunkers of Nostradamus that his prophecies were retroactive. In other words, his obscure history of the future is actually regurgitated past events. This initial thesis is turgid but, strangely enough, documents a number of Nostradamus successful "predictions" about the future.

c. 1730s French commentaries by Jean Vallier (1731), Nicolas de Malezieu (1733).

c. 1740s Italian commentaries (1740) and French editions of the prophecies published by Garnier (1741), Oudot (1742, 1744), and commentaries by Gachet d'Artigny (1749).

c. 1750s Commentaries by François Nau (1755), Toussaint-Gaspard Taconet (1759).

c. 1760s A German translation of Nostradamus the Younger's fraudulent predictions (1760), a commentary by Monseigneur Comte de Provence (1766), and an Italian to French translation of the real Nostradamus' *Les Propheties de M. Michel Nostradamus* (1769).

1775 An English author (unknown) accurately predicts the American Revolution and its successful outcome based on his study of Nostradamus. This is the first of many recorded examples to come of interpreters using Nostradamus to make a successful forecast while putting into question whether such success comes from divining Nostradamus' prophecy or is due to a gift of the commentator's insight projected over Nostradamus' cloudy verses.

1781 The papacy of Pope Pius VI officially condemns and blacklists Nostradamus' prophecies in all its translations.

1789 Just before the catastrophe of the French Revolution, Chez Gattey publishers of Paris turn out *La Vie et le Testament ... de Nostradamus* (*The Life and Testament ...*). Pierre-Joseph de Haitze, in the 1720s, or an author under the spurious name Edme Chavigny probably wrote it. Its biographical research relies heavily on a second unpublished manuscript by Palamèdes Tronc de Coudoulet.

1791 French revolutionary guards ransack Nostradamus' grave. Some of his bones are eventually recovered and re-entombed in the chapel of St. Roch (patron saint of plague victims) in Salon's Collegiale St.-Laurent, where they remain to this day.

1792 The first French Republic is proclaimed and a new calendar system established.

Late 1790s In Paris, a copy of *Les Propheties de M. Michel Nostradamus* is put on public exhibition. It is opened to a page in the Epistle to Henry II highlighting Nostradamus' prophecy concerning the year 1792 as a time perceived to be a renovation of the age requiring the creation of a new calendar system.

1790–1815 The French Revolution and the subsequent dictatorship of Napoleon Bonaparte rekindle French interest in Nostradamus' prophecies as it appears that out of a number of his vague verses there seem to be clear and detailed references to many of the people and intimate events of the Revolution and Napoleonic years. There are at least nine commentaries during this period, including. D'Odoucet (1790) and Madame "H.D." (1800), who cite Nostradamus auguring the French Revolution. Dr. Belland and Théodore Bouys find the rise and significance of Napoleon Bonaparte in his quatrains.

1808 German poet and dramatist Johann Wolfgang von Goethe publishes *Faust.* In the opening chapter, when Faust conjures up Mephistopheles, he cries:

> Fly! Up, and seek the broad, free land!
> And this one Book of Mystery
> From Nostradamus' very hand,
> Is't not sufficient company?
> When I the starry courses know,
> And Nature's wise instruction seek,
> With light of power my soul shall glow,
> As when to spirits spirits speak.
> 'Tis vain, this empty brooding here,
> Though guessed the holy symbols be:
> Ye, Spirits, come – ye hover near –
> Oh, if you hear me, answer me![3]

1813 M. David, Mayor of Salon erects a stone plaque honoring Nostradamus' tomb as the final resting place of one who had foreseen the French Revolution.

1820 The fraudulent Prophecy of Olivarius (Orval), attributed to Nostradamus, first appears in Mlle M.A. Le Normand's memoirs recounting her life as the Empress Josephine

Bonaparte's private card reader. Normand claims this prophecy attributed to Nostradamus was carried around by Napoleon on his campaigns.

1839 The fraudulent Prophecy of Orval is another forecast from the 1540s from "Olivarius" recovered and copied in 1823 by Henri Dujardin from a little booklet published in 1544. Eugène Bareste prints it again in 1840 but admits he cannot find its 16th-century source.

1840 Eugène Bareste's *Nostradamus* not only comments on the prophecies but also launches what Edgar Leoni cites as the first attempt at a "scientific biography."

1860–63 The many articles of F. Buget continue the quest to reveal the documented – as opposed to the propagated – life of Nostradamus.

1862–78 A French curé named H. Torné (who takes the pseudonym Torné-Chavigny because he claimed to be a direct descendant of Jean-Aymes de Chavigny on his mother's side) floods the writing market with interpretations that make him the greatest 19th-century Nostradamian propagator of French royalist causes. All of them unfulfilled. This zealot influenced Victor Hugo, and his writings convinced Pope Pius IX that Napoleon III was the "Beast of the Apocalypse."

1867 Anatole Le Pelletier prints his monumental study of Nostradamus. His commentaries are considered by many Nostradamians to be the best mix of propaganda and scholarship from the 19th century. Rather than Napoleon III, Le Pelletier believes the "antichrist" is Garibaldi, the Italian revolutionary. However, beyond his checkered interpretive skills, Le Pelletier establishes the first foundations for future etymological glossaries for Nostradamus' vocabulary used for his prophecies.

1891 Charles A. Ward publishes *Oracles of Nostradamus* in England. The book will become one of the most widely read

English commentaries of the 20th century. His views are a derivative of the Le Pelletier commentary.

1909 Nostradamus' house in Salon and the town's old quarter suffer damage from the great Vernègues earthquake.

1913 Graf Karl von Klinckowström publishes his bibliography of the earliest surviving works of Nostradamus.

1914–22 World War I (1914–18) stimulates interest in Nostradamus on either side of the Franco-German trench line. German Nostradamians Kniepf and Loog fire their interpretations at the French, explaining why Imperial Germany will win; French Nostradamians Nicoullaud, Demar-Latour, Gaffront and Larmor publish their counter-barrage. After 1918, the French writers publish further commentaries celebrating their victory by interpretation.

1926 Dr. Christian Wöllner publishes *Das mysterium des Nostradamus*. It is the first serious study of potential time windows for the fulfillment of Nostradamus' astrological predictions.

1927 In Pierre V. Piobb's *Le Secret de Nostradamus* ... is one of the first attempts at finding and using one all-encompassing code to unlock the obscure prophecies. As with all attempts of code-breakers to come, his theories work rather well on specific examples seen in hindsight, but fail utterly when applied to future events.

1933 Jacques R. Boulenger publishes a biography of Nostradamus in Paris. Seventy years will pass before another classic biography is released on the life of Nostradamus.

1936 Henry James Forman defines Nostradamus as "Europe's greatest prophet" in his classic on forecasting and forecasters *The Story of Prophecy*.

1937–9 As the Second World War approaches interest in Nostradamus mounts in France. Publications appear in Portugal, Sweden, and Spain. French commentators Emil Ruir and Dr. E. de Fontbrune have mixed success predicting the catastrophes about to befall a world descending into war. Beyond this, Riur, a staunchly right-wing royalist and devout Catholic, waxed apocalyptic predicting the conversion of Israel, the reign of God and the Church of Christ at the end of the world. Both are modern proponents of the Nostradamian cult of Henry V – a future king who will free the French from its republics and restore the monarchy.

Late 1939 Magda Goebbels, the wife of Josef Goebbels, the Propaganda Minister of the Third Reich, loved to take a copy of Von Loog's German interpretation of Nostradamus to bed with her. She nagged Goebbels under the covers about prophecies of a "captain of Greater Germany" who Nostradamus called "Hister." She may have also brought to her husband's attention Dr. H.H. Kritzinger's interpretation of Germany's next war with England in Century 3, Quatrain 57. According to Lemesurier, other German interpreters suggested a war would come in 1939 involving Poland, France, Germany, and Britain, as was the case.

7–10 November 1939 Karl Ernst Krafft, a Swiss citizen, Nostradamus commentator, and a fervent believer in the Nazi Party, moved to Germany to offer his already well-known and respected astrological and intuitive services. While working for Himmler's Secret Service as an astrological consultant, Krafft submitted a paper at the beginning of November 1939 warning of an assassination threat hovering over Hitler's stars between 7 and 10 November. Horoscopes on the Führer were forbidden, so the paper was filed and locked away. On the evening of 8 November, Hitler made his annual speech at the Munich Beer Hall, the scene of the 1923 Putsch. Mainstream historians say that pressing business forced him to cut short his speech. Hitler himself would relate to intimates that he felt a strong premonition to leave. Eight minutes after Hitler and a number of other key Nazi leaders left the hall, a time-bomb hidden in a pillar behind the rostrum exploded, killing seven and wounding 63. On hearing about the Führer's close brush with death, Krafft reminded Himmler's office of his forecast, and where it was filed. At this, the Gestapo arrested him and brought him to Berlin. Krafft was released to Joseph Goebbels, who set him to work on the Nostradamus project as chief interpreter. It is said that Century 6, Quatrain 51 helped Krafft pinpoint the time and place of the assassination attempt.

5 December 1939 Entry in Joseph Goebbel's diary: "Oberst von Hacken has produced a new translation of Nostradamus. Marvelously useful for our propaganda abroad. I shall take steps immediately."[4]

1940 Charles Reynaud-Plense includes new biographical data in his *Les Vraies Centuries et Prophéties ... Nostradamus.*

9 January 1940 Joseph Goebbels' diary: "I will set up a committee to deal with Nostradamus and astrology. It will supply the necessary material for my propaganda."[5]

16 January 1940 Goebbels' diary: "A lot of work. Thrash out Nostradamus verses in co-operation with the Intelligence Service for us in France and neutral countries. Every little bit helps."[6]

Latter half of 1940 A pro-Nazi propaganda pamphlet, written by a certain "Norab," published in Stockholm, surfaces across the United States.

c. 1941 After the French Revolution and Napoleonic era, the escalation of the European conflict into a full-fledged world war brings the second great historical peak of interest in Nostradamus beyond France's borders. In this year commentaries appear from James Laver and Rolfe Boswell, as well as American author Lee McCan's famous myth and fact mixing account *Nostradamus: The Man Who Saw Through Time.*

Karl Ernst Krafft's propaganda pamphlets bending Nostradamus to fit the future whims of the Nazi cause are published in Spain and appear across Europe. However, his fate took a turn for the worse in this year when Rudolph Hess, Nazi Party leader, Third Deputy of the Third Reich, and follower of the occult, flew to England on a self-deluded errand of astrologically or psychically approved peace. Hitler instigates a purge of occultists and astrologers. While in prison the Gestapo coerces Krafft to continue his writing of National-Socialistically correct interpretations of Nostradamus.

c. 1941–3 Across the English Channel, allied propagandists work for the British Prime Minister Winston Churchill, such as Louis de Wohl, and more capable astrologers such as John Watkins. According to the latter, Churchill played prophetic editor of Nostradamus, doctoring the prophecies to make Britain's destiny look better than it was.

1942 More efforts to make Nostradamus predict the outcome for one side or the other of World War II, including works by André Lamont (U.S.A.), James Laver (U.K.), Stewart Robb (U.S.A.), and skeptical attacks against Nostradamus by Dr. Edgar Leroy (in occupied Provence). Lamont and Robb would document some prophetic successes as to the fate of Hitler and the outcome of the war. Leroy would begin fomenting his opinion that Nostradamus was a drunkard who composed prophecies based on private and historical data while bingeing on wine.

19 May 1942 Goebbels in his diary writes: "Brendt [Ingomar Brent, one of Goebbels' yes men and closest lieutenants] handed in a plan for occultist propaganda to be carried on by us. We are getting somewhere. The Americans and English fall easily to this kind of propaganda. We are therefore pressing into service all-star witnesses of occult prophecy. Nostradamus must once again submit to being quoted."[7]

1942–3 After the United States enters the Second World War, Metro-Goldwin-Meyer Studios (MGM) draft Nostradamus for a series of glitzy film shorts called *Nostradamus Says So, More About Nostradamus, Further Prophecies of Nostradamus,* and *Nostradamus IV.* The MGM propaganda department intended to stretch his prophecies – and the facts – across the silver screen to persuade the American theater audience that even the prophet Nostradamus foresaw the triumph of democracy over Nazi Germany and Imperial Japan. Thus, we see the beginning of movies and documentaries becoming a key medium for spreading the Nostradamus phenomenon around the world. The exposure will have mixed results. On the one hand he becomes a household name and his prophecies become globally known; however, the new notoriety will plunge the understanding of his vision deeper into a morass of hearsay, propagandized lies, and yellow journalistic sensation.

January 1945 Karl Ernst Krafft dies. His work on Nostradamus had opened doors for him in the Reich – first to the propaganda ministry, then to a prison cell. In the end his inability to find a genuine prediction supporting Nazi victory stretched him tight as a string. Finally, he succumbed to a nervous breakdown and in January 1945 died from typhus while on his way to Buchenwald concentration camp.

1946 Garcia de Montpellier writes and performs a radio drama on Argentinian radio on the life of Nostradamus.

1947 Henry C. Roberts produces *The Complete Prophecies of Nostradamus* (which are neither complete, nor taken from accurate sources). Riur publishes *Nostradamus: Ses Prophéties, de nos jours à l'an 2023* wherein he sees Nostradamus marking the year 2023 as the time the white race and Christian civilization will lose their dominant role on the face of Earth.

1950 This is the year André Lamont, writing in 1941, believed Nostradamus foresaw another war in the Far East. The Korean War began in this year.

Raoul Busquet publishes *Nostradamus, sa famille, son secret*. Among other skeptical inquiries, he further runs with Leroy's theory that Nostradamus was a drunk. Jean de Fontbrune prints *L'Étrange XXᵉ siècle vu par Nostradamus* (*The Strange 20th Century Seen by Nostradamus*.)

1956 G. Gustafsson in Stockholm publishes *Europas framtid enligt Nostradamus*.

1961 Edgar Leoni publishes his momentous work of scholarship *Nostradamus: Life and Literature*. It becomes the foundation for most scholarship or flights of interpretative commentary for the rest of the 20th century.

1973 Erika Cheetham publishes *The Prophecies of Nostradamus*. Her highly successful interpretations of the quatrains (if not the complete works of Nostradamus) launch what some might call the present-day "golden age" of worldwide interest in Nostradamus the man, his myth, and his prophecies. Beginning in the 1970s, dozens of amateur studies, and a few serious attempts, flood book markets across the world.

1974 Al Stewart writes the song "Nostradamus," which ends with the famous chorus: "Man, Man, your time is sand, your ways are leaves upon the sea/I am the eyes of Nostradamus, all your ways are known to me."

1976 Fantasy illustrator Bruce Pennington prints his series of apocalyptic paintings inspired by the prophecies of Nostradamus in his book *Eschatus: Future Prophecies from Nostradamus' Ancient Writings*.

1981 Orson Welles narrates *The Man Who Saw Tomorrow*. It becomes what is so far the definitive documentary on the life and predictions of Nostradamus. It includes a prediction that the 27-year war of the Third Antichrist will begin after 1999. Its popularity sees the documentary regularly reissued and updated in video for 20 years.

1982 Leoni's book is reissued under the new title *Nostradamus and His Prophecies*.

1983–4 Jean-Charles de Fontbrune publishes the widely trans-lated *Nostradamus, Historien et prophète,* then a follow-up volume.

1984 *Nostradamus: Prophecies of Present Times* by David Pitt-Francis.

1985 *The Further Prophecies of Nostradamus* (Cheetham).

1987 John Hogue publishes the first magazine-style, fully-illustrated study of the prophet's life and prophecies entitled *Nostradamus and the Millennium.* It becomes a bestseller in nine countries, with 630,000 copies printed. A number of copycat "clone" versions of the unique design style appear in the coming years.

1989 Arkansan author, Dolores Cannon, claims to "channel" the living Nostradamus back in the 16th century in her three-volume commentary *Conversations with Nostradamus.* Her interpretations, however, rely heavily on the work of other translators, such as Cheetham and Lamont, who, it is safe to say, did not claim to talk with the prophet across a wide ocean of time. Other publications for this year: *The Final Prophecies of Nostradamus.* (Cheetham), and *Bibliographie Nostradamus* (Michel Chomarat with Larouche).

1990 James Randi publishes *The Mask of Nostradamus.* This book is the most significant, if less skeptical and more cynical, inquiry into the life and work of the prophet since Dr. Edgar Leroy.

1991 V.J. Hewitt and Peter Lorie publish *Nostradamus: The End of the Millennium,* documenting magnificently unsuccessful evidence that they have broken a code unlocking the secrets of Nostradamus' prophecies.

1992 J.H. Brennan issues *Nostradamus: Visions of the Future* providing a less biased and refreshing insight into the occult aspects of the prophet's life.

1993 With the millennium approaching there is a surge of Nostradamus books, including: *Nostradamus, Lettres – Inédites* (Jean Dupèbe), *Nostradamus 1: Countdown to Apocalypse* (English ed., J.-C. Fontbrune), *Nostradamus 2:*

Into the Twenty-First Century (English ed., J.-C. Fontbrune),
Les Dernières Victoires de Nostradamus (V. Ionescu),
Nostradamus: Prophecies Fulfilled ... (Francis X. King),
Nostradamus: The Next 50 Years (Peter Lemesurier),
Nostradamus: ses origines, sa vie, son oeuvre (reprint: Leroy),
Nostradamus: The Millennium and Beyond (Peter Lorie),
Orus Apollo (reprint: Michel Nostradamus), and *Les
Prophecies ... 1557 ed.* (Nostradamus, trans. by Chomarat).

1994 A busy year for literary and media attention. Significant
books published in this year include: *Nostradamus: The New
Revelations* (Hogue), *Nostradamus* (Knut Boeser's noveliza-
tion of the Orion Classic movie produced this year),
Nostradamus: The Key to the Centuries (V.J. Hewitt, sans
Lorie), *Keys to the Predictions of Nostradamus* (Bardo Kidogo
– aka, Barry Popkess), *Les Ultimes Prophéties de Nostradamus*
(J. Mareuil).

Spring 1994 NBC television broadcasts a two-hour special across
the Untied States called *Ancient Prophecies*. The quasi-
documentary, with its spectral, floor-lit scholars (including
this author), and its melodramatic re-enactments, led the
TV dish denizens of over 20 million homes in a journey
through the collective visions of doomsday. In the first hour
after it aired, NBC received 35,000 calls before the phone
system overloaded and had to be shut down. Due to its
unexpected success, *Ancient Prophecies* enjoyed a rare re-
broadcast in less than a month and once again scholarly
projections of Nostradamus lived to predict on Prime Time
Sunday across North America to high national ratings.

c. October 1994 In the article "Who will be first among us"
(*Time*, 10/26/94) there is an account of a conversation at
lunch between Pope John Paul II and a bishop from
Senegal. "In Africa," the bishop said, "people are talking a
lot about your succession. After you, they say there will be
a black Pope." John Paul said, "You seem very well

informed." To which the bishop replied, "Yes, I read it in Nostradamus!"

c. November 1994 Members of the NFL football team, the Green Bay Packers, declare on ESPN TV that Nostradamus foresaw their victory against the Chicago Bears.

c. 1995 The year's list of new commentaries includes: *Nostradamus: The Final Reckoning* (Lemesurier), *Nostradamus' Prophecies for Women* (Peter Lorie with Maschetti), *Ansi parlait Nostradamus* (E. Mézo), and *Nostradamus Magic Eye* (Thing Enterprises).

January 1995 Orion Classics releases the first feature film of the prophet's life (appropriately named *Nostradamus*), starring Tcheky Karyo, F. Murray Abraham, Julia Ormond, and Rutger Hauer. The movie drew some of its interpretive ideas from this author's first book. These include the dramatic climax depicting a fleet of space ships from Earth preparing to land and colonize a distant planet in the far future. It is a good example of how interpretations of this or any author have been made to play a part in the Nostradamus mythos.

Autumn 1995 *Nostradamus: Prophet of Doom* (Greystone) appears on U.S. cable channel Arts and Entertainment's popular series *A & E's Biography*. It will become one of the top three most-watched biographies of the first 500 shows of this long-running series.

"Nose"-tradamus (a Seattle sportscaster in costume) predicts unsuccessfully the Mariners baseball team winning the pennant. Jay Leno, host of *The Tonight Show* (a nationally broadcast night talk show) begins his series of comic parodies of the prophet called "Nostra-dumb-ass."

1997 John Hogue publishes *Nostradamus: The Complete Prophecies*, the first full translation and commentary of the major prophecies and presages in 36 years. Peter Lemesurier publishes the comprehensive *Nostradamus Encyclopedia*. David

Ovason in *The Secrets of Nostradamus* may have introduced another theory-cum-myth that Nostradamus coded his prophecies by using the secret "Green Language" of the Provençal Troubadours.

April 1997 The approach of the millennium brings renewed and mostly sensational interest in Nostradamus from the television media. *NBC Dateline* broadcasts a segment on Nostradamus, flashing one of this author's book covers on national U.S. television and declaring that Nostradamus predicted the end of the world in the year 2000. (Clearly, no one at NBC opened the author's book to see Nostradamus slotting doomsday for the year 3797.)

August 1997 The Fox Channel shows *Prophecies for the Millennium* on national U.S. television. This author appears in a segment on Nostradamus prophecies purported to foretell a future terrorist attack on New York. There is a dramatization of annihilation of the World Trade Center towers by a small atomic bomb detonated by terrorists.

1999 The year sees a whole plethora of works on Nostradamus across the world and Nostradamus web sites increase by the thousands.

July 1999 Global interest surges when the time of Nostradamus' detailed and dated prophecy (Century 10, Quatrain 72) for a "king of Terror" descending from the skies in "1999 and seven months" arrives. Nothing seems to happen, beyond that summer's exceedingly chaotic and violent weather around the world.

2 August 1999 John Hogue reports in the *Seattle Times* his theory that the "king of Terror" is not a person but the phenomenon called "Global Warming."

11 August 1999 A great eclipse passes over Europe, Turkey, and the Middle East all the way to Gujarat in India. It appears that in a number of predictions Nostradamus described the trail of its shadow and other important details of this pre-millennium eclipse in a number of prophecies.[8] In brief, interpretations generally weave the theme that this eclipse marks a turning point in history. A new 27-to-30-year travail for civilization is expected to come heralded by great climatic disruptions and earthquakes. (Coincidence at least played into the prophecy as major earthquakes wracked countries in the shadow of the eclipse. Turkey suffered a 7.4 quake at the end of August 1999, with equally large aftershocks killing tens of thousands. Greece also suffered massive earthquakes that autumn. In early 2001, a quake devastated the entire Indian state of Gujarat.)

September 1999 Interpreters and fans of Nostradamus desperate to find some important objective support for his King of Terror/July 1999 prophecy stretch his French to cover the double entendre of *sept mois* for "September month." Nothing significant happens.

July 2000 One last try for the interpreters to make hay out of the 1999 prophecy believe "1999 and seven months" means 1999 "plus" seven months. Nothing significant happens.

2000 The millennium brings an explosion of interest for Nostradamus on the World Wide Web. There are over 40,000 web pages and sites

11 September 2001 The terrorist attack on the twin towers of the World Trade Center rekindles global attention and controversy because of prophecies attributed to Nostradamus purportedly forecasting the attack. After "9/11" the number of Nostradamus web pages and sites expands to over 140,000.

2002 Several commentaries appear incorporating updates and theories on future trends following the "9/11" terrorist attacks. The books include *Nostradamus: The New Millennium* (Hogue) and *Nostradamus, Prophecies for America* (Ovason).

2003 The 500-year anniversary of Nostradamus' birth sees a number of books published around the world about his life and prophecies. Amazon.com lists nearly 250 new and used book commentaries, video documentaries and audio book titles – most of these published after 1995.

Notes

[A full rendering of the bibliographical information in these notes can be found in the Select Bibliography.]

INTRODUCTION:
AN ECCENTRIC MAN FOR ALL SEASONS

1. The original French version taken from the 1568 Benoist Rigaud Edition of *Les Propheties de M. Michel Nostradamus* reads:

    Cinq & quarante degrés ciel bruslera,
    Feu approcher de la grand cité neufue,
    Instant grand flamme esparse sautera,
    Quand on voudra des Normans faire preuue.

    (6Q97)

    Iardin du monde aupres du cité neufue,
    Dans le chemin des montaignes cauees:
    Sera saisi & plongé dans la Cuue,
    Beuuant par force eaux soulfre enuenimees.

    (10Q49)

2. Some mention of Nostradamus' family background and the life of his brother appear in Jehan de Nostredame's *Les Vies des plus celebres et anciens poetes provensaulx*, 1575.
3. Important milestones in the life of his father appear in César de Nostredame's *L'Histoire et chronique de Provence* (1st ed., 1614).
4. In later life Jean-Aymes (Aimé) de Chavigny wrote the first surviving biographical account and character study of his master in *La Première Face du Janus françois, contenant*

sommairement les troubles, guerres civiles et autres choses
mémorables, advenues en la France et ailleurs, dès l'an de salut
1534, jusques à l'an 1589, fin de la maison Valésienne. Extraite
et colligée des centuries et autres commentaires de M. Michel de
Nostredame, iadis conseillier et médecin des rois Henry II,
Francoys II et Charles IX. A la fin est adiousté un discours de
l'advénement a la couronne de France du roy très-chrestian à
present regnant: ensemble de sa grandeur et prosperité à venir. Le
tout fait en françois et latin pour le contentement de plusieurs ...
dedié au roy. A Lyon, par les héritiers de Pierre Roussin (1594).

5. Etienne Jaubert was the source of some of the most interesting – yet potentially apocryphal – stories in *Eclaircissement*
   des veritables Quatrains de Maistre Michel Nostradamus,
   Docteur et Professeur en Medecine, Conseiller et Medecin ordi-
   naire, des Roys Henry II. François II. & Charles IX. grand
   Astrologue de son temps, & specialement pour la connoissance
   des choses futures (1656).

   Edgar Leoni believes his book was published in
   Amsterdam as the first and last of an intended serialization
   in 19 booklets, covering 71 quatrains Jaubert applied to
   events for the years 1555–60. Copies can be found at the
   Harvard University and New York Public libraries.

6. Theophilus de Garencières wrote the first English interpretation of Nostradamus' major prophetic work. See *The true*
   prophecies; or, Prognostications of Michael Nostradamus, physi-
   cian to Henry II. Francis II. and Charles IX. kings of France, and
   one of the best astronomers that ever were. A work full of curiosi-
   ty and learning. Translated and commented ..., London, 1672.

   Copies exist in Harvard, Williams, Illinois and Michigan
   college libraries and in Sacramento, New York, and Newark
   public libraries and a number of private collections. Leoni
   tells us Houdini's copy sits in the US Library of Congress.

7. F. Buget, in his articles in the *Bulletin du Bibliophile et du*
   Bibliothécaire (Paris, 1860–63), claimed to have seen the first

Coudoulet manuscript, which at the time was in the library of Comte de Lagoy of Aix. Dr. Bossy, the former mayor of Salon and great-grandson of Coudoulet, showed Buget the second manuscript, which was noted for similar and perhaps copied biographical information that one finds in the Haitze work, blended with that of the first manuscript.

8.   Edgar Leoni, *Nostradamus and his Prophecies,* 1961.
9.   Michel Chomarat's diligent and exhaustive recovery of surviving records, manuscripts, and papers of Nostradamus and his works makes him the pre-eminent archivist of the prophet. See *Bibliographie Nostradamus (avec la collaboration de Jean-Paul Laroche), Bibliotheca Bibliographica Aureliana CXXIII,* 1989.
10. Pierre Brind'Amour edited and interpreted the recently rediscovered first Macé Bonhomme (1555) edition of Nostradamus' major prophecies. See *Nostradamus, Les Premières Centuries ou Propheties (édition Macé Bonhomme de 1555) Edition et commentaire de l'Epître à César et des 353 premiers quatrains* (1996).
11. See *The Nostradamus Encyclopedia: The Definitive Reference Guide to the Work and World of Nostradamus,* 1997, Peter Lemesurier.
12. See *Nostradamus: ses origines, sa vie, son oeuvre* by Dr. Edgar Leroy (reprinted 1972).
     Leoni describes him as a "fanatical Nostradamus-hater."
13. James Randi, *The Mask of Nostradamus,* 1990.
14. "You're in the Lap of History," Malcolm Jones, *Newsweek* (1/27/03), p. 64.
15. *The Biography of J.R.R. Tolkien: Architect of Middle Earth,* Daniel Grotta, p. 44.

CHAPTER ONE:
BORN IN THE LAND OF TROUBADOUR KINGS

1. *Holly Horrors*, James A. Haught, p. 43.

2. *Nostradamus Encyclopedia*, Lemesurier, p. 26.

3. A notary of Avignon, Jacques Giraud, recorded and witnessed on 12 May 1455 that Petro de Nostra Domina was an inhabitant of Avignon, a year after the king's edict. In addition, an attached note says: *Pro Petro de Nostra Domina Olim cum judeus esset vocato Vidono Gassonet obligatio* ("Obligation for Pierre de Nostredame who was called Guy Gassonet, from the time he was Jewish").

4. *Nostradamus Encyclopedia*, Lemesurier, p. 26.

5. *Histoire de Juifs*, Depping, pp. 334–5.

6. There is a record of an ennobled and baptized Jewish physician of King Réné named Abraham Solomon. See *L'Encyclopédie du Département des Bouches-du-Rhône*, p. 357.

7. Charles Reynaud-Plense, *Les Vraies Centuries et Prophéties de Michel Nostradamus ... Colligées des premières éditions imprimées à Lyon en 1558–1605 et, à Troyes en 1611, et à Leyde en 1650, avec sa Vie, et un Glossaire Nostradamique*, 1940.

8. René was titular King of Naples, Sicily and Jerusalem, Duke of Anjou, Lorraine and Bar, and Count of Provence and Piedmont.

9. *Nostradamus: The Man Who Saw Through Time*, Lee McCann, p. 8.

10. *Mémoires de L'Institut historique de Provence*, Vol. 17, 1941, reprinted by Busquet in 1950.

    Lee McCann in his book *Nostradamus, The Man Who Saw Through Time*, p. 6, lists some commonsense reasons why Nostradamus was not Jewish. If Jews were tolerated within Provence, his widening fame across the French and European realms that were intolerant to Jews should have exposed him to a rich record of virulent anti-Semitic attacks beyond those enemies calling him a charlatan and sorcerer. McCann also cites no record of his secretary, Chavigny, mentioning his Jewish heritage, nor does any admission come from commentator Theophilus Garencières, "who states that all his life he had been in contact with people who either knew all about Nostradamus or thought they did." Possibly Chavigny did not mention it because he was far less intimately connected to Nostradamus than he claims, and he did not know about this secret. On the other hand, perhaps he knew *too* much, and preferred not to reveal the yellow stigma of the Star of David in his biographical account, as it would harm Chavigny's reputation if readers came to know that his master was a Jew.

11. Changes in French fashions of spelling have seen the names of Nostradamus' parents go through a number of changes: for example, *Jaume* becomes *Jeaumet*, and *Jacques*, *Reynière* is *Renée* in many biographies.

12. The archives at Aix-en-Provence list the names of Jean de Saint-Rémy and Pierre de Nostredame on the roll of taxes levied on the "new Christian community" by 12 December 1512, 11 years later. Even though David Pitt-Francis (*Nostradamus: Prophecies of Present Times?*, p. 14) believes the conversion of Nostradamus and his family came to pass in that year, when Nostradamus was nine, other scholars cite the snail pace of local bureaucrats of the 16th century in disseminating pertinent changes in census information.

13. Astrologer Dr. Louis Turi, in his book *The Power of the Dragon*, passionately disputes any speculative calculation beyond the general time of "noon" by both astrologer Jeff Green and myself, explaining that the suffering and exhausted midwife bringing Michel into the world probably had neither the time, the clock, nor the education to record the exact time needed for plotting ascendants. This concept overlooks certain facts. By this time, clocks and coil spring watch works had already existed for at least a half-century.

The archival records indicate that Jaume de Nostredame was well-heeled enough financially to have some kind of early clock to record the time of birth. He may have owned an early watch shaped like a drum or ball that was worn suspended from a belt or kept in a pocket. A number of horoscopes of the early 16th century record the ascendant and the exact time of birth. John Dee's chart is just one of many examples on record. Still, to say his birth took place two or three minutes after noon is speculation, for watches and clocks at that time possessed only one hand that told time to the nearest quarter hour or unit of five minutes. See *The Power of the Dragon* (Chapter on "Famous Dragon Charts," p. 120).

14. *Ibid.* Dr. Louis Turi gives one of the best astrological interpretations of the natal chart of Nostradamus. Dr. Turi's technique, called Divine Astrology, is based on disciplines of casting charts that were far more prevalent at the beginning of the 16th century, when Nostradamus was born.

15. Chavigny records for posterity a comprehensive character study of Nostradamus from recollections when the latter was between 51 and 63 years old. "He was a little under medium height, of robust body, nimble and vigorous. He had a large and open forehead, a straight and even nose, gray eyes which were generally pleasant but which blazed when he was angry and a visage both severe and smiling, such that along with his severity a great humanity could be seen; his cheeks were ruddy, even in his old age, his beard was long and thick, his health good and hearty (except in his old age) and all his senses acute and complete. His mind was good and lively, understanding easily what he wanted to; his judgment was subtle, his memory quite remarkable. By nature he was taciturn, thinking much and saying little, though speaking very well in the proper time and place: for the rest, vigilant, prompt and impetuous, prone to anger, patient in labor. He

slept only four to five hours ..." See *La Première Face du Janus françois* ... (1594).

16. *Histoire de France*, Michelet, vol. ii, p. 277.

17. *Anne of Geierstein*, Scott, p. 228–9.

18. *La Première Face du Janus françois* ..., Jean-Aymes (Aimé) de Chavigny.

19. I cannot find a surviving quote from Nostradamus himself specifying whether his paternal or maternal ancestors – or both – were the source of his purported gift of sight. In his Preface and Epistle letters in his work *Les Propheties*, he only speaks of his gift as *la parolle hereditaire de l'occulte prédiction* or coming from *mes antiques progeniteurs* respectively. See *Les Propheties* (Benoist Rigaud, ed., 1568): Preface, p. 3; and *Les Propheties* (Benoist Rigaud, ed., 1568): *A L'Invictissime ... Henry Roi de France* ... (i.e., Epistle to Henry II), pp. 6–7.

  Stewart Robb sourced this gender-specific lineage from Bareste and Le Pelletier. Lemesurier and Joseph Robert Jochmans cite family accounts.

20. *New English Bible*, Oxford Study Edition, p. 433.

21. *Key to the Future*, Boscolo, p. 5

22. *Preface oe M. Michel Nostradamus à ses Propheties. Ad Caesarem Nostradamum filium, Vie & felicité* (1 March 1555). See English translation in *Nostradamus: The Complete Prophecies*, Hogue, pp. 44–5.

23. *Nosradamus Now*, Jochmans, p. 34.

24. Nostradamus' coat-of-arms consists of a gules (red) quartered shield. The first and fourth quarters have a broken wheel of gold with eight rays; the second and third quarters have the detached head of an eagle in sable (black). The latter is the device of the Saint-Rémy family (Nostradamus' maternal family). The Nostradamus family motto written on a parchment scroll below the shield is "*Soli Deo*" ("to God alone" or "only to God").

CHAPTER TWO: THE ITINERANT APOTHECARY

1. See *Society and Culture in Early Modern France*, Davis, p. 112.
2. *Sages and Seers*, Manly P. Hall, p. 29.
3. *The true prophecies; or, Prognostications of Michael Nostradamus* ..., London, Theophilus de Garencières, 1672.
4. *Sages and Seers*, Manly P. Hall, p. 29.
5. Speculation abounds as to what works Nostradamus would have read, and when, in his quest for knowledge. In order to pinpoint the written sources of Nostradamus' basic foundations in the humanities, Bardo Kidogo takes the special spellings and classical information Nostradamus used as the basis for metaphors found in his future prophetic writings. Kidogo believes Nostradamus' study of drama would have included reading in Greek the plays of Aeschylus. For his extensive knowledge of classical geography his source had to be the geographies of Pausanias and Strabo; for mythology, Hesiod; and, for history, Homer, Thucydides, and Xenophon. Natural histories would see him study Pliny the Elder and perhaps the Younger. Kidogo considers other fundamental sources of his liberal education to be Ammianus Marcellinus (for ancient Balkan and Middle Eastern history); Gaius Julius Caesar (for rhetoric and Western Roman history); Plutarch (for general mythology, philosophy, classical travelogues, and social studies – note that Plutarch was the intellectual foundation for many European Renaissance figures); Cornelius Tacitus (for histories); and Ovid (for poetry and creative writing). See *Keys to the Predictions of Nostradamus*, Kidogo, pp. 35–7.

   References to the "Law of More" in Nostradamus' prophecies indicate he may have read the Latin volume of Sir Thomas More's *Utopia* as early as his studies at Avignon, as it was published in 1516.
6. *The Scientific Renaissance 1450–1630*, Boas, p. 168.

7. According to its author, *Traité des fardemens et confitures* was completed 1 April 1552. It may have been first published as early as that year but no copy survives. There are a number of surviving editions of the bestseller of the 16th century from 1557 onwards under different titles, such as *Excellent & Moult Utile Opuscule* ..., or *Le Vray et Partaict Embelissement de la Face et Conservation du Corps* .... The book is divided into two parts, sometimes with a preface or proeme included.

8. The original French spelling in the Plantin 1557 Antwerp edition of the book has *planetes* rather than *plantes*. Lemesurier poses that this is possibly a Freudian slip from our astrologer/doctor. David Ovason believes he means the search to understand the influence of "planets" – i.e. the astrological properties of healing (See *The Secrets of Nostradamus*, p. 22). It is more likely a slip of typesetting, overlooked or even shrugged off by the proofing editor. The state of editorial discipline, added to the travel and time constraints in 16th century publishing deadlines, rarely allowed the author a chance to proofread a final copy for editorial errors before publication.

9. Paracelsus believed his medical insights went the next step beyond the 1st-century Alexandrian school of medicine championed by Aulus Cornelius Celsus.

10. *The Civilization of Europe in the Renaissance*, Hale, p. 287.

11. *Beloved Son Felix: The Journal of Felix Platter, a Medical Student in Montpellier in the Sixteenth Century*, 1552–7, Platter, p. 38.

12. *The Civilization of Europe in the Renaissance*, Hale, p. 503.

13. *Medieval Prostitution*, Rossiaud, p. 9, and "Discipline and Respectability: Prostitution and the Reformation in Augsburg," *History Workshop Journal*, 19, p. 4.

14. See the definitive list of geographical locations in the prophecies in Leoni's *Nostradamus and His Prophecies*, pp. 540–46.

15. See *Nostradamus: The Complete Prophecies*, Hogue, 6Q100dp ('duplicate' Century 6, Quatrain 100), p. 500.
16. *Ibid.* See 5Q66 (pp. 415–16); 9Q9 (pp. 696–7).
17. *Ibid.* See 4Q94 (p. 368); 8Q21 (pp. 635–6).
18. René Choppin, jurist, recounting a suit brought by the Faculty of Medicine at Paris against a peasant woman practicing folk medicine. See *Traité de Privileges des Personnes Vivans aux Champs* (1575), in *Oeuvres* (Paris, 1662).
19. *Traité des fardemens et confitures*, Nostradamus, Book 1 (*Le Vray et Parfaict Embellissement de la Face …*), ch. XXVI, p. 24.
20. *Ibid*, p. 24. The quote is a variation in second person singular translated from the French third person singular from the 1557 Plantin edition.
21. *Ibid*, ch. XXVII, pp. 26–7.
22. *Ibid.*
23. *Provence: A Country Almanac*, Louisa Jones, p. 163.

CHAPTER THREE: THE TURNING OF THE DREAM

1. *Nostradamus Encyclopedia*, Lemesurier, p. 28.
2. Then again, it is possible Nostredame had no licence at all and that was apparently not a problem. Eleven months after Nostredame enrolled at Montpellier, the ledger of new students records another famous fellow student, François Rabelais. He attained entry to the University as an unlicensed and self-taught expert in theoretical medicine.
3. *Traité des fardemens et confitures*, Nostradamus, Book 1 (*Le Vray et Parfaict Embellissement de la Face …*), ch. XXVI, p. 24.
4. *Sages and Seers*, Hall, p. 38.
5. *Ibid*, p. 39.
6. *La Première Face du Janus françois …* Jean-Aymes (Aimé) de Chavigny.
7. *Moon Mistress: Diane de Poitiers*, Jehanne d'Orliac, pp. 130–31.
8. *Society and Culture in Early Modern France*, Natalie Zemon Davis, p. 124.

9. Lemesurier in *Nostradamus and Beyond* tells us the young doctor married a girl named Henriette d'Encausse, but he does not explain how he came to this conclusion, nor does he mention her name in his subsequent work, *The Nostradamus Encyclopedia*.

10. *Nostradamus*, Jacques Boulenger, Excelsior, Paris, 1933.

11. Michel Chomarat reports that it was the work of the 18th-century engraver, Aure (or Aurèlle) Billette. See *Cahiers Michel Nostradamus*, No. 3/Fevrier 1985/40F.

12. *Sages and Seers*, Hall, p. 40, probably derived from Boulenger's *Life of Nostradamus*.

13. Reynier presided over the notorious case of Arnaud du Tilh who in 1548 was tried for suspicion of impersonating Armand Guerre and enjoying the latter's property and wife. Tilh nearly convinced the court that he was the soldier returned from war years earlier to claim his rightful property and eager intimacy of his wife, until the real peg-legged and impotent article hobbled into the courtroom to claim wife and hearth. Tilh was hanged for his fraud.

CHAPTER FOUR: THE PLAGUE DOCTOR

1. *Sages and Seers*, Hall, p. 45.

2. *Traité des fardemens et confitures*, Book II (*La Seconde Partie ... confitures ...*), ch. VII, p. 49, 1557 edition.

3. *Ibid*, Book II, *La maniere de faire A Maistre Iean de Nostredame ...*, p. 39.

4. *Nostradamus Now*, Jochmans, p. 37.

5. *Civilization of Europe in the Renaissance*, Hale, p. 165.

6. *Nostradamus Now*, Jochmans, pp. 3, 7. *Orus Apollo* did not find a publisher until the 20th century.

7. *The Keys to the Predictions of Nostradamus*, Kidogo, p. 35.

8. *Sages and Seers*, Hall, p. 45.

9. *Ibid*, p. 46.

10. *Nostradamus Encyclopedia*, Lemesurier, p. 30.

11. *Sixteenth Century Europe: Expansion and Conflict*, Richard Mackenny, pp. 240–42, and *The Dictionary of Wars*, George C. Kohn, pp. 223–4.

12. *Sages and Seers*, Hall, p. 47.

13. The medieval Irish St. Malachy (1094–1148) wrote 111 Latin mottos and a 112th coda, each representing the succession of 112 popes remaining from his own time until Judgment Day. After Pope John Paul II, there are only two future popes left on his list. For a comprehensive examination of the prophecies of St. Malachy and other Catholic seers, see *The Last Pope: The Decline and Fall of the Church of Rome*, Hogue, Element Books.

14. *Traité des fardemens et confitures*, Book I (*Le Vray et Parfaict Embellissement …*), ch. XXVII, p. 27.

15. "Aix" is an abbreviation for *Aquae Calidae Salluviorum*, the Roman name given to the settlement of the Celtic Salyens and subsequent Roman spa town constructed around thermal springs. The hot waters run at a constant temperature of 34°C and are rich in radioactive, oligometallic, hardy, salted minerals, purported to heal cardiovascular complaints, rheumatism, nervous disorders, and obesity. Aix had also been famous for its many natural springs and ancient fountains. Nostradamus would have utilized its many founts of fresh water for cleansing the town.

16. Jehan de Nostradamus became Procurer of the Parliament of Provence later in the mid-1550s. There is no documentation supporting any supposition that he used his brother's success in saving Aix as political capital, nor is there anything on record disproving it.

17. Themis in Greek mythology is the personification of Justice. She is the goddess and guardian of the law and harmony of nature established by the gods.

18. *L'Histoire et Chronique de Provence*, César de Nostredame, p. 772.

19.   The only surviving copies of Nostradamus' 1559 Almanac are those translated in 1559 in Elizabethan English. For clarity's sake, I have modernized much of the spelling of these excerpts from the John Day edition (1559). The excerpts highlight passages on diet; the bracketed insertions for clarification are mine:

> The next way to preserve the body from this infirmity is to open a vein or purge, to flee from the corrupt air, to use abstinence, moderate diet, exercise, also [avoiding] long sleep, of often eating and drinking when as nature require it not this make the body prepared to the pestilence. [In other words, eating and sleeping too much will stress the body and make you more prone to pestilence.] ... And in all the time of his fever, let him neither sleep, eat, or drink.
>
> After the fever ended, let him be dried with warmth and clean clothes. And if he desires to eat, give him a little broth made of chicken, or such like, but no great quantity. [Note that fatty meats, such as beef, are excluded.]
>
> Let him keep his chamber for certain days after, and have merry company, and music, using perfumes in his chamber with mastic, myrrh, obidan, Frankincense ...
> *An Excellent treatise, Showing such perilous, and contagious infirmities, as shall ensue, in 1559 and 1560 ... by Master Michael Nostradamus, Doctor in Phisicke, and translated into English at the desire of Laurentius Philotus, Tyl.*

20.   *Traité des fardemens*, Part I (*Le Vray et Parfaict Embellissement* ...), ch. VIII, pp. 10–12.

21.   Lemesurier considers the term *le charbon* used by Nostradamus and his contemporaries as a slang for the

bubonic plague to be another medical myth of the Nostradamus story fostered by modern Nostradamian authors such as Erika Cheetam and her "imitators." (See *Nostradamus Encyclopedia*, p. 46.) Actually, Cheetam was correct. This term *le charbon* was used for the pestilence in the 16th century. It is documented on page 104 of the highly respected *Dictionnaire du moyen français* by Larousse (ed.): *Charbon* comes from the Latin *Carbo, -onis*. A free translation from the Larousse dictionary into English defines this word recorded as far back as the medieval French of 1190 as the "carbon pestilence; infectious malady of men and animals that manifests from carbon-like (coal covered, coaly) tumors." In modern French, the word is applied to the coal-like pustules seen on the victims of anthrax.

Nostradamus frequently calls the black pustules "carbons" in his famous plague account. See *Traité des fardemens*, Part I (*Le Vray et Parfaict Embellissement...*), ch. VIII, pp. 10–12, 2nd edition, 1557.

22. *Les Propheties de Michel Nostradamus*, Century 1, Quatrain 25 (1555). Lemesurier disputes my translation, but he bases his argument on what is, in my view, a prejudiced stretch in translation based on words of the first edition of the prophecy that Nostradamus apparently corrected in later editions.

23. *Traité des fardemens et confitures*, Nostradamus, Book 1 (*Le Vray et Parfaict Embellissement de la Face ...*), ch. VIII, p. 10.

24. *Ibid.*

25. The English translation of Nostradamus' 1559 Almanac does prescribe modest bleeding ("opening a vein") as long as the patient is deemed strong enough and the time of year is right: "The cure of this sickness is to open a vein if the age of the patient, strength, and time of the year agree hereto, near to the place where the swelling appears (if there be any) else in the part where he feeleth most grief ..." *An Excellent treatise, Showing such perilous, and contagious infirmities, as*

shall ensue, in 1559 and 1560 ... by Master Michael Nostradamus, Doctor in Phisicke, and translated into English at the desire of Laurentius Philotus, Tyl.

26. 2 Samuel 5:6: "Then the Lord laid a heavy hand upon the people of Ashdod; he threw them into distress and plagued them with tumors, and their territory swarmed with rats. There was death and destruction all through the city."

27. *The Elixirs of Nostradamus*, Kurt Boeser, p. xx.

28. *Traité des fardemens et confitures*, Nostradamus, Book 1 (*Le Vray et Parfaict Embellissement de la Face ...*), ch. VIII, p. 12.

29. *Nostradamus: Le mage de Salon*, Christian Kert, p. 23.

30. *Traité des fardemens et confitures*, Nostradamus, Book II (*La Seconde Partie ... confitures ...*), ch. XXX, p. 77. The latter half of the original quote is so gramatically odd that it required this very free translation.

31. Bareste in his account mistakes Antoine Sarrazin, the son, for Phillipe Sarrazin.

CHAPTER FIVE:
THE RENAISSANCE OF NOSTRADAMUS

1. Her name is spelled a number of different ways in public records: Anne *Pons, Ponce, Ponsart* and *Pousart* Gemelle. *Gemelle* (old French for the Latin *gemellus* "twin; double" or *Gemina*) may be her nickname. Women of the 16th century kept their maiden names after marriage, only qualifying that they were the widow or wife of so-and-so when it was necessary. The slightly more eccentric among them kept these nicknames, such as *Gemelle*, for public record.

2. A&E (Arts and Entertainment) Channel's highly popular "Biography" series perpetuates a centuries-long visual myth of mistaken identity, placing César's self-portrait on the cover of their DVD and video cassette copies of their *Biography of Nostradamus*, which remains the third most popular show of their first 500 biographies. Many publishers make the same

mistake on book covers, the most recent example being the English edition of the spurious work of Ottario Cesare Ramotti: *The Nostradamus Code.*

3. *Nostradamus and His Prophecies*, Leoni, p. 23.
4. *Traité des fardemens et confitures*, Nostradamus, Book 1 (*Le Vray et Parfaict Embellissement de la Face ...*), ch. XI, p. 13.
5. *Ibid*, Book II (*La Seconde Partie ... confitures ...*), ch. XXX, p. 75.
6. The inscription reads:

1556

NOSTRADAMUS A LOGE ICI

OU IL HA LE PARADI,

LENFER LE PURGATOIRE

JE MAPELLE LA VICTOIRE.

QUI M'HONORE AURA LA GLOIRE.

QUI ME MEPRISE AURA LA RUINE ENTIERE

(The following loose English translation tries to restore an approximation of the rhythm and rhyme lost in other translations:)

Nostradamus to rest did he

Where Paradise came to be,

Hell and also Purgat'ry.

My name is victory.

Who honors me glory to he.

Who scorns me shall ruin see.

7. A *synecdoche* is a Latin word-play convention wherein a town represents a state, such as saying "those of Washington D.C." when you mean "those of America."
8. See *Nostradamus: The Complete Prophecies*, Hogue, Century 10, Quatrain 8.

9. *Ibid,* Century 2, Quatrain 74.

10. *Nostradamus Encyclopedia,* Lemesurier, p. 155.

11. For example, a less poetic but literal English translation of Century 2, Quatrain 93 reads: "Very near the Tiber [River] the Goddess of Death threatens. Shortly after the great flood, the head of the church [the pope] will be taken prisoner and cast out. Castle [of St. Angelo] and the palace [of the Vatican] in flames." See *Nostradamus: The Complete Prophecy,* Hogue, pp. 223–4.

12. Nostradamus could have taken Varro of Ancient Rome as an inspiration for his "Pasteur" prophecy, as Varro had considered infinitesimal particles (which germs resemble) as the carriers of pestilence.

13. *Traité des Fardemens,* Book 1 (*Le Vray et Parfaict Embel …*), ch. XXXIII, p. 39.

14. The Latin passages quoted by Nostradamus in his later writings strongly hint that he possessed the de Tourne 1549 edition of *De mysteriis Aegyptiorum.* The Wizard's Bookshelf published a fine English translation by Thomas Taylor.

15. *Nostradamus: The Complete Prophecies,* Hogue (The Preface …), p. 58, PF91–3.

16. *De Daemonibus,* Michel Constantine Psellos.

17. *Nostradamus: The Complete Prophecies,* Hogue (The Preface …), p. 58, PF49.

18. *Ibid,* p. 42, PF46–7.

19. Anne gave birth to Madeleine (c. 1551–1623), César (c. 1554–c. 1630), Charles (1556–1629), André (1557–1601), Anne (1558–c. 97), and Diane (1561–1630).

20. *Nostradamus: The Complete Prophecies,* Hogue (The Preface …), p. 44, PF49–52.

21. *Ibid.*

22. The first surviving publishing record for Nostradamus' annual Almanac begins with the 1553 edition (Chaussard, Lyon); followed by the 1554 edition ("Bertot," Lyon); 1555

edition (Brotot, Lyon), and following. Volant would merge with Brotot to produce most of the Almanacs printed from 1558 to 1567.

23. It is in his Almanac publications that we have the first surviving record of Michel de Nostredame presenting himself in print as *Nostradamus*. Surviving archival records before this indicate he sometimes signed himself as *Michel nostra domina*.

24. So says Chavigny in *La Première Face du Janus*.

25. The archives in Salon include a notarized receipt from two Lyon printers for a royalty of 20 gold crowns to Nostradamus for the sale of almanac and prognostications for 1562.

CHAPTER SIX: A HISTORY OF THE FUTURE

1. *Nostradamus: Le mage de Salon*, Christian Kert, p. 10.

2. Latin for "in jest." By the way, *lingua* in *bucca* means "tongue" in "cheek."

3. See *Nostradamus: The Complete Prophecies*, Hogue, The Preface to César, pp. 30–33.

4. This desert of stones inspired classical mythologists to imagine it was once the scene of a pitched battle between the Greek demi-god Hercules and a whole army of Ligurians. Hercules held his own against his attackers until, wounded and weaponless, he cried to the heavens for his father, Zeus, to send him aid. Zeus is said to have opened the skies with a cloudburst of stones and buried the entire Ligurian army under the 15 meters (50 feet) of rocks and gravel that make the flat expanse of the Grande Crau.

5. The public records of Salon show Nostradamus from 1556 through 1566 signing off on a sizable investment of 688 crowns divided in the following installments by year: 1556 – 200 crowns; 1560 – 288 crowns; 1562 – 100 crowns; with Anne Ponsarde signing off another 100 crowns circa 1566, sometime after the death of her husband.

6. The records misspell the name "Brotot."

7. *L'Histoire et chronique de Prouence*, César de Nostredame, p. 774.

8. *Ibid.*

9. No other documentation or dating of the appearance of these two deformed creatures exists outside of César de Nostredame's second-hand account.

10. Century I, Quatrain I from the original Macé Bonhomme edition of 1555. The principal 1568 Benoist Rigaud edition (the first volume posthumously printed that achieved Nostradamus' dream of containing all of his prophecies in one book, rather than in the serialized and fragmentary editions preceding it) has the following editorial corrections (or in some cases botched corrections) that one assumes came to Rigaud's editors from Nostradamus himself prior to his death in 1566: line 1, no comma; line 2, *sur* rather than *sus*; line 3, *fait* rather than *faict*.

11. A more literal, albeit unpoetic, translation for Century I, Quatrain I would read:

    Being seated at night in secret study
    Resting alone upon the brass tripod:
    A minute flame comes forth from the solitude
    Making successful that which should not be believed in vain.

12. Century 2, Quatrain I from the original Macé Bonhomme edition of 1555 diverges from later editorial "corrections" in the 1568 Benoist Rigaud edition as follows: in line 1, *La verge* differs from the Rigaud editorial error, *Laverge*, and *BRANCHES* is in upper-case in Rigaud without a comma. Perhaps the latter was a specific change asked for by Nostradamus. In line 3, the Bonhomme edition's erroneous *tremissent* becomes *fremissent* in Rigaud's edition (or, in modern spelling, *fremissant* – "to quiver; to shudder,") – a clear

example of Nostradamus catching an editorial error and having it corrected later on. In line 3, the "n" is missing in *manches* and is indicated by the wrong accent symbol (´ instead of ˜) in the Bonhomme *máches*. This error Rigaud corrected. It seems the latter had more "n" typefaces, which Lyonnais printers of the 16th century for some reason often had in short supply.

13. The literal apposed to the freely poetic translation for Century 2, Quatrain 1 would read:

The divining wand in hand is placed in the middle
   of Branchus
With water, he moistens the hem (of his robe) and foot:
Fear! A voice quivers through his long sleeves:
Divine splendor. The divine one sits nearby.

14. See *Iamblichus on the Mysteries of the Egyptians, Chaldeans, and Assyrians* (*De mysteriis Aegyptiorum* ...), translated by Thomas Taylor, ch. XI, pp. 143–5.

15. Century 3, Quatrain 2 as printed in the 1568, Benoist Rigaud edition, including a free English translation approximating the rhyme. A literal translation would read:

The divine word will give to the essence, [that which]
Contains heaven and earth. The hidden gold in the
   mystic deed:
Body, soul and spirit having all powerful,
All is beneath his feet as at the feet of heaven.

16. Century 4 Quatrain 25 as printed in the 1568, Benoist Rigaud edition with the approximate English rhyme. The literal translation:

Sublime essence forever visible to the eye,
Come to cloud the conscious mind for reasons of their own:
Body and forehead together, senses and the overseeing ego
    become invisible,
As the sacred prayers diminish.

17. See *Nostradamus: The Complete Prophecies*, Hogue, The
     Preface to César, pp. 34–42.

18. *Hidden Harmony*, Osho, p. 70.

19. See *Nostradamus: The Complete Prophecies*, Hogue, The
     Preface to César, pp. 50–53.

20. Only in the Epistle to Henry II (written in 1558 as a preface
     to the final three centuries of his planned ten) does
     Nostradamus share some conclusions stemming from his
     mathematical calculation of history's future timeline. Indeed,
     he crunches numbers – and the reader's understanding –
     detailing two divergent cycles of time. In the first, he starts a
     countdown to the seventh millennium and the apocalypse in
     1242 and puts the dawn of the seventh millennium at 2242.
     Towards the end of his Epistle, he passes us through the
     number mill again with 1826 as the beginning of the count-
     down that brings some revelatory disaster for, and transfor-
     mation of, humanity in the year 2826. If that was not clear
     enough, there are a number of quatrains, specifically the
     famous doom-laden prophecy of Century 10, Quatrain 72,
     that imply a more traditional millennialism for the hammer
     of the apocalypse to fall in or shortly after the year 1999.

21. *Nostradamus Encyclopedia*, Lemesurier, "Nostradamus and
     the Muslim Invasion of Europe," pp. 148–50.

22. *La Première Face du Janus françois ...*, Chavigny (1594).

23. Many interpreters, including myself, have tried to unveil just
     whom Nostradamus defined as "common people" in his
     visions. To do so one must consider his social filters as a class-
     bound royalist of the 16th century. He had a fear of the

common rabble; perhaps as a royalist he projected that fear to its conclusion in a vision that saw the peasants and rabble eventually bringing down their kings and ruling the Earth (*the advent of the common people*). If this fear was actually a prophecy, as he obviously believed it was, then it is possible he foresaw the fall of a future French king in the French Revolution (as many sympathetic Nostradamians believe), or even saw the advent of something he feared but we "commoners" of today know and accept as democracy.

24. See *Nostradamus: The Complete Prophecies*, Hogue, The Preface to César, pp. 32–3.

25. Words and phrases are scrambled to construct other words and phrases using the same letters; for example: *rapis* becomes *Paris*; *chyren* is a word-play of the contemporary king of France, Henry II's, Latinized name – *Henryc*. Phonetics allow for *V* to become *U*, *Y* or become *I*, *S* to become *C*, *I* to be *J*, and so on. Nostradamus made his own variations for switching or replacing letters. One or two letters can be dropped; for example, *Noir* becomes *roi* – "king." Letters can be added and/or changed: *Hadrie* becomes *Henrie*, the anagram believed by sympathetic translators of Nostradamus' prophecies to be Henry, King of Navarre, and the future Henry IV of France.

26. Nostradamus' poetry uses a number of classical Greek and Latin grammatical devices.

Aphaeresis: Elimination of one or more letters and sounds from the beginning of a word, as in *paroir* for *apparoir* (to appear).
Apocope: Omission of the last sound or syllable or a word; for example, *Orl.* for *Orléans*. Nostradamus sometimes takes further liberties and omits the rest of a phrase. For example, *corn* for *corne d'aboncance* (a cornucopia).
Ellipsis: Exclusion of words and phrases that are understood or taken for granted by the 16th-century reader.

Epenthesis: Insertion of a letter or syllable into a word; for example: *Timbre* for *Tibre* (the Tiber River).

Hyperbaton: Transposition or inversion of the natural order. Nostradamus consistently scrambles the natural order of his sentences and verse lines.

Metathesis: Transposition of letters, sounds, or syllables within a word. For example, the Old French *mezan* is transposed from the Latin *mensa* (month). Nostradamus often does this to preserve rhyme.

Metonymy: A figure of speech in which an idea is evoked or named by means of a term designating some associated notion. The word *Mars* has a metonymical designation for *war*; *scepter* can imply a *king*, *hunger* can mean a *general famine*.

Prothesis: Insertion of an extra letter or syllable at the beginning of a word. For instance, *expectacle* (*ex* added to *spectacle* [spectacle]).

Synecdoche: A grammatical trick in Greek and Latin to make the part represent the whole. For example: *Paris* stands for *France*, *Boristhenes* for the *Ukraine* or perhaps even *Russia*.

Syncope: Shortening of a word by the omission of a sound, letter, or syllable from the middle of the word. For example, Nostradamus abbreviates a number of his future-tense verbs: *donra* for *donnera*, *monstra* for *monstrera*, and so on.

27. ... *Composees plustost d'vn naturel instinct, accompagné d'une fureur poëtique.* See my translation and interpretation, *Nostradamus: The Complete Prophecies*, Epistle to Henry II, pp. 546–7.

28. In *Nostradamus: The Complete Prophecies* (p. 27) I explained translating the occult narrative technique in the following way: "Certain mystics use an unusual cadence or a nebulous and turgid writing style as a device to shake us out of our usual mental habits so we can look beyond the words to that

which cannot be said [directly]. By editing Nostradamus for the sake of comfort and clarity, his well-intentioned interpreters may be doing him a disservice."

29. See *Nostradamus: The Complete Prophecies*, Hogue, The Preface to César, pp. 32–5.

30. *Ibid*, pp. 42–5.

31. *Ibid*, pp. 46–7.

32. *Ibid*, pp. 46–9.

33. *Ibid*, pp. 48–9.

CHAPTER SEVEN: THE QUEEN'S ORACLE

1. The *imprimatur* was an official privilege sought by publishers across France and dispensed by representatives of the king before a book could be published within the kingdom of France. A manuscript must first pass the scrutiny of royal authorities to see whether its assertions were offensive to the Catholic faith, or to the person of the king. If deemed politically and spiritually correct, the publisher would receive a letter of endorsement that often found itself printed on the fore page of the book. This royal *privelège* was an early form of copyright, granting the publisher sole rights for a certain period of time to reprint or sell the book in the area under the Lord Governor's jurisdiction. Thus, a publisher had to pass a similar censorship check before receiving a royal privilege to sell his book in each province of the French Realm.

2. A literal and unrhymed translation of Century 1, Quatrain 10 reads:

The serpent's coffin is put in a vault of iron,
Where seven children of the King are held:
Their ancestors will rise from the depths of hell,
Before dying lamenting at seeing the fruits of their line dead.

3. The literal translation of Century 1, Quatrain 35 reads:

> The young lion will overcome the older one
> On the field of combat in single battle:
> He will pierce his eyes through a golden cage
> Two wounds made one, then he dies a cruel death.

4. Today, the population of Paris numbers 8.8 million.

5. James Randi, the renowned "skeptic," estimates the number as high as 30,000 – a clear exaggeration of one too many zeros. If he were correct, then roughly one in five Parisians was a conjuror. See *The Mask of Nostradamus*, p. 21.

6. *Essay on Prophecy*, Sir Francis Bacon, quoted from *The Story of Astrology*, Manly P. Hall, p. 26.

7. See *Nostradamus: The Complete Prophecies*, Hogue: 2Q79 (*grand CHIREN*), 4Q34 (*Roy Chyren*), 6Q27 (*Chyren Selin*), 6Q42 (*grand Selin*), 6Q70 (*Chyren*), 6Q78 (*grand Selin*), 8Q54 (*Chyren-Selin*), 9Q41 (*grand Chyren*), and 10Q53 (*grand Selin*). A further dozen or more quatrains may generally implicate "the great king" (*Chyren Selin*) or *l'Ogmion* (the Celtic Hercules) as Henry II in their prophecies.

8. *Les Propheties de M. Nostradamus*, Macé Bonhomme edition, 1555.

9. A literal translation of Century 2, Quatrain 79 could read:

> The man with the curly black beard through ingenuity,
> Will subdue the cruel and proud people:
> The great CHYREN will take from afar,
> All those captured by the banner of the Turkish crescent.

10. *Les Propheties …*, Macé Bonhomme edition, 1555.

11. A literal translation of Century 4, Quatrain 34 could read:

The great one from a foreign land led captive,
By gold-enchained offered to King Chyren:
He who in Ausonia, Milan will lose the war,
And all his army put to fire and sword.

12. *The Letter to Jean Morel,* Nostradamus, *Fonds latin,* no. 8589, French National Library.

13. *The American Heritage Dictionary* defines gout as a disturbance of uric acid metabolism occurring predominantly in males, characterized by arthritic attacks, capable of becoming chronic and producing deformity, and precipitated by minor trauma, as by ill-fitting shoes, excessive consumption of food or alcohol, etc. In Nostradamus' day, doctors believed gout was caused by drops of morbid humors, ergo the Old French word *gote* (from the Latin *gutta*) meaning "drop."

14. Chavigny is the only source for this story. See *Vie et testament de Nostradamus* in *La Première Face du Janus françois ...* (1594).

15. The quatrains listed below were already in print when Nostradamus drew their horoscopes. The list includes the Valois child, Century-and-Quatrain indexing, and in the parentheses, the general theme of this author's interpretation. For a comprehensive examination, consult the following predictions by their index numbers in *Nostradamus: The Complete Prophecies*.

Francis II [François] (1543–60): 1Q10 (no heirs); 1Q13 (targeted for abduction by Huguenot princes during the Conspiracy of Amboise); 1Q68 (too young and immature to rule); 1Q85 (long dead before the assassination of Henry III ends the male Valois bloodline).
Elizabeth de Valois, [Queen of Spain] (1545–68): 1Q10 (no heirs).
Claude de Valois (1547–75): 1Q10 (no heirs).

Charles IX (1550–74): 1Q10 (no heirs); 1Q68 (too young to rule); 1Q78 (called a weak degenerate); 1Q85 (will die before Henry III is assassinated); 2Q11 (a harsh rule, he is immature); 3Q25 (manipulated by Huguenots in his cabinet to move away from an alliance with Catholic Spain); 3Q41 (pardoned the chief perpetrator of the Conspiracy of Amboise, Prince Louis de Condé, who later foments future civil wars until he is killed at Jarnac – the details of Condé's death described); 4Q47 (depicts the notorious incident when Charles stood on a Louvre balcony, firing his harquebus at fleeing and unarmed Huguenot men, women and children during the St. Bartholomew's Day Massacre in 1572).

Henry III [Duc d'Anjou] (1551–89): 1Q10 (no heirs); 1Q36 (described as a degenerate, a civil war-mongerer, destined to die); 1Q68 (too immature to rule); 1Q78 (called a weak degenerate); 1Q85 (details events leading up to his assassination); 2Q11 (was immature and unbalanced into adulthood because of unexpected death of his father, Henry II); 2Q34 (fratricidal intrigues); 2Q43 (the appearance of a malevolent comet will come when he fights a three-way civil war between the Huguenots, the Catholic League and forces of the throne – which would make this the passing of the comet of 1577, to be exact); 2Q88 (cornered in the siege of Paris by Henry of Navarre in 1590); 3Q50 (suffered a popular rebellion in Paris, then a siege); 3Q51 (Château Blois mentioned as the scene of the assassination of Duc de Guise; this murder set the stage for his own assassination); Presage 7 from the Almanac for 1555 (Henry III would be the last male Valois to die, supplanted by Henry of Navarre at the end of the ninth and final civil war).

Marguerite de Valois (1553–1615): 1Q10 (no heirs), 1Q78 (at odds with treacherous brothers, Charles IX and Henry III. They instigated the Saint Bartholomew's Day massacre, murdered her Protestant wedding guests and nearly murdered her groom, Henry of Navarre).

Hercules [Duc d'Alençon] (1554–84): 1Q10 (no heirs); 2Q34 (fratricidal intrigues).

16. *Nostradamus: The Future Foretold,* James Laver, pp. 49–50.

17. Rasputin, a Russian mystic monk, hypnotist and faith healer, became an influential favorite of the Russian Imperial family of Czar Nicholas and Czarina Alexandria. The latter was especially under his sway after he purportedly healed the Czarevitch Alexis from a bout of hemophilia. Rasputin had sent the Czar a letter at the outbreak of World War I in August 1914, warning him not to join the conflict, because Russia would lose and the war would see an end to the Romanov reign. Nicholas tore up the note. Later, Rasputin's hypnotic influence over the Czar and Czarina was blamed in part for Russia losing the war. By 1916, he sensed the end was near and composed a letter to the Czarina predicting that if peasants assassinated him then the Romanov reign would thrive; however, if princes killed him, the peasants would rebel and not one member of her family would be left alive after 18 months. Princes did kill Rasputin and all the royal family were dead in 18 months. Cheka red guards shot them all by order of Lenin during the Russian Revolution.

18. *Essay on Prophecy,* Bacon.

19. Nostradamus was answering Morel's letter, which angrily demanded repayment of the money loaned to Nostradamus for his first lodgings in Paris. Nostradamus explained that he had discussed this issue with the queen and apparently was under the false assumption for these many years that she had followed through with repayment.

20. Note that he does not mention his journey to Blois. Perhaps Catherine sent him on his astrological errand under a cloak of secrecy.

21. *The Letter to Jean Morel,* Nostradamus, *Fonds latin,* no. 8589, French National Library.

22. *The Fate of the Nations*, Arthur Prieditis, p. 9.

23. *Nostradamus Encyclopedia*, Lemesurier, p. 36.

24. Claude de l'Aubespine, who translated the letter of Luc Gauricus into French (from Latin) for Henry, mentioned the king's reply in his *Histoire particulière del la Cour de Henry II* (Archives Curieuses de la France, s. I, vol. III, 1835, pp. 295–6); the courtier Brantôme also confirmed that the conversation between the King and Montgomery took place.

CHAPTER EIGHT: NOTORIOUS SUCCESS

1. Leoni believes these were already on the bookstalls by the latter half of 1556 (See *Nostradamus and his Prophecies*, p. 26). Chomarat reports that an edition containing complete Centuries 1, 2, 3, 4, plus 99 quatrains of Century 6 and 40 quatrains of Century 7, can no longer be found. Rather than the usual title *Les Propheties de M. Nostradamus*, this 1556 edition published by Sixte Denyse might have gone by the title *Le quatrains ou propheties de Nostradamus*. See *Bibliographie Nostradamus*, Chomarat, p. 19.

2. The full title was: *Paraphrase de C. Galen, sus L'exortation de Menodote, aux estudes des bonnes Artz, mesmement Medicine: Traduict de Latin en Francoys, par Michel Nostradamus*. This was another successful literary effort. After 1557, du Rosne rapidly printed a second and third edition in 1558 and 1559.

3. *Nostradamus Encyclopedia*, p. 90.

4. Century 1 Quatrain 19, Macé Bonhomme edition, 1555.

5. The literal translation:

When the serpents will come to encircle the altar,
The Trojan blood is vexed by the Spanish:
Because of them a great number will be made to suffer.
The chief flees, hidden in the swamp within the swamp.

6. Century 4, Quatrain 8, Macé Bonhomme edition, 1555.

7. The literal translation:

   The great city by assault both prompt and swift,
   Surprised at night, guards intercepted:
   The guards and watchmen of St. Quentin,
   Massacred guards and the front gates broken.

8. Some biographers claim John Calvin's right-hand man, Théodore de Bèze, was the author.

9. *La Premiere Invective du Seigneur Hercules le François, contre Monstradamus, Taduicte de Latin. A Paris, De l'Imprimerie de Simon Calvarin, ruë S. Iean de Beauvais, à la enseigne de Vertu. 1558.* For a complete facsimile see *Cahiers Michel Nostradamus*, No. 5–6, 1987–8, Michel Chomarat.

10. These ideas generally can be found in *La Premiere Invective du Seigneur Hecules le François, contre Monstradamus.* Of course, the author of these demands, as well as many other pamphlets denouncing Nostradamus, did not have the courage to write his true name.

11. See *Nostradamus: The Complete Prophecies*, Hogue (Epistle to Henry II), pp. 548–9.

12. *Ibid,* EP165–7, pp. 597–9.

13. *Queen's Conjuror*, Benjamin Woolley, p. 60.

14. *Ibid.* p. 60.

15. *The Little Ice Age: How Climate made History, 1300–1850*, Brian Fagan, p. 85.

16. *Traité des fardemens*, Preface (trans. from German): "To the Most Serene Highness ... Lady Christina, former Queen of Denmark, Sweden and Norway and Duchess of Milan, Lorraine and Barr ..." German trans. Mertz, 1572 (Manger, Augsburg publishers). Reissued and translated into English by Kurt Boeser as *Elixirs of Nostradamus*, pp. xxv–xxvi.

17. *Bibliographie Nostradamus*, Chomarat (avec la collaboration de Jean-Paul Laroche, Bibliographica Aureliana), pp. 26, 35.

18.   *Moon Mistress, Dianne de Poitiers,* D'Orliac, p. 288.

19.   *Ibid.*

CHAPTER NINE: FAME AND INFAMY

1.   On 22 November 1963, a few minutes before President Kennedy's motorcade drove into Dealey Plaza in Dallas, Texas, Jeane Dixon was in Washington D.C. having lunch with friends at the Mayflower Hotel. Witnesses report that Dixon suddenly became so distraught that she could not touch her food. "Something dreadful is going to happen to the President today," she declared. Throughout the month, Dixon's friends had noticed her increasing concern about the fate of the young President Kennedy. She had been making accurate and documented predictions about him for over a decade. She had attained notoriety for her vision, recorded in 1956 by Jack Anderson, publisher of *Parade* magazine, in which she saw the White House with the shimmering numbers *1-9-6-0* hovering above it. Pulled like a magnet, her consciousness floated toward the main door, where a young man with striking blue eyes stood upon the threshold. An inner voice impressed upon her that this young man, a Democrat, would be elected President in 1960 and was destined to die violently while in office.

Jeane Dixon and her friends looked up as the orchestra at the Mayflower suddenly stopped playing and the conductor announced that someone had just taken a shot at the President. Her friends tried to comfort her, saying that he must have avoided danger. "No," she replied, "The President is dead ... you will learn that he is dead."

2.   *Les Propheties ...,* Macé Bonhomme edition (1555).

3.   A literal, unrhymed translation reads:

In the year that France has a one-eyed king,
The court will be in very great trouble.
The great man from Blois will kill his friend,
The kingdom put into evil difficulty and double doubt.

4. The Salic code of laws, derived from the ancient Salian Franks, also prohibited a woman from ever sitting in place of a male king on the French throne. No queen or queen mother in French history exerted more influence, or came closer to breaking the Salic Law, than Catherine de' Medici.

5. Jeane Dixon (1918–97), called America's first lady of prediction, was born in a Wisconsin village, one of seven children to German immigrant parents. As a child, she could not decide whether to become a nun or an actress. Some might say she accomplished both, becoming the fast-talking television prognosticating personality, as well as a nonsmoking, teetotaling devout Catholic who regularly attended mass and dedicated much of her time to helping elderly people and disadvantaged children.

In 1946, Dixon became a respected world-syndicated horoscope columnist for predicting the partition of India down to the very day, one month before it happened. She also forewarned the world of the 1964 Alaskan earthquake. Her predictions concerning the assassination of President John Kennedy rank among the greatest predocumented and prepublicized forecasts in history. Although her work afterwards was marred by her need to deliver thousands of predictions for the tabloids (most of them failures – such as the Soviets getting to the moon first), Dixon did successfully predict Sino-Soviet border clashes for 1969 and the fall of the Berlin Wall. The latter was indeed broken down to rubble that became souvenirs, as she had foretold. She numbered many famous celebrities and public figures as her astrological clients, including Nancy Reagan.

Perhaps prompted by Dixon's successes in predicting John Kennedy's assassination, some sympathetic believers in Nostradamus' powers to foresee the future think that he foresaw Dixon herself in Quatrain 26 of Century 1 in her attempt to warn the President:

Le grand du fouldre tumbe d'heure diurne,
Mal & predict par porteur postulaire:
Suiuant presage tumbe d'heure nocturne,
Conflict Reims, Londres, Etrusque pestifere.

A literal translation (from the Benoist Rigaud edition, 1568), free of the beclouding constraints of translating into English rhyme would read:

The great man will be struck down in the day by a
    thunderbolt,
The evil deed predicted by the bearer of a petition
According to the prediction another falls at night time.
Conflict in Reims, London, and pestilence in Tuscany.

It is coincidentally true at least that President John Kennedy was shot shortly after 12 noon in Dallas, Texas, on 22 November 1963 (or "struck down in the day by a thunderbolt"). His brother, Senator Robert Kennedy was assassinated a few minutes after 1 a.m., moments after his victory speech in the 1968 presidential primary ("another falls at night time"). The French word *porteur* ("bearer") can also be applied as a double meaning for "tramp" or "hobo." Many Kennedy assassination conspiracy theories try to unravel the unsolved mystery of five men masquerading as tramps who were arrested in the Dallas, Texas, railway yard adjacent to Dealey Plaza and the Grassy Knoll, the place where conspiracy buffs believe the third and fatal shot killing the President was fired. Alternatively, since "petition" is derived from the Latin *postularius* – demanding, claiming, or petitioning – the "bearer of the petition" could be Dixon. Nostradamus may have chronicled her unsuccessful attempt to forewarn the President, and, later, Senator Robert Kennedy, who was her friend. The last line dates Robert Kennedy's murder through events occurring around that time: student riots in France and London during 1968–9 ("Reims" is a synecdoche for France) and the 1966 Florence flood, when authorities feared that pestilence in Tuscany would follow the disaster.

Nostradamians who were near-contemporaries of the prophet believe this prophecy accurately forecast another set of politically powerful brothers, the sons of his contemporary, François Duc de Guise, assassinated by Henry III at Château Blois in 1588. Henry de Guise was stabbed in the king's bedroom at night, and the Cardinal de Guise killed the following day in broad daylight. There was, however, no pestilence in Tuscany in 1588, but there was indeed "conflict" in France (if "Reims" stands for the whole country) and in "London" (standing for England), which fought off the threat of the Spanish Armada in 1588.

6. A selection of Nostradamus' notoriously foggy astrological readings survives. They are mostly Latin missives, dating from 1556 to 1565. Jean Dupèbe in his book *Nostradamus – Lettres Inédites* gives summarized examples of these. Professional skeptic James Randi draws a few example letters (to L. Tubbe) from this single source of surviving letters to paint Nostradamus as a crank astrologer (See *The Mask of Nostradamus*, pp. 104–15). Yet Randi does not seem able to explain how someone so unscrupulously vague could compete with more lucidly versed astrologers and win the favor of so many publishers, write bestselling astrological prognostications in a dozen almanacs, and claim a queen of France and later Princess Marguerite of Savoy as his ever-faithful

clients. One would hope that the quest to find a "crank" astrologer on the evidence of what appears to be one eccentric and not-so-successful client–astrologer relationship does not imply the scent of a "rank" cynical inquiry. A handful of letters in a life filled with thousands of correspondences is simply not enough data by which one can draw such sweeping and altogether disparaging conclusions.

7. In his natal chart is a powerful T-square aspect of the Aries ascendant and Virgo descendant at 90 degrees from the Midheaven conjunction. The Moon in its detriment in Scorpio would make him touchy about learning disabilities. Alongside other aspects showing he would work hard to overcome his learning disabilities, the Moon in Scorpio would ever shadow him with temptations to overcompensate and defend these privately self-condemned flaws.

8. *Les Significations de l'Eclipse, qui sera le 16. Septembre 1559 …* p. 3. A good facsimile of this pamphlet can be studied in *Présages de Nostradamus*, Bernard Chevignard, pp. 445–60.

9. Epistle to Henry II (signed by Nostradamus in June 1558). See *Nostradamus: The Complete Prophecies*, EP33–4, pp. 553–4.

10. *L'Histoire et Chronique de Provence*, César de Nostredame, p. 783.

11. *Catherine de' Medici and the Lost Revolution*, Ralph Roeder, p. 187.

12. *Les Propheties …*, Macé Bonhomme edition (1555).

13. The literal translation of 1Q13:

The exiles because of anger and intestinal hatred
Will inflict a great conspiracy against the King:
Secretly they will place enemies as a threat,
And his own old ones, sedition against them.

14. All the representations in French of the presage quatrains displayed in this book coming from Nostradamus' Almanacs are drawn from those collected and edited by Chavigny for his book *La Première Face du Janus françois* ... published in 1594. Chavigny listed presages collected from Nostradamus' almanacs. This Presage "for April [1560]" is usually referred to as Presage 50.

    Espeüillera is an example of a composite word Nostradamus used to describe two actions ("exposing" and "frightening") with one word – *(a)* Old French. *espewirer*, to frighten; *(b)* Provençal *espelhar*, to expose, to strip, despoil.

15. A literal translation of Presage 50 would read:

    With the place chosen, the Shaved Ones will not be
        contented,
    Led from Lake Geneva, unproven,
    They will cause the old times to be renewed:
    They will expose and frighten off the plot so well hatched.

16. The French text comes from the post-mortem *Les Propheties* ..., Benoist Rigaud edition, 1568.

17. A literal translation of 8Q52:

    The king of Blois to rule in Avignon,
    From Amboise and the Seine, [he] will come the length of
        the Indre:
    Talon at Poitiers, sacred wings to ruin,
    Before Boni.

18. *Les Propheties* ..., Benoist Rigaud edition, 1568.

19. Century 10, Quatrain 39 in a more literal translation:
    The first son, widow, unfortunate marriage,
    Without any children, two islands in discord,

Before eighteen years, still a minor,
For the other one betrothal happens while even younger.

20. Suriano's letter is filed in the Bibliothèque National, Paris,
     under *Manuscript du fonds, italien* #1721-4-193.
21. See *Négotiations diplomatiques de la France avec la Toscane*
     (Paris, 1865), vol. III, p. 428.
22. This Presage is #57 in the Chavigny list of *Janus françois*,
     p. 244:

Les duels laissez, supremes alliances,
Razes grand mort, refus fait à l'entrée:
De retour estre bien fait en oubliance,
La mort du iuste à banquet perpetrée.

An unrhymed translation reads:

The mourning left behind, supreme alliances,
Great Shaven One dead, refusal given at the entrance:
Upon return kindness to be in oblivion,
The death of the just one perpetrated at a banquet.

In 1997, I gave the following interpretation (*Nostradamus:
The Complete Prophecies*, p. 857):

> Rather than chronicling the death of François II for
> December, this presage seems to hiccup forward in
> time 14 years to the final days of 1574 and the foreseen
> death of Charles de Guise, Cardinal de Lorraine
> ("Great Shaven One"). He died at age 49 from catching
> a cold from walking barefoot while leading a holy
> procession of flagellating monks. His death was given
> little official notice. Even his bitter rival, Catherine de
> Medici, hearing the news when sitting down for dinner,

was at pains to make a post-mortem statement which had any weight. After a few perfunctory reflections that had no effect on her guests, she hissed loudly, "Today has died the wickedest of men!" and attacked her dinner with gusto. But his ghost is said to have haunted her. A week later, while at dinner, Catherine let out a cry and dropped her wine glass. She swore she had seen the cardinal's ghost. For weeks afterwards she passed through a strange state of mourning. Unable to stop thinking about him, she suffered that perverse and intimate loss that only those who have survived the death of a lifetime enemy can feel. Catherine's mourning would be "left behind" and replaced with foreboding for her favorite son, Henry III, soon to be coronated king of France. He was emotionally high strung and quickly discouraged. He had returned from Poland already chafing to get out from under the domination of his mother, who wanted to wage a fifth civil war with the Huguenots. By December 1574 he had decided to negotiate with the Protestant Confederacy and make peace ("supreme alliances").

Time shifts forward once again and the final two lines move us ahead to the last months of 1588. Their chilling poetry gives us a view of how Henry III would later seal his end by plotting to assassinate his chief rival, the petty-royal Henry de Guise. In fairness to the king – who, all faults aside, Nostradamus acknowledges as the "just" blood royal to be sitting on the throne – Guise's desire to assassinate him was mutual. An Italian actor acting as the king's informant was present at a dinner given by Henry de Guise's brother, the Cardinal de Guise. A toast was proposed to Henry de Guise: that he should become the next King of France ("death ... perpetrated at a banquet"). The king would "return" the "kindness" upon Henry de Guise and the Cardinal when they returned to the king's country residence at Château Bois, and have both men assassinated. This deed would precipitate his own assassination in the following year.

23. This Presage is #24 in the Chavigny list from *Janus françois*, p. 78:

Puisné Roy fait, funebre epithalame,
Sacrez esmeus, festins, iceux, soupi Mars:
Nuit larme on crie, hors on conduit la Dame,
L'arrest & pache rompu de toutes pars.

The literal and unrhymed translation:

The young King makes a funeral wedding song,
Holy one stirred up, feasts, of the said, Mars dormant:
Night of tears they cry, they conduct the lady outside,
The arrest and peace broken on all sides.

The following interpretation can be found in *Nostradamus: The Complete Prophecies*, p. 824:

Line 1 opens the year [1558] with a blend of near and distant-future outcomes for the limpid young Dauphin of fourteen years. This is the near-future François II, who was married to the fifteen-year-old Mary, Queen of Scots in April of 1558. At the time of his marriage [his] sickliness was already a major concern. The riddle ties a wedding song with a funeral dirge, adequately foreseeing the unconsummated marriage to be. In little over two years the honeymoon of these genuinely in-love royals would come to an unconsummated end with the Dauphin's death from a number of physical complaints. It is believed his physical maturity was so stunted that he was still pre-pubescent before his untimely death at eighteen.

24. This Presage is #33 in the Chavigny list from *Janus françois*, p. 56:

Jeux, festins, nopces, mort Prelat de renom.
Bruit, paix de tresue pendant l'ennemy mine:
Mer, terre & ciel bruit, fait du grand Brennon,
Cris or, argent, l'ennemy l'on ruyne.

A literal translation reads:

Games, feasts, nuptials, death, Prelate of renown.
Noise, peace of truce while the enemy threatens:
Sea, land and sky noise, deed of the great Brennus,
Cries gold, silver, the enemy they ruin.

The following interpretation was logged in *Nostradamus: The Complete Prophecies*, p. 829–30:

> Sometime in the previous year [1557] Nostradamus wrote a description of the wedding celebrations for the Dauphin and Dauphine, François II and Mary Queen of Scots, although he records them a few months late. Once again he tags another omen of death onto the end of the wedding party. The renowned "Prelate" is the former vice-legate to Bologna, Giovani Angelo de Medici, who became Pope Pius IV after the death of Paul IV in 1559 [and not at the end of 1558 as marked here]. Line 2 is correct; peace would follow the truce between Spain and France. The "enemy" that "threatens" could be the

Corsairs and Ottoman Turks, but most likely it is the Spanish, who would hold much power over France after the Treaty of Cateau-Cambrésis in 1559.

Line 3 falls back on a classical metaphor. "Brennus" was a Cisalpine Gallic chieftain who conquered Rome in 390 B.C. It seems Nostradamus is beating around the classical underbrush again with his magic wand, trying to chase out a wish-fulfilling tiger of a prophecy that his own great Brennus, Henry II, will conquer Rome and banish the Spanish from Italy. This, like all other prophetic promises of Henry II resuming his military adventures in Italy, would remain unfulfilled. [Perhaps] Nostradamus' prophetic bias has him misinterpreting his signs and portents of the successful conquest of Italy and Rome by Napoleon over 235 years later.

25. *Archives Nationales*, K 1494, #27.

26. *Rélations des Ambassadeurs Vénitiens* ... (Paris, 1838), vol. 1, p. 425. Suriano's original second letter on the subject of Nostradamus no longer exists. It was recopied in the 18th century. This was a common practice of archivists over the centuries, and would not even venture a hint of suspicion if the subject of the letter was less controversial than Nostradamus.

27. *Les Propheties* ..., Benoist Rigaud edition, 1568.

28. A literal translation for Century 8, Quatrain 17:

Those at ease will suddenly be cast down.
The world put into trouble by three brothers.
The enemies will seize the marine city,
Famine, fire, blood, plague, all evils doubled.

29. *Les Propheties* ..., Benoist Rigaud edition, 1568.

30. A literal translation for Century 8, Quatrain 46:

Paul the Celibate shall die three leagues from Rome,
The next two [Popes?] fled the oppressed Tarascan monster:
For Mars will make the most horrible throne,
The Cock and the Eagle of France, the three brothers.

31.   Modern scholars project a different set of popes and brothers
      on this prophecy. The following interpretation comes from
      Nostradamus: The Complete Prophecies, pp. 651–2:

> Charles de Fontbrune and Kidogo offer an intriguing
> interpretation. *Pol menfolee* stands for the Polish pope
> John Paul II. First, *Pol* stands for *Pollone*, the ancient
> word for Poland or, in this case, Paul the Pole. Then
> one adds an *a* to *m(a)nfolee* ("celibate") signifying John
> Paul II. This is another of Nostradamus' parallels to the
> earlier prophecies of Saint Malachy. Second, Fontbrune
> thinks Nostradamus invented the compound word
> *mansol* out of the Latin *manus* (man's work, travail,
> labor, etc.), and *sol* (the Sun). Kidogo refines the com-
> pound word to get the Latin *mens solis*, the astrological
> meridian over which the sun reaches its highest posi-
> tion at noontime. Both interpretations link *Pol
> menfolee* to Saint Malachy's prediction that John Paul
> II would be called *De Labore Solis*, or the Sun's Labor,
> since he was born during a solar eclipse.
>
>   Nostradamus could be telling us that the pope in
> office at the time of this writing (April 1996) will also
> end his days at the Castel Gondolfo, outside of Rome.
> "The next two" popes would then be the last two on
> Saint Malachy's list before doomsday, whom he calls
> *Gloria Olivae*, the Glory of the Olive, and *Petrus
> Romanus*, Peter of Rome. They both flee the Tarascon
> monster, a creature Kidogo interprets as Wormwood,
> which in Russian is "Chernobyl." One decade ago in

April 1986, mankind suffered the worst nuclear disaster in history when the Chernobyl nuclear power plant exploded and disgorged radiation around the world. This quatrain may warn of a worse nuclear disaster to come during the reign of the next two popes ...

The final line seems to be a general dating for modern France in the latter half of the 20th century. The three brothers are American president John F. Kennedy and US president hopefuls Senators Robert and Edward Kennedy.

32. *Les Propheties ...*, Benoist Rigaud edition, 1568.
33. A literal translation for 9Q36:

The great king captured by the hands of a young man,
Not far from Easter, confusion, thrust blow [of the] knife:
Perpetually captive times what lightning on the top,
When three brothers will be wounded and murdered.

34. *Les Propheties ...*, Macé Bonhomme edition (1555).
35. A literal translation of 1Q97:

That which iron [sword] or fire [shot] did not know how
    to accomplish,
Will be managed by a sweet-speaking tongue in council:
The King will be made to contemplate the dream seen
    while sleeping,
Because [of] the enemy at the fire, in warlike blood.

36. This Presage is #58 in the Chavigny list from *Janus françois*, p. 80:

Le Roy Roy n'estre, du Doux la pernicie,
L'an pestilent, les esmeus nubileux:

Tien qui tiendra des grands non leticie,
Et passera terme de cauilleux.

A literal translation of the full prophecy reads:

The King, King, not to be, destruction by the Clément one,
The year pestilent, the beclouded stirred up:
For the great nobles every man for himself, no joy:
And the term of the mockers will pass.

The "King, King not to be" is Henry III, who was king of
Poland before he ascended the French throne. He met a brutal end, leaning close to hear a whispered message from an
seemingly agreeable and gentle Dominican. Le Pelletier was
the first to pose that *Doux la pernicie* is the key decoding the
assassin's name and pernicious action of regicide in line 1.
Clemency is one of the Old French definitions for the noun
douceur. Nostradamus used the Latin *pernicies* in a double
pun implying the destruction, ruin, disaster, and calamity
that regicide entails – a capital crime considered most
heinous in the 16th century. Le Pelletier suggests that
Nostradamus translated the phrase *Tien' qui tiendra* from the
Latin *teneat qui tenebit,* or "every man for himself." A perfect
description of the chaos Henry III's death left behind. France
was a land without a king for five more years of civil war.

Although 1561 did see a pestilence arise in Nice, and both
1561 and 1589 would prove to be "beclouded" and "stirred up"
with riots and rebellion between believers of the Catholic
Christ and the Protestant Christ, the presage better refers to
the chaos of 1589. With Henry III's murder the House of
Valois had fallen, leaving the greatest nobles, Mayenne
of Guise and Henry de Navarre, to fight a free-for-all battle
for the French throne. The "mockers" are the fanatic
Catholic and anti-royalist leaders of the Paris "Sixteen," who

would be ruthlessly overthrown by Mayenne. Before this happened, their followers began the year 1589 participating in a macabre parade celebrating their freedom from Henry III's rule after he fled the city. Men, women, and children marched and danced through the streets of Paris stark naked in the dead of winter ("the mockers will pass").

37. Palamèdes Tronc de Coudoulet is the source for this account published in the 18th century. It was passed down the generations to him from its original source, Pierre Tronc de Coudoulet, a crony of Nostradamus in Salon.

38. *Mask of Nostradamus*, Randi, pp. 110–11.

39. See *Bibliographie Nostradamus*, Chomarat, p. 36: *Almanach Nouveau, Pour l'An. 1562. Composé par Maistre Michel Nostradamus* ... (Guillaume le Noir, & Jehans Bonfons, publishers).

40. Lemesurier says he was summoned by command of Catherine de' Medici to see the Duke and Princess of Savoy residing in Turin. See *Nostradamus Encyclopedia*, p. 38.

41. The handwriting of the original letter is a casualty of crumbling parchment; however, the copy made in 1714 does present the unique and turgid cadence of Nostradamus' hand.

CHAPTER TEN: TWILIGHT TRIUMPH

1. "Presage for the Year 1562," from *Prognostication nouvelle, Pour l'an mille cinq cents soixante deux*, Nostradamus (Anotione Volant, & Pierre Brotot, Lyon). This Presage is #66 in the Chavigny list from *Janus françois*, p. 86.

2. The First War of Religion (March 1562–March 1563) rapidly developed after the Massacre of Vassy, with Catholic and Huguenot bands and armies snatching up towns in a number of raids across France. The Huguenots mobilized an army, led by Condé and Coligny, which seized Orléans. Catholic armies invaded the Huguenot stronghold of

Normandy, investing Rouen. By December, a bloody and indecisive battle was fought at Dreux by a Catholic army commanded by Montmorency, against a force of Huguenots led by Condé. Both commanders were captured by the other side. At the siege of Rouen, Antoine de Bourbon was assassinated. François de Guise invested Orléans with a Catholic force but was also assassinated. It was left to the prisoners, Condé and Montmorency, to negotiate the Peace of Amboise, granting limited freedoms for Protestants if they joined forces with the crown to expel the English, who had seized La Havre with Huguenot support.

Some Nostradamians believe the Battle of Dreux is mentioned in Quatrains 56 and 57 of Century 9. If this is true, they predate the events by four years. The following literal translations and interpretations appear in *Nostradamus: The Complete Prophecies*, pp. 729–30 (the original French is from *Les Propheties ...*, Benoist Rigaud 1568 edition):

Century 9, Quatrain 56:

Camp pres de Noudam passera Goussan ville,
Et à Maiotes laissera son enseigne,
Conuertira en instant plus de mille,
Cherchãt les deux remettre en chaine & legne.

The army near [H]oudam will pass Goussainville,
And to the eager soldiers they will leave its ensign,
They will convert in an instant more than a thousand,
Searching for the two to return them back in fetters
    and wood.

Houda[n] and Goussainville are both west of Paris. The latter was little more than nine miles northeast of Dreux, where the Huguenot and Royal armies clashed in the First War of

Religion in 1562. The battle began with a collision of Huguenot and royalist cavalry. The commander of the royalist army, Anne de Montmorency, the constable of France, was captured along with several dozen troopers and some cavalry standards ("ensign"). The Huguenot cavalry led by Admiral Coligny sought to exploit its advantage with a counterattack but was repulsed by Catholic infantry. Line 3 hints that either 1,000 Huguenots will be killed – converted instantly from life to death in the failed attack – or they are captured and later request conversion the Catholicism. The final line paints a picture of Huguenot troopers with chained and manacled hands held fast by heavy wooden stocks ("fetters and wood").

Century 9, Quatrain 57:

Au lieu de DRUX vn Roy reposera,
Et cherchera loy changeant d'Anatheme,
Pendant le ciel si tresfort tonnera,
Portee neufue Roy tuera soymesme.

In the place of Dreux a King will repose,
And will search for a law changing Anathema,
While the sky so very loudly will thunder,
[At] the new gate the King will kill himself.

In the following year (1563) after the royalist victory at Dreux, Queen Regent Catherine de' Medici, acting in the name of her pubescent son, Charles IX, cooled the passions of the first civil war by issuing the Edict of Amboise, which granted freedom of worship to the Protestant nobility and gentry. This arrangement satisfied neither Huguenot nor Catholic ("Anathema" to both sides). The thunder of cannon and harquebus would rend the air in eight more civil wars.

Charles IX never committed suicide. One could say, metaphorically at least, that such edicts were suicidal to his future. History records that nine years later the 23-year-old king, physically and emotionally exhausted, died of a cold in 1574. It is believed the sensitive nervous system of Charles IX broke down from guilt over being bullied by his mother into ordering the Saint Bartholomew's Day massacres two years earlier.

3. "Presage for January," from *Prognostication nouvelle, Pour l'an mille cinq cents soixante deux*, Nostradamus (Anotione Volant, & Pierre Brotot, Lyon). This is Presage #67 in the Chavigny list from *Janus françois*, pp. 196, 200.

4. "Presage for August," 1561, from *Almanach pour l'An mil cinq cens soixante & un* (Barbe Regnault, Paris). This Presage is #64 in the Chavigny list from *Janus françois*, pp. 266–8).

There is much dispute between Nostradamians concerning whether the Presage quatrains can or even should be considered beyond the timeframe defined by Nostradamus. Certainly there is strong circumstantial evidence supporting a belief in Nostradamus seeing an event correctly but dating it incorrectly. Sometimes a seemingly clear forecast may be off by decades in its timing.

5. The following quatrains may detail the deaths of the following figures in the Wars of Religion. (Note that all page references to interpretations are for *Nostradamus: The Complete Prophecies*):

Antoine de Bourbon: 4Q88 (pp. 364–5).
François de Guise: Presages 23 (pp. 538–9), 68 (p. 866), and 82 (pp. 874–5).
Anne de Montmorency: Presage 113 (pp. 892–3).
Louis I, Duc de Condé: 3Q41 (pp. 254–5), Presage 88 (p. 878).
Gaspard de Coligny: 5Q83 (pp. 426–7), 9Q79 (pp. 743–4).

Charles de Guise, Cardinal de Lorraine: Presage 57 (pp. 857–8).

6. *Les Propheties ...*, Benoist Rigaud edition, 1568.

7. An unrhymed and more literal translation for 6Q63 would read:

The lady left alone in the realm,
Her unique [husband] first extinguished on the bed of honor:
For seven years she will weep with grief,
Then a long life and good fortune for the kingdom.

8. Full title: *Prophetie Merveilleuse commençant ceste presente Année, & dure jusques en l'An de grand'Mortalité, que l'on dira M.d.lxvijj.*

9. These editions being: le Noir & Bonfons (Paris) and the Volant & Brotot (Lyon). See *Bibliographie Nostradamus*, Chomarat, pp. 35–7.

10. Full title: *Le Remede tres utile contre la peste et toutes fievres pestilentielles, avec la maniere d'en guérir; aussi la singulière recepte de l'oeuf dont usoit l'empereur Maximilian premier du nom* (Guillaume Nyverd, publisher, 1561).

11. See *Bibliographie Nostradamus*, Chomarat, p. 38.

12. Lemesurier poses that Nostradamus was possibly too embarrassed to write to Catherine de' Medici for her original copy, which he "undoubtedly sent her." (See *Nostradamus Encyclopedia*, p. 89.) Lemesurier, however, does not provide evidence that the queen ever had anything more than the special first printings of the Rosne editions of Century 7 without the missing 60 quatrains.

13. Full title for the Ménier edition: *Les Propheties de M. Michel Nostradamus: Don't il y en a trois cens qui n'ont encores esté imprimées, lesquelles sont en ceste presente edition. Reueues et additionées par l'Autheur pour l'An mil cinq cens soixante et un,*

de trente neuf articles à l'a dernier Centurie. Par Pierre Ménier, portier de la porte Sanct Victor. Printed circa 1588, according to Chomarat, Klinckowström, Leoni, and Parker.

14. Bibliophiles believe Pierre Duruau of Troyes printed the following publication in 1605:

Les Propheties de M. Michel Nostradamus. Reueuës & corrigées sur la coppie Imprimée à Lyon par Benoist Rigaud. 1568 [Portrait] M.DCV.

Les Propheties de M. Michel Nostradamus. Centurie VIII. IX. X. Qui n'auoient esté premierement Imprimées: et sont en la mesme edition de 1568

Predictions Admirables pour les ans courans en ce siecle. Recueillies des Memoires de feu M. Michel Nostradamvs, vivant Medecin du Roy Charles IX., & L'vn des plus excellens Astronomes qui furent iamais. Presentées au tres-grand Inuincible & tres-clement Prince Henry IIII, vivant Roy de France & de Nauarre. Par Vincent Seue de Beaucaire en Languedoc, dés le 19. Mars 1605, au Chasteau de Chantilly, maison de Monseigneur le Connestable de Montmorency.

15. The surviving quatrains for Century 11 are numbered 91 and 97, implying a full volume was composed before his death in 1566. Century 12's surviving quatrains are numbered 4, 24, 36, 52, 55, 56, 59, 62, and 65, indicating Nostradamus composed at least two-thirds of a twelfth volume before either age or disinterest overtook him.

16. *Bulletin du Bibliophile* (1862), p. 784.

17. Sixian 6 gives a detailed prediction for the conspiracy of the Duc de Biron in 1602 – far too detailed, making it appear retroactive and perhaps implying that the Sixians were composed sometime in 1602 through 1605.

18. Leoni says the letter can be found in *Les Correspondants de Peiresc* (Marseilles, 1880).

     Leroy narrows his origins down to Anne de Nostredame, who married a "Pierre de Seva" of Toulon (see *Nostradamus: Ses origines, Sa vie, Son oeuvre*, Tableau généalogique no. 3).

19. *Nostradamus: Ses origines, Sa vie, Son oeuvre*, Leroy, Tableau généalogique no. 1 through no. 6.

20 *Nostradamus Encyclopedia*, Lemesurier, pp. 148–9.

21. Could a true son of Nostradamus be the forger? Leoni points out that César would live another 25 years after the Sixians were published and was "much less interested in the prophecies of his father than he was in the social position his father's reputation gave him." (See *Nostradamus and His Prophecies*, p. 50.) Therefore he was unconcerned whether the Sixians were true or false, as long as they enhanced the reputation and perhaps the myth of his father.

22. *Catherine de' Medici and the Lost Revolution*, Roeder, p. 356.

23. *Ibid*, p. 354.

24. *Ibid*, pp. 354–5.

25. Divination via the reading of moles requires that one take into account the color, location and shape of moles on the body. Light moles denote luck; black warn of challenges to overcome. Virtue and goodness dot the body in round moles; a destiny of wealth blemishes one with oblong moles. Moles on one's backside signify a lack of ambition, but an easygoing disposition. Spots on one's belly denote overindulgence in food, wine, money and love affairs. The reason beauty marks on the chin were so *en vogue* stems from blemishes advertising to others your first-rate character – loving, honest, competent, and so on. However, it would be best to hide one's bemoled fingers in a glove, for they would indicate a naturally dishonest character and a predilection to exaggerate because of an inability to face the truth in life.

26. *Mémoires pour servir à l'histoire de France*, Cologne, 1718, vol. II, p. 2.

27. *Henry of Navarre: Henry IV of France*, Lord Russell of Liverpool, p. 24.

28. Note that César, the patriotic Provençal, considers France a foreign territory his father visited when traveling to Paris in 1555.

29. *L'Histoire et chronique de Provence*, César de Nostredame, pp. 801–2.

30. *Archives nationales*, K 1503, #37.

31. *Ibid*, #30.

32. *L'Histoire et chronique de Provence*, César de Nostredame, p. 802.

CHAPTER ELEVEN: FROM LIFE TO AFTERLIFE

1. *Almanach pour l'An M.D.LXVII. Composé par feu Maistre Michel de Nostredame Docteur en medecine conseillet [!] & medecin ordinaire du Roy. Avec ses amples significations, ensemble les explications de l'Eclypse merveilleux & tout formidable qui sera le IX. d'avril proche de l'heure de Midy.* A Lyon Par Benoist Odo, Avec privilege [c. 1566].

2. *Bibliographie Nostradamus*, Chomarat, p. 48.

3. Michel Chomarat produced a fine facsimile. See *Cahiers Michel Nostradamus*, no. 5–6, 1987–8. Textes réunis et présentés par l'Association des Amis de Michel Nostradamus B.P.54,/69396 Lyon Cédex 03.

4. Nostradamus to Io. [Johannes] Lobbettius, 13 December 1565. See *Nostradamus – Lettres Inédites* [LI], p. 163.

5. *Ibid.*

6. *Ibid.* No French copy of the Almanac for 1564 remains. See *Nostradamus Bibliographie*, Chomarat, p. 41. The Presages from this Almanac do survive and were reproduced by Chavigny.

7. Presage for May 1566. This Presage is #124 in the Chavigny list from *Janus françois*, pp. 152, 218, and 230–32:

Entre peuple discorde, intimitié brutale,
Guerre mort de grands Princes, plusieurs pars d'Italie:
Vniverselle playe, plus fort occidentale,
Tempore bonne et pleine, mais fort seche et tarie.

A literal translation:

Between people discord, brutal enmity,
War, death of great Princes, several parts [of Italy]:
Universal plague, more strong (in the) western,
Times good and full, but very dry and exhausted.

The following interpretation for the first three lines comes from *Nostradamus: The Complete Prophecies*, Hogue, p. 900:

> Although later editions add "of Italy" to line 2, I believe this better chronicles events in France, either retro-actively as a Chavigny addition or prophetically as Nostradamus' view of 1566. This year did see the death of one "great Prince" if you could call Suleiman the Magnificent of the Ottoman Empire such. The "universal plague" of religious hatreds may be implied here. And it was worse towards the west of Provence in the Huguenot-dominated regions of the French southwest. [See the text for the interpretation of the final line.]

8. Presage for July 1566. This Presage is #125 in the Chavigny list from *Janus françois*, pp. 152–4:

Par pestilence & feu fruits d'arbres periront,
Signe d'huiie abonder. pere Denis non gueres:
Des grands mourir, mais peu d'estrangers saillirõt,
Insult, marin barbare, & dangers de frontieres.

A literal translation:

Through pestilence and fire, fruits of [the] trees will perish,
Signs of oil to abound. Father Denis not scarce:
Some great ones to die, but few foreigners will sally forth
    in attack,
Offense, Barbarian marines, and dangers at the frontiers.

The following interpretation comes from *Nostradamus: The
Complete Prophecies*, pp. 901–2:

> Here we have a forecast of tree blight, which one might
> expect to find in a prophecy for an almanac. But the
> buds of spring and summer promise a good olive oil crop
> for the fall. As we know the Turkish sultan did die in his
> tent bed on 5 September just before the final victorious
> assault on Sziget. If Nostradamus means "few foreigners"
> sallying forth against France, he is right. But during this
> time Suleiman the Magnificent had amassed the might-
> iest Ottoman army to date and hurled it against the
> Christian states in the Balkans. Raids by corsairs along
> the Riviera were endemic so it is easy to predict such
> "offenses" from Barbary pirates ("Barbarian marines")
> landing onshore and carrying off people and loot. If
> anyone feared "dangers at the frontiers" of France it was
> the Huguenots, who believed the Spanish were plotting
> with French Catholics to wipe them out. I render the
> task of disclosing who father Denis is to anyone more
> familiar with French Provençal history than myself. I'll
> only speculate that the good "Father" is the Cardinal
> de Lorraine working for the House of Valois, symbol-
> ized by their sepulchre at Saint "Denis."

9. *Présages de Nostradamus,* Chevignard, pp. 189–90, quoted from *Recueil de Presages prosaique de M. Michel de Nostradame,* Chavingy (1589).

10. Presage for April 1567. This Presage is #134 in the Chavigny list from *Janus françois,* p. 178:

Par grandes maladies, religion fachée,
Par les enfans & legats d'Ambassade:
Don donné à indign, nouuelle loy laschée,
Biens de vieux peres, Roy en bonne contraue.

A literal translation:

Through great maladies, religion offended,
Through the infants and gifts of the Embassy:
Gifts given to a worthless one, new law relaxed,
Goods of old fathers, King in good country.

11. The judgment of being "a worthless one" could be a jibe aimed at Charles IX himself. Nostradamus may have secretly taken his honor to be a gift from the king's mother. Although he had respect for the title of "king," his prophecies throughout the centuries tag Charles as the *noir/roi* (or the black-evil-king) of the Saint Bartholomew's Day Massacre to come. The presage speaks of a "new law" relaxed. This could be the Treaty of Amboise proscribing religious tolerance. Thus if vigilance against intolerance was "relaxed" then Nostradamus predicted civil war near. In any case, Nostradamus with foresight had accurately tagged 1567 as the year the second War of Religion began.

12. *Fonds Bonnemant,* no. 298, of the Catalogue of Manuscripts from the Municipal Library of Arles, under the division *Testaments Curieux.*

13. *Nostradamus and His Prophecies,* Leoni, p. 35.

14. The itemized list of funds included: 36 rose nobles; 101 simple ducats; 79 Angelots; 126 double ducats; 4 old crowns; 2 gold lions in the form of old crowns; 1 crown King Louis (most likely a valued heirloom); 1 gold medal worth 2 crowns; 8 German florins; 10 imperials; 17 marionettes; 8 half-crowns; 1,419 crowns; 1,200 crown-pistolets; and finally, 3 pieces of gold said to be Portuguese, worth 36 crowns.

15. The will was attested by the following witnesses, many of whom, besides Marc and Suffren, might have been among Nostradamus' friends and close business associates: Martin Mason, consul; Jehan Allegret, treasurer; Palamède Marc, Esquire, Lord of Châteauneuf; Guillaume Giraud, the noble Arnaud d'Amraines; Jaumet Viguier, Esq.; and Vidal de Vidal, Friar Superior of the Convent of St. Francis. Another friend/business acquaintance not present but recorded as a legal witness was the burger Joseph Raynaud. The order of witness signatures after Michel Nostradamus was as follows: Mason, Allegret, Friar Superior Vidal, Balthezar d'Amirane, P. Marc, J. de Viguier, Guilhaume Giraud, and the notary, Roche.

16. This Presage is #133 in the Chavigny list from *Janus françois*, p. 208:

Les ennemys publics, nopces & mariages,
La mort apres, l'enrichy par les morts:
Les grands amys se monstrer au passage,
Deux sects iargonner, de surpris tards remords.

A literal translation:

The public enemies, nuptials and marriages,
Death after, he grown rich through the deaths:
The great friends will show themselves in the passage,
Two sects to talk jargon, from surprise remorse later.

Chavigny believes this is about the future marriage of Henry of Navarre and the events of the St. Bartholomew's Day Massacre in 1572, and how Henry would later profit and inherit the throne from the deaths of Charles IX and Henry III. See *Pleiades*, p. 113.

17. The Presage for May 1567. This Presage is #135 in the Chavigny list from *Janus françois*, pp. 202, 285:

Du pere au fils s'approche: Magistrats dits seueres,
Les grands nopces, ennemys garbelans:
De latens mis auant, par la foy d'improperes,
Les bons amis & femmes contre tels groumelans.

A literal translation:

From the father it approaches the son: Magistrates called
　　severe,
The great nuptials, enemies to mangle:
Concealed, put in front, through the faith of reproaches,
The good friends and women against the grumblings.

Chavigny again applies it to the marriage of Henry of Navarre to Marguerite [Margot] de Valois and the resulting St. Bartholomew's Day massacre. See notes: *Présages de Nostradamus*, Chevignard, pp. 185–6.

18. The Presage for June 1567. This Presage is #136 in the Chavigny list from *Janus françois*, pp. 152, 164:

Par le thresor, trouué l'heritage du pere:
Les Roys & Magistrats, les nopces, ennemys:
Le public mal veillant, les Iuge & Maire,
La mort, peur & frayeur: & trois Grands à mort mis.

A literal translation:

Through the treasure, found – the heritage of the father:
The Kings and Magistrates, the nuptials, enemies:
The public malevolent, the Judge and Mayor,
The death, fear and terror: and three Great Ones put to death.

Chevignard also thinks some of this is generally about Nostradamus' final days (see *Présages de Nostradamus*, p. 186); however, I hold to my interpretation for the last three lines on pp. 906–7 of *Nostradamus: The Complete Prophecies*:

> The reference to "nuptials" could transport us a few years ahead to 1572, during the stifling hot dog days of August in Paris, when King Charles IX gave the sweating hand of his sister, Marguerite de Valois, to the garlic-perfumed paw of Henry, King of Navarre. The people of Catholic Paris were in a malevolent, muggy mood, and thanks to the schemes of Catherine de' Medici and Henry de Guise, their mutual rival, Admiral Gaspard de Coligny, would be assassinated along with thousands of Marguerite's Huguenot wedding guests on the night of "death, fear and "terror" – Saint Bartholomew's Eve. As a consequence of this massacre the "three Great Ones" are put to death in the coming decades of civil war: Henry III, Henry de Guise and much later, Henry de Navarre after he takes the French throne as Henry IV of France.

19. This Presage is #137 in the Chavigny list from *Janus françois*, p. 178. A literal translation would read:

Again the death approaches [him], Royal gift and Legacy,
He will prepare what is, through old age in decay:
The young heirs in suspicion of no legacy,
Treasure found in plasters and kitchen cookery.

20. This Presage is #140 in the Chavigny list from *Janus françois*, p. 212:

    The Kings and Magistrates through the deaths, the hand [power]* to place,
    Young girls sick, and of the Great Ones body swells:
    All through languors and nuptials, enemy serfs for the master.
    The public sad, the Composer all swelled up.

    * A poetic interpretation of the old French *main* (hand) can mean the hand of power; ergo "hand" equals power in this interpretation.

21. See *Nostradamus: The Complete Prophecies*, Hogue, 5Q94, pp. 433–4.
22. *Ibid.* "Hister" is mentioned in 2Q24, 4Q68, 5Q29, Presage 29, and Presage 31.
23. *Ibid,* 6Q49.
24. *Ibid,* 5Q45, pp.399–400.
25. *Ibid,* 4Q80.
26. *Traité des fardemens et confitures*, Nostradamus, Book 1 (*Le Vray et Parfaict Embellissement de la Face* ...), ch. XXVI, p. 24.
27. Century 9, Quatrain 7 as printed in the 1568, Benoist Rigaud edition:

    Qui ouurira le monument trouué,
    Et ne viendra le serrer promptement:
    Mal luy viendra & ne pourra prouué,
    Si mieux doit estre Roy Breton ou Normand.

    The literal translation:

He who will open the tomb discovered,
And who does not close it promptly:
Evil will come to him and one will be unable to prove,
If it would be better to be a Breton or Norman king.

28. Mea culpa! Lemesurier is correct to chide me and other Nostradamians who did not read this phrase *une tombe ou monument contre la muraille* more carefully. Nostradamus' tomb and monument were set "against" the wall. Therefore, he was not stood upright in the church "against" the wall, unless he was propped upright "against" the wall. Alas, the church and the first tomb of Nostradamus were destroyed, so the myth lives on to exasperate those who dot their "Ts" and cross their eyes.

29. One legend has Nostradamus sealed against the church wall while still alive, and if you listen closely it is not "Nostra-doormouse" scratching behind the wall, but the quill of Nostradamus writing new prophecies. (They must be the prophecies the supermarket tabloids publish.)

   The coming centuries had their share of peasants' and wives tales of Nostradamus haunting Salon at night. Others concerned themselves with a secret document hidden in his coffin containing the key to unlocking the code to all his prophecies. Sometime in the 17th century – the date keeps changing – the city consuls of Salon decided to move the body of their most famous citizen to a more prominent wall of the church. The tight corner between the wall and the altar of St. Martha had become a popular place for contemplating the man and his prophecies. Indeed, even Louis XIII and Louis XIV had meditated before his tomb in 1622 and 1660, respectively, with Cardinal Mazarin and the latter's mother Anne of Austria in attendance. It is said the consuls overseeing the breaking of the wall and the removal of the coffin took a quick, careful look inside to see if any secret paper was there. It contained no paper of any kind, but there was one surprise. It is claimed that around the skeleton's neck hung a medallion inscribed with the date of the exhumation. Of course, the medallion has been conveniently lost, and the date keeps changing depending on who tells the story. If the legend were true, it would have amused Nostradamus to see how the leading citizens of Salon responded to the practical joke he had devised so many years before.

I would like to add a new urban legend. The last time I visited fair Salon and the tomb of Nostradamus I could have sworn I heard the old fellow murmuring to himself beyond the marble plaque. I knocked on the wall and asked him (in my slow and labored French, of course) what he was doing. He replied with a lazy Provençal drawl, "I am erasing my prophecies." Puzzled, I asked why, to which he growled, "Because I'm decomposing, you idiot!"

30. M. David most likely did not know whether Nostradamus foresaw the French Revolution or not; however, most Nostradamians believe his forecasts of the French Revolution number among his greatest prophetic successes. Beyond his successful prediction about the creation of the French Revolutionary Calendar in "1792" there are dozens of quatrains that supposedly foretell the following: the year the revolution began (1Q3); the "500" Fédérés storming the Tuilleries Palace (9Q35); a very detailed account of Louis XVI and his family's thwarted escape, with the route they took and the town in which they were captured mentioned outright (9Q20); the guillotine and the Reign of Terror to come (9Q20); the execution of Louis XVI and Queen Marie Antoinette (1Q57, 4Q85); and the execution of Robespierre, which brought an end to the Terror (8Q41). See *Nostradamus: The Complete Prophecies*, Hogue.

31. In 1813, Nostradamus' surviving bones were reinterred in the neighboring 14th/15th-century Church of the Collégiale

St.-Laurent. Mayor David had a tombstone erected, the beginning of which, Leoni remarked, "must have caused the prophet to roll over in his nearby tomb":

> In the Year 3 of Liberty the tomb of Nostradamus, who honored Salon, his native land, and whose memory will always be dear to French patriots because of his predictions of the reign of Liberty, was opened. The citizens anxious to save his precious remains divided them amongst each other; with great pains the municipality has been able to recover part of them, which this tomb contains. It makes a gift of them to posterity, as well as of the portrait of this celebrated man and that of his son, the historian, painted by himself.

Mayor David obviously did not read Nostradamus' unflattering predictions this avowed royalist from the 16th century made about the French Revolution. Nor does David have the date in the revolutionary calendar right. The "Year 3" in the Revolution's new calendar is around the time our royalist Nostradamus' bones were plundered by the so-called "French patriots" of this dedication.

32. *Les Vraies Centuries*, Reynaud-Plense, p. 26.

33. Century 6, Quatrain 100 as printed in the 1568 Benoist Rigaud edition. A literal translation reads:

> May those who read this verse consider it profoundly,
> Let the profane and ignorant herd keep away:
> And all Astrologers, Idiots and Barbarians stay far away,
> May he who does otherwise, let him be subject to the
>   sacred rite.

34. The following wordplays are:

Mabus = sbaM = Sudam = Saddam Hussein

(The dictator of Iraq, responsible for starting two bloody wars in the Persian Gulf, and for using chemical weapons on the Iranians and the Kurds. You can decode Mabus into Saddam by using the laws of reverse lettering, and adding redundant letters.)

Mabus = Maabus = Usaam b = Usama b(in) = Usama bin Laden

(The messianic founder of the al-Qaeda terrorist network responsible for the terrorist attacks on New York and Washington, D.C., on 11 September 2001. You can decode Mabus by applying a more correct phonetic representation of the Arabic pronunciation of his name, plus using the law of subtracting redundant letters.)

Mabus = MaBus = a M Bus = g. W. Bus(h)

(The U.S. President elected in 2000, who launched a war in the Middle East in early 2003 to liberate Iraq. You can decode Mabus into his name by turning the letters "m" and "a" upside down to make "g" [George] "W" [Walker]. Add the silent 16th-century Latinized-French "h" in Bus[h].)

For these or any other candidates to fulfill the supposed Third Antichrist prophecies of 2Q62 and 8Q77, they must be among the first to fall in the 27-year third world war they would trigger early in the new millennium. (See *Nostradamus: The New Millennium*, Hogue, pp. 175–213.) Once they "soon die" or are "soon annihilated" there will come a "terrible destruction of people and animals."

35. Presage for November 1567. This Presage is #141 in the Chavigny list from *Janus françois*, p. 154. The literal translation:

On his return from the Embassy, the King's gift put in place.
He will do nothing more. He will be gone to God.
Close relatives, friends, brothers by blood,
[Will find him] completely dead near the bed and the bench.

Chavigny claimed to have recovered two more Presages: one
for December (see *Recueil,* XII, pp. 347, 696) and a Presage
for "The end of the year" (see *Recueil,* XII, pp. 379, 699).
These presages seem to list a number of coded personal messages that must have made sense to Nostradamus' intimate
relations, but in general would remain a mystery to all those
outside his inner family circle. Possibly, they work as some
kind of post-mortem denouement forecast. He predicted his
sons would eventually study in Paris, and that a positive resolution would come concerning some undisclosed sickness
perhaps suffered by his wife along with an end to disputes
within the family about his estate and his "secrets."

CHRONOLOGY: LIFE AND AFTERLIFE

1. *L'Histoire universelle* (Maillé, 1616–20) by Théodore-Agrippa
    d'Aubigné, grandfather of the wife of Louis XIV (Madame
    de Maintenon).
2. *Nostradamus: The Complete Prophecies,* Hogue, pp. 236–7.
3. *Faust,* Johann Wolfgang von Goethe, (Bayard Taylor, trans.),
    p. 43.
4. *Geobbels Diaries 1939–41,* Josef Goebbels, translated and edit-
    ed by Fred Taylor, B.P. Putman's Sons, New York, 1982.
5. *Ibid.*
6. *Ibid.*
7. *Geobbels Diares 1942–1943,* edited and translated with intro-
    duction by Louis P. Lochner, Doubleday, New York, 1948.
8. *Nostradamus: The Complete Prophecies,* Hogue: 3Q17 (pp.
    241–2), 3Q34 (p. 251), 5Q41 (p. 397), 5Q64 (p. 414–15), 6Q6
    (pp. 442–3), and EP87 (pp. 570–71).

Select Bibliography

Bareste, Eugène, *Nostradamus*, Paris, 1840

Boas, Marie, *The Scientific Renaissance 1450–1630*, London, 1962

Boeser, Knut, ed., *The Elixirs of Nostradamus: Nostradamus' Original Recipes for Elixirs, Scented Water, Beauty Potions and Sweetmeats*, Moyer Bell, Wakefield, 1996

Boeser, Knut, *Nostradamus*, HarperSanFrancisco, New York, 1994

Boscolo, Renucio, *Nostradamus, Key to the Future*. Abbot Press, Burlingame, CA, 1984

Boulenger, Jacques, *Les grands illuminés: Nostradamus*, Excelsior, Paris, 1933

Brennan, J.H., *Nostradamus, Visions of the Future*. Aquarian Press/HarperCollins, London, 1992

Brind'Amour, Pierre (ed. & commentaire), *Nostradamus – Les Premières Centuries ou Propheties (édition Macé Bonhomme de 1555)*, Droz, Genève, 1996

Buget, F, *Etude sur les Prophèties de Nostradamus. Biographes et commentateurs. Oeuvres et adversaires. Editions des Prophéties. Moyens de distinguer celles du XVIe siècle de leurs nombreuses confrefaçons. Ce qu'on doit penser de l'homme et de son oeuvre.* Paris, 1860–63. (*Bulletin du Bibliophile et du Bibliothécaire*. 1860, pp. 1699–1721; 1862, pp. 68–94, 241–68, 383–412, 657–91; 1862, pp. 761–85; 1863, pp. 449–73, 513–30, 577–88)

Burman, Edward, *The Inquisition: Hammer of Heresy*, Dorset Press, New York, 1984

Cartwright, Frederick F., *Disease and History*, Dorset Press, New York, 1972

Castiglione, Baldesar, *The Book of the Courtier*, Penguin, New York, 1967

Castleden, Rodney, *World History: A Chronological Dictionary of Dates*, Shooting Star Press, New York, 1993

Chavigny, Jean-Aymes (Aimé) de, *La Première Face du Janus françois, contenant sommairement les troubles, guerres civiles et autre choses mémorables, advenues en la France et ailleurs, dès l'an de salut 1534, jusques à l'an 1589, fin de la maison Valésienne. Extraite et colligée des centuries et autres commentaires de M. Michel de Nostredame, iadis conseillier et médecin des rois Henry II, Francoys II et Charles IX. A la fin est adiousté un discours de l'advénement a la couronne de France du roy très-chrestian à present regnant: ensemble de sa grandeur et prosperité à venir. Le tout fait en françois et latin pour le contentement de plusieurs ... dedié au roy.* A Lyon, par les héritiers de Pierre Roussin, 1594

Chevignard, Bernard, *Présages de Nostradamus*, Éditions du Seuil, 1999

Chomarat, Michel, *Bibliographie lyonnaise des Nostradamus suivie d'un inventaire des manuscrits relatifs à la famille Nostradamus*, Lyon, 1973

Chomarat, Michel (avec la collaboration de Jean-Paul Larouche), *Bibliographie Nostradamus XVIᵉ–XVIIᵉ–XVIIIᵉ siècles*, Éditions Valentin Koerner, Baden Baden, 1989

Chomarat, Michel (Dir.), *Cahiers Michel Nostradamus, Textes réunis et présentés par l'Association des Amis de Michel Nostradamus*, Lyon: Nº1/Mars 1983, Nº3/Février 1984, Nº2/Février 1985, Nº4 /Juillet 1986, Nº5–6/1987–8

Chomarat, Michel, *Nostradamus entre Rhône et Saône*, Lyon, 1971

Chomarat, Michel, *Supplément à la Bibliographie lyonnaise des Nostradamus suivie d'un inventaire des estampes relatives à la famille Nostradamus*, Lyon, 1976

Choppin, René, *Traité de Privileges des Personnes Vivans aux Champs* (1575), in *Oeuvres* (Paris, 1662)

Cook, Theodore Andrea, *Old Provence*, Interlink Books, New York, 2001 (first published 1905)

Coudoulet, Palamèdes Tronc de, *Abrégé de la Vie de Nostradamus, suivi d'une nouvelle découverte de ses quatrains; par le sieur Palamèdes Tronc de Coudoulet de la ville de Sallon*. Aix, Adibert. [c. 1701]. The existence of this manuscript was reported by Bareste in note, p. 9 (*Opuscule fort rare*), and by Buget (*Bulletin du Bibliophile*, 1860, pp. 1716–18).

Cowan, Alexander, *Urban Europe 1500–1700*, Arnold (A member of the Hodder Headline Group), London, 1998

Davis, Natalie Zemon, *The Return of Martin Guerre*, Harvard University Press, Cambridge, MA, 1983

Davis, Natalie Zemon, *Society and Culture in Early Modern France*, Standford University Press, Stanford, 1975

Debus, Allen G., *Man and Nature in the Renaissance*, Cambridge University Press, New York, 1978

De Rosa, Peter, *Vicars of Christ: The Dark Side of the Papacy*, Crown, New York, 1988

Dunn, Richard S., *The Age of Religious Wars, 1559–1689*, W.W. Norton & Company, New York, 1970

Dupèbe, Jean, *Lettres Inédites*, Librairie Droz S.A., Genève, 1983

Durby, George (ed.), *A History of Private Life: Revelations of the Medieval World*, Belknap Press of Harvard University Press, Cambridge, MA, 1988

Durrell, Lawrence, *Provence*, Arcade Publishing, New York, 1990

Elliott, J.H., *Imperial Spain: 1469–1716*, St. Martin's Press, New York, 1964

Fagan, Brian, *The Little Ice Age: How Climate Made History, 1300–1850*, Basic Books, 2000

Febvre, Lucien, *Life in Renaissance France*, Harvard University Press, Cambridge, MA, 1977

Fontbrune, Jean-Charles de, *Nostradamus, Countdown to Apocalypse*, Henry Holt & Company, New York, 1983

Fontbrune, Jean-Charles de, *Nostradamus 2, Into the Twenty-First Century*, Henry Holt & Company, New York, 1984

Fontbrune, Dr Max de, *La Prédiction mystérieuse de Prémol*, Michelet, Sarlat, 1939

Fontbrune, Dr Max de, *Les Prophéties de Nostradamus Dévoilées. Lettres à Henry Second*, Adyar, 1937

Forman, Henry James, *The Story of Prophecy in the Life of Mankind*, Tudor Publishing Company, New York, 1940

Francis, David Pitt, *Nostradamus, Prophecies of Present Times?* Aquarian Press, Wellingborough, Northamptonshire, 1986

Fraser, Antonia, *Mary Queen of Scots*, Delacorte Press, New York, 1978

Gail, Marzieh, *Life in the Renaissance*, Random House, New York, 1968

Garencières, Theophilus de, *The true prophecies; or, Prognostications of Michael Nostradamus, physician to Henry II. Francis II. and Charles IX. kings of France, and one of the best astronomers that ever were. A work full of curiosity and learning. Translated and commented ...*, London, 1672

Gattey, Charles Neilson, *Visionaries and Seers*, Prism Press, Dorset, 1977

Geobbels, Josef (Fred Taylor, ed. & trans.), *Goebbels Diaries 1939–1941*, B.P. Putnam's Sons, New York, 1982

Geobbels, Josef (Louis P. Loucher, ed. & trans.), *Goebbels Diaries 1942–1943*, Doubleday, 1948

Gibson, Walter B. & Litzka, R., *The Complete Illustrated Book of Divination and Prophecy*, Arrow Books, London, 1989

Greengrass, Mark, *France in the Age of Henri IV*, Longman, New York, 1984

Grun, Bernard, *The Timetables of History: A Horizontal Linkage of People and Events*, Touchstone Books, Simon & Schuster, New York, 1982

Grotta, Daniel, *The Biography of J.R.R. Tolkien: Architect of Middle Earth*, Running Press, Philadelphia, 1992

Haitze, Pierre-Joseph de, (aka Pierre Joseph), *La Vie de Nostradamus. Par Pierre Joseph. De Filiis quoque Issachar, viri eruditi, qui noverant singula tempora.* Paralip. Lib. I. Cap. 12. v. 32. A Aix, Chez la Veuve de Charles David, & Joseph David, Imprimeur du Roy & de la Ville. 1711. [This book was mentioned in the commentaries of Arbaud, Bareste and Buget. Chez Gattey, Paris edition of 1789, was the last known edition.]

Hale, John, *The Civilization of Europe in the Renaissance,* Simon & Schuster, New York, 1993

Hall, Angus, *Signs of Things to Come,* Danbury Press/Aldus Books, London, 1975

Hall, Manly P., *Sages and Seers,* The Philosophical Research Society, Inc., Los Angeles, CA, 1975

Hall, Manly P., *The Secret Teachings of All the Ages: An Encyclopedic Outline of Masonic, Hermetic, Qabbalistic and Rosicrucian Symbolical Philosophy. Being an Interpretation of the Secret Teachings concealed within the Rituals, Allegories and Mysteries of all Ages,* The Philosophical Research Society, Inc., Los Angeles, CA, 1977

Hall, Manly P., *The Story of Astrology: The Belief in the Stars as a Factor in Human Progress,* The Philosophical Research Society, Inc., Los Angeles, CA, 1977

Haught, James A., *Holy Horrors: An Illustrated History of Religious Murder and Madness,* Prometheus Books, Buffalo, NY, 1990

Hibbert, Christopher, *The House of Medici: Its Rise and Fall,* William Morrow & Co., New York, 1975

Hogue, John, *Nostradamus: The Complete Prophecies,* Element Books, HarperCollins, London, 1997

Hogue, John, *Nostradamus: The New Millennium,* Element Books, HarperCollins, London, 2002

Iamblichus (Thomas Taylor, trans.), *Iamblichus on The Mysteries of the Egyptians, Chaldeans, and Assyrians*, Wizards Bookshelf, San Diego, 1984

Jacobi, Jolande (ed. & trans.), *Paracelsus: Selected Writings, Bollingen Series XXVIII*, Princeton University Press, Princton, 1951

Jaubert, Etienne, *Eclaircissement des veritables Quatrains de Maistre Michel Nostradamus, Docteur et Professeur en Medecine, Conseiller et Medecin ordinaire des Roys Henry II. François II. & Charles IX. grand Astrologue de son temps, & specialement pour la connoissance des choses futures*, [Amsterdam], 1656

Jochmans, Joseph Robert, *Nostradamus Now, Prophecies of Peril and Promise for the 1990's – And Beyond*, Sun Books/Sun Publishing, Santa Fe, NM, 1993

Jones, Louisa, *Provence: A Country Almanac*, Stewart, Tabori & Chang, New York, 1999

Josephus, Flavius (William Whiston, A.M. trans.), *The Works of Flavius Josephus, the Learned and Authentic Jewish Historian and Celebrated Warrior, to which is added, Three Dissertations, concerning Jesus Christ, John the Baptist, James the Just, God's Command to Abraham*, Milner and Company, London, 1737

Kelly, J.N.D. *The Oxford Dictionary of Popes*, Oxford University Press, London, 1989

Kert, Christian, *Nostradamus: Le Mage de Salon*, Éditions Les Centuries, Salon de Provence

Kidogo, Bardo, *The Keys to the Predictions of Nostradamus*, Foulsham, London, 1994

King, Francis W., *Nostradamus: Prophecies Fulfilled and Predictions for the Millennium & Beyond*, St. Martin's Press, New York, 1994

Kingston, Jeremy, *Healing Without Medicine*, Danbury Press/Aldus Books, London, 1975

Kinross, Lord, *The Ottoman Centuries, The Rise and Fall of the Turkish Empire*, Morrow Quill Paperbacks, New York, 1977

Kohn, George C., *Dictionary of Wars*, Anchor Books/Doubleday, New York, 1986

Ladurie, Emmanuel Le Roy (Brian Pearce, trans.), *Jasmin's Witch*, George Braziller, New York, 1987

Laver, James, *Nostradamus; or, The Future Foretold*, London, 1942 (and 1950 in paperback)

Lemesurier, Peter, *Nostradamus and Beyond*, Sterling Publishing Co., New York, 1999

Lemesurier, Peter, *The Nostradamus Encyclopedia: The Definitive Reference Guide to the Work and World of Nostradamus*, St. Martin's Press, New York, 1997

Leoni, Edgar, *Nostradamus, Life and Literature*, 1961 (reissued) *Nostradamus and his Prophecies*, Wings Books, New York, 1982

Le Pelletier, Anatole, *Les Oracles de Nostradamus, astrologue, médecin et conseiller ordinaire des rois Henry II, François II et Charles IX*, Le Pelletier, 40, rue d'Aboukir, Paris, 1867, 2 vols

Leroy, Dr. Edgar, *"Les origines de Nostradamus"*, *Mémoires de l'Institut historique de Provence*, vol. 18, Marseille, 1941

Lord Russell of Liverpool, *Henry of Navarre: Henry IV of France*, Praeger Publishers, New York, 1969

Mackenney, Richard, *Sixteenth Century Europe: Expansion and Conflict*, St. Martin's Press, New York, 1993

Mathers, S. Liddell MacGregor (trans.), *The Key of Solomon the King (Clavicula Salomonis)*, Samuel Weiser, Inc., York Beach, ME, 1972

McCann, Lee, *Nostradamus, The Man Who Saw Through Time*, Greenwich House/Crown, New York, 1984

Mémoires de L'Institut historique de Provence, vol. 17, 1941, reprinted by Busquet, 1950

Nebenzahl, Kenneth, *Atlas of Columbus and the Great Discoveries*, Rand McNally, New York, 1990

Nostradamus, Michel/Jean Lobetius, *Epistola Michaelis Nostradami ad Iohan. Lobetium [...] Salonae Petraeae Provinciae Saluniesium Nicephorae XII. Decembris, die autem ante natalem meum secunda.* [dans: Monumenta pietatis et literaria virorum in republica et literaria illustrium selecta, édité par L. C. Mieg et D. Nebel]. Francoforti 1701

Nostradamus, Michel de, *Hiéroglyphes de Horapollo (Texte inédit établi et commenté par Pierre Rollet)*, Marcel Petit, Raphèle-Lès-Arles, 1993

Nostradamus, Michel de, *Traité des fardemens et confitures* [also known as] *Le Vray et Parfaict Embellissement de la Face, & conservation du corps en son entierc:ontenant [!] plusieurs Receptes secretes & desirées non encore veues. Par M. Michel Nostradamus. La Seconde Partie, Contenant la façon et maniere de faire toutes confitures liquides, tant en succre, miel, qu'en vin cuit. Ensemble deux façon pour faire le syrop rosat laxatif: & pour faire le sucre candi, penites & tourrons d'Hespaigne,* (Anvers, Christophe Plantin, c. 1557), Imp. sur les presses des Imprimeries Réunies de Senils pour le compte de Gutenberg Reprint, 1979

Nostredame, César de, *L'Histoire et chronique de Provence* (first ed. 1614)

Nostredame, Jehan de, *Les Vies des plus celebres et anciens poetes provensaulx*, 1575

Orliac, Jehanne d', *The Moon Mistress, Diane De Poitiers, Grant' Sénéchalle de Normandy*, J.B. Lippincott Company, London, 1930

Osho, *The Hidden Harmony: Discourses on the Fragments of Heraclitus*, Rebel Press, Cologne

Ovason, David, *The Secrets of Nostradamus: A Radical New Interpretation of the Master's Prophecies*, HarperCollins Publishers, New York, 2001

Oxford Study Edition (Samuel Sandmel, gen. ed.), *The New English Bible with the Apocrypha*, Oxford University Press, New York, 1976

Pachter, Henry M., *Paracelsus, Magic into Science*, Henry Schuman, New York, 1951

Pagnani, Lelio (introduction), *Cities of the World (Civitates orbis terrarum): Europe and America*, Magna Books, Leicester, 1990

Pagnani, Lelio (introduction), *Cities of the World (Civitates orbis terrarum): Europe – Africa – Asia*, Magna Books, Leicester, 1990

Pagnani, Lelio (introduction), *Cosmography (Cosmographia tablae): Maps from Ptolemy's Geography*, Magna Books, Leicester, 1990

Platter, Felix, *Beloved Son Felix: The Journal of Felix Platter a Medical Student in Montpellier in the Sixteenth Century, 1552–7*, trans. Seán Jennet, London, 1963

Prieditis, Arthur, *The Fate of the Nations: Nostradamus' Vision of the Age of Aquarius*, Llewellyn Publications, St. Paul, MN, 1982

Potter, David (ed. and trans.), *The French Wars of Religion: Selected Documents*, Macmillan Press, London, 1997

Quigly, Isabel (trans.), *Paris and Its People: An Illustrated History*, Methuen & Co, London, 1953

Roeder, Ralph, *Catherine de' Medici and the Lost Revolution*, Garden City Publishing, New York, 1939

Rabelais, François, *The Complete and Authentic Works of Rabelais*, The Bibliophilist Society, c. 1920

Ramotti, Ottario Cesare (Tami Calliope, trans.), *The Nostradamus Code: The Lost Manuscript that Unlocks the Secrets of the Master Prophet*, Destiny Books, Rochester, NY, 1998

Randi, James, *The Mask of Nostradamus*, Charles Scribner's Sons, New York, 1990

Reynaud-Plense, Charles, *Les Vraies Centuries et Prophéties de Michel Nostradamus. Colligées des premières éditions imprimées à Lyon en 1558-1605 et, à Troyes en 1611, et à Leyde en 1650, avec sa Vie, et un Glossaire Nostradamique*, 1940

Rizzi, Silvana, *Provence: Past and Present*, Friedman/Fairfax, MetroBooks, New York, 2001

Robb, Stewart, *Prophecies on World Events by Nostradamus*, Liveright Publishing Corporation, New York, 1961

Roper, Lyndal, "Discipline and Respectability: Prostitution and the Reformation in Augsburg," *History Workshop Journal*, 19, 1985, pp. 3–28

Rossiaud, Jacques, *Medieval Prostitution*, (trans. Lydia G. Cochrane), Blackwell Publishers, Oxford, 1988

Scott, Sir Walter, *Waverly Novels, Vol XLV: Anne of Geierstein; or, The Maiden in the Mist – II*, Fisher, Son, & Co., London; and Quai Des Grands Augustine, Paris, 1838

Tannahill, Reay, *Food in History*, Crown Trade Paperbacks, New York, 1988

Thurston, Herbert, S.J., *The War & the Prophets: Notes on certain Popular Predictions Current in this Latter Age*, P. J. Kenedy & Sons, New York, 1915

Toland, John, *Adolf Hitler*, Doubleday & Company, New York, 1976

Torné-Chavigny, H., *Réédition du livre de prophéties de Nostradamus ...*, 1862 edition, expanded in 1872

Turi, Dr. Louis, *The Power of the Dragon*, Startheme Publications, 1996

Wilson, Colin, *Mysterious Powers*, Danbury Press/Aldus Books, London, 1975

Woolley, Benjamin, *The Queen's Conjuror: The Science and Magic of Dr Dee*, HarperCollins, London, 2001

Ward, Charles A., *Oracles of Nostradamus*, London, 1891

Name and Subject Index

ML   10/03